This book is to be returned

Books are to be returned on or before
the last date below.

- 9 APR 1991

2 5 APR 1996   2 1 SEP 1993

2 1 SEP 1993

1 2 JUN 1991   1 FEB 1996

1 5 DEC 1992

06 DEC 1991

1 7 NOV 1993

2 6 JAN 1993

1 9 MAY 1994

28 JAN 1992
28 APR 1992

1 5 MAR 1993

1 5 JUN 1992

- 6 APR 1999

1 9 MAY 1993

2 8 MAR 2001

24 NOV 1992   1 5 JUN 1993   2 1 MAR 2002

Principles of
Digital Data
Transmission

Principles of Digital Data Transmission

Second Edition

A. P. Clark, *MA, PhD, DIC, MIERE, CEng*
Department of Electronic and Electrical Engineering,
Loughborough University of Technology

PENTECH PRESS
(London : Plymouth)

First published 1976
by Pentech Press Limited
Estover Road, Plymouth
Devon PL6 7PZ

First edition 1976
Reprinted 1978
Second edition 1983

British Library Cataloguing in Publication Data

Clark, A. P.
  Principles of digital data transmission. 2nd ed.
  1. Digital electronics   2. Telecommunication
  Apparatus and supplies
  I. Title
  621.38′043   TK5103

ISBN 0–7273–1613–3
ISBN 0–7273–1614–1 Pbk

Printed in Great Britain
Typeset by Mid-County Press, London, SW15

Preface to second edition

Since the writing of the first edition of Principles of Digital Data Transmission, considerable changes have taken place in the design of data-transmission systems, involving both new modulation methods and detection processes. Although most of these changes have been concerned with the higher transmission rates, which are not studied in detail in this book, they have significantly affected the relative importance of the basic topics considered here. For instance, through the use of large scale integrated circuits it is now possible to implement relatively cheaply quite complex processes, provided only that a sufficient number of the devices are produced. This means that the practising engineer must now be more closely concerned with 'optimum' systems, since such systems are no longer of purely academic interest. Thus it has been felt appropriate to expand considerably the treatment of detection processes, which has involved the inclusion of an additional chapter on the principles of the coherent and incoherent detection of AM, FM and PM signals. Particular emphasis is placed here on the relationship between the different detection processes and the 'optimum' detector that minimizes the probability of error. The background material provided by this chapter has been made the foundation for a considerably expanded treatment of FM signals and their detection, in the following chapter. The performance of a discriminator detector for FM signals is considered here in some detail, and more complex signals such as MSK and offset QPSK are also studied, and their relationships with FSK and PSK signals are explained. Where possible, values are given for the relative tolerances to noise of the systems studied.

The other major changes that have been made to the book involve a more detailed study of both HF radio links and multi-level signals, together with a simplified derivation of the optimum transmitter and receiver filters in Chapter 14. Each of the remaining changes involves either the inclusion of some additional material or else some further explanation or description that has been found to be desirable as a result of some years experience in teaching from the book. The basic philosophy behind the structure of the book and the treatment of the material has been left unchanged, although inevitably some mathematical analysis has now had to be included in the first eleven chapters.

The reason why about one third of the material in Chapters 12–16 is concerned with partial response channels deserves some further comment. This is partly because of the very great practical importance of such channels, but partly also because the study of these channels provides an excellent introduction to more sophisticated data-transmission systems involving equalizers or more complex detection processes. Throughout this book the main emphasis is on basically simple detection processes, in which a signal element is detected on its own, as it arrives, and in which no correction is made in the detector for signal distortion introduced in the transmission path. The study of more sophisticated systems such as adaptive equalizers and near-maximum-likelihood detectors is beyond the scope of this book, these topics being considered in detail by the Author in Reference 422, which is a study of more advanced data-transmission systems. In the Author's experience, attempts at simplifying these topics by reducing the depth to which they are taught, generally results in making them even more difficult to understand, so that they are best taught in some detail or not at all! Furthermore, by omitting from the book the topics just mentioned, the reader is not required to have any understanding of vectors or matrix algebra, thus bringing the book within the range of understanding of many engineers who would otherwise have found the subject matter unduly difficult. Unfortunately, any theoretical treatment of data-transmission systems that is not purely qualitative and therefore rather superficial must involve the use of random variables and random processes and so require some quite abstract theory. Inevitably, therefore, the Chapters 12–16 are of considerably greater theoretical difficulty than the Chapters 1–11 (with the possible exception of the new Chapter 6). In an attempt to simplify the description here and so to reduce the disparity between the two parts of the book, the material in Chapters 13–15 is presented in the form of worked examples of steadily (but not too rapidly) increasing difficulty, the new topics being introduced at the appropriate points. Thus, for example, Chapter 13 describes simple applications of the theoretical results developed in Chapter 12 and is aimed partly at illuminating these results. By this means, some of the more difficult parts of the theory, involving the coding and detection of signals and the computation of error probability, are repeated several times in different applications, thus helping to clarify the basic principles involved. This method of presenting the theory has been found to be most effective in practice.

A. P. Clark

Preface to first edition

This book is the outcome of some lecture courses in digital communications presented over the past five years to both undergraduate and postgraduate students in the Department of Electronic and Electrical Engineering of Loughborough University of Technology.

The book is written mainly for private study by practising and student engineers who are interested in the design and development of data-transmission systems. It is concerned primarily with basic principles and techniques rather than with details of equipment design.

Part 1 of the book (Chapters 1–11) is a non-mathematical survey of the properties of the voice-frequency channels formed by telephone circuits and HF radio links, and of the various techniques that have been used or proposed for the transmission of digital data over these channels. The different techniques are compared and descriptions are given of the preferred data-transmission systems. The voice-frequency channels are important not only in their own right but also because they introduce most of the different types of noise and distortion experienced over many other channels. The study of data-transmission over these channels is therefore relevant to many other applications.

Part 2 of the book (Chapters 12–16) is a theoretical analysis and comparison of various different signals that may be used for the transmission of digital data. Both baseband and modulated-carrier signals are studied, with particular emphasis on some of the baseband signals that may be obtained over partial-response channels and by correlative-level coding. Matched-filter detection is studied in some detail as is the related topic of the optimum combination of transmitter and receiver filters.

Part 2 of the book presents the theoretical analysis necessary for the full understanding of the more important topics studied in Part 1. An idealised system is assumed in Part 2, not only to facilitate the theoretical analysis but also to bring out a number of interesting relationships that exist between the different signals studied.

A total of some 474 references, suitably classified according to the topics covered, are provided to enable the reader to pursue in more detail the particular topics that are relevant to the subject matter of the book but are only briefly mentioned here.

The book is concerned primarily with the situation where it is required to transmit digital data as simply and effectively as possible over a given channel but without necessarily achieving an exceptionally high transmission rate. The systems studied use basically simple detection processes and do not involve the more sophisticated techniques such as adaptive equalizers. The proper study of the latter requires rather more specialised mathematics than is considered appropriate for this book, so that a detailed consideration of these techniques has not been included here. The book attempts to establish as clearly as possible the important properties of the different digital signals that may be used for the transmission of data, and to compare these properties in such a way that the most suitable modem design for any given application can be determined.

Part 1 of the book is written at a relatively elementary level and assumes only a limited knowledge of mathematics. Part 2 assumes a basic (but not advanced) understanding of Fourier transforms, probability theory, random variables, random processes and in particular the Gaussian random process, signal transmission through linear systems, the sampling theorem and linear modulation methods. The book is suitable for presentation as part of a course on digital communications, at either a final-year undergraduate or first-year postgraduate level.

Many of the results and conclusions presented in Part 1 of the book are the outcome of a study of practical data-transmission systems carried out by the author from 1956–1965 and again from 1969–1970, while working at Plessey Telecommunications Research Ltd., Taplow, Buckinghamshire. The author is grateful for the opportunity that was provided to undertake this work. The author would also like to thank Professor J. W. R. Griffiths for his encouragement in the later part of the work and for providing the necessary facilities for its completion.

A. P. Clark

Contents

1 Introduction   1

    1.1   Organization of book   1
    1.2   The first law of data transmission   2
    1.3   Power-density spectrum   3
    1.4   Baseband signals   4
    1.5   Modulated-carrier signals   6
    1.6   Signal alphabet and information content   8
    1.7   Serial and parallel systems   9
    1.8   Transmission rates   10

2 Distortion   11

    2.1   Definitions   11
    2.2   Telephone circuits   12
    2.3   Private and switched telephone lines   15
    2.4   Attenuation and delay distortions over telephone circuits   17
    2.5   HF radio links   20
    2.6   Attenuation and delay distortions over HF radio links   22

3 Noise   25

    3.1   Basic types of noise   25
    3.2   Noise over telephone circuits   25
    3.3   Noise over HF radio links   27

4 Transmission of timing information   32

    4.1   The need for timing information   32
    4.2   Synchronous systems   32
    4.3   Start-stop systems   35
    4.4   Comparison of systems   37

5 Modulation methods 38

5.1	The need for modulation	38
5.2	AM, FM and PM signals	39
5.3	Relative tolerances to additive white Gaussian noise of AM, FM and PM systems	41

6 Ideal detection processes 49

6.1	Optimum detection of a received signal message	49
6.2	Optimum detection of an m-level signal element	50
6.3	Optimum detection of an m-level FM or PM signal-element	54
6.4	Ideal coherent detection of an m-level FSK signal	55
6.5	Ideal coherent detection of an m-level PSK signal	57
6.6	Ideal coherent detection of an m-level ASK signal	60
6.7	Principles of ideal incoherent detection	62
6.8	Ideal incoherent detection of an m-level FSK signal	63
6.9	Ideal coherent detection of an m-level ASK signal	67
6.10	Ideal incoherent detection of an m-level PSK signal	69

7 Practical detection processes 76

7.1	Coherent detection	76
7.2	Incoherent and noncoherent detection	83
7.3	Selection of preferred systems	93

8 Transmission rates 100

8.1	Maximum transmission rate	100
8.2	Baseband signals	101
8.3	AM signals	103
8.4	PM signals	105
8.5	FM signals	107
8.6	Comparison of FM and PM systems	109

9 Binary data-transmission systems for use over telephone circuits 112

9.1	Comparison of systems	112
9.2	Complete synchronous serial systems	114
9.3	Asynchronous systems	119
9.4	Synchronous serial PM system	120
9.5	Asynchronous serial FM system	125

10 Multilevel data-transmission systems for use over telephone circuits 129

10.1	Double-sideband systems	129
10.2	Vestigial-sideband systems	132
10.3	Adaptive systems	133

11 Data-transmission systems for use over HF radio links 138

11.1	Parallel systems	138
11.2	Conventional FDM systems	139
11.3	Overlapping-spectra FDM systems	140
11.4	Effects of multi-path propagation	143
11.5	Time guard bands	145
11.6	Collins Kineplex system	147
11.7	APR systems	150
11.8	Serial systems	152

12 Matched-filter detection 154

13 Rectangular baseband signals 168

13.1	Binary signals	168
13.2	Detection of a binary polar signal-element	170
13.3	Error probability in the detection of a binary polar signal-element	172
13.4	Detection of a binary unipolar signal-element	174
13.5	Quaternary polar signals	176
13.6	Quaternary unipolar signals	179
13.7	The Gray code	180
13.8	Comparison of signals	180

14 Rounded baseband signals 182

14.1	Introduction	182
14.2	Optimum design of transmitter and receiver filters	186
14.3	Model of the data-transmission system	192
14.4	Rectangular spectrum	195
14.5	Spectrum with a sinusoidal roll-off	200
14.6	Raised-cosine spectrum	201

15 Partial-response channels 207

15.1 Introduction 207
15.2 Cosine spectrum 208
15.3 Sine spectrum 211
15.4 Cosine^2 spectrum 214
15.5 Sine^2 spectrum 216
15.6 Cancellation of intersymbol interference 218
15.7 Precoding 221
15.8 Cosine and sine spectra 222
15.9 Cosine^2 and sine^2 spectra 230
15.10 Assessment of systems 233
15.11 Partial-response channels formed by
      correlative-level coding 237

16 Modulated-carrier signals 246

16.1 Model of the data-transmission system 246
16.2 ASK signals 248
16.3 PSK signals 255
16.4 FSK signals 259
16.5 Comparison of signals 271

References 273

Index 296

1

Introduction

1.1 Organization of book

The most widely used communication channel is undoubtedly the voice-frequency channel designed for the transmission of speech[1-45]. This passes a band of frequencies from approximately 300 to 3000 Hz. Almost all major towns and cities throughout the world are interconnected by the telephone network, using voice-frequency channels[1-31]. With the rapidly increasing use of computers and the corresponding increase in the quantity of digital data transmitted to and from the larger computer installations, there is considerable interest in using the telephone network for the transmission of digital data. It seems likely that over the coming years there will be a steady increase in the ratio of digital data to speech signals, carried by the telephone network.

For communication between isolated locations and over long distances, voice-frequency channels over HF radio links are often used[32-45]. In some important applications these are the most cost effective communication channels for the transmission of digital data.

In Chapters 2 to 11 we shall be concerned with two main types of voice-frequency channel: *telephone circuits* and *HF radio links*. A telephone circuit is, of course, a connection (voice-frequency channel) between one subscriber (user) and another, over the telephone network. We shall be concerned with the problems involved in transmitting digital data over these channels, and with the techniques for achieving satisfactory operation. We shall study the design of the *modem* (modulator-demodulator) which both generates the digital data signals that are transmitted over a voice-frequency channel to another location, and also detects the digital data signals transmitted back from that location, often (but not always) over a different voice-frequency channel. The emphasis throughout will be on basic principles rather than on the detailed designs of particular modems.

1

We shall *not* be concerned with the design of the voice-frequency channel itself or with techniques for improving its characteristics.

An important point that requires to be mentioned here is that the basic types of noise and distortion experienced over typical voice-frequency channels include those experienced over many other quite different transmission paths, so that the study of digital data transmission over voice-frequency channels is in fact relevant to many other applications.

Chapters 1–11 present an elementary survey of the more important problems involved in transmitting digital data over voice-frequency channels and of the basic techniques that can be used to overcome these problems. Considerable emphasis is given to the fundamental principles, methods of operation and relative performances of various detection processes, the use of mathematical analysis being kept to a minimum. For the reader wishing to pursue particular points in more detail, an extensive list of references is provided. These are, for the most part, grouped according to the subject matter and placed in chronological order within each group, in order to facilitate their use.

In Chapters 1 to 11, simple intuitive explanations are provided where possible for the results quoted. Where no simple explanations are available, the results are presented without further justification. The reader must not therefore expect every statement in this part of the book to follow directly or logically from the preceding discussion. The aim of this method of presentation is to collect together the more important results and relationships, without the distraction of detailed mathematical analysis, in the hope that the reader may thereby be enabled to see the wood for the trees! Indeed, the whole purpose of the Chapters 1 to 11 is to give the reader a sense of values, so far as data-transmission is concerned, so that he can discriminate between the things that matter and those that do not. The detailed theoretical analysis, needed for the full understanding of some of the more important topics in Chapters 1 to 11, is given in the Chapters 12 to 16.

Before pursuing the study of data-transmission systems, there are some important fundamental points that require clarification and some frequently used terms that need to be defined. The remainder of this chapter is devoted to this end.

1.2 The first law of data transmission

In designing any data-transmission system there is an important principle known as the first law of data-transmission that needs at all times to be born in mind. This law is of quite general application and can be stated in two different ways: 'you cannot eat your cake and have it' or 'you cannot get something for nothing'. For instance, if you improve the tolerance of a modem (the transmitter and receiver of a data-transmission system) to a particular type of noise or distortion, you will almost certainly reduce its tolerance to some other type of noise or distortion, or, at best, increase its complexity. For any improvement in one respect there is always a degradation in another. The assumption here, of course, is that the original modem is a reasonable design and with no basic design faults. Obviously, if a modem is designed on the basis of some incorrect assumptions, then its performance in one respect can often be improved at no cost in any other. Thus, any new technique that promises to give an improvement in some particular aspect of the performance of a modem must always be carefully checked to determine its disadvantages. A good technique is one which gives a useful improvement in an area that is important and whose disadvantages or weaknesses lie in areas that do not matter or are, at least, less important. The design of a modem is in fact always a compromise between several conflicting requirements, so that the art of modem design is the ability to select the techniques that give advantages in the areas that matter most and whose disadvantages lie in the areas that matter least. One of the questions that the first part of this book attempts to answer is: what are these areas?

1.3 Power-density spectrum

Any time-varying signal with a given shape or waveform can be considered alternatively as a set of frequency components (separate sine-waves with different frequencies) which occupy a certain range of frequencies. The frequency components form the *spectrum* of the signal and are given by the Fourier transform of the signal waveform. In the spectrum of a given signal waveform, both the amplitudes and phases of the individual frequency components are defined. The range of frequencies occupied by the spectrum gives the *bandwidth* of the signal. In general, the more slowly a signal varies in time, the lower are the frequencies of its frequency components and so the lower are the frequencies occupied by its spectrum. The more rapidly a signal varies in time, the higher are these frequencies. The components of the transmitted signal, carrying the individual symbols of the transmitted data, are pulses of suitable shape and (for practical purposes) finite duration. The pulses are known as *signal elements*. As a rule, any reduction in the signal bandwidth tends to lengthen the transmitted signal elements, since, for a given pulse shape, the width of the frequency spectrum is inversely proportional to the duration of the pulse.

The spectrum (Fourier transform) of the transmitted signal, corresponding to a given message (sequence of symbols or element values), is not normally the same as the spectrum of the transmitted signal corresponding to any other message. It is assumed here, for the purpose of the comparison, that the message of finite duration is repeated continuously to give a resultant signal of infinite duration. The transmitted signal now has a *line* spectrum, with a set of *discrete* frequency components, whose levels are measured in units of *power* rather than *energy*. As the length of the message increases and assuming that the digital data are random in nature (without repetitive sequences), so the *average power* in any given unit bandwidth tends towards a given value, which is the same as that obtained with any other message of the type being considered. In the limit, as the duration of a message tends to infinity, its spectrum becomes *continuous*, with a given relationship between the average power per unit bandwidth and frequency, that is, with a given *power-density spectrum*. The power at any particular frequency is now vanishingly small, which is why the power *density* and not the power is considered.

It is conventional, on the grounds of mathematical convenience, to evaluate the power-density spectrum over both positive and negative frequencies, to give a two-sided power density spectrum. For the present, however, we shall consider instead the one-sided power density spectrum, which shows directly the variation of power density (power per unit bandwidth) with frequency. This has the property that the area beneath the curve and bounded to the left and right by two different frequencies, gives the average power over the frequency range bounded by the two frequencies. Clearly, the area under the whole of the curve gives the average signal power.

1.4 Baseband signals

The simplest digital data signal contains a sequence of signal elements (units or pulses of the data signal) where each element is binary coded, having the choice of two possible shapes which correspond to the element values 0 and 1. Each signal element has the same duration of T seconds and follows immediately after the preceding element, so that the signal element rate is $1/T$ elements per second or bauds. An example of such a signal is shown in Figure 1.1.

This is a binary antipodal baseband signal, where the element value 0 is represented by a signal value k, and the element value 1 is represented by a signal value $-k$. A baseband signal is one whose

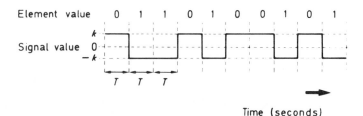

Fig. 1.1   Rectangular binary baseband signal

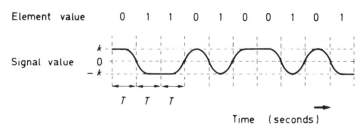

Fig. 1.2   Rounded binary baseband signal

spectrum usually extends to zero frequency (d.c.) or to very low frequencies, and which carries information (data) in terms of its *values* at certain points. Thus the above waveform could alternatively be shaped as in Figure 1.2. At the receiver, each signal element is here sampled at its mid point in time and each sample has a value $\pm k$.

It can be seen that the second of the above two waveforms does not contain as rapid variations with time as does the first waveform, so that its spectrum does not extend to such high frequencies. Both waveforms, however, contain the same slower variations, so that their spectra do not differ greatly at the lower frequencies. Both spectra extend to zero frequency. Clearly, the second of the two waveforms has a narrower bandwidth, so that it achieves a higher ratio of transmission rate to signal bandwidth, and in this sense it makes a more efficient use of bandwidth.

Differential coding may alternatively be used to give the signal waveform in Figure 1.3. An element value 1 is represented here by a *change* in value between adjacent signal elements, and an element value 0 by no change. Again, a rounded waveform could be used instead, such that an element value 1 is represented by a change in the sample values of two adjacent elements, and an element value 0 by no change.

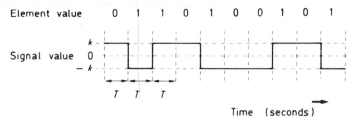

Fig. 1.3   Differentially coded binary signal

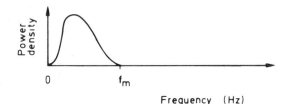

Fig. 1.4   Spectrum of baseband signal

1.5   Modulated-carrier signals

In order to obtain satisfactory transmission over a typical voice-frequency channel, signal waveforms of the types just considered could not in general be used. The reasons for this are considered in Section 5.1. The baseband signal now modulates a suitable sine-wave carrier, using amplitude, frequency or phase modulation (AM, FM or PM), and the modulated-carrier signal is then transmitted over the voice-frequency channel. The *signal carrier* is the sine wave which carries the transmitted data in terms of the amplitude, frequency or phase of this sine wave. At the receiver, the baseband data signal is extracted from the received modulated-carrier signal, by a suitable demodulation process, and the demodulated baseband signal is then detected to give the sequence of data element values.

Consider a baseband signal with the power-density spectrum shown in Figure 1.4. The power density here is zero at d.c. and at frequencies above f_m Hz.

The baseband signal is used to amplitude modulate a sine-wave carrier with frequency f_c Hz, so that the amplitude (level) of the carrier varies as the baseband signal. This gives a double sideband AM signal with the power-density spectrum shown in Figure 1.5.

The impulse at f_c Hz (shown by the arrow in Figure 1.5) indicates that there is a non-zero frequency component at f_c. The upper

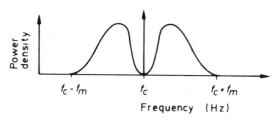

Fig. 1.5   Spectrum of double sideband AM signal

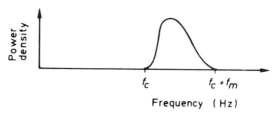

Fig. 1.6   Spectrum of single sideband suppressed carrier AM signal

sideband (part of the spectrum above f_c) is the spectrum of the baseband signal, unchanged in shape but shifted up in frequency by f_c Hz. The lower sideband (part of the spectrum below f_c) is the 'reflection' of the upper sideband in the carrier frequency f_c. It is assumed here that $f_c > f_m$.

If now the lower sideband and the carrier frequency are removed by a filter, which passes the upper sideband through unchanged, the signal becomes a single sideband suppressed carrier AM signal, with the spectrum shown in Figure 1.6.

The spectrum of the single sideband suppressed carrier AM signal is simply the spectrum of the baseband signal shifted up in frequency by f_c Hz. Although the *shape* of the spectrum is unchanged, the *levels* of all frequency components may have been increased or decreased by a fixed amount. A single sideband suppressed carrier AM signal may alternatively use the lower sideband of the original double-sideband signal.

The double sideband AM signal and the single sideband suppressed carrier AM signal are each produced by a process of *linear modulation*. If either of these signals is multiplied by a sine-wave carrier with frequency f_c Hz and with the same phase as that of the signal carrier (whether present or suppressed), and if the resultant signal is passed through a filter which removes all frequency components above f_m Hz, without affecting the frequency components below f_m Hz, then the resultant signal is the original baseband signal, with perhaps a change in level. This is a process of *linear demodulation*.

1.6   Signal alphabet and information content

The signal alphabet of a digital signal is the number of *different* symbols or element values which may be transmitted. Thus, when there are m different signal elements, the signal alphabet is of size m and the signal is said to be an m-level signal. The term 'level' here does not refer to the signal amplitude, which may of course be constant. The simplest digital signal is clearly a 2-level or binary signal. A careful distinction must be made between the transmitted *waveform* of a signal element, which is considered here as the *signal element* itself, and the *symbol* that is represented or carried by the signal element, which is here referred to as the *element value*. In the case of simple baseband signals there is a unique relationship between the element value and the corresponding *signal value*, as is shown in Figures 1.1–1.3. In the latter case it is sometimes convenient to consider the *symbol* represented by a signal element to be the *signal value* itself, since there is a unique one-to-one relationship between the two. This is done in Chapters 12–15.

Consider a sequence of m-level signal elements, where $m = 2^n$ and n is a positive integer. The m-level data symbol that determines the element value of a signal element can now be represented by a sequence of n binary digits (bits), each of which has a possible value of 0 or 1, there being a unique one-to-one relationship between the symbol and n binary digits. Thus, for example, if $m = 8$ and the possible values of a data symbol are $0, 1, 2, \ldots, 7$, then $n = 3$ and the corresponding sequences of 3 binary digits can be taken to be 000, 001, 010, $\ldots$, 111. The m-level symbol is here *coded* into the corresponding sequence of n binary digits, where

$$n = \log_2 m \qquad (1.1)$$

If the data symbols (element values) are statistically independent and equally likely to have any of their possible values, then so also are the binary digits into which these are coded. Each binary digit now carries *one bit of information*. A 'bit' here is a unit measure of information and is not to be confused with the binary digit itself. However, throughout this book it is assumed that the transmitted data symbols are statistically independent and equally likely to have any of their possible values, so that the number of binary digits into which a data symbol can be coded becomes the same as the number of bits of information carried by the data symbol. The term 'bit' can therefore be taken to have either meaning. Clearly, the information content per signal element is n bits, where n is given by Equation 1.1. If now the signal-element rate is B bauds (elements per second), the transmission rate (information rate) of the signal is $B \log_2 m$ bit/s (bits per second). Thus the transmission rate can be increased by raising the signal-element rate B, the number of levels m, or both of these together.

In applications where there is severe noise and distortion, a binary signal is normally used because this gives the best tolerance to these effects for a given degree of equipment complexity. Multi-level signals (signals having more than two levels) are normally only used where binary signals do not permit the required transmission rate to be achieved over the available frequency band.

1.7 Serial and parallel systems

A serial system is one in which the transmitted signal comprises a sequential stream of data elements whose frequency spectrum occupies the whole of the available bandwidth.

A parallel system is one in which two or more sequential streams of data elements are transmitted simultaneously, so that at any instant two or more data elements are being transmitted, and the spectrum of an individual data stream (data channel) normally occupies only a part of the available bandwidth. The data channels are in general synchronously multiplexed, so that the individual data signals have the same element duration and are in element synchronism (the elements starting and ending together).

A serial system is in general considerably less complex than a parallel system, largely because of the inevitable duplication of equipment in a parallel system, particularly at the receiver, where the different frequency channels must be separated from each other. The one application where there is sometimes less equipment involved in parallel systems, is a data collection system which may use one or two receivers fed from any one or two of say a hundred different transmitters. The complexity of the receivers is here obviously unimportant compared with that of the transmitters, and under these conditions a parallel system need not be under any disadvantage on grounds of economy. Again, over HF radio links, where there may be very severe signal distortion and where cost is relatively unimportant, parallel systems are sometimes more suitable. However, for applications over telephone circuits, a serial data-transmission system is nearly always to be preferred to a parallel system, on grounds of both economy and performance.

1.8   Transmission rates

The following transmission rates have been accepted as preferred standards for use over voice-frequency channels: 600, 1200, 2400, 4800 and 9600 bit/s. Whereas the transmission rates of 600 and 1200 bit/s can be achieved relatively easily even over poor channels, the rates of 4800 and 9600 bit/s require the use of more sophisticated techniques, even over relatively good channels. Binary signal elements are normally used at transmission rates of 600 and 1200 bit/s, and 4-level (quaternary) signal elements are used at 2400 bit/s. At 4800 and 9600 bit/s, 8- or 16-level signal elements may be used, or other signal alphabets of the same order of magnitude.

2

Distortion

2.1 Definitions

The *attenuation characteristic* of a channel is the variation of attenuation with frequency, when a constant level sine-wave, with adjustable frequency, is fed over the channel.

The *attenuation distortion* in a given frequency band is the variation of attenuation over that frequency band.

The *bandwidth* of a channel is the range of frequencies (frequency band) over which the attenuation does not exceed some specified value, usually 3, 6 or 20 dB above its lowest value.

A *voice-frequency channel* has ideally a negligible attenuation over the frequency band 300–3000 Hz, but does not necessarily pass any frequencies outside this band.

The *group-delay characteristic* of a channel is the variation of group delay (envelope delay) with frequency. The group delay at a given frequency is the delay in transmission of energy at that frequency. It is measured as the delay in transmission of a slowly varying envelope (peak value) of a sine wave having the given frequency.

The *delay distortion* in a given frequency band is the variation of group delay over the frequency band.

The attenuation and group-delay characteristics of a channel give some idea of the signal distortion introduced by that channel. The *signal distortion* is the change in the shape of the transmitted signal, resulting from the attenuation and group-delay characteristics of the channel. Changes in the shape of the transmitted signal, caused by other effects, are generally classed as *noise* and are not considered in this chapter.

Certain types of change in the shape of the signal, caused by the attenuation and group-delay characteristics of the channel, are not important and are often not classed as distortion. These are: a time delay in the received signal relative to the transmitted signal, resulting from a constant (time-invariant) delay in transmission, a constant

11

change in signal level (amplitude), and a constant change in the phase of the signal carrier (where a modulated-carrier signal is transmitted).

2.2 Telephone circuits

A telephone circuit connecting one subscriber (user) to another is normally made up of two or more links connected in tandem (end-to-end). These links are usually of three distinct types: unloaded audio, loaded audio or carrier[1-31]. Microwave links are often used, and for long distance telephone circuits, satellite links and sometimes HF radio links.

A long telephone circuit of several hundred miles in length, may, for example, contain the following arrangement of individual links: unloaded audio, loaded audio, carrier, carrier, loaded audio, unloaded audio. Clearly, the types of distortion to be expected over a telephone circuit will usually be a combination of the distortions introduced by the different individual links[1-31,97].

Unloaded audio links are generally very short (not more than two or three miles) and comprise a pair of wires with impedance 600 Ω. Because of their short length, they have a good frequency response, with some attenuation distortion and negligible delay distortion over the voice-frequency band. The attenuation increases as the square root of the frequency, over the voice-frequency band, and is typically about 2 dB per mile, in the centre of the band, with a variation of about 1.5 dB over the band. The delay distortion per mile, over the voice frequency band, is of the order of 20 μs and is quite negligible. It is the high attenuation per mile that prevents the use of long unloaded audio links.

Loaded audio links may be very much longer (up to about a hundred miles). They comprise a pair of wires with impedance 600 Ω and with inductances (often 44 or 88 mH) inserted at regular intervals (typically 2000 yds). Their attenuation characteristics resemble that of a low-pass filter, such that up to a certain frequency (often below 3000 Hz) there is only small attenuation (less than 1 dB per mile) and above this frequency the attenuation increases rapidly with frequency. Thus the attenuation over the centre of the voice-frequency band is reduced by the loading coils, in return for a greatly increased attenuation over the higher frequencies. Not only is the response of the link restricted at high frequencies, but the group delay increases towards the high frequency end of the band, to give a delay distortion of the order of 200 μs per mile over the range of frequencies for which there is only small attenuation. The attenuation and delay distortions introduced by a loaded audio link increase with its length, and the longer links introduce considerable attenuation and delay distortions at the high frequency end of the band.

Carrier links may be very much longer than loaded audio links. A process of single sideband suppressed carrier amplitude modulation is used here to shift the signal frequency band to higher frequencies, for transmission over a wideband channel which may be a coaxial cable or open wire line. This channel carries several signals, each using a different frequency band, in an arrangement of frequency-division multiplexing (FDM). At the other end of the carrier link, each of the multiplexed signals is first isolated from the others by means of a band-pass filter, and a process of linear demodulation is then used to restore the signal to the voice-frequency band.

The modulation process at the transmitter first multiplies the voice-frequency signal by a sine wave with the appropriate frequency, to give a double sideband signal centred on this frequency. The sideband required for transmission is then isolated by means of a filter. The process of linear demodulation first multiplies the received single-sideband signal by a sine wave with ideally the same frequency as that used at the transmitter, and the required voice-frequency signal is then isolated by means of a filter.

The filters involved in the processes of modulation and demodulation in a carrier link have an effect on the demodulated voice-frequency signal, at the output of the link, equivalent to that of a high-pass filter with a cut-off frequency in the range 100–300 Hz. They also restrict the high-frequency components of the demodulated signal, but to a much less significant degree. Thus a carrier link has a restricted low-frequency response, and appreciable delay distortion is introduced at the low-frequency end of the band before the attenuation becomes large. The distortion introduced in a carrier link originates in the terminal equipment and does not depend on the length of the link.

If the sine wave carriers, used for modulating and demodulating the signal in a carrier link, do not have exactly the same frequency, the frequency spectrum of the signal at the output of the carrier link is shifted by an amount equal to the difference between the two carrier frequencies, but the shape of the spectrum remains otherwise unchanged. This is known as *frequency offset*. The frequency offset over carrier links may have a value up to ± 5 Hz, but usually lies within the range ± 1 Hz. Although this offset may be regarded as a form of signal distortion, it is best described as a noise signal and is considered further in Chapter 3.

Microwave and satellite links are in general engineered to much tighter specifications than are loaded audio and carrier links. Their attenuation and delay characteristics, as well as their noise properties, are usually less harmful to data-transmission systems than are those of the poorer loaded audio and carrier links, nor do they introduce any very serious effects of a different nature to those obtained over loaded audio and carrier links. In other words, a data-transmission system capable of satisfactory operation over a poor telephone circuit, containing loaded audio and carrier links, should normally give satisfactory operation over the corresponding telephone circuit in which one or more of the loaded audio and carrier links are replaced by microwave or satellite links[1-31]. It is therefore sufficient to ensure that a data-transmission system can operate satisfactorily over the likely combinations of loaded audio and carrier links. For this reason, microwave and satellite links will not be considered further here, nor, for similar reasons, will PCM links.

HF radio links are considered separately from telephone circuits, because they have rather different properties and because they are normally used for point-to-point working or for isolated communication networks, and not often as part of the general telephone network[32-45].

Loaded audio links of more than a few miles in length require repeaters (amplifiers) to offset the attenuation introduced by the line. Over a long loaded-audio link, the repeaters are spaced at regular intervals along the line. Where an appreciable gain is required for an individual repeater, an amplifier is used. Since this only passes the signal in one direction, two amplifiers are in fact required, one for each direction of transmission. Thus a 4-wire line is needed, two wires to carry signals in one direction and the other two wires to carry signals in the reverse direction. Carrier circuits also operate with separate go and return channels, using separate processes of modulation and demodulation for the two channels, so that carrier circuits also require 4-wire lines.

Most subscribers, however, are connected to the local exchange via a single pair of wires, carrying signals in both directions. Thus where a telephone circuit contains repeaters or carrier links, arrangements must be made to couple 2-wire lines to 4-wire lines. This is achieved by means of hybrid transformers, connected as in Figure 2.1.

A hybrid transformer, when correctly matched, feeds signals from the 2-wire line to the 'transmit' terminals of the 4-wire line, and it feeds signals from the 'receive' terminals of the 4-wire line to the 2-wire line. It does not, however, feed signals between the 'receive' and 'transmit' terminals of the 4-wire line. Unfortunately, hybrid transformers are often mismatched and the result of this is that signals from the 'receive' terminals of the 4-wire line are passed (with some attenuation) to the 'transmit' terminals. When both hybrid transformers are mismatched, a signal can pass right round the loop

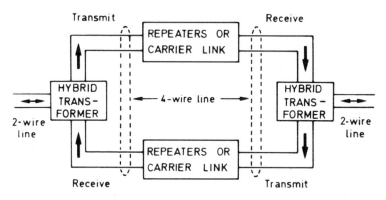

Fig. 2.1 Interconnection of 2-wire and 4-wire lines

and appear at the output of the 2-wire line, at the receiving end, as the main signal followed by a series of echoes (copies or replicas of this signal). The echoes have steadily increasing delays and steadily decreasing levels, causing the signal to be dispersed (spread out) in time. This is known as 'listener echo' and can introduce serious signal distortion in a transmitted data signal. For instance, when the loop delay exceeds the duration of a transmitted signal-element, the corresponding received signal-element appears as a sequence of separate pulses of steadily reducing levels and sometimes varying shapes. When the loop delay is less than the element duration, the individual echoes overlap. The received signal-element is now continuous but may have a duration of two or three times that of the transmitted element. It is clear that when a continuous sequence of signal elements is transmitted, each received element will overlap the following elements and therefore interfere with them. This is an effect known as *intersymbol interference*.

For really high quality data-transmission over a telephone network, 4-wire working must be used throughout the network and including the subscriber terminals.

2.3 Private and switched telephone lines

Telephone circuits may be divided into two distinct groups: private and switched lines. A private line is one which is rented permanently or on a part-time basis by a subscriber. It is not connected through any of the automatic switches in the exchange and it is also disconnected from the exchange battery supplies which are used for d.c. signalling and various other purposes. The private line is also checked for its overall attenuation-frequency characteristic to ensure a reasonable frequency response.

A switched line, that is a line on the public network, is the circuit obtained when using an ordinary telephone to set up a call, either by dialling a number or through the local exchange operator. The line is connected through a number of switches and, via transmission bridges, to the exchange battery supplies. The transmission bridges provide the required d.c. connection to the batteries together with a.c. isolation from these, and they both increase the attenuation over the voice-frequency channel and further reduce the low frequency response. In addition, a switched line is made up of a number of separate links, each chosen at random from sometimes quite a large number. It is therefore obviously not possible to check the frequency characteristics of complete circuits, since far too many possible combinations of the individual links are involved. Instead, only the frequency characteristics of the individual links are checked. One of the results of this is that it is possible over any such telephone circuit to obtain serious mismatches between individual links.

Each mismatch reflects a portion of the signal reaching it, with the result that when there are two or more mismatches along one line, a portion of a signal, reflected back from a mismatch near the receiving end of the line, will be reflected forward again by a mismatch nearer the transmitting end, and a portion of this signal will eventually reach the receiver as an echo of the main signal. Thus each received signal-element comprises the main component of the element (received via direct transmission over the line) followed by several echoes, which are attenuated and delayed with respect to the main component. Each echo is of course the component of the received signal which has travelled via a different combination of the mismatches along the line. In principle, this is the same effect as that which occurs when a pair of hybrid transformers are mismatched, as described in Section 2.2. These are both examples of *multipath propagation*, where the transmitted signal can reach its destination over two or more different paths, usually having different attenuations and delays. Multipath propagation causes time dispersion of each received signal-element, resulting in intersymbol interference.

Any given set of echoes in the received signal corresponds to (or indicates the presence of) the appropriate combination of attenuation and delay distortions. When the echoes are not small compared with the main signal component, they indicate the presence of severe attenuation and delay distortions. A single large echo, for instance, corresponds to a large sinusoidal ripple superimposed on both the attenuation and group-delay characteristics, where the wavelength of the ripple (measured along the frequency scale) is inversely pro-

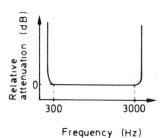

Fig. 2.2   Ideal attenuation-frequency characteristic

portional to the delay of the echo. When the ripple wavelength along the frequency scale is of the same order as the bandwidth of the voice-frequency channel, the ripple cannot be recognised as such by the presence of alternating peaks and troughs, and the presence of the ripple effectively reduces the bandwidth of the channel. There is also usually an increase in both the attenuation and delay distortions over the frequency band passed by the channel.

On account of the reflections caused by mismatching, the attenuation and delay distortions experienced over switched lines may be appreciably more severe than those over private lines. The 'listener echoes' caused by mismatched hybrid transformers can of course occur on both private and switched lines. Another important reason for the inferior frequency characteristics of a typical switched line is, of course, the fact that no attempt is made to check and correct the characteristics of the complete line (contrary to the case of a private line) which means, for example, that the steadily increasing attenuation with frequency introduced by the two unloaded audio links (one at each end) tend to appear in the resultant attenuation-frequency characteristics.

2.4   Attenuation and delay distortions over telephone circuits

Figure 2.2 shows the attenuation-frequency characteristic of an ideal voice-frequency channel. Frequencies below 300 Hz and above 3000 Hz are not required for the intelligible reception of speech and the attenuation of the channel may therefore increase rapidly at frequencies below 300 Hz and above 3000 Hz.

Figure 2.3 shows the typical attenuation-frequency characteristic of a telephone circuit containing both audio and carrier links[3,25]. The whole of the frequency band from 300 to 3000 Hz is here available for transmission but there is a gradually increasing attenuation at frequencies above about 1100 Hz.

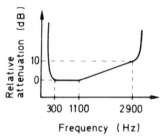

*Fig. 2.3   Typical attenuation-frequency
characteristic*

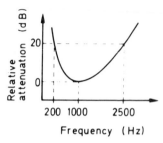

*Fig. 2.4   Attenuation-frequency
characteristic of a poor circuit*

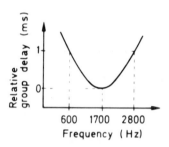

*Fig. 2.5   Typical group-delay
frequency characteristic*

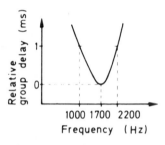

*Fig. 2.6   Group-delay frequency
characteristic of a poor circuit*

Figure 2.4 shows the attenuation-frequency characteristic of a poor circuit containing both audio and carrier links[3,25]. Frequencies above 2500 Hz cannot be used here and there is severe attenuation distortion within the available frequency band.

Figures 2.3 and 2.4 demonstrate the characteristic property of telephone circuits which is a rising attenuation with frequency, for frequencies above about 1000 Hz. The attenuation at 1000 Hz may be as much as 30 dB for a switched line, but it is unlikely to exceed 15 dB for a private line.

Figure 2.5 shows a typical group-delay frequency characteristic for a circuit containing both loaded-audio and carrier links[3,25]. The group delay increases towards the lower and upper ends of the frequency band, there being a delay distortion of about one millisecond in the frequency band 600–2800 Hz. The better circuits tend to have a smaller increase in group delay at the lower frequencies, say only $\frac{1}{2}$ ms at 600 Hz.

Figure 2.6 shows the group-delay frequency characteristic of a poor circuit containing both loaded audio and carrier links[3,25]. The characteristic shows a delay distortion of 1 ms in the frequency band 1000–2200 Hz. Over the very worst switched telephone lines, the delay distortion in this frequency band can be about 2 ms.

There is a very wide spread in the frequency characteristics of different telephone circuits, so that although the five characteristics just considered give some idea of the attenuation and delay characteristics likely to be experienced, the characteristics of any particular circuit may differ appreciably from these[1-31]. In particular, most telephone circuits show a ripple in both the attenuation and delay characteristics. The ripple is caused by multipath propagation, which results from reflections at mismatches along the line, and the presence of a ripple indicates that the received signal is dispersed in time.

Any variations of attenuation and group delay with frequency, subject to the restriction that the attenuation is extremely high over all frequencies above a certain value, correspond to multipath propagation with an infinite number of echoes, where the time delay between adjacent echoes is vanishingly small. A good example of this, of course, is the voice-frequency channel, which is a band-pass channel of bandwidth less than 3000 Hz. Its impulse response (response to an infinitely narrow unit positive impulse) is a continuous rounded waveform of duration not less than $\frac{1}{3}$ ms. The output waveform here is built up of an infinite set of adjoining echoes of the input impulse, where an echo may be a positive or negative pulse of vanishingly short duration and of any finite value. It can be seen that for any other input pulse waveform, the corresponding set of echoes (each with the same waveform as the input pulse) is obtained at the output of the channel.

Thus the attenuation and delay characteristics of the types shown in Figures 2.2–2.6 themselves cause time dispersion of the received signal, and this time dispersion usually increases with the attenuation and delay distortions in the signal frequency band. The time dispersion of the signal elements limits the rate at which the signal can be transmitted (in elements per second) for an acceptable level of intersymbol interference. It is clear, therefore, that a considerably lower signal element rate is obtainable over a telephone circuit with the frequency characteristics of Figures 2.4 and 2.6 than over a circuit with the characteristics of Figures 2.3 and 2.5.

Not only do switched lines tend to have more pronounced ripples on their attenuation and delay characteristics than do private lines, but the smoothed shapes of their characteristics may sometimes resemble Figures 2.4 and 2.6, whereas those of private lines are unlikely to be very much worse than Figures 2.3 and 2.5. For the poorest switched lines, the attenuation at 2000 Hz may be 20 dB greater than that at 1000 Hz, giving a total bandwidth of only

1800 Hz. This is 500 Hz less than that shown in Figure 2.6 and compares with a minimum bandwidth of some 2400 Hz likely to be experienced over the very worst private lines. Private lines using 4-wire working throughout (and therefore containing no hybrid transformers) have a minimum bandwidth of about 2800 Hz. Thus the maximum signal-element rate obtainable with a digital signal over switched lines is in general appreciably lower than that over private lines.

Tests over telephone circuits have shown that the time dispersion of a digital signal, resulting from all causes, does not often exceed 6 ms, but it can occasionally be very much greater[1-31]. Thus, even at the lowest signal element rate of 600 bauds, an individual signal element is likely to be lengthened so that it overlaps and therefore causes intersymbol interference in up to five of the immediately neighbouring elements. However, the dispersed portion of a signal element (that portion of the element causing intersymbol interference) usually contains only a fraction of the total element energy, the major part of the energy lying in the correct time interval. Thus a suitable binary signal, with an element rate of 600 bauds, gives correct operation over the very large majority of telephone circuits.

Nonlinear distortion of the transmitted data signal begins to have a noticeable effect on the detection of the received data signal only at the higher transmission rates. This distortion is harmonic distortion in which the significant components are the second and third harmonics. There does not appear to be any simple or cost-effective method of removing the harmonic components that lie within the signal frequency band, although the level of these components is reduced if the transmitted data signal has no discrete frequency components (carrier or pilot tones) and if there is not a large ratio of peak to mean power levels in this signal[502]. Nonlinear distortion effects do not appear to be very serious in the U.K. telephone network, but they may need to be taken into account at the highest transmission rate of 19.2 kbit/s.

2.5 HF radio links

The voice-frequency signal fed to the radio transmitter for transmission over an HF radio link, modulates a carrier in the frequency band 3–30 MHz, using a process of single sideband suppressed carrier amplitude modulation. This shifts the signal spectrum, which has a bandwidth of about 3 kHz, to the required band in the HF spectrum. At the other end of the radio link the received signal is multiplied by a sine-wave carrier with nominally the same frequency

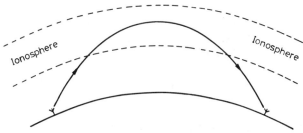

Fig. 2.7 Single-path propagation

as that used at the transmitter, and the resultant signal is filtered to remove the high-frequency components. This is a process of linear demodulation that shifts the signal spectrum back to the voice-frequency band, to give a signal which is ideally the same as that fed to the radio transmitter at the other end of the link. The process of shifting the signal spectrum to the HF band and back again (using linear modulation and demodulation) are basically the same as the corresponding processes used in a telephone carrier link. Since the two carrier frequencies, used for modulating the demodulating the signal, do not necessarily have exactly the same frequency, the spectrum of the voice-frequency signal obtained at the output of the radio receiver may be shifted by 1 or 2 Hz relative to the original signal spectrum at the input to the radio transmitter. In other words, the HF radio link may introduce a frequency offset of 1 or 2 Hz into the voice-frequency signal.

Several voice-frequency signals may be transmitted over a single HF radio link, the signals being frequency division multiplexed in a manner similar to that used over telephone carrier circuits.

An HF radio signal reaches the receiver aerial via a sky wave that has been reflected by the ionosphere, as illustrated in Figure 2.7. The ionosphere is a region of ionized particles, which include free electrons, and it extends from some 50 km to over 700 km above the earth's surface[480]. The ionization is caused by the action of the sun's radiation on the upper atmosphere of the earth. The free electrons act as reflectors for HF radio waves, and their density (and hence their ability to reflect radio signals) varies with height, the greatest density being normally at a height in the neighbourhood of 300 km. The density does not, however, usually increase steadily with height until the greatest density is reached, but generally has two or three regions in which the density reaches a local maximum. These regions are known as *ionized layers*. During the day time the ionosphere has three main ionized layers, each of which could, under the appropriate conditions, reflect an HF radio wave. The layers are known as the E, F_1 and F_2 layers, whose heights are, respectively, around 100, 200 and 250–350 km[480]. The density of free electrons in the F_2 layer is greater than that in the F_1 layer, which, in turn, is greater than that in the E layer. At night the F_1 layer tends to fade out such that the F_1 and F_2 layers effectively coalesce into a single F layer, which has a height of around 300 km. The E layer again has a lower density of free electrons than the F layer and occasionally almost disappears. During the day time there is a fourth ionized layer of relatively small ionization density, known as the D layer, whose height is typically 50–90 km[480]. This layer cannot be used to reflect an HF radio wave and it tends to attenuate sky waves that are reflected from any of the E, F_1 and F_2 layers. The ionosphere is never completely stable, and when it is disturbed by solar flares the density of the free electrons is represented more nearly as clouds on a windy day than as smooth layers. As a general rule, the higher the frequency of the radio signal or the more nearly vertical the direction of the transmitted sky wave, the greater the height at which the wave is reflected. For any given angle of the transmitted sky wave, no reflection takes place at frequencies above a certain value. The height at which reflection takes place, for a sky wave having a given frequency and a given transmitted direction, can vary considerably over a 24 hour period or, for a particular time of day, over a period of a year. The critical frequency above which reflection does not take place can show a similar large variation over the two time periods just mentioned.

We are concerned here with the generation and detection of digital data signals, where these are transmitted over an HF radio link, and not with the design of the radio equipment itself. Thus the equipment considered here is the modem that generates and detects the data signals in the voice-frequency band.

2.6 Attenuation and delay distortions over HF radio links

Whereas the attenuation and delay characteristics of telephone circuits do not vary much with time, so that these are essentially time-invariant channels, the attenuation and delay characteristics of HF radio links may vary considerably with time in an effect known as *frequency selective fading*. This is caused by multipath propagation of the transmitted HF radio wave, when it travels from the transmitter to the receiver via two or more different paths with appreciably different transmission delays. For example, the transmitted radio signal may travel from the transmitter to the receiver via two sky waves which are reflected at two different layers in the ionosphere and

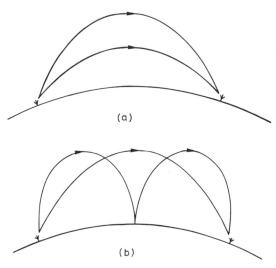

Fig. 2.8   Multipath propagation: (a) reflection from different layers of the ionosphere, (b) different number of hops

therefore at very different heights, the difference being typically of the order of one or two hundred kilometres. Alternatively the transmitted radio signal may travel from the transmitter to the receiver via both one and two hops, that is, being reflected either once or twice from the ionosphere. There is a difference of typically one or two milliseconds between the transmission delays of the two paths, which are as illustrated in Figure 2.8 for the two cases just mentioned. For a relative transmission delay of τ seconds between the signals received over the two paths (sky waves), a ripple is superimposed on each of the attenuation and group-delay characteristics of the voice-frequency channel, with peaks regularly spaced at intervals of $1/\tau$ Hz. The closer the levels of the two signals the greater the attenuation and group-delay peaks, and a change in the relative carrier phases of the two signals shifts the location of these peaks in the frequency characteristic. The two reflected sky waves may be subjected to Rayleigh fading and Doppler shifts, which are forms of multiplicative noise and are considered further in Chapter 3. The effects of these changes is to cause the attenuation peaks to move across the frequency characteristic and also to change in level[32-45,481]. A further interesting effect that introduces a little group-delay distortion into the received signal is the fact that for any one sky wave the effective height of the ionosphere tends to increase with frequency, causing the transmission delay to increase with frequency. Occasionally it decreases with frequency, causing the corresponding decrease in transmission delay with frequency.

For most of the time there are four or fewer sky waves of significant level and having significantly different delays in transmission. With four sky waves the behaviour of the HF radio link is more complex than that with two sky waves, but the same basic effects occur. Thus considerable attenuation and delay distortions can be obtained, these appearing as sharp peaks moving across the corresponding frequency characteristics[32-45,481]. The time dispersion of a transmitted signal-element, caused by multipath propagation, does not usually exceed 8 ms and is most often less than 3 ms[36,37,481]. However, in a 600 bit/s serial system, a large fraction of the element energy may lie in the dispersed portion of the element. Not only can this distortion be considerably more severe than that normally experienced over telephone circuits, but it is time varying, with fading rates typically in the range 5–50 fades per minute. The signal distortion caused by the radio equipment itself is not normally very significant.

The design of a modem for use over HF radio links is influenced mainly by the need for the optimum available tolerance to attenuation and delay distortions, so that complex techniques are often used. Over telephone circuits it is more important to minimize the cost of the equipment, and complex techniques are not often used.

3

Noise

3.1 Basic types of noise

The noise obtained on telephone circuits may be classified into two distinct groups: additive noise in which a waveform is added to the transmitted signal, and multiplicative noise in which the transmitted signal is modulated by the interfering waveform. The multiplicative noise itself may be further subdivided into amplitude and frequency modulation effects[1-31,97].

When the interfering waveform reaches a sufficient level, its effect is to cause the receiver to interpret incorrectly the received signal and so of course to introduce errors at the receiver output. Additive noise becomes less effective in producing errors as the signal level is increased, whereas multiplicative noise has the same effect in producing errors regardless of the signal level.

3.2 Noise over telephone circuits

The different types of noise are as listed below[314,328].

(1) Additive noise
      Impulsive noise
      Speech and signalling tone crosstalk
      White noise
(2) Amplitude modulation effects
      Modulation noise
      Transient interruptions
      Sudden level changes
(3) Frequency modulation effects
      Frequency offset
      Sudden phase changes
      Phase jitter

Impulsive noise comprises short bursts of random additive noise, often with a duration of the order of 20 ms, over typical telephone circuits. Individual noise pulses (bursts) frequently occur in groups, sometimes in quick succession but more often relatively widely scattered. Impulsive noise is the predominant type of noise over switched lines where its effects will often swamp those of the other types of noise. It is also sometimes important over private lines. Impulsive noise on switched lines is usually introduced both by direct pick up from the electromechanical switches in an exchange, and through common impedance coupling via the exchange batteries to the switches, other equipment and telephone circuits fed from these. The common impedance coupling via the batteries may often be the most important source of impulsive noise. Since private lines are not connected either to the switches or to the battery supplies, the level of impulsive noise over switched lines is in general very much higher than that over private lines.

Speech and signalling tone crosstalk result from stray coupling with other telephone circuits. They are not normally important in causing errors except at unusually low signal levels or under definite line fault conditions.

White noise is a steady background noise of low level and relatively wide bandwidth. It only produces errors at very low signal levels and is not normally a significant source of errors.

Over some private lines containing carrier links and particularly at the higher signal levels, modulation noise probably causes a large number of the errors. This appears as amplitude modulation of the signal by band-limited white noise and it normally occurs in short bursts, each lasting up to one or two seconds and causing a scattered group of errors over its duration[97]. Modulation noise may be caused both by microphonic effects when equipment is knocked or shaken, and also by inter-modulation effects when common amplifiers in the carrier link are temporarily overloaded.

Transient interruptions appear as complete breaks in transmission lasting usually from 1 to 100 ms. Over some of the longer and more complex private-line telephone circuits, these transient interruptions could be responsible for a considerable number of the errors obtained, although over the shorter telephone circuits they are not likely to be important.

Sudden signal level changes, usually of the order of 1 to 2 dB but sometimes even exceeding 5 to 6 dB, may occur several times a day. Again this effect will tend to become more frequent and serious over the longer and more complex telephone circuits, and to be less important over the shorter circuits.

Frequency modulation effects occur only over telephone circuits containing carrier links. The frequency offset may have a value up to

± 5 Hz but usually lies in the range ± 1 Hz. Sudden phase changes may occur from time to time and may involve a large change of phase, occurring almost instantaneously. Phase jitter appears as the phase modulation of the received signal carrier by the mains frequency and its harmonics, giving peak to peak values of the resultant phase variations that are normally less than 15° but sometimes up to as much as 30° or more. A significant 250 Hz component has often been observed. Phase jitter is probably caused by the action of nonlinear effects (possibly in repeaters) on the data signal when in the presence of an appreciable mains-frequency interference-signal picked up from the power supplies. Phase jitter is not usually important at transmission rates up to 4800 bit/s, but at transmission rates of 9600 bit/s and above it can seriously degrade the performance of a data-transmission system.

Switched lines have the same amplitude and frequency modulation effects and additive noise as private lines, but they have in addition a high level of impulsive noise which may often mask the other types of noise present.

Experimental and theoretical considerations have shown that although the tolerance of a data transmission system to white Gaussian noise is not necessarily an accurate measure of its actual tolerance to the additive noise over telephone circuits, the relative tolerances to white Gaussian noise of different data transmission systems are nevertheless a good measure of their relative tolerances to this additive noise[297-367]. Since Gaussian noise lends itself well to theoretical calculations and is also easily produced in the laboratory over the required frequency range, the relative tolerances of different data transmission systems to Gaussian noise are a very useful measure of their relative tolerances to the additive noise over telephone circuits.

Whereas over switched lines the majority of the noise is additive, over private lines amplitude and frequency modulation effects can predominate, and these must therefore also be considered. Thus the relative performances of different data-transmission systems over telephone circuits may be assessed on the basis of their tolerances to Gaussian noise and to both amplitude and frequency modulation effects, due weight being given to the relative frequencies and severities of the different types of noise represented by these.

3.3 Noise over HF radio links

The different types of noise are as listed below[32-45].

(1) Additive noise

        Atmospheric noise
        Impulsive noise
        Interference from other radio signals
(2) Amplitude modulation effects
        Flat fading
(3) Frequency modulation effects
        Frequency offset

The main source of additive noise is atmospheric noise caused by lightning discharges. This occupies a frequency band from very low frequencies to around 30 MHz, at the input to the radio receiver[3 26]. The radio receiver band-limits the received signal to a bandwidth of about 3 kHz, in an essentially linear process. It follows therefore that at any instant the band-limited signal contains components originating from several lightning discharges, which can be assumed to be statistically independent sources. From the central-limit theorem, the band-limited noise signal is approximately equivalent to a Gaussian signal, at least over the range of values in the neighbourhood of the mean (that is, near zero). At values away from zero, the probability density of the noise signal begins to depart from the Gaussian probability density, the discrepancy becoming appreciable along the tails. Although the additive noise signal at the input to the receiver of the data modem is not truly Gaussian, it is normally of a sufficiently random nature and sufficiently close to band-limited Gaussian noise, that a modem, having a better tolerance to additive Gaussian noise than another, will almost certainly have a better tolerance to atmospheric noise.

Impulsive noise in HF radio links is usually man made interference and therefore only becomes really important in built up areas or where the radio receiving equipment is close to a source of electrical interference.

An increasingly serious problem in the transmission of digital signals over HF radio links is interference from other radio signals whose spectra overlap that of the wanted signal. For this reason it is important not only to use a narrow-band signal but also to ensure that the bandwidth of the receiver filter is no wider than is absolutely necessary for the satisfactory reception of the data signal.

A modem having the best tolerance to additive white Gaussian noise will in general also have the best overall tolerance to the atmospheric and impulsive noise normally experienced over HF radio links. The different signal designs and detection processes considered for HF radio links will therefore be compared on the assumption that the additive noise is Gaussian. The tolerance of a modem to an interfering radio signal can conveniently be assessed by measuring its tolerance to an interfering tone whose frequency is adjusted, in turn, to different points within the signal frequency band.

Flat fading is the variation with time of the received signal level and is, in fact, always accompanied by the corresponding frequency modulation effect, that appears as a slowly and randomly varying frequency offset applied to the received signal carrier. Flat fading occurs when a radio signal (sky wave) is reflected from just one layer of the ionosphere and reaches the receiver aerial via one hop. The situation is in fact a little more complex than this in that a sky wave reflected from a given layer in the ionosphere is often composed of two sky waves reflected at noticeably different heights, which are often close enough not to cause significant frequency selective fading. This is the result of the so-called, magneto-ionic splitting of the transmitted sky wave into the ordinary and extraordinary rays (that are reflected at slightly different heights) and it is caused by the action of the Earth's magnetic field[480,481]. When reference is made to *different* sky waves in Section 2.5, the two sky waves just mentioned are considered as *one*. In the following discussion, only a *single* reflected sky wave is, for convenience, considered, and in the presence of magneto-ionic splitting of a sky wave, the comments apply separately to each of the ordinary and extraordinary rays.

The ionosphere acts as a large number of different reflectors at different (but not widely different) heights and introducing different attenuations, to give a large number of reflected waves with different levels and carrier phases. The average height of the different reflectors need not be constant, so that there may be a resultant steady increase or decrease in the effective height of the ionosphere. The relative heights of the reflectors and their attenuations may now vary slowly and in a random manner. Variations in the relative heights of the reflectors cause the corresponding variations in path lengths and hence in the relative delays of the reflected waves, leading to slow and random variations in the relative carrier-phases of the reflected waves. Any two of these therefore sometimes tend to add and at other times tend to cancel, leading to a random variation in the level of the resulting wave. The variations in level and phase of the many different reflected waves cause Rayleigh fading of the overall resultant reflected wave. The envelope of this wave varies according to a Rayleigh distribution and its phase varies according to a uniform distribution. So long as the total variation in the relative time delay in transmission of the different reflected waves is small compared with the duration of an individual signal-element, which is usually the case under the conditions assumed here, there is no change in *shape* of the (short term) power-density spectrum of the received signal with time. This implies that the fading affects all parts of the signal spectrum equally and leads to the term 'flat fading'. The reduction in level of the received signal due to flat fading is most often less than 20 dB but is occasionally up to 40 dB or more. Fading rates are usually in the range 3–15 fades per minute (typically 3–6 fades per minute) but may occasionally increase to as much as 1 or 2 fades per second[481].

In addition to amplitude and frequency modulation effects, HF radio links also introduce time modulation effects which are known as Doppler shifts. A steadily increasing path length, caused by a steady increase in the height of the ionosphere, has the effect of stretching out (slowing down) the received signal in time. Similarly, a steadily reducing path length, caused by a steady decrease in the height of the ionosphere, has the effect of compressing (speeding up) the received signal in time. Random variations in the effective height of the ionosphere produce the corresponding random variations in the rate of arrival of the received signal waveform, which is therefore modulated in time. Since the transmitted HF radio signal has a bandwidth of 3 kHz and a carrier frequency in the range 3–30 MHz, it is a narrow-band signal. It can be shown that the Doppler shifts are now approximately equivalent to frequency modulation effects. The combination of these with the small frequency offset introduced by the radio equipment, results in a frequency offset of the received voice-frequency signal, which varies slowly with time and most often has a value in the range ± 2 Hz[32–45,481], but is occasionally up to ± 10 Hz or more, when the ionosphere is disturbed. No constant frequency offset in the radio equipment is assumed here. Since slow random variations in the effective height of the ionosphere normally occur during fading, the latter is generally accompanied by the corresponding random variations in the frequency offset (as has previously been mentioned). It is evident that the received signal here is modulated both in amplitude and frequency, the modulating waveforms having only very low frequency components. Thus the bandwidth of the received signal is very slightly increased. The increase in bandwidth is known as 'frequency spread', the value of frequency spread being around 0.1 Hz under mild fading conditions and around 0.5 Hz under poor fading conditions. Frequency spreads of up to 1 or 2 Hz are, however, likely to be experienced sufficiently often for it to be important that the modem has an adequate tolerance to these.

Whereas the predominant form of additive noise over telephone circuits is impulsive noise, over HF radio links it is atmospheric noise which resembles additive white Gaussian noise. Again, HF radio links do not often introduce such rapid changes in amplitude or phase as occur over telephone circuits. Although the amplitude and phase changes over an HF radio link may at times be very large, they normally take place relatively slowly. The main exception to this is during very deep fades, when the signal is in any case very seriously attenuated.

4

Transmission of timing information

4.1 The need for timing information

A digital signal on its own has very little meaning in the absence of the corresponding timing information. A receiver normally has prior knowledge of the duration of an element, that is, of the element rate, but it rarely if ever has prior knowledge of the positions of the element boundaries. Without this information, correct detection of the received data signal is impossible. The necessary timing information must therefore be transmitted with the data signal, and the receiver must always have a means of extracting from the received signal a timing waveform which determines the element boundaries. This can be done in various ways, depending upon the nature of the data signal[46-93].

4.2 Synchronous systems

A synchronous system is one in which the transmitter and receiver are operating continuously at the same numbers of signal elements per second and are maintained, by correction, in the desired phase relationship[46-86].

The transmission of timing information in a synchronous system may be achieved in two different ways. In the first of these the timing information is transmitted by a completely separate signal, which may use a separate modulated carrier or may be imposed on the signal carrier itself, using a different modulation method to that used for the data signal. Sometimes even the same modulation method may be used[192]. The essential requirement of this or of any other method is of course that the timing waveform at the receiver should not be affected by frequency modulation effects over the transmission path. For this reason a single unmodulated carrier, on its own, cannot be used.

The above method has the important property that the correct transmission of the timing information is in no way dependent on the sequence of data element values being transmitted, so that no restriction need be placed on the data signal in order to ensure the correct transmission of the timing information. It has, however, certain disadvantages. Firstly, because an additional signal is transmitted, there is an inevitable increase in the complexity of both the transmitter and the receiver. Secondly, the presence of the separate timing signal often implies a lower level for the data signal and therefore a lower tolerance of the latter to additive noise. There is always a limit on either the peak or the mean transmitted signal power. Thirdly, there may sometimes be a degree of interference between the signal carrying the timing information and the data signal, thus reducing the tolerance of the system to both noise and distortion. Fourthly, where the spectrum of the timing signal does not lie within the frequency band occupied by the data signal, the phase of the timing waveform obtained in the receiver relative to that of the demodulated data signal, is dependent on the group-delay characteristic of the transmission path. Over HF radio links, where the delay characteristic may vary considerably with time, satisfactory operation is unlikely to be obtained with such an arrangement. Over telephone circuits, the timing waveform at the receiver must now always be correctly re-phased relative to the demodulated data signal, for any new transmission path having a different group-delay characteristic or for any significant change in the group-delay characteristic of the path used. However, one important requirement for a data-transmission system is that once the equipment has been adjusted it should be capable of operating correctly over any one of possibly a large group of different telephone circuits, without further readjustment. Such arrangements for transmitting the timing information, where the phase of the timing waveform at the receiver relative to that of the demodulated data signal is a function of the group-delay characteristic of the transmission path, are not therefore suitable for use over telephone circuits.

The timing information can alternatively be transmitted by the data signal itself. The timing waveform at the receiver is here derived from the transitions in the demodulated data signal, and the timing waveform is then used in the detection of the latter signal. It is now necessary to restrict the length of sequences in the data signal during which there are no transitions in the demodulated baseband signal. Otherwise excessive phase-errors may occur in the timing waveform, whose phase is controlled by the transitions in the demodulated baseband signal. Such an arrangement clearly cannot handle all possible sequences of data element values and it is not therefore a transparent system. It does, however, overcome the various weaknesses of the other arrangement, essentially because no additional timing signal is transmitted.

In a serial system, the second method of transmitting the timing information is normally to be preferred, whereas in a parallel system, a separate timing signal should be used.

With either method of transmitting the timing information, the receiver has an accurate prior knowledge of the signal element rate so that in the generation of the timing waveform, the signal carrying the timing information is filtered through a very-narrow-band filter. This removes practically all the noise components, to give a timing waveform having the correct phase and essentially free from jitter, even when there is an unusually low signal/noise ratio. A phase-locked oscillator with a very stable natural frequency is normally used in place of a simple filter, and performs essentially the same operation. Its output is shaped to give a rectangular timing waveform. In a correctly designed synchronous system, long before there is appreciable jitter in the timing waveform at the receiver, the error rate in the detected data signal with correct sampling, will have risen well above the maximum acceptable value.

The timing waveform is extracted from the received signal and is used to sample the demodulated data signal at the optimum points, to give an undistorted binary data signal (the detected data signal) which together with the timing waveform provide the required output signals.

The method of extracting the timing waveform at the receiver from the demodulated baseband data signal may be clarified by the following example, The demodulated data signal in the receiver, for a binary coded system, has two different voltage levels, one representing the binary value 0 and the other representing the binary value 1, as shown in Figure 4.1. Strictly speaking, this is the demodulated waveform (usually rounded in shape) after it has been compared with a threshold voltage and set positive when above the threshold and negative when below. In other words, it is the demodulated waveform after it has been sliced along the threshold level and amplified. The transition between a '0' and a '1' or vice versa occurs at the junction between two adjacent demodulated signal elements, and therefore, if the received signal element rate is known at the receiver, these transitions can be used to phase correctly a timing waveform of the correct frequency which is already generated by an oscillator. Alternatively, the transitions may be used themselves both to generate and correctly phase the timing waveform, as in Figure 4.1.

Demodulated data signal

Timing waveform

Detected data signal

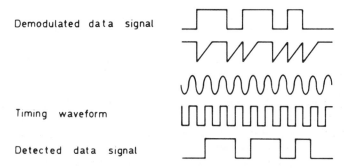

Fig. 4.1   Generation of timing waveform

Each transition in the demodulated waveform is here used to generate
a negative-going triangular pulse. The waveform comprising these
pulses has a very strong frequency component not only at the correct
signal element rate but also in the correct phase. This frequency
component is filtered out using a narrow-band filter and it is then
suitably shaped to produce the timing waveform. This, as can be seen
from the diagram, is phased so that the positive-going edges sample
each demodulated signal element centrally. At each sampling instant
a bistable circuit is set to the corresponding state, and the rectangular
binary output signal from this circuit is the detected data signal.

Clearly, the receiver has prior knowledge of the signal element rate,
in terms of the centre frequency of the pass band of the narrow-band
filter. The phase of the output sine-wave from this filter, at any instant,
is dependent on a number of the preceding transitions in the
demodulated waveform, so that the phase of the timing waveform is
the running average of the phase indicated by these transitions. This,
of course, reduces the effect of noise on the timing waveform. The
longer the averaging (or integration) period used in the generation of
the timing waveform, the smaller is the effect of noise on this
waveform, but the more accurate must be the prior knowledge of the
element rate at the receiver. Hence the more stable must be both the
oscillator that determines the element rate at the transmitter and the
filter or phase-locked oscillator used to extract the timing waveform
at the receiver.

4.3   Start-stop systems

A start-stop system is defined as one in which each group of data
elements, corresponding to a character or alphabetic symbol, is
preceded by a start signal which serves to prepare the receiving

mechanism for the reception and detection of a character, and is followed by a stop signal which serves to bring the receiving mechanism to rest in preparation for the reception of the next character[92,93].

The data signal is here divided into separate groups of elements, where the signal elements in a group are transmitted sequentially and at a steady rate. Each group of data elements is preceded by a timing signal (the start signal) which is allocated solely to the transmission of timing information. Two adjacent groups of data elements are separated from each other by an arbitrary time interval, which may vary considerably from one pair of adjacent elements to another. Where there is a fixed number of elements in a group (character), the stop signal is redundant and is therefore often omitted, or made the same as the standby signal transmitted between adjacent characters.

At the receiver, each timing signal is used to generate a discrete series of timing pulses which are used to sample the following group of demodulated data elements, to provide at the receiver output the detected data signal together with the associated timing waveform.

The receiver here has an accurate prior knowledge of the time intervals between adjacent elements in a group, but it has no prior knowledge of the time intervals between adjacent groups. The correct sampling of the data elements in a group is therefore critically dependent on the accurate detection of the preceding timing signal. Any error in the detection of this timing signal produces a corresponding error in the sampling of each of the following demodulated data elements. Since the element energy and therefore the tolerance to additive noise of an individual timing signal cannot in practice be made very much greater than that of a data element, the timing waveform in the receiver of a start-stop system can be seriously affected by both noise and distortion.

In a truly asynchronous system, the individual data elements are transmitted with arbitrary time intervals between adjacent elements, and the time interval may vary considerably from one pair of adjacent elements to another[399]. A separate timing signal may be transmitted shortly before each data element, to prepare the receiver for the detection of the element. Alternatively, the arrival of a data element may be detected from the element itself, by arranging that the signal transmitted for a data element of any value is always different from the signal transmitted during the intervals between data elements. As before, the timing waveform used to sample any demodulated data element at the receiver, is critically dependent on the accurate detection of the corresponding timing signal, so that the timing waveform can be seriously affected by both noise and distortion. Such a system is, of course, a special case of a start-stop system, with only one data-element associated with each timing signal.

4.4 Comparison of systems

In a start-stop system, the generation of the timing waveform for a character is initiated immediately the start signal has been detected. There is therefore a negligible delay at the start of the transmission of the data signal, since no special synchronizing characters are required in the data signal. A synchronous system, however, requires a certain minimum time at the beginning of each transmission,, when a synchronizing signal is sent to the receiver, to adjust the phase of the timing waveform to its correct value.

In a start-stop system the group of data elements following a timing signal normally comprises a 'character', so that the first, second, third, etc., element in each character is identified directly from its position in the group. However, in a synchronous system a special character-synchronizing code is required at the beginning of each transmission to enable the equipment fed from the receiver to identify the first, second, third, etc., element in each character[87-91]. Thus the equipment required for a start-stop system may sometimes be less complex than that for the equivalent synchronous system.

There are, however, two rather serious disadvantages associated with start-stop systems. Firstly, except for extremely short data messages, the average data-element rate of these systems cannot be as great as that obtainable in the equivalent synchronous systems. This follows because of the special timing signals which are interspersed between the data signals in start-stop systems. Secondly, whereas in a synchronous system the timing waveform is essentially unaffected by noise and distortion, the timing waveform in a start-stop system can be seriously affected. The latter system therefore inevitably has a lower tolerance to both noise and distortion.

Since there is normally no very significant difference in the complexity of the different systems, a synchronous system should always be used where possible.

5

Modulation methods

5.1 The need for modulation

The information which it is required to transmit over a voice-frequency channel is most often initially contained in a binary rectangular signal in which one level represents the value 0 and another level represents the value 1. The main function of the data modem, at the sending end of the channel, is to convert this rectangular signal into the form most suitable for transmission over the channel, and at the receiving end of the channel it is to convert the latter waveform back again into the original rectangular signal.

The rectangular data signal cannot itself be transmitted satisfactorily over a typical voice-frequency channel for the following reasons. Firstly, whatever the signal element rate, a significant proportion of the signal power will usually be lost in transmission, and secondly, the received signal at the other end of the channel will normally be so severely distorted as to make satisfactory detection impossible. The most compelling single reason for the transmission of modulated-carrier signals over voice-frequency channels, however, is the existence of frequency-modulation effects over many of these channels. Any shift (frequency offset) in the spectrum of a baseband data signal in general makes it impossible to detect the signal correctly. Thus, even where it is possible to shape the spectrum of a baseband signal to match the attenuation characteristic of the channel and so avoid the attenuation and distortion effects just mentioned, any frequency offset introduced by the channel prevents the correct detection of the baseband signal.

Where a private-line telephone circuit is less than about 15 miles long and is not connected through a repeater or any telephone carrier equipment, it may be possible to obtain a d.c. connection between the two ends of the line, which now passes all the low frequencies with little or no distortion. Under these conditions, a suitably rounded form of the rectangular data signal could be transmitted directly over the circuit.

Except where otherwise stated, it is assumed that a synchronous serial binary data-transmission system is used, but most of the discussion applies equally well to the corresponding parallel systems. The emphasis here is on transmission rates of 600 and 1200 bit/s, over a voice-frequency channel. These transmission rates are achieved quite satisfactorily by binary signals, which would always be used here in preference to multilevel signals. The latter involve greater equipment complexity and in the present applications they usually give no improvement in performance.

5.2 AM, FM and PM signals

A modulated sine-wave carrier may be expressed by the following equation:

$$s(t) = a(t) \sin \left\{ 2\pi \int_0^t f(\tau)\, d\tau + p(t) \right\} \qquad (5.1)$$

This waveform contains three different parameters which are variable quantities and which may be used to carry information. These are the amplitude $a(t)$, the instantaneous frequency $f(t)$ and the phase $p(t)$. In any simple process of modulation, one of these parameters is made to vary with the modulating waveform, so that the information present in the modulating waveform is transferred to that parameter of the sine-wave carrier, the other two parameters ideally remaining constant.

Consider ideal double-sideband binary signals using *rectangular* modulating waveforms with an element duration of T seconds, and assume the ideal arrangement of each modulation method. The amplitude modulated (AM) signal uses 100% amplitude modulation. It transmits an element '0' by the absence of the signal carrier (no signal) and an element '1' by the presence of the signal carrier. The frequency modulated (FM) signal transmits an element '0' by a given carrier frequency and an element '1' by another carrier frequency differing by $1/T$ Hz from the first carrier frequency. There is no phase change here in the signal carrier at the boundary between two signal-elements. The phase modulated (PM) signal uses the same carrier frequency for the two binary elements, with a phase difference of 180° between the carriers of the two elements. This is also a suppressed carrier AM signal, whose two binary elements are antipodal (the negatives of each other).

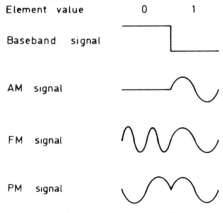

Fig. 5.1   Basic types of modulation

The three modulation methods are illustrated in Figure 5.1. The modulating waveform here is the rectangular binary baseband signal which contains two adjacent elements, the first of which carries the binary value 0 and the second of which carries the binary value 1.

In practical PM systems using a binary signal, the carrier phase may be shifted by a large and often variable amount in transmission, so that an element transmitted as a '0' may well arrive at the receiver as a '1' and vice versa. To overcome this difficulty, differential coding may be used, in which a '1' is transmitted as a 180° phase shift in the carrier between two adjacent signal elements, and a '0' as no phase shift between these elements. Alternatively, the phase of the received signal carrier corresponding to a '0' or a '1' may be determined at the beginning of each transmission, by sending here a continuous series of '0's' or '1's' or some other convenient code. The phase of the carrier, corresponding to a '0' or a '1' at any later point during transmission, may then be remembered by suitable means, so long as the phase variations of the carrier, resulting from frequency modulation effects in the channel, are not rapid enough to be confused with real transmitted phase changes between adjacent signal elements.

The particular arrangements of the AM, FM and PM signals just described will be assumed in the following discussion. Although in the comparison of the different systems it is assumed that there is no significant band limiting of the transmitted signals, the relative tolerances of the different systems to additive and multiplicative noise are not seriously affected when some band-limiting is applied to the transmitted signals, just so long as this is symmetrical with respect to the centre of the signal frequency band and does not introduce significant delay distortion.

AM, FM and PM signals are often referred to as ASK, FSK and PSK signals, respectively, where A, F and P mean 'amplitude', 'frequency' and 'phase', as before, and SK means 'shift keyed'. This terminology is, however, often associated with the important case where a rectangular modulating waveform is used, since 'shift keyed' tends to imply instantaneous or very rapid changes of the modulating waveform at the signal-element boundaries and no change over the duration of any signal element. All FM and PM signals to be studied in any detail in this book are assumed to have rectangular modulating waveforms and so could also, on this basis, be considered as FSK and PSK signals. This is not, however, true for AM signals, where the modulating waveform is sometimes taken to be rounded in shape. Of course, when FSK and PSK signals are bandlimited by passing them through the appropriate band-pass filters, the original rectangular envelopes of the individual signal elements become rounded in shape, leading to the corresponding envelope variations and hence amplitude modulation in the resulting FSK and PSK signals. However, the modulating waveforms of the filtered FSK and PSK signals may still be rectangular in shape. On the other hand, both the modulating waveform and envelope of the corresponding filtered ASK signal are rounded in shape, these being, of course, the same waveform. Throughout this book the terms AM, FM and PM will be used to include both rectangular and rounded modulating waveforms and both rectangular and rounded envelopes of an individual signal element. The terms ASK, FSK and PSK will be taken to imply a rectangular modulating waveform and a rectangular envelope of an individual signal element, the envelope being therefore constant over the duration of the element, as in Figure 5.1. By this means a distinction can be made between this important class of signals and the remainder.

Extensive studies have been carried out over the past 30 years on AM systems[94-102], FM systems[103-182] and PM systems[183-243] using digital signals. Not only have the properties of these systems been studied under a wide range of conditions but the basic modulation methods have themselves been developed and refined[94-243]. We are here concerned only with the elementary properties of simple AM, FM and PM signals.

5.3 Relative tolerances to additive white Gaussian noise of AM, PM and FM systems

A data-transmission system is said to have an advantage of x dB in tolerance to additive noise over another system, if, for the same

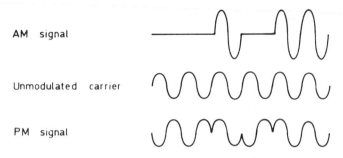

AM signal

Unmodulated carrier

PM signal

Fig. 5.2　An AM signal shown as the sum of a PM signal and an unmodulated carrier

transmission rate and for the same average or peak transmitted power level in the two systems, a noise power level at the receiver input of the first system, which is x dB greater than that for the second system, results in the same error rate in the detected element values of the two systems. Digital data-transmission systems normally operate at low error rates of the order of 1 in 10^5.

A binary AM signal, having a rectangular modulating waveform, is the sum of an unmodulated carrier signal and a PM signal, as shown in Figure 5.2.

The unmodulated carrier and PM signal here both have half the peak amplitude of the AM signal. The binary PM signal is of course a suppressed carrier AM signal, and is obtained by subtracting the carrier from the AM signal. The relationship between AM and PM signals illustrated in Figure 5.2 holds for any whole or fractional number of carrier cycles per signal element.

Since the carrier in Figure 5.2 is unmodulated, it is of no help in the detection of the data signal. Thus the data is carried entirely by the PM signal, and the optimum detection process for the AM signal involves the optimum detection of the PM signal. But the PM signal has half the peak amplitude of the AM signal, so that in applications over voice-frequency channels where the transmitted signals are peak power limited and therefore have a fixed *peak* amplitude, the PM signal component of a transmitted AM signal has half the peak amplitude of a transmitted PM signal, and the tolerance of the corresponding AM system to additive Gaussian noise is 6 dB below that of the corresponding PM system. It is assumed that rectangular and not rounded modulating waveforms are used here and that a transmitted signal-element is equally likely to have either binary value. Again it can be seen that half the transmitted power of the AM signal is carried by the PM signal and the remaining half by the unmodulated carrier, so that only half the transmitted power is used in the detection of the AM data signal. Thus in applications where the transmitted signals are limited by their average power, the tolerance to additive Gaussian noise of the AM system is 3 dB below that of the PM system.

A binary FM signal, which has a rectangular modulating waveform and a whole number of half cycles of the carrier in each of the two binary signal-elements, with one of the two binary elements having a whole number of carrier cycles more than the other and with no phase change in the carrier at the boundary between two signal elements, is the sum of two complementary AM signals as shown in Figure 5.3. Each of these AM signals is, in turn, the sum of an unmodulated carrier and a binary PM signal, where the unmodulated carrier and PM signal both have half the power of the AM signal. The total power of the two PM signals is equal to the sum of their individual power levels. Similarly, the total power of the two unmodulated carriers is the sum of their individual power levels. Thus half the power of the FM signal is carried by the two PM signals and the remaining half by the two unmodulated carriers. The transmitted data is carried entirely by the two PM signals, and the optimum detection process for the FM signal involves the optimum detection of the two PM signals. It may readily be shown that the detection of either signal is unaffected by the presence or absence of the other, and the tolerance to additive white Gaussian noise in the optimum detection of the *two* signals is the same as that in the optimum detection of a single binary PM signal of the same element rate and with a power level equal to the sum of the powers of the two signals. Alternatively, the two PM signals together form a binary antipodal signal of the same element rate and with a power level equal to half that of the FM signal. The tolerance to additive white Gaussian noise in the optimum detection of the binary antipodal signal is the same as that in the optimum detection of a binary PM signal of the same element rate and power level. Clearly, only half the power of the FM signal is used in the detection process, so that the tolerance to additive white Gaussian noise of the FM system is 3 dB below that of the corresponding PM system.

It is interesting to observe that in the extreme case of the class of FM signals illustrated in Figure 5.3, when one of the two carrier frequencies becomes zero and the constant level (d.c.) corresponding to this zero frequency is also zero, the FM signal degenerates into an AM signal.

A binary FM signal, which has a rectangular modulating waveform, with one cycle of the signal carrier in one of the two binary elements and half a cycle in the other, is similar to a PM signal, as shown in Figure 5.4[161]. As before, there is no phase change in the

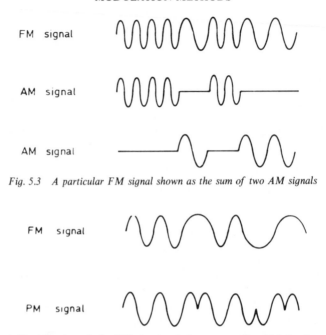

Fig. 5.3   *A particular FM signal shown as the sum of two AM signals*

Fig. 5.4   *A particular FM signal and the corresponding PM signal*

carrier at the boundary between two elements of the FM signal. It can be seen that if the PM signal is passed through a low-pass filter which suitably attenuates the frequency components above the signal carrier frequency but without changing the phase of the carrier, the PM signal becomes rounded in shape and closely resembles the FM signal, except that the element boundaries of the PM signal occur at the mid points of the corresponding elements of the FM signal. The filtering of the PM signal does not significantly affect its tolerance to additive Gaussian noise, when detected by the optimum detector (Chapter 7), so that this detector can be used also for the FM signal, with effectively the same tolerance to noise. In other words, the FM signal is equivalent to a filtered PM signal.

It can be seen that in this FM signal, the phase of the signal carrier over any signal element is shifted by 180° (that is, the signal element is replaced by its negative) if the binary value of *any one* of the preceding signal elements is changed. With the previous FM signal, as in Figure 5.3, the carrier phase over any signal element is *independent* of the binary values of the preceding elements. Although the particular FM signal in Figure 5.4 has some unique properties that are not shared by other FM signals, it is itself a member of an important class of FM

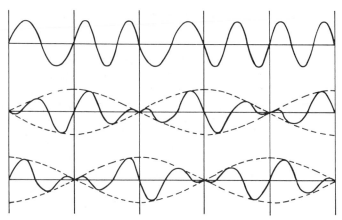

Fig. 5.5 *MSK signal and its two constituent binary PM signals*

signals known as MSK (minimum shift keyed) signals that are in fact both FSK and PM signals[482-490].

An MSK signal is a binary FSK signal in which, of course, the instantaneous carrier frequency and envelope are both constant over the duration T of a signal element, and where the frequency shift (in Hz) between the two values of the instantaneous carrier frequency, f_0 and f_1, is

$$f_1 - f_0 = \frac{1}{2T} \tag{5.2}$$

In addition, either or both of the following two conditions should be satisfied:

$$f_0 = \frac{l}{2T} \tag{5.3}$$

where l is a positive integer, or

$$f_0 \gg \frac{1}{T} \tag{5.4}$$

where $1/T$ is the signal element rate in bauds. As is illustrated in Figure 5.5, such a signal is in fact the sum of two binary PM signals with the same carrier frequency but with the two carriers in phase quadrature (that is, at an angle of 90°). The duration of a PM signal element is $2T$ seconds and the two binary PM signals are offset in time by T seconds, such that a boundary between two adjacent elements in one signal lies half way between the two nearest boundaries in the

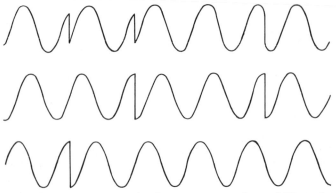

Fig. 5.6   *Offset QPSK signal and its two constituent binary PSK signals*

other. The envelope of each binary signal element is shaped as a half cycle of a sine wave. Differential coding must be used for each binary PM signal. The two binary signals are orthogonal (Equation 6.26), such that neither interferes in the optimum detection of the other. The optimum detection of such signals is considered in Chapters 6 and 7. Thus, if the detector handles the MSK signal as the sum of the two binary PM signals and carries out the optimum detection process separately on each of these, the tolerance to additive white Gaussian noise is the same as that in the optimum detection of the corresponding binary PM signal, having the same power level and information rate (bit rate) as the MSK signal. Since the MSK signal has a constant envelope and generally a narrower bandwidth than the corresponding binary PM signal, it is of considerable practical importance.

If now the envelopes of the two PM signals in Figure 5.5, that together make up the MSK signal, are made rectangular, without otherwise changing the PM signals, the latter become PSK signals and the resultant signal becomes an offset QPSK (quaternary PSK) signal as shown in Figure 5.6. This is a PSK signal but not an FSK or FM signal, since the instantaneous carrier frequency over each signal element is now constant at the same value for every element.

The carrier frequency f_c should here satisfy either or both of the following two conditions:

$$f_c = \frac{l}{2T} \tag{5.5}$$

where l is a positive integer, or

$$f_c \gg \frac{1}{T} \qquad (5.6)$$

where $1/T$ is the signal element rate in bauds. Since the maximum phase shift of the offset QPSK signal is $90°$ instead of $180°$ as in each constituent binary PSK signal, its bandwidth becomes somewhat narrower than that of the corresponding QPSK signal in which the two constituent binary PSK signals (with carriers in phase quadrature) are in element synchronism.

The MSK and offset QPSK signals are both members of a large class of signals which are formed by two offset binary PM signals, with the same carrier frequency but in phase quadrature, the different members of the class being formed by different shaped envelopes of the binary PM signals[482-490]. All members of this class, other than the offset QPSK signal itself, are both FM and PM signals and all have approximately the same tolerance to additive white Gaussian noise as that of a binary PM signal with an element rate of $1/T$ bauds. The members of this class of signals do not necessarily have constant envelopes.

In a typical FM signal, one of the two binary elements does not have a whole number of carrier cycles more than the other, a common value being around 0.7 cycles. Again, there is no phase change at the boundary between two signal-elements. Such an FM signal no longer has any discrete frequency (unmodulated carrier) components, suggesting that *all* the received signal power can be used in the detection of the received signal-elements. Furthermore, the wrong detection of a received signal-element means that the following received elements do not have the expected carrier phases. This fact can be used in the detection process to assist in the location and correction of the error that has occurred, and so to give a better tolerance to noise. Indeed, if an optimum detection process is used with such an FM signal, the detection process operating not only over the duration of the given received signal-element, whose value is being determined, but also over n of the following received signal-elements (where $n \geq 4$), rather than operating separately on the individual received signal-elements, it appears that the tolerance to additive white Gaussian noise may be improved to a little over 1 dB better than that for the optimum detection of the corresponding binary PM signal[176,495]. The detection of a received signal-element now spans the duration of $n + 1$ consecutive received elements, thus delaying by nT seconds the detection of the wanted element. With n sufficiently large and at high signal/noise ratios, a near optimum detection process for the wanted signal-element, which is rather simpler than that just mentioned, involves the detection of the whole sequence of $n + 1$ elements and the selection of the final detected value of the wanted element as its value in the detected sequence. The principles behind this detection process are considered further in Sections 6.1 and 6.3. Unfortunately, the detection process is likely to be very complex to implement and it is therefore not really suitable for applications over telephone circuits, where the cost of a modem is of critical importance.

The binary PM signal is unique in that it is an antipodal signal, the two possible forms of a signal element being the *negatives* of each other. This means that for a given element energy, the distortion or mutilation that can be tolerated by a received signal-element, before it can no longer be distinguished from the incorrect one of its two possible forms, is greater than that for any other binary signal. Furthermore, *all* the received signal energy can here be used effectively in the separate detection of an individual received element value, which is not so for any other binary signal.

It is interesting now to summarize the important conclusions that have been reached concerning the AM, FM and PM signals, of the types corresponding to those in Figures 5.2 and 5.3. These conclusions are derived more rigorously in Chapter 16, with a more precise statement of the conditions assumed. First, it is necessary to mention the two different situations that are often found in practice.

In applications over voice-frequency channels where *any* sequence of binary element values may be transmitted, the *peak* power of the signal fed to the channel is limited at a specified value. Where the digital data is itself random in nature, or else has been scrambled (or recoded) to produce a nearly random sequence, the *average* power of the signal fed to the channel is limited at the specified value.

Where the transmitted signal level is limited by the peak power of the signal, a binary PM signal gains a 3 dB advantage, in tolerance to additive white Gaussian noise, over a binary FM signal, and the latter gains a 3 dB advantage over a binary AM signal. Where the transmitted signal level is limited by the *average* power of the signal, a binary PM signal gains a 3 dB advantage over both the binary FM and the binary AM signals[197,303,306,320]. Rectangular modulating waveforms and envelopes, an approximately equal number of the two binary element values in a transmitted message, and optimum detection processes, are assumed for the three signals.

6

Ideal detection processes

6.1 Optimum detection of a received signal message

Suppose that a signal message involving a sequence of signal elements is received in the presence of bandlimited additive white Gaussian noise. The noise is assumed to be bandlimited to a frequency band that extends over the whole of that of the data signal and to have a constant power spectral density (average power per unit bandwidth) over its frequency band. The maximum-likelihood detection process for the received signal message selects as the detected message the possible sequence of transmitted signal-element values (data symbols) for which there is the minimum mean-square difference between the corresponding received data signal, for the given signal distortion introduced by the equipment filters and transmission path but in the absence of noise, and the signal actually received. The detection process must, of course, extend over the *whole* of the received data signal, and it is assumed that no other signals are transmitted immediately before or after the given message. If the different possible received messages are equally likely, the maximum likelihood detection process minimizes the probability of error in the detection of the received message[422].

Suppose now that the signal elements comprising the message are equally likely to have any of their possible values and are furthermore statistically independent, which means not only that the *value* of any one signal element (that is, the data symbol carried by the element) in no way influences the value of any other, but also that the value of any one signal element in no way influences the actual *waveform* of any other. Under these conditions the optimum detection of the received message can be achieved by the optimum detection of each individual received signal-element on its own, provided only that there is no intersymbol interference in a detection process.

Consider next a message formed by a sequence of binary FSK signal-elements, with an element duration of T seconds and a frequency shift (between the two possible values of the instantaneous frequency) of $0.7/T$ Hz. Even though the signal elements are equally likely to take on either binary value and the element values (data symbols) are statistically independent, the actual *waveform* of an individual signal-element is dependent on the waveforms of the preceding elements and therefore on their binary values, which implies that the detection of this element value must be able to assist in the detection of the previous element values, and vice versa. It follows from this that the optimum detection of the received message cannot be achieved by the separate detection of each individual received signal-element, where the detection of any one signal element does not involve, at the same time, the detection of any other signal elements. It also means that the optimum detection of any sequence of such signal elements, must involve the detection of the *whole* sequence.

6.2 Optimum detection of an *m*-level signal element

The aim of this section is to derive, by means of simple intuitive arguments involving the minimum of mathematics, the optimum detection process for a received data signal. In the interests of clarity and with a view to illuminating the more important basic principles, certain sacrifices have been made in mathematical rigour. Fully rigorous derivations of these results can be found elsewhere[71,423,475].

Suppose that a received *m*-level signal element has the waveform $s_h(t)$, where $h = 0, 1, \ldots, m - 1$ and is the element value, that is, the data symbol carried by the signal element. Suppose also that the signal element is received in the presence of stationary zero-mean additive white Gaussian noise, and that it is equally likely to have any of its *m* possible values and therefore any of the *m* corresponding waveforms. No particular assumptions are for the present made concerning the *m* possible waveforms of the signal element, so that the waveforms may have widely differing shapes and energies. The $(i + 1)$th of the *m* possible waveforms is $s_i(t)$, where i is the corresponding element value, and it is assumed that, for $i = 0, 1, \ldots, m - 1$,

$$s_i(t) = 0 \quad \text{for } t < 0 \text{ and } t > T \tag{6.1}$$

Furthermore, it is assumed that the $\{s_i(t)\}$ are, for practical purposes, bandlimited signals, having some given 'effective' bandwidth. Strictly speaking, of course, they have infinite bandwidth as a result of their finite time duration, but all signals of interest here undergo a negligible change when bandlimited to a sufficiently wide frequency band. Clearly, the waveforms $\{s_i(t)\}$ may be baseband or modulated carrier signals, and in the latter case the modulating waveforms may be rectangular or rounded, provided only that Equation 6.1 is satisfied. (Small curly brackets, as in $\{s_i(t)\}$, designate a set.)

It is assumed here (and throughout this book) that neither the amplitude nor the instantaneous frequency of $s_i(t)$ can tend to infinity, and that the energy of $s_i(t)$ (even when not confined to a time interval of T seconds) is strictly finite. Furthermore, all signals are real valued. For convenience, the source and load impedance of every signal is taken to be one ohm and purely resistive, and the signal value is measured in volts or amps. Thus the instantaneous signal power, at any given instant in time, is the square of the corresponding signal value, and the signal energy over any given time interval is simply the integral of the square of the signal waveform over this interval.

The detection process for a received signal element is here taken to be optimum in the sense that the probability of error in the detection of the signal element is minimized under the condition that the signal element is received on its own (in the absence of other signal elements). This is equivalent to the case where the signal element is one of a stream of received elements which are statistically independent (in the sense described in Section 6.1) and do not overlap in time. For the optimum detection of the received signal-element, the receiver must have prior knowledge of $s_i(t)$, for $i = 0, 1, \ldots, m - 1$, which is taken to be the case. This means, of course, that the receiver can generate $s_i(t)$ for each i. Since true white Gaussian noise has infinite bandwidth, it has an infinite average power level and so is not physically realisable. To avoid this difficulty the noise waveform is considered to have a constant power spectral density over the whole of the effective frequency band of the data signal, the noise power density decaying to zero at frequencies well away from the edges of the frequency band of the data signal, such that the noise is bandlimited white Gaussian noise. The noise waveform is designated $w(t)$.

It can be shown that there is no loss in performance of an optimum detector when the frequency components of the white Gaussian noise that lie outside the frequency band of the data signal are removed. This result follows from the fact that the noise and data signals are statistically independent (an assumption made throughout this book) and from the fact that, when Gaussian noise is fed to two filters whose passbands are disjoint (do not overlap), the two output noise signals are statistically independent Gaussian random processes[423,475]. Clearly, the portion of the original white Gaussian noise that has been removed in forming the bandlimited white Gaussian noise is statistically independent of the bandlimited noisy data signal and so cannot help in the detection process.

The received bandlimited noisy data signal is

$$r(t) = s_h(t) + w(t) \tag{6.2}$$

and the receiver must determine h from $r(t)$ with the minimum probability of error. Now, given $r(t)$ and assuming (correctly or incorrectly) that $s_i(t)$ is the received data signal, where i has one of the values $0, 1, \ldots, m-1$, the corresponding estimate of the received noise waveform $w(t)$ is

$$w_i(t) = r(t) - s_i(t) \tag{6.3}$$

It can be shown that, if there are two possible bandlimited white Gaussian noise waveforms $\{w_i(t)\}$, for two different values of i taken from $0, 1, \ldots, m-1$, then the one of the two that is the more likely to be the one actually received is that for which

$$\int_0^T w_i^2(t)\, dt$$

is the smaller[475]. Strictly speaking the function $w_i^2(t)$ should be integrated over the time interval from $-\Delta$ to $T + \Delta$, where Δ is positive and is the minimum separation between points on $w(t)$ that can, for practical purposes, be considered to be statistically independent. This follows because the optimum detector must consider all portions of the received noise waveform that are in any way influenced by the received waveform $r(t)$ over the duration of $s_h(t)$, that is, from 0 to T. However, provided that the frequency band of the bandlimited white Gaussian noise is sufficiently wide and, in particular, that it includes the whole of the effective frequency band of every $s_i(t)$, the value of Δ becomes so small that it can be set to zero with no noticeable effect on the detection process.

Now, under the assumed conditions, the value of i most likely to be correct (equal to h) can be taken to be that for which $s_i(t)$ is closest to $r(t)$ in the sense that it minimizes the parameter[478]

$$
\begin{aligned}
D_i &= \int_0^T (r(t) - s_i(t))^2 \, dt \\
&= \int_0^T (r^2(t) + s_i^2(t) - 2r(t)s_i(t)) \, dt \\
&= \int_0^T r^2(t) \, dt + \int_0^T s_i^2(t) \, dt - 2 \int_0^T r(t)s_i(t) \, dt \tag{6.4}
\end{aligned}
$$

In Equation 6.4,

$$\int_0^T r^2(t)\, dt$$

is the energy of the received waveform over the time interval 0 to T and is independent of i,

$$\int_0^T s_i^2(t)\, dt$$

is the energy of $s_i(t)$, which may or may not be independent of i, and

$$\int_0^T r(t)s_i(t)\, dt$$

is the *time correlation* of $r(t)$ and $s_i(t)$ over the time interval 0 to T. Obviously the optimum detector could operate by evaluating

$$D_i = \int_0^T (r(t) - s_i(t))^2\, dt \tag{6.5}$$

for $i = 0, 1, \ldots, m - 1$, and taking as the detected element value (the detected value of h) the value of i for which D_i is minimum.

If the additive noise is coloured (and not white) Gaussian noise, which means that the power spectral density of the noise varies over its bandwidth in some way with frequency, the optimum detection of the signal element value can be achieved by first passing the received signal $r(t)$ through a 'noise-whitening' filter[475]. The transfer function of this filter over the frequency band of the noise is proportional to the square root of the reciprocal of the noise power density, so that (from Equation 12.10), the power density of the noise signal at the output of the filter is constant over its bandwidth, giving bandlimited white Gaussian noise. It is assumed here that the power density of the noise does not decay to zero at any points within its frequency band. If a zero-mean Gaussian random process is fed to a time invariant linear filter, the output signal from this filter is also a zero-mean Gaussian random process[475]. The optimum detection process for the element-value h (Equation 6.2) is now carried out on the signal at the output of the noise-whitening filter, bearing in mind that the m possible waveforms $\{s_i(t)\}$ of the received signal-element have been changed, so that the detector must operate with the corresponding changed waveforms.

All of the results derived in this section apply equally (under the given assumptions) to the case where $s_i(t)$ is itself a sequence of signal elements, that is, a received message over the time interval 0 to T and such that the m possible waveforms $\{s_i(t)\}$ are given by all combinations of the possible element values in the sequence. Since m can become extremely large here, special techniques must be employed to minimize the number of operations involved in the detection process, but even with the aid of such techniques it may not be possible to reduce the equipment complexity to an acceptable level. The detection processes to be considered in detail in this book are basically simple processes where each received signal element is detected separately as it arrives, the detection of any one signal element not, at the same time, involving the detection of any other.

The optimum detector can exploit the relationships between the different possible signal waveforms $\{s_i(t)\}$ in the various ways now to be described, in order to reduce the complexity of the detection process.

6.3   Optimum detection of an m-level FM or PM signal-element

Where the received signal $s_h(t)$ is an element of an FM or PM signal, the energy

$$\int_0^T s_i^2(t)\,dt$$

of a possible signal-element $s_i(t)$ (for $i = 0, 1, \ldots, m-1$) is normally independent of i, so that only the term

$$-2\int_0^T r(t)s_i(t)\,dt$$

in Equation 6.4 is dependent on i. Thus the value of i (the possible element value) most likely to be correct is now that which maximizes

$$\int_0^T r(t)s_i(t)\,dt$$

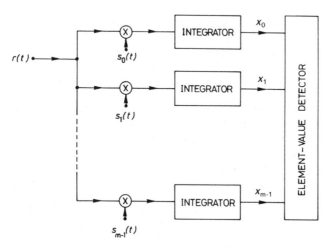

Fig. 6.1   Optimum detector for an m-level FM or PM signal element

As mentioned before, this is the time correlation of $r(t)$ and $s_i(t)$ over the time interval 0 to T. The envelope of $s_i(t)$ may here have any shape, which could be rectangular or rounded and could even be a function of i, provided only that the element energy is independent of i and Equation 6.1 is satisfied. The detector can now be implemented as in Figure 6.1, where

$$x_i = \int_0^T r(t)s_i(t)\,dt \qquad (6.6)$$

for $i = 0, 1, \ldots, m - 1$, and the element-value detector selects the value of i for which x_i has the most positive value.

6.4   Ideal coherent detection of an m-level FSK signal

In the case of an m-level FSK signal the waveform $s_i(t)$ in Figure 6.1, over the time interval 0 to T and for $i = 0, 1, \ldots, m - 1$, becomes

$$s_i(t) = \begin{cases} \sqrt{2} \cos(2\pi f_i t + \phi), & 0 < t < T \\ 0, & \text{elsewhere} \end{cases} \qquad (6.7)$$

where f_i is the instantaneous frequency of the signal carrier and ϕ is the carrier phase at time $t = 0$. It is assumed here that $f_i \gg 1/T$ for each i. The detection process of Figure 6.1 is optimum for the detection of an isolated received signal-element ($s_h(t)$ in Equation 6.2) or else when the signal element is one of a continuous stream of elements, each of duration T, and when ϕ is independent of the element values of any of the preceding signal-elements.

A continuous stream of FSK signal-elements can be transmitted, with element boundaries at the time instants $T, 2T, 3T, \ldots$, and each element can be detected in the manner previously described, using the appropriate portion of duration T of the received waveform $r(t)$. When the $\{f_i\}$ are now spaced at regular intervals of $1/T$ Hz, the phase angle ϕ at the start of any signal element, is independent of the element values of the preceding signal-elements, which means that a continuous reference carrier (sine wave) with the appropriate frequency and phase can be fed to each multiplier, thus simplifying the implementation of the detector. Since the received FSK signal here can itself be considered as the sum of m complementary ASK signals (Section 5.3), the received signal contains discrete frequency components at the m frequencies $\{f_i\}$ and with the appropriate phases, which can be used at the receiver to synchronize the m reference carriers in both frequency and phase[71]. Clearly, the detection of any one signal-element does not provide any information which can be used to improve the detection of any other, so that, under the assumed conditions, the optimum detection of the whole sequence of signal elements (the complete message) is given by the optimum detection of each individual element, in turn, where the detection of any one signal-element does not involve the detection of any others. When the $\{f_i\}$ are not spaced at intervals of $1/T$ Hz or any integral multiple of this, the detection process of Figure 6.1 is only optimum in the sense that it is the best detection process under the constraint that each signal element is detected separately, without involving the detection of any others. The process assumes a prior knowledge of the signal carrier phase at the start of an element detection process, as before, but this now implies the correct detection of all preceding signal elements in the received message, which was not required before. Without the correct detection of these elements, the detector could not, in general, have a correct knowledge of the carrier phase, ϕ, at the start of the signal element, since the carrier phase is now dependent on the preceding element values. Correct knowledge of the carrier phase at the start of the message would be obtained here by means of the appropriate synchronization procedure[71]. In spite of the limitation of the detection process just mentioned it is the ideal form of the conventional coherent detector. As has been mentioned in Section 6.1, the optimum detection process, that minimizes the probability of error in the detection of the whole received message, under the assumed conditions, involves (at least, in principle) the detection of the whole message in a single detection process. Even when the implementation of this detection process has been reduced to its simplest form and rendered slightly suboptimum[422,506,509,510] (details of which are beyond the scope of this book), it is still considerably more complex than the corresponding simple approximation to a coherent detector, which detects each received signal-element separately and is described in Section 7.2. For this reason the optimum detection process would only be considered for those applications where the cost of the equipment was not critical. The principles of the optimum detection process are considered in detail elsewhere[176,422,479,498] and will not be considered further here.

6.5 Ideal coherent detection of an *m*-level PSK signal

In the case of an *m*-level PSK signal the waveform $s_i(t)$ in Figure 6.1, for $i = 0, 1, \ldots, m - 1$, becomes

$$s_i(t) = \begin{cases} \sqrt{2} \cos\left(2\pi f_c t + \dfrac{2\pi i}{m} + \phi\right), & 0 < t < T \\ 0, & \text{elsewhere} \end{cases} \quad (6.8)$$

where f_c is the carrier frequency and ϕ is a phase shift that is independent of i. Since $s_i(t)$ differs from $s_h(t)$ only in the phase of the signal carrier, the carrier frequency being now the same for each of the *m* different signal-elements, a considerable simplification can be introduced into the optimum detector, as follows. The *m* multipliers in Figure 6.1 are replaced by just two multipliers to give the arrangement of Figure 6.2, where the output signals, y_p and y_q, from the two integrators, are processed as shown to give x_i, for $i = 0, 1, \ldots, m - 1$. The reference carriers $\sqrt{2} \cos 2\pi f_c t$ and $-\sqrt{2} \sin 2\pi f_c t$ have unit power level and are for convenience taken to have zero phase shift at time $t = 0$ (the value of this phase shift not affecting the performance of the detector). The phase of the reference carrier $-\sqrt{2} \sin 2\pi f_c t$ leads that of the carrier $\sqrt{2} \cos 2\pi f_c t$ by 90°.

The received signal, over the time interval 0 to T, is now

$$r(t) = \sqrt{2} \cos\left(2\pi f_c t + \frac{2\pi h}{m} + \phi\right) + w(t) \quad (6.9)$$

from Equations 6.2 and 6.8, so that

$$y_p = \int_0^T r(t)\sqrt{2} \cos(2\pi f_c t)\, dt \quad (6.10)$$

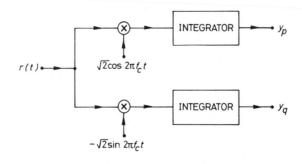

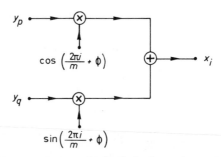

Fig. 6.2   Modification to Figure 6.1 for the ideal coherent detection of an m-level PSK signal

which simplifies to

$$y_p = T \cos\left(\frac{2\pi h}{m} + \phi\right) + z_p \qquad (6.11)$$

where

$$z_p = \int_0^T w(t)\sqrt{2} \cos\left(2\pi f_c t\right) dt \qquad (6.12)$$

It is assumed here that

$$f_c = \frac{l}{2T} \qquad (6.13)$$

where l is an integer greater than unity. Alternatively, or in addition,

$$f_c \gg \frac{1}{T} \qquad (6.14)$$

Similarly,

$$y_q = T \sin\left(\frac{2\pi h}{m} + \phi\right) + z_q \tag{6.15}$$

where

$$z_q = \int_0^T w(t)(-\sqrt{2} \sin 2\pi f_c t) \, dt \tag{6.16}$$

Thus,

$$
\begin{aligned}
x_i &= y_p \cos\left(\frac{2\pi i}{m} + \phi\right) + y_q \sin\left(\frac{2\pi i}{m} + \phi\right) \\
&= T \cos\left(\frac{2\pi h}{m} + \phi\right) \cos\left(\frac{2\pi i}{m} + \phi\right) \\
&\quad + T \sin\left(\frac{2\pi h}{m} + \phi\right) \sin\left(\frac{2\pi i}{m} + \phi\right) + z_x \\
&= T \cos\left(\frac{2\pi(h - i)}{m}\right) + z_x
\end{aligned}
\tag{6.17}
$$

where

$$z_x = z_p \cos\left(\frac{2\pi i}{m} + \phi\right) + z_q \sin\left(\frac{2\pi i}{m} + \phi\right) \tag{6.18}$$

It can be shown that z_p, z_q and z_x are Gaussian random variables with zero mean and the same variance.

In the absence of noise, x_i (Equation 6.17) is most positive (maximum) when $i = h$. Thus, as in Figure 6.1, the element-value h is detected as the value of i for which x_i is most positive.

A continuous stream of PSK signal-elements with boundaries at the time instants $T, 2T, 3T, \ldots$ can be transmitted and each element value can be detected in the manner just described, using, for each detection process, the appropriate portion of duration T of the received waveform $r(t)$. When the reference carriers $\sqrt{2} \cos 2\pi f_c t$ and $-\sqrt{2} \sin 2\pi f_c t$ have the same instantaneous frequency as the received signal carrier, as is assumed here, the phase angle ϕ between the received signal carrier (when $h = 0$) and the reference carrier, does not change from one signal-element to the next, so that the quantities

$$\left\{\cos\left(\frac{2\pi i}{m} + \phi\right)\right\} \quad \text{and} \quad \left\{\sin\left(\frac{2\pi i}{m} + \phi\right)\right\}$$

in Figure 6.2 do not change, which simplifies the detection process. Techniques are available for extracting the two reference carriers from the received signal in such a way that $\phi = 2\pi l/m$, where l has one of the values $0, 1, \ldots, m - 1$, but is not known at the receiver[71]. This means that l must be determined during the synchronization process at the start of transmission or else differential coding must be used at the transmitter and the corresponding differential decoding applied to the detected data signal at the receiver. In differential coding, the element-value h is transmitted as a *phase change* of $2\pi h/m$ radians in the signal carrier between two adjacent signal-elements.

6.6   Ideal coherent detection of an *m*-level ASK signal

In the case of an m-level ASK signal the received waveform $r(t)$ (Equation 6.2), becomes

$$r(t) = a_h u(t) + w(t) \tag{6.19}$$

where

$$u(t) = \begin{cases} \sqrt{2} \cos (2\pi f_c t + \phi), & 0 < t < T \\ 0, & \text{elsewhere} \end{cases} \tag{6.20}$$

$$a_h = k_0 + 2kh \tag{6.21}$$

$$h = 0, 1, \ldots, m - 1 \tag{6.22}$$

and k is a positive constant. a_h is the data symbol that carries the transmitted information, and, as before, h is equally likely to have any of its m possible values. When $k_0 = 0$ the signal is a double sideband ASK signal, and when $k_0 = -(m - 1)k$, the signal is a double sideband suppressed carrier ASK signal. It is assumed furthermore that one or both of the Equations 6.13 and 6.14 hold for the ASK signal. As before, $w(t)$ is a bandlimited white Gaussian noise waveform whose frequency band extends over the whole of the effective bandwidth of the data signal.

The received signal can now be rewritten as

$$r(t) = y_h u(t) + v(t) \tag{6.23}$$

where

$$y_h = a_h + z \tag{6.24}$$

$$w(t) = zu(t) + v(t) \tag{6.25}$$

and $v(t)$ is a Gaussian random process that contains no component proportional to $u(t)$, any such component being considered as part of $zu(t)$. z is the appropriate Gaussian random variable. The relationship between $v(t)$ and $u(t)$ is expressed mathematically as

$$\int_0^T u(t)v(t) \, dt = 0 \tag{6.26}$$

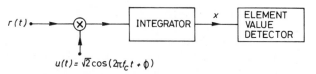

$$u(t) = \sqrt{2}\cos(2\pi f_c t + \phi)$$

Fig. 6.3   Ideal coherent detector for an m-level ASK signal

which means that the waveforms $u(t)$ and $v(t)$ are orthogonal over the time interval 0 to T.

The parameter D_i in Equation 6.5 now becomes

$$D_i = \int_0^T (a_h u(t) + w(t) - a_i u(t))^2 \, dt$$

$$= \int_0^T ((y_h - a_i)u(t) + v(t))^2 \, dt$$

$$= (y_h - a_i)^2 \int_0^T u^2(t) \, dt + \int_0^T v^2(t) \, dt \qquad (6.27)$$

from Equation 6.26. But $u(t)$ and $v(t)$ are independent of i, which means that D_i is minimum for the value of i that minimizes $|y_h - a_i|$, where $|y|$ is the modulus (absolute value) of y. Furthermore,

$$\int_0^T u^2(t) \, dt = E \qquad (6.28)$$

which is known at the receiver (since, of course, $u(t)$ is known), and

$$\int_0^T r(t)u(t) \, dt = \int_0^T (y_h u(t) + v(t))u(t) \, dt$$

$$= y_h E \qquad (6.29)$$

from Equations 6.26 and 6.28. Thus the optimum detection process for determining h from $r(t)$ is as shown in Figure 6.3, where

$$x = y_h E \qquad (6.30)$$

from Equation 6.29. The element-value detector here takes as the detected value of h the possible value of i for which $|x - a_i E|$ is minimum, since this minimizes $|y_h - a_i|E$ and therefore also $|y_h - a_i|$, as required.

For a binary ASK signal-element, $a_i = 0$ or $2k$, and for a binary suppressed carrier ASK signal-element, which is also a binary PSK signal-element, $a_i = \pm k$. The optimum detection process is in each case as shown in Figure 6.3 and is considered further in Sections 7.1 and 16.2.

It can be shown that the random variable z and the random process $v(t)$ (Equation 6.25) are statistically independent, as are also these two and the data-symbol a_h (Equation 6.24), so that no useful information is lost in discarding $v(t)$, which is done in Equations 6.29 and 6.30. Similarly, no useful information is lost in ignoring the portions of the received noise-signal $w(t)$ outside the time interval 0 to T, again because these portions of the noise signal and that inside the given time interval are, for practical purposes, statistically independent. The latter, of course, holds for each of the Figures 6.1–6.3.

A continuous stream of ASK signal-elements can be transmitted, with element boundaries at the time instants $T, 2T, 3T, \ldots$, and each element can be detected in the manner just described, using the appropriate portion of duration T of the received waveform $r(t)$. So long as the reference carrier has the correct instantaneous frequency f_c, as is assumed here, the phase angle between the received signal carrier and the reference carrier, does not change from one signal-element to the next. Thus a continuous reference carrier can be fed to the multiplier and techniques are available for adjusting its instantaneous frequency and phase to their values assumed in Figure 6.3[71].

6.7 Principles of ideal incoherent detection

An ideal incoherent detector makes no use of any prior knowledge of the signal carrier phase at the start of a detection process, and subject to this constraint it achieves the best available tolerance to additive white Gaussian noise. The performance of such a detector is independent of the signal carrier phase at the start of the detection process. However, any phase change introduced by the transmission path into the received signal carrier *during* the detection process for a received signal-element is likely to degrade the tolerance of the detector to additive noise and, under the appropriate conditions, if the phase change is sufficiently severe, it can itself cause an error in the detection of the received signal-element. Thus, although incoherent detection greatly increases the tolerance of a data-transmission system to frequency-modulation effects, relative to coherent detection, it does not render it totally immune to these effects.

It is assumed in Sections 6.8–6.10 that an ASK, FSK or PSK signal-element is received in the presence of bandlimited additive white Gaussian noise, under the conditions described in Sections 6.2–6.5. As before, a signal element has a rectangular modulating waveform, a constant envelope and a constant instantaneous carrier-frequency over its duration, which is T seconds. No inter-symbol interference is now experienced in the optimum incoherent detection of a signal element when this is one of a continuous stream of such elements. The incoherent detection of an ASK or FSK signal-element extends over the duration T of that element, whereas the incoherent detection of a PSK signal-element extends over the duration of both the immediately preceding signal-element and the given element, that is, over a period of $2T$. The tolerance to noise of an incoherent detector for an FSK signal, whose frequency shift is around $0.7/T$ Hz, can be improved significantly by extending the duration of an element detection process so that this includes some of the preceding and some of the following received signal-elements[176]. The detection process is, however, very complex and, for this reason, will not be considered further here.

6.8 Ideal incoherent detection of an m-level FSK signal

The ideal incoherent detector for an m-level FSK signal-element is derived from the optimum detector shown in Figure 6.1, through a replacement of each multiplier and following integrator (Figure 6.4(a)) by the arrangement in Figure 6.4(b). Thus, the received waveform, over the time interval 0 to T, is

$$r(t) = s_h(t) + w(t) \tag{6.31}$$

where

$$s_h(t) = \sqrt{2} \cos (2\pi f_h t + \phi) \tag{6.32}$$

from Equations 6.2 and 6.7. As before, $w(t)$ is the bandlimited white Gaussian noise and $h = 0, 1, \ldots, m - 1$ is the element value. Also $f_h \gg 1/T$ for each h. The output signals from the two integrators in Figure 6.4(b) are

$$y_{p,i} = \int_0^T r(t) \sqrt{2} \cos 2\pi f_i t \, dt \tag{6.33}$$

and

$$y_{q,i} = \int_0^T r(t) (-\sqrt{2} \sin 2\pi f_i t) \, dt \tag{6.34}$$

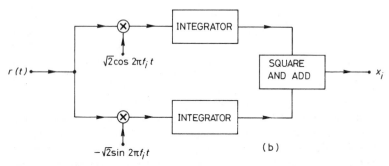

Fig. 6.4 *Modification to Figure 6.1 for the ideal incoherent detection of an FSK signal. (a) Multiplier and following integrator in coherent detector; (b) corresponding arrangement in incoherent detector*

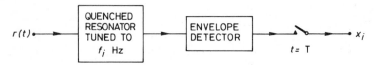

Fig. 6.5 *Alternative arrangement to that in Figure 6.4(b)*

and the output signal from the square-and-add circuit is

$$x_i = y_{p,i}^2 + y_{q,i}^2 \tag{6.35}$$

It can be shown that x_i, for each i, is independent of the carrier phase ϕ of the signal element, at the start of the detection process, so that the operation of the element-value detector is clearly unaffected by ϕ. The element value detector selects the value of i for which x_i has the greatest value. Now, of course, x_i cannot be negative.

An alternative implementation of the ideal incoherent detector is achieved through replacing the arrangement in Figure 6.4(b) by that in Figure 6.5. The quenched resonator here is an infinite-Q tuned circuit resonant at f_i Hz, as shown in Figure 6.6. The current into and the voltage across this tuned circuit are both set to zero at a time just before $t = 0$, by closing the switch and at the same time

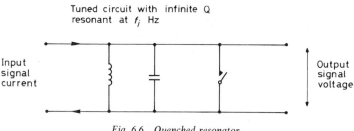

Fig. 6.6   Quenched resonator

reducing the Q of the coil to some appropriately low value. At time $t = 0$, the switch is opened and the Q of the tuned circuit is set to infinity (by means of an amplifier and sufficient positive feedback, not shown in Figure 6.6). The received signal $r(t)$ is fed as the input current to the tuned circuit over the time interval 0 to T, and the envelope of the sinusoidal voltage across the tuned circuit is measured by the envelope detector. The latter is implemented as a full-wave rectifier followed by a low-pass filter, as, for instance, shown in Figure 7.4. The value (magnitude) of the envelope at time $t = T$ is measured and fed to the output as the signal x_i. The same basic operation as that just described is carried out simultaneously by each of m circuits as in Figure 6.5, for $i = 0, 1, \ldots, m - 1$. As before, the element-value detector selects the value of i for which x_i has the greatest value. In practice it may be necessary to use two quenched resonators and envelope detectors for each i, in place of the one in Figure 6.5, the two being used alternately, so that while one quenched resonator is operational, the other is being reset (quenched).

The operation of this incoherent detector is illustrated in Figure 6.7, which shows the waveforms at the output of the quenched resonator tuned to f_0 Hz and the corresponding waveforms at the output of the following envelope detector, for the case where $m = 2$ and the two carrier frequencies, f_0 and f_1, are such that

$$f_1 - f_0 = \frac{1}{T} \tag{6.36}$$

It is assumed here that there is no noise in the received signal. It can be seen from Figure 6.7 that, at the sampling instant $t = T$, the output signal from the envelope detector, following the receipt of a carrier with frequency f_1 Hz, is $x_1 = 0$. In other words, a quenched resonator gives no response to a possible received carrier frequency other than that to which it is tuned. This condition is satisfied in the general case of an m-level FSK signal where the frequency shift

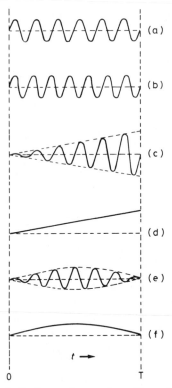

Fig. 6.7   Waveforms in the incoherent detector for a binary FSK signal, where the detector employs quenched resonators. (a) Input signal when carrier frequency is f_0 Hz; (b) Input signal when carrier frequency is f_1 Hz; (c) Output of quenched resonator tuned to f_0 Hz when a signal carrier with frequency f_0 Hz is received; (d) Output of following envelope detector; (e) Output of quenched resonator tuned to f_0 Hz when a signal carrier with frequency f_1 Hz is received; (f) Output of following envelope detector

between any two possible carrier frequencies is an integral multiple of $1/T$ Hz, and the tolerance of the incoherent detector to additive white Gaussian noise now reaches its maximum value, for the given received element energy. When a possible carrier frequency of the FSK signal is not very much greater than $1/T$ Hz, the envelope of the output signal from the corresponding quenched resonator is no longer sufficiently well defined for correct operation, so that the previous incoherent detector (Figure 6.4(b)) should now be used in preference to the quenched-resonator detector. For the best tolerance to noise under these conditions, not only should the frequency shift between adjacent possible carrier frequencies be $1/T$ Hz but

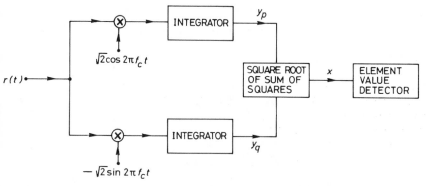

Fig. 6.8   Ideal incoherent detection of an m-level ASK signal

each possible carrier frequency should itself be an integral multiple of $1/2T$ Hz.

The quenched resonator and envelope detector in Figure 6.5 form what is known as an 'incoherent matched filter' for the received signal-element $s_i(t)$, and the two incoherent detection processes just described are equivalent in that they achieve the same result, although in different ways. The principles and properties of a 'matched filter' are considered in Chapter 12.

6.9   Ideal incoherent detection of an m-level ASK signal

The received waveform $r(t)$ (Equation 6.2) now satisfies Equations 6.19–6.22 together with Equations 6.13 and 6.14 and the other conditions mentioned in Section 6.5. Thus

$$r(t) = a_h u(t) + w(t) \tag{6.37}$$

where

$$u(t) = \begin{cases} \sqrt{2} \cos{(2\pi f_c t + \phi)}, & 0 < t < T \\ 0, & \text{elsewhere} \end{cases} \tag{6.38}$$

and a_h takes on any one of m different given values regularly spaced at intervals of $2k$. The ideal incoherent detector for the m-level ASK signal-element is shown in Figure 6.8, and it is interesting to compare this with the corresponding ideal coherent detector in Figure 6.3. The relationship between these two is closely related to that between the incoherent and coherent detectors for an FSK signal-element, as shown in Figure 6.4.

The output signals from the two integrators in Figure 6.8 are

$$y_p = \int_0^T r(t)\sqrt{2} \cos 2\pi f_c t \, dt \qquad (6.39)$$

and

$$y_q = \int_0^T r(t)(-\sqrt{2} \sin 2\pi f_c t) \, dt \qquad (6.40)$$

Equations 6.39 and 6.40 simplify to

$$y_p = a_h T \cos \phi + z_p \qquad (6.41)$$

and

$$y_q = a_h T \sin \phi + z_q \qquad (6.42)$$

where z_p and z_q are noise components. The output signal from the circuit that takes the square root of the sum of the squares of its two input signals y_p and y_q is

$$x = \sqrt{(y_p^2 + y_q^2)} \qquad (6.43)$$

and this simplifies to

$$x = |a_h|T + z \qquad (6.44)$$

where $|a_h|$ is the modulus (absolute value) of a_h and z is the resultant noise component (which is not now independent of a_h). As for x_i in Equation 6.35, x is independent of ϕ. The element value detector selects as the detected value of a_h its possible value a_i for which the corresponding possible value of x in the absence of noise ($|a_h|T$ in Equation 6.44) is closest to the actual value of x. Clearly, for satisfactory operation, a_h must be nonnegative, which means that a suppressed carrier ASK signal cannot be used here. Strictly speaking, the arrangement just described is not quite optimum, although at high signal/noise ratios it comes close enough, for practical purposes, to achieving the minimum error rate for an incoherent detector[328,477]. For the optimum performance, the decision thresholds, which are here assumed to be placed half way between adjacent possible values of x, in the absence of noise, and against which x is compared in the element-value detector, should be slightly raised, the increase being greater at the lower thresholds and becoming greater at the lower signal/noise ratios[328].

An alternative implementation of the ideal incoherent detector in Figure 6.8, which is suitable when $f_c \gg 1/T$, is the corresponding quenched-resonator detector, as shown in Figure 6.9. The quenched resonator and following envelope detector operate exactly as those in Figures 6.5–6.7, and x is the value (magnitude) of the envelope of

Fig. 6.9 Alternative incoherent detector for an m-level ASK signal

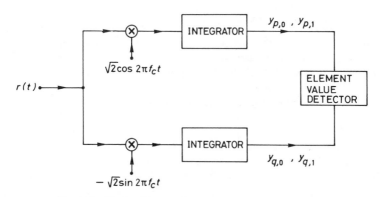

Fig. 6.10 Ideal incoherent detection of an m-level PSK signal

the sinusoidal voltage across the tuned circuit at time $t = T$. The element-value detector operates in a similar manner to that in Figure 6.8. The two incoherent detection processes are equivalent in that they achieve the same result, although in different ways.

6.10 Ideal incoherent detection of an m-level PSK signal

The incoherent detection of an m-level PSK signal element is normally referred to as 'differentially-coherent' detection and can be achieved as shown in Figure 6.10. Differential coding must be used here in the data signal, such that the element-value h is transmitted as a phase change of $2\pi h/m$ radians in the signal carrier between two adjacent signal-elements. The incoherent detector operates over the duration of the two adjacent signal-elements to determine the value of h. Thus the received waveform involved in the detection process is now

$$r(t) = s_h(t) + w(t) \qquad (6.45)$$

where

$$s_h(t) = \sqrt{2} \cos\left(2\pi f_c t + \frac{2\pi g}{m} + \phi\right), \quad -T < t \leqslant 0 \quad (6.46(a))$$

$$s_h(t) = \sqrt{2} \cos \left(2\pi f_c t + \frac{2\pi(g+h)}{m} + \phi \right), \quad 0 < t \leqslant T \qquad \text{(6.46(b))}$$

$$s_h(t) = 0, \qquad\qquad\qquad\qquad\qquad \text{elsewhere} \qquad \text{(6.46(c))}$$

$$g = 0, 1, \ldots, m-1 \qquad\qquad\qquad\qquad \text{(6.47)}$$

$$h = 0, 1, \ldots, m-1 \qquad\qquad\qquad\qquad \text{(6.48)}$$

and both the carrier frequency f_c and the phase angle ϕ are independent of the element-value h. The waveform $s_h(t)$ here comprises two adjacent signal-elements and one or both of the Equations 6.13 and 6.14 are assumed to be satisfied, as before. The output signals from the two integrators in Figure 6.10 are

$$y_{p,0} = \int_{-T}^{0} r(t)\sqrt{2} \cos 2\pi f_c t \, dt \qquad\qquad \text{(6.49)}$$

$$y_{p,1} = \int_{0}^{T} r(t)\sqrt{2} \cos 2\pi f_c t \, dt \qquad\qquad \text{(6.50)}$$

$$y_{q,0} = \int_{-T}^{0} r(t)(-\sqrt{2} \sin 2\pi f_c t) \, dt \qquad\qquad \text{(6.51)}$$

$$y_{q,1} = \int_{0}^{T} r(t)(-\sqrt{2} \sin 2\pi f_c t) \, dt \qquad\qquad \text{(6.52)}$$

which simplify to

$$y_{p,0} = T \cos \left(\frac{2\pi g}{m} + \phi \right) + z_{p,0} \qquad\qquad \text{(6.53)}$$

$$y_{p,1} = T \cos \left(\frac{2\pi(g+h)}{m} + \phi \right) + z_{p,1} \qquad\qquad \text{(6.54)}$$

$$y_{q,0} = T \sin \left(\frac{2\pi g}{m} + \phi \right) + z_{q,0} \qquad\qquad \text{(6.55)}$$

$$y_{q,1} = T \sin \left(\frac{2\pi(g+h)}{m} + \phi \right) + z_{q,1} \qquad\qquad \text{(6.56)}$$

where $z_{p,0}$, $z_{p,1}$, $z_{q,0}$ and $z_{q,1}$ are noise components. It may readily be shown that

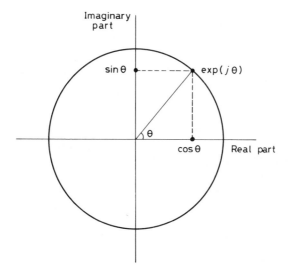

Fig. 6.11 *Real and imaginary parts of exp(jθ)*

$$y_{p,1}y_{p,0} + y_{q,1}y_{q,0} = T^2 \cos \frac{2\pi h}{m} + z_c$$

$$= a \cos \frac{2\pi h'}{m} \qquad (6.57)$$

and

$$y_{q,1}y_{p,0} - y_{p,1}y_{q,0} = T^2 \sin \frac{2\pi h}{m} + z_s$$

$$= a \sin \frac{2\pi h'}{m} \qquad (6.58)$$

where z_c and z_s are the resultant noise components (which are not now independent of the data signal). The parameters a and h' are the appropriate quantities that satisfy Equations 6.57 and 6.58, and the latter are clearly independent of f_c and ϕ.

It can be seen from Figure 6.11 that $T^2 \cos(2\pi h/m)$ and $T^2 \sin(2\pi h/m)$ in Equations 6.57 and 6.58 are the real and imaginary parts, respectively, of

$$T^2 \exp(j2\pi h/m)$$

where $j = \sqrt{-1}$, so that together the two terms uniquely determine h. Similarly,

$$y_{p,1}y_{p,0} + y_{q,1}y_{q,0} \quad \text{and} \quad y_{q,1}y_{p,0} - y_{p,1}y_{q,0}$$

are the real and imaginary parts, respectively, of

$$a \exp (j2\pi h'/m)$$

where a is a noisy estimate of T^2 and h' is a noisy estimate of h. The parameter h' is, of course, not normally an integer.

To determine the value of i (possible value of h) that agrees most closely with $y_{p,0}$, $y_{p,1}$, $y_{q,0}$ and $y_{q,1}$ in Equations 6.57 and 6.58, the receiver forms $\exp (j2\pi i/m)$ and selects i from its possible values such that the angle $2\pi i/m$ is closest to the angle $2\pi h'/m$. Thus the receiver selects i to minimize the angle $2\pi(h' - i)/m$. But it can be seen from Figure 6.11 that, when the magnitude of θ is minimum (whether θ is positive or negative), the real part of $\exp (j\theta)$, which is $\cos \theta$, is maximum. Furthermore, this result is not affected if $\exp (j\theta)$ is multiplied by some positive quantity a that is independent of θ. It follows that the receiver must select i so that the real part of $a \exp (j2\pi(h' - i)/m)$ is maximum (most positive). Now the real part of $a \exp (j2\pi(h' - i)/m)$ is

$$a \cos \frac{2\pi(h' - i)}{m} = a \cos \frac{2\pi h'}{m} \cos \frac{2\pi i}{m}$$

$$+ a \sin \frac{2\pi h'}{m} \sin \frac{2\pi i}{m} \qquad (6.59)$$

which is therefore the quantity that i must be selected to maximize. In the absence of noise, Equation 6.59 becomes

$$T^2 \cos \frac{2\pi(h - i)}{m} = T^2 \cos \frac{2\pi h}{m} \cos \frac{2\pi i}{m}$$

$$+ T^2 \sin \frac{2\pi h}{m} \sin \frac{2\pi i}{m} \qquad (6.60)$$

and $T^2 \cos (2\pi(h - i)/m)$ has the maximum value T^2 when $i = h$.

As can be seen from Equations 6.57–6.59, in the ideal incoherent detection of the element value h of $s_h(t)$, the detector evaluates

$$x_i = (y_{p,1}y_{p,0} + y_{q,1}y_{q,0}) \cos \frac{2\pi i}{m}$$

$$+ (y_{q,1}y_{p,0} - y_{p,1}y_{q,0}) \sin \frac{2\pi i}{m} \qquad (6.61)$$

for $i = 0, 1, \ldots, m - 1$, and selects as the detected value of h the value of i for which x_i is greatest (most positive). In the case of a binary signal-element, $m = 2$ and

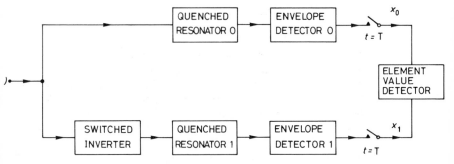

Fig. 6.12   Alternative incoherent detector for a binary PSK signal

$$x_i = (y_{p,1}y_{p,0} + y_{q,1}y_{q,0}) \cos \pi i \qquad (6.62)$$

so that the binary value h of $s_h(t)$ is detected as 0 or 1 depending upon whether

$$y_{p,1}y_{p,0} + y_{q,1}y_{q,0} > 0 \quad \text{or} \quad < 0 \qquad (6.63)$$

respectively.

An alternative implementation of the ideal incoherent detector in Figure 6.10, for the particular case of a binary PSK signal-element, is as shown in Figure 6.12. Each quenched resonator here is an infinite-Q tuned circuit (as in Figure 6.6) and is resonant at the signal carrier frequency f_c Hz. Each tuned circuit is released from a short circuit at the start of the signal element preceding the one being detected, that is, at time $t = -T$, and the detection process extends over a period of $2T$, until time $t = T$. The switched inverter allows the input signal $r(t)$ through unchanged to the quenched resonator 1, over the duration of the first signal-element, that is, for $-T < t < 0$. Over the duration of the second signal-element, that is, for $0 < t < T$, the switched inverter feeds $-r(t)$ to the quenched resonator 1. The signals at various points in Figure 6.12, over the detection process just considered, are as shown in Figure 6.13, for the case where a binary value 1 is transmitted as a $180°$ phase change in the signal carrier at time $t = 0$, and assuming no noise in the received signal. At the sampling instant $t = T$, the output signal x_0 from the envelope detector 0 has the value zero, whereas x_1, at the output of the envelope detector 1, has a large positive value. Had there been no phase change in the signal carrier at time $t = 0$ (representing the binary value 0), x_1 would have been zero and x_0 would have had a large positive value. The element-value detector in Figure 6.12 detects the binary element value as 0 or 1, depending upon whether $x_0 > x_1$ or $x_1 > x_0$, respectively. Two circuits as

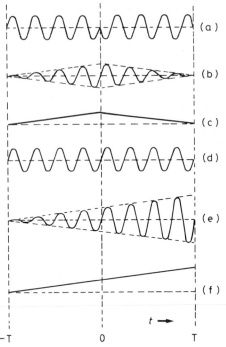

Fig. 6.13 Waveforms in the incoherent detector for a binary PSK signal, where the detector employs quenched resonators. (a) r(t): (b) output of quenched resonator 0: (c) output of envelope detector 0: (d) output of switched inverter: (e) output of quenched resonator 1: (f) output of envelope detector 1

shown in Figure 6.12 are required, the detected element values being determined alternately by these circuits.

The quenched resonator 0 and envelope detector 0 in Figure 6.12 form an incoherent matched filter for the two consecutive signal elements involved in the detection process, when there is no phase change in the signal carrier between these two elements. The switched inverter, quenched resonator 1 and envelope detector 1 form an incoherent matched filter for the two signal elements, when there is a phase change in the signal carrier between them. Furthermore, the two pairs of received signal elements just mentioned are clearly orthogonal over the period $2T$ of the detection process. But in the case of the corresponding binary FSK signal, with an element duration of T seconds and a frequency shift of $1/T$ Hz between the two carrier frequencies, the ideal incoherent detector employing quenched resonators (Figure 6.5) operates over a period of only T

seconds (see Figure 6.7). Again, the detector involves two incoherent matched filters, but matched here to the two possible waveforms of an *individual* received signal-element, these waveforms being orthogonal over the period T of the detection process. It is now evident, from the similar properties both of the FSK and PSK signals and of the corresponding detection processes, that, at a given average power level and a given element rate, the binary PSK signal gains an advantage of 3 dB in tolerance to additive white Gaussian noise over the binary FSK signal. This is essentially because the energy of the data signal involved in the detection of a PSK signal element is twice that in the detection of an FSK signal element.

7

Practical detection processes

7.1 Coherent detection

In coherent detection of a digital signal the receiver makes use of a prior knowledge of the phase of the signal carrier in an element detection process. The principles of the coherent detection of a signal element received in the presence of additive white Gaussian noise are considered in Sections 6.4–6.6, and the detectors shown in Figures 6.1–6.3 are coherent detectors.

An important problem with all coherent detectors is that they assume a prior knowledge at the receiver of the different possible waveforms of a received signal-element, whereas, in practice, this information (or at least a part of it) must be derived from the received signal itself. For a binary AM signal with a rectangular modulating waveform, as, for instance, shown in Figure 5.1, the receiver generates from the received signal a reference carrier having the same frequency and phase as the signal carrier[71,244–266]. The reference carrier is usually extracted directly from the received signal by means of a phase-locked loop (Figure 7.8) that operates essentially as a narrow-band filter extracting the discrete frequency component from the received AM signal. The portion of this reference carrier over the duration of any received signal-element is used in the detection of the corresponding element-value, by means of the coherent detector shown in Figure 7.1. The received waveform, over the time interval 0 to T, is

$$r(t) = a_h\sqrt{2} \cos\left(2\pi f_c t + \phi\right) + w(t) \tag{7.1}$$

where $a_h = 0$ or $2k$ for $h = 0$ or 1, respectively, h being the binary value of the signal element received over the given time interval, and $w(t)$ is the noise waveform. The output signal x from the integrator, at time $t = T$, is here

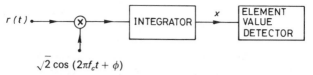

Fig. 7.1   Coherent detector for a binary AM signal

$$x = \frac{1}{T} \int_0^T r(t)\sqrt{2} \cos (2\pi f_c t + \phi)\, dt \qquad (7.2)$$

When f_c satisfies one or both of the Equations 6.13 and 6.14, as is assumed, Equation 7.2 simplifies to

$$x = a_h + v \qquad (7.3)$$

where

$$v = \frac{1}{T} \int_0^T w(t)\sqrt{2} \cos (2\pi f_c t + \phi)\, dt \qquad (7.4)$$

Thus x is an estimate of a_h, and, in the absence of noise, $x = a_h$.

The coherent detector now operates as follows. The reference carrier is used to multiply the received signal and the resultant product is multiplied by $1/T$ and integrated over each element period, to give at the end of this period a linear estimate of the value of the corresponding rectangular modulating waveform. The output of the integrator is, of course, reset to zero at the start of each element period. In the absence of noise and distortion, the output signal from the integrator, at the end of an element period, has the value $2k$ when a burst of carrier (representing the element value 1) is received, and it has the value zero when no signal (representing the element value 0) is received. The output signal from the integrator is fed to the element value detector where it is compared with a threshold level of k, at the end of each element period. Whenever the output signal from the integrator, at the end of an element period, exceeds k, the binary value of the signal element is detected as 1. Whenever the output signal is less than k, the element binary value is detected as 0.

In the absence of multiplicative noise that prevents the correct operation of the coherent detector, the detector minimizes the probability of error in the detection of an element of a binary AM signal, where this has a rectangular modulating waveform and is received in the presence of additive white Gaussian noise, assuming that the binary element values are statistically independent and equally likely. In other words, the coherent detector achieves the best available tolerance to additive white Gaussian noise for the given AM signal.

The coherent detector for a binary PM signal is as described for the AM signal but with certain changes. The received waveform, over the time interval 0 to T, is again given by $r(t)$ in Equation 7.1 and x is again given by Equation 7.3. The data-symbol a_h, however, has one of the two values $\pm k$ and no longer itself carries the binary value of the corresponding signal-element, for reasons that will be made clear shortly. The binary PM signal is, of course, also a binary suppressed carrier AM signal.

The reference carrier cannot now be isolated directly from the received signal, by means of a narrow-band filter or phase-locked oscillator tuned to the carrier frequency, as is done for the AM signal, since the received PM signal does not contain a discrete frequency component at the signal carrier frequency. A simple method of extracting the reference carrier from the received signal is to full-wave rectify the latter and isolate from the rectified signal the fundamental frequency component at twice the carrier frequency. This is fed to a frequency divider to give a carrier frequency component which has a phase angle of $0°$ or $180°$ with respect to the carrier in any received signal element. Alternative techniques are available for extracting the reference carrier, but they all result in the same uncertainty in the phase of the carrier[244-266]. The effects of this uncertainty can be eliminated by using differential coding at the transmitter, so that an element value 1 is transmitted by a change of phase between two adjacent signal elements, and an element value 0 by no change of phase. It does not now matter which of the two phases is adopted by the reference carrier. The use of differential coding will be assumed here.

In the absence of noise and distortion, the output signal from the integrator at the end of an element period now has a value $\pm k$, where k corresponds to one of the two binary signal elements and $-k$ to the other. The detector compares the output signal from the integrator, at the end of an element period, with a threshold level of zero. When the output signal is positive, the signal element is detected as $+$, and when the output signal is negative, the signal element is detected as $-$. The detection process for a received signal element is completed by comparing its detected sign with that of the preceding element. If the signs are different, the element binary value is detected as 1, and if the signs are the same, the element binary value is detected as 0.

The coherent detector achieves the best available tolerance to additive white Gaussian noise for the binary PM signal, under similar conditions to those assumed for the binary AM signal.

The coherent detection of a binary FM signal requires two coherent detectors of the type described for the AM signal, tuned to the two carrier frequencies used by the FM signal. There is, however, only one element-value detector. This compares the output signals from the two integrators, at the end of each element period, and detects the binary value as that corresponding to the carrier frequency giving the greater output.

The coherent detector achieves the best available tolerance to additive white Gaussian noise for a binary FM signal in which one of the two binary elements has a whole number of carrier cycles more than the other, assuming similar conditions to those for the binary AM signal.

The coherent detector for the binary FM signal involves considerable equipment complexity, particularly when one of the two binary elements does not have a whole number of carrier cycles more than the other. This is because, for the satisfactory operation of the FM system, it is important that there are no phase discontinuities at the boundaries between adjacent signal-elements, so that the phase of the carrier over any signal element is now a function of the previously transmitted element values. The two reference carriers needed for each element detection process cannot therefore be extracted from the received signal by simple filtering, but require additional and complex equipment. Coherent detection of an FM signal is not therefore normally used.

In the coherent detection of an AM signal, the received signal is first amplified and set to a predetermined level, by an automatic gain controlled amplifier. This is necessary to ensure that the threshold level, used in the element-value detector, has the correct value k, bearing in mind that the signal attenuation over a typical voice-frequency channel is likely to have any value from 0 to 40 dB, and may of course vary with time.

In the coherent detection of a PM signal, either an automatic gain controlled amplifier or an amplifier limiter may be used to set the received signal to the predetermined level. An amplifier limiter gives a rectangular output waveform, obtained by taking a very narrow slice of the signal, about the value zero, and amplifying the sliced signal to the required level. This signal is treated in the coherent detector in the same way as the corresponding unsliced signal from the automatic gain controlled amplifier.

Whatever modulation method is used for the transmitted signal, the receiver cannot normally itself have prior knowledge of the phase of the received signal carrier, so that this prior knowledge (in the form of a reference carrier, which is required for coherent detection) must be derived from the received signal. In order to minimize the jitter in the reference carrier caused by noise, the reference carrier must be filtered through a narrow-band filter. In practice, a phase-locked oscillator is normally used in place of a filter, but its basic function is the same. The effect of the narrow-band filtering on the reference carrier is to prevent the reference carrier from following (or responding to) rapid phase changes in the received signal carrier. A sudden large phase change in the received signal carrier therefore causes incorrect detection over several received signal elements, before the phase of the reference carrier has responded to this change and has been appropriately adjusted. On the other hand, a frequency offset of up to ± 5 Hz introduces only a small phase error in a well designed phase-locked oscillator, provided that the frequency offset varies only very slowly with time, and this is usually the case over telephone circuits. Thus a coherent detector has a good tolerance to the frequency offsets normally experienced here in the received signal.

In a serial AM data-transmission system, a rounded modulating waveform is normally used in place of the rectangular waveform so far assumed, in order to minimize the bandwidth of the transmitted signal. In a serial binary PM system the bandwidth is normally reduced by rounding the *envelope* of each signal element, rather than the modulating waveform, such that the PM signal is now perhaps better considered as a suppressed-carrier AM signal with a rounded modulating waveform. The rounding of the envelope of each individual element of a PM signal is produced by appropriately bandlimiting the corresponding PSK signal, the phase modulating waveform remaining rectangular. If instead the modulating waveform of the binary PM signal is rounded, the envelope remaining constant, the PM signal becomes also an FM signal, since the instantaneous frequency of the carrier is no longer constant over a signal element. There is in fact a large class of such signals with potential use over satellite links, where a bandlimited constant envelope signal is required[482-490]. Except where specifically stated to the contrary, it is assumed throughout this book that the *modulating* waveform of an FM or PM signal is *rectangular*.

In the optimum coherent detection of a binary AM or suppressed-carrier AM signal, where the envelope (and hence also the modulating waveform) of an individual signal-element is rounded, the integrator in Figure 7.1 is replaced by a suitable low-pass filter. The shape of the modulating waveform used at the transmitter and the response of the low-pass filter are together selected so that there is a sinusoidal transition from one binary value to the other, at the output of the low-pass filter. Thus a typical output

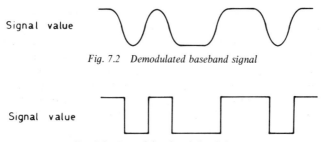

Signal value

Fig. 7.2   Demodulated baseband signal

Signal value

Fig. 7.3   Demodulated and sliced data signal

signal from the low-pass filter is shaped as in Figure 7.2, and this is the demodulated baseband signal.

In the element-value detector, the demodulated baseband signal is sliced at a threshold level half way between the positive and negative peaks of the signal, and the sliced signal is amplified to give the rectangular waveform shown in Figure 7.3. This is the demodulated and sliced data signal, but *not* the detected data signal.

The positive and negative going transitions in the rectangular waveform of Figure 7.3, occur at the boundaries between certain of the adjacent pairs of signal elements in this waveform, and are used to control the phase of the element timing waveform. Although individual transitions may be displaced in time, due to the effects of noise and distortion, the average phase of the transitions gives the correct phase (or positions) of the element boundaries and hence the correct phase for the element timing waveform.

The rectangular waveform of Figure 7.3 is sampled by the element timing waveform, at the mid-point in time of each signal element, to give the rectangular output data signal, which appears as the rectangular waveform in Figure 7.3 but delayed by $\frac{1}{2}T$ seconds (half the element period). Since the demodulated data signal in Figure 7.2 is compared with the threshold level to give the rectangular waveform in Figure 7.3, it follows that whenever this rectangular waveform is positive, the demodulated data signal lies above the threshold, and whenever this rectangular waveform is negative, the demodulated data signal lies below the threshold. Clearly, the value of the rectangular waveform in Figure 7.3, at each sampling instant, gives the detected binary value of the corresponding signal element. Thus the output data signal, obtained by sampling the rectangular waveform of Figure 7.3, carries the detected binary values. This signal is undistorted but may have errors. It can be seen that the coherent detector provides both the timing waveform and the detected data signal.

At the mid point in time of a signal element in the rectangular waveform of Figure 7.3, when the signal element is sampled, the value of the rounded waveform of Figure 7.2 is normally at a positive or negative peak, and coincides with the *end* of the corresponding received signal element. To a first approximation, the low-pass filter can be considered to perform a process of integration over a period of T seconds, so that its output signal at any instant is equal to the integral of its input signal over the preceding T seconds. Thus at the sampling instant of a signal element, the value of the rounded waveform can be considered to be the integral of the product of the received signal and reference carrier, over the corresponding element period of T seconds, just as shown for the integrator in Figure 7.1.

The description of a low-pass filter as an integrator gives a good idea of the essential function of the filter. It is, however, somewhat of an over-simplification. Although a typical low-pass filter does in fact integrate its input signal over a period of around T seconds, it does not weight the different parts of the input signal equally, but usually gives much more weight to those parts of the input signal in the middle of the integration period and correspondingly less weight to those at the beginning and the end. It is this weighting which results in the rounded waveform for the demodulated data signal, instead a more nearly triangular waveform which would be obtained if true integration (with equal weighting) were used. Furthermore, most practical filters introduce an additional delay into the output signal, which is, for convenience, neglected here.

Where an integrator is used in the coherent detector, the timing waveform must be derived independently of the coherent detector, in a separate process, since the timing waveform is itself required to initiate and terminate the integration over each element period. The integrator output signal must be reset to zero at the start of each element period, and it must be sampled at the end of each element period, immediately before being reset to zero again. Thus, in a serial system, the use of an integrator in place of a low-pass filter for the coherent detector, results in a considerable increase in equipment complexity. Furthermore, because of the need to limit the bandwidth of the transmitted signal to the bandwidth of the channel, a rectangular modulating waveform cannot normally be used for the transmitted signal. With a rounded modulating waveform, the optimum process of coherent detection uses the appropriate low-pass filter in place of the integrator, in Figure 7.1. It follows that, in a serial system, the most cost-effective arrangement of coherent detection uses a low-pass filter and extracts the timing waveform from the demodulated and sliced data signal.

In a parallel system, the timing information is usually transmitted via a separate timing signal, so that a separate process must in any case be used to extract the timing waveform at the receiver. Since the nominal bandwidth of an individual data signal is now small compared with the bandwidth of the channel, a relatively wider bandwidth may frequently be used for each individual data signal, thus permitting the use of rectangular modulating waveforms. Under these conditions, a coherent detector employing an integrator becomes the most cost-effective detector.

7.2 Incoherent and noncoherent detection

In incoherent detection of a digital signal the receiver has no prior knowledge of the phase of the signal carrier at the start of an element detection process, or, at least, makes no use of any such knowledge. It follows that the operation of an incoherent detector is not affected by the phase relationship between the received signal carrier over the portion of the received signal involved in an element detection process and the signal carrier over any other portion of the received signal. *Noncoherent* detection is here taken to be a compromise between coherent and incoherent detection, having therefore a performance that lies somewhere between that of coherent detection and that of incoherent detection. In practice, *incoherent* (rather than noncoherent) detection is normally used for AM and PM signals, whereas *noncoherent* detection is normally used for FM signals. The principles and basic techniques of the ideal incoherent detection of ASK and PSK signals are considered in Sections 6.9 and 6.10. The techniques of incoherent and noncoherent detection now to be described are simple methods that are or have been employed in practice and are cost effective. Practical incoherent detectors for AM and PM signals do not in general achieve quite as good a tolerance to noise as the corresponding ideal incoherent detectors but they are simpler to implement.

With any detector, whether coherent, incoherent or noncoherent, it is essential that the received signal is first fed through a band-pass filter to remove as much noise as possible outside the signal frequency band. This is necessary for two reasons. Firstly, in any incoherent or noncoherent detector the demodulation process is essentially nonlinear and such that noise frequency components in the received signal that lie outside the frequency band of the data signal can give rise to noise frequency components in the demodulated waveform, which lie inside the frequency band of the corresponding demodulated baseband data signal and so cannot be removed by the post-demodulation low-pass filter. Secondly, high level wide band noise that has frequency components well outside the frequency band of the received data signal, is often present at the input to a modem. If the components of this noise that lie outside the frequency band of the data signal are not removed by the input band-pass filter, they can cause overloading of the input circuits of the modem and so degrade the performance of the detector, regardless of whether this is coherent, noncoherent or incoherent. If noise frequency components outside the frequency band of the data signal cause overloading, new frequency components are introduced, some of which are more than likely to lie inside the frequency band of the data signal and will therefore not be removed by any subsequent filtering in the receiver. Hence it is assumed throughout the following discussion that the input signal to each detector has been filtered in an appropriate band-pass filter.

Incoherent detection of an AM signal is envelope detection. A typical detector is shown in Figure 7.4. The received signal is first amplified and set to a predetermined level, by an automatic gain controlled (AGC) amplifier. It is then full-wave rectified and the rectified signal is filtered by a low-pass filter, to give the demodulated baseband signal which is a rounded waveform. The presence of signal carrier over a received element period represents the element value 1 and gives a negative output signal from the low-pass filter at the end of the element period. The absence of signal carrier over a received element period represents the element value 0 and gives a positive output signal from the filter at the end of the element period. The output signal from the low-pass filter at any instant is the suitably weighted running average of its input signal over a period of around T seconds (the element duration). More accurately, the output signal is *proportional* to this running average.

The output signal from the low-pass filter is fed to the element timing and detection circuit, where it is sliced along the threshold level and amplified, to give a rectangular waveform. The positive level in this waveform represents the element value 0, and the negative level the element value 1. The rectangular waveform is the demodulated and sliced data signal. It is used to control the phase of the element timing waveform, which is generated by a suitable phase-locked oscillator. The demodulated and sliced data signal is sampled by the timing waveform at the mid-point of each element, to give the rectangular output data signal, which carries the detected element values.

The detection of a binary FM signal is normally achieved by means of the arrangement shown in Figure 7.5. This uses a discriminator whose output signal is ideally proportional to the

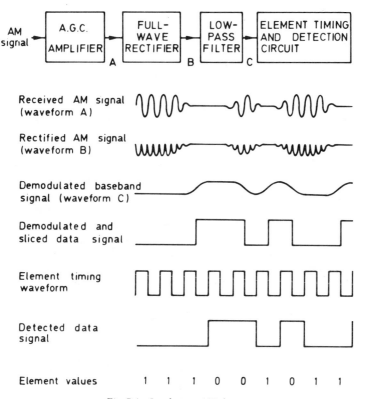

Fig. 7.4   Incoherent AM detector

Fig. 7.5   Noncoherent FM detector

instantaneous frequency (rate of change of phase) of the received
FM signal. The high frequency components in the output signal
from the discriminator are removed in the low-pass filter to give a
rounded demodulated baseband signal (similar to the waveform C
in Figure 7.4) and this is fed to the element timing and detection
circuit. The latter operates as previously described.

The tolerance to additive white Gaussian noise of the detector in
Figure 7.5 usually lies somewhere between that of an ideal coherent
detector (Section 6.4) and that of an ideal incoherent detector

(Section 6.8). An FM-discriminator detector is therefore classed here as a noncoherent detector. In the ideal incoherent detection of a binary FSK signal-element, in which the element duration is T seconds and the frequency shift between the two carrier frequencies is $1/T$ Hz, the tolerance to additive white Gaussian noise is about 3 dB below that of the corresponding binary PSK system using ideal incoherent detection (Section 6.10) and about 4 dB below that of the corresponding binary PSK system using ideal coherent detection. A frequency shift of $1/T$ Hz in the FSK signal gives the best available tolerance to white Gaussian noise when ideal incoherent detection is used. In a conventional FSK modem operating at 600 or 1200 bit/s, the frequency shift in the binary FSK signal is $2/3T$ Hz, and the tolerance to additive white Gaussian noise with ideal incoherent detection is nearly 5.5 dB below that of the corresponding binary PSK system using ideal coherent detection. An error rate of 1 in 10^4 in the detected element-values is assumed here.

The binary FSK signal giving the best available tolerance to additive white Gaussian noise, when ideal coherent detection is used at the receiver, has a frequency shift of $0.715/T$ Hz between the two carrier frequencies, this being 0.715 times the signal element rate of $1/T$ bauds. The tolerance to additive white Gaussian noise of this system is 2.15 dB below that of the corresponding PSK system with coherent detection at the receiver, and is some 2.8 dB better than if ideal incoherent detection is used for the FSK signal. Clearly, a useful improvement in performance can be gained here by replacing the incoherent detector with a noncoherent detector having a tolerance to noise closer to that of a coherent detector.

T. T. Tjhung and P. H. Wittke have shown[337] that the noncoherent detector of Figure 7.5, when used with a binary FSK signal having a frequency shift of $0.7/T$ Hz and with the appropriate receiver filter can achieve a tolerance to additive white Gaussian noise only 2.25 dB below that of the corresponding PSK system employing coherent detection at the receiver. An error rate of 1 in 10^4 is assumed here. Thus, for practical purposes, this arrangement can be considered to achieve coherent detection of the received FSK signal. Most of the power of the given FSK signal is contained in a frequency band whose width is $1.2/T$ Hz, that is, 1.2 times the signal element rate. The band-pass filter used here ahead of the discriminator (and not shown in Figure 7.5) has a rectangular transfer function with a linear phase characteristic and a bandwidth of $1.2/T$ Hz centred on the FSK signal spectrum. The filter has unit gain over its pass-band and zero gain outside, and it passes most of the signal power. The low-pass filter (following the discriminator)

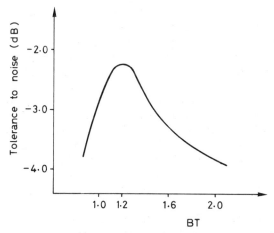

Fig. 7.6   Tolerance to additive white Gaussian noise of FSK system relative to that of the corresponding PSK system

has a rectangular impulse response of duration T (Figure 13.5), and the filter is equivalent to an integrator that operates on a received signal-element over its duration, as is shown in Equation 13.5 and Figure 13.6.

If the bandwidth, B Hz, of the band-pass filter ahead of the discriminator is adjusted to different values, the tolerance of the FSK system to additive white Gaussian noise, relative to that of the corresponding PSK system with ideal coherent detection, varies with the bandwidth of the filter as shown in Figure 7.6. An error rate of 1 in 10^4 in the detected element-values is assumed, as before, and the corresponding PSK signal is not bandlimited at the input to the coherent detector.

In practice it is difficult or complex to implement a band-pass filter with a rectangular transfer function, a Gaussian transfer function (or, at least, an approximation to it) being much easier to achieve. With such an input filter, the optimum bandwidth (measured between the 3 dB points) is now $1/T$ Hz, and the tolerance to additive white Gaussian noise is only 0.1 dB below the best obtainable with the rectangular transfer-function filter[337]. When the binary FSK signal has the very slightly suboptimum frequency shift of $2/3T$ Hz, as in a conventional 600 or 1200 bit/s modem, the further loss in tolerance to noise is a little under 0.05 dB. Thus, in a 1200 bit/s binary FSK modem using carrier frequencies of 1300 and 2100 Hz, it should be possible to achieve a tolerance to additive white Gaussian noise of no more than about 2.5 dB below that of

Fig. 7.7   Zero-crossing FM detector

the corresponding PM modem using coherent detection. Allowance has been made here for the small possible reduction in tolerance to noise due to the fact that the lower carrier frequency is only a little greater than $1/T$ Hz.

The simplest detector for a binary FM signal is a 'zero-crossing' detector which is shown in Figure 7.7 and operates as follows. The received and filtered FM signal is first fed through an amplifier limiter, which amplifies a narrow slice of the received signal, the slice being centred on a signal value of zero, to give a rectangular output waveform. Each transition of the latter waveform corresponds to a zero crossing of the input signal and, in the zero crossing detector, it is used to generate a positive (or negative) pulse whose leading edge coincides with the zero crossing. The resulting stream of pulses is fed to a low-pass filter whose output signal is the demodulated baseband signal at the output of the zero-crossing detector in Figure 7.7. The higher the carrier frequency of the FM signal the greater the density of the pulses and so the more positive (or negative) is the corresponding output signal from the zero-crossing detector. The output signal is a measure of the average pulse density over the preceding period of about T seconds and is therefore also a measure of the average instantaneous frequency of the received FM signal over this period. The output signal is a rounded waveform, as in Figure 7.2, and is fed to the element timing and detection circuit which gives the detected data signal, as previously described (Figure 7.4).

If the time interval between two adjacent zero crossings of the FM signal is τ seconds, the average instantaneous carrier frequency of the FM signal over this period is $1/2\tau$ Hz. As the number of carrier cycles per signal element increases, so the change in instantaneous frequency over the time interval τ tends to decrease, and the zero-crossing detector approximates more closely to an ideal discriminator detector. However, when there are only one or two cycles of the signal carrier per signal element, there can be quite large changes in instantaneous frequency over the time interval between two adjacent zero crossings, so that the zero-crossing detector no longer approximates well to an ideal discriminator detector.

In a 1200 bit/s binary FM modem using carrier frequencies of 1300 and 2100 Hz, the tolerance to additive white Gaussian noise of a zero-crossing detector, as in Figure 7.7, generally lies in the range

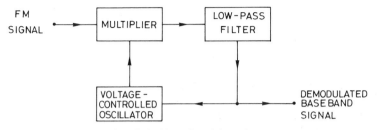

Fig. 7.8   *Phase-locked-loop demodulator for an FM signal*

of 4–6 dB below that of the corresponding binary PM system with coherent detection, assuming here that the transmission path does not itself introduce significant signal distortion. For the best performance in this range, a carefully designed and perhaps rather complex band-pass filter is required at the receiver input[143]. This filter is of only just sufficient bandwidth to pass the bulk of the signal power. Where a simpler filter with a somewhat wider bandwidth is used, the tolerance of the system to additive white Gaussian noise is likely to lie in the range of 5–6 dB below that of the corresponding PM system with coherent detection. Such a system has a tolerance to additive white Gaussian noise quite similar to that of the ideal incoherent detector (this being about 5.5 dB below that of the PM system), but it is very much simpler to implement.

It is clear that when the FM signal has only one or two carrier cycles per signal element (as is the case here for the 1200 bit/s FM signal under consideration), ideal discriminator detection cannot be achieved on this signal after it has been passed through an amplifier limiter or slicer. The spectrum of the FM signal should now be shifted up in frequency so that there are at least some 10 cycles of the signal carrier per signal element. The signal should then be fed through an amplifier limiter and next to an FM discriminator. The latter could be implemented as a zero-crossing detector, which now approximates well to an ideal discriminator detector. The tolerance to additive white Gaussian noise of this arrangement can be made to approximate as closely as required to that of an ideal discriminator detector.

The zero-crossing detector in the arrangement just described may be replaced by the more sophisticated phase-locked-loop detector shown in Figure 7.8. When appropriately designed this should give the best available detection of the received FM signal that can be achieved by means of an FM discriminator. When the frequency shift in the binary FSK signal is $2/3T$ Hz, as is assumed here, a further improvement of some 2.5–4 dB in tolerance to additive white Gaussian noise can be achieved by delaying the detection of a signal element and involving in its detection the detection also of several of the immediately following signal elements[176,422].

Such techniques are considered in Sections 6.1 and 6.4. The detection processes are, however, really too complex for applications over telephone circuits, and will therefore not be considered further here.

The phase-locked loop in Figure 7.8 attempts to maintain a phase angle of 90° between the carrier at the output of the voltage-controlled oscillator and that of the received FM signal. With a high-level input FM signal and the appropriate low-pass filter, the signal at the input to the voltage-controlled oscillator should be effectively the same as the modulating waveform at the transmitter or, at least, a low-pass filtered form of this. If the received FM signal has only one or two cycles of the carrier per signal element and is fed through an amplifier limiter at the input of the phase-locked loop, there may be a reduction in tolerance to additive white Gaussian noise of up to about 1 dB, due to the loss of information (distortion) introduced by the amplifier limiter. If a simple zero-crossing detector is used here in place of the phase-locked-loop detector, there is typically a further loss of between 1 and 2 dB in tolerance to Gaussian noise.

With any FM-discriminator detector, as the bandwidth of the receiver input filter is reduced, so is the noise level at the output of the discriminator, but at the same time the distortion in the demodulated waveform is increased. The best performance is obtained with the appropriate balance between the two effects. The inferior performance of the zero-crossing detector, relative to the detector employing an amplifier limiter and a phase-locked loop, is due, at least in part, to the greater signal distortion introduced in the zero-crossing detector.

An alternative approach towards achieving a good tolerance to additive white Gaussian noise with a binary FM signal is a technique described by J. Salz[476]. The optimum FM signal here has a frequency shift of $1/2T$ Hz and is filtered at the transmitter in such a way as to increase the signal power density towards the edges of the signal frequency band (the power density being measured here relative to that of the corresponding FSK signal). This enables the attenuation of the receiver filter to be increased towards the edges of the signal frequency band, while still giving the required FSK signal at the filter output. Thus there is a steadily increasing attenuation of the noise frequency components at the output of the receiver filter, as the frequency is further removed from the centre of the signal frequency band. An ideal discriminator detector is used at the receiver. Since the level of the demodulated signal at the output of the discriminator increases as the input carrier frequency is moved further from the centre of the signal frequency band, it is evident that the sensitivity of the discriminator to a noise frequency component increases as its frequency approaches the edge of the signal frequency band. Thus, by attenuating most severely these noise frequency components that cause the greatest interference in the demodulated FM signal, an improved tolerance to noise is achieved.

The transmitted FM signal here does not have a constant envelope and so it is not also an FSK signal. The FM signal is in fact modulated both in frequency and in amplitude. It has been shown that, with the optimum transmitter and receiver filters and with an ideal discriminator detector at the receiver, the tolerance of the system to additive white Gaussian noise is only 0.25 dB below that of the corresponding binary PM system[476].

The weakness of the arrangement just described is that some not entirely straightforward filtering of the transmitted FM signal is required. Furthermore, as is mentioned in Section 5.3, an FSK signal with a frequency shift of $1/2T$ Hz (and having, of course, a constant envelope) is in fact also an MSK signal, which, in turn, is the sum of two binary PM signals that are in phase quadrature and offset in time, as shown in Figure 5.5. The coherent detection of the two binary PM signals gives the same tolerance to additive white Gaussian noise as that obtained in the coherent detection of a conventional binary PM signal, and so gives a tolerance to noise 0.25 dB better than that of the previous system. On the other hand, if the MSK signal is treated as an FSK signal, the tolerance to additive white Gaussian noise with coherent detection is 3 dB below that of the corresponding binary PM signal, and with incoherent detection it is about 7.5 dB below. Thus the optimum discriminator detection of an MSK signal gives a tolerance to additive white Gaussian noise of around 3 dB below that of the coherent detection of the corresponding binary PM signal. The tolerance to additive white Gaussian noise is in every case quoted at an error rate of 1 in 10^4 in the detected element values. The reason why coherent detection of an MSK signal, treating this as the sum of two binary PM signals, gains 3 dB in tolerance to noise over coherent detection of the MSK signal, treating this now as an FSK signal, is essentially because in the former case a detection process extends over a period of $2T$, twice that in the latter case, thus enabling the detector to

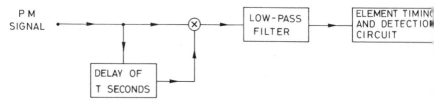

Fig. 7.9   Incoherent PM detector

exploit fully the available prior knowledge of the received modulated-carrier signal, which is not possible over a period of only T.

The ideal incoherent detection of a PM signal (strictly speaking, a PSK signal) is carried out as described in Section 6.10. The detection process for a binary PM signal, with a rectangular modulating waveform and a rounded (or rectangular) envelope for each individual element, is often implemented in a slightly different manner, as shown in Figure 7.9. It is assumed here that there are a whole number of half cycles of the signal carrier per signal element, with at least one complete cycle, the element duration being T seconds, as before. This means that the signal carrier frequency is $l/2T$ Hz, where l is an integer greater than unity. Over the duration of any signal element its waveform is multiplied by that of the preceding element. The output signal from the multiplier at any instant is positive or negative, depending upon whether the signs of the two input signals at this instant are the same or different, respectively. The detector can be greatly simplified by first slicing and amplifying the received PM signal in an amplifier limiter, to give a rectangular input signal waveform. The linear multiplier in Figure 7.9 now becomes a simple exclusive-OR gate. With either arrangement, the output signal from the low-pass filter, at any instant, is the weighted average of the input signal over the preceding period of around T seconds. When a signal element has just been received, the output signal from the low-pass filter is a measure of the average phase change in the signal carrier between the element just received and the preceding element. When the carrier phase is the same at all corresponding points over the two signal elements, the output signal from the low-pass filter (immediately following the receipt of the second element) has its maximum positive value. When the carrier phase in one of the two signal elements is shifted by 180° with respect to that in the other, at all corresponding points over the two elements, the output signal from the low-pass filter has its most negative value. When on average the carrier phase in one of the two signal elements is less than 90° out of phase with that in the other, the output signal from the low-pass filter (immediately following the receipt of the second element) is positive. When on average the carrier phase in one of the two signal elements is more than 90° out of phase, the output signal is negative. The output signal from the low-pass filter is a rounded waveform, as in Figure 7.2, and is fed to the element timing and detection circuit which gives the detected data signal, as previously described. The detector in Figure 7.9 may not be quite optimum[492].

Since a binary PM signal is normally differentially coded, a binary value 1 being sent as a phase change between two adjacent elements and a binary value 0 as no phase change, it can be seen that the incoherent detection of a PM signal not only detects the signal but also decodes it, to give a negative output level for a binary value 1 and a positive level for a binary value 0. On account of the basic structure of the incoherent detector, it is often referred to as a differentially coherent detector.

When a received binary AM or PM signal has a rectangular envelope for each signal element, in place of the rounded envelope assumed here, the low-pass filter in the detector is replaced by an integrator. This, of course, requires the timing waveform to be extracted from the received signal by a separate process, and, in the case of a serial system, it results in a considerable increase in equipment complexity. Since true rectangular envelopes are not normally used for serial AM and PM signals, the most cost-effective detectors for serial systems are similar to those described, using low-pass filters. As has previously been mentioned, a PM signal with a rounded or rectangular envelope is also a suppressed carrier AM signal with a rounded or rectangular modulating waveform, respectively. Unless specifically stated to the contrary, the modulating waveform of a PM or FM signal is always assumed to be rectangular.

In a parallel system, the timing information is usually transmitted via a separate timing signal and rectangular envelopes are often used. Under these conditions an incoherent detector employing an integrator becomes the most cost-effective detector.

7.3 Selection of preferred systems

Consider a binary signal-element $s_h(t)$ received in the presence of a noise waveform $w(t)$ to give the received waveform

$$r(t) = s_h(t) + w(t) \tag{7.5}$$

where $s_h(t)$ is equally likely to be $s_0(t)$ or $s_1(t)$ and $w(t)$ is a stationary Gaussian random process with zero mean and a constant two-sided power spectral density of $\frac{1}{2}N_0$ over the whole of the frequency band of the data signal. Clearly, N_0 is the average noise power per unit bandwidth of the data signal (that is, per Hz of the one-sided signal spectrum). It is assumed that $s_h(t)$ extends over the time interval from 0 to T seconds (with $s_h(t) = 0$ for $t < 0$ and $t > T$) and that the average energy of $s_h(t)$ is E. The data-symbol h ($= 0$ or 1) carries the binary value of the received signal-element.

Table 7.1 gives the expressions for the probability of error in the detection of the element binary value from $r(t)$, for different signals and both coherent and incoherent detection processes. The FSK signal here has a frequency shift of $1/T$ Hz. The function $Q(y)$ is given by

$$Q(y) = \int_y^\infty \frac{1}{\sqrt{2\pi}} \exp\left(-\tfrac{1}{2}v^2\right) dv \qquad (7.6)$$

and the error probabilities for coherent detection are derived in Chapter 16. The error probabilities for incoherent detection are derived elsewhere[303,320,328,475-477]. The ideal coherent and incoherent detectors for ASK, FSK and PSK signals are described in Chapter 6. The expression for the probability of error in the incoherent detection of an ASK signal holds only at high signal/noise ratios, and the optimum decision threshold, employed in the element-value detector of Figure 6.8 or 6.9, is now approximately half way between the two possible signals (values of x) at the input to this detector in the absence of noise (see Section 6.9). At lower signal/noise ratios, the optimum decision threshold is raised somewhat. It is assumed here that the decision threshold is set exactly half way between the two possible signals at the detector input, in the absence of noise, and, under this condition, the error probability becomes steadily greater than that given by $\frac{1}{2}\exp(-E/2N_0)$ as the signal/noise ratio is reduced, the expression holding reasonably well for error probabilities below 1 in 10^4 [477]. The improvement in tolerance to Gaussian noise at an error probability of 1 in 10^4, achieved by using the optimum decision threshold in place of that assumed here, is 0.4 dB and decreases steadily towards zero as the error probability is reduced[328].

When the frequency shift in the binary FSK signal is not necessarily $1/T$ Hz, the error probability with coherent detection is

$$P_e = Q\left(\sqrt{\left\{\frac{E(1-\rho)}{N_0}\right\}}\right) \qquad (7.7)$$

where

$$\rho = \frac{1}{E} \int_0^T s_0(t)s_1(t)\, dt \qquad (7.8)$$

The parameter ρ is the cross-correlation coefficient for the two possible signal-element waveforms $s_0(t)$ and $s_1(t)$, each with energy E. It can readily be shown that, for a frequency shift of Δ/T Hz,

$$\rho = \frac{\sin 2\pi\Delta}{2\pi\Delta} \qquad (7.9)$$

It is assumed here that each of the two possible values of the signal carrier frequency is much greater than $1/T$ Hz.

In the case of a binary PSK signal, where the carrier phase shift between the two possible signal-elements $s_0(t)$ and $s_1(t)$ is ϕ radians, the error probability with coherent detection is again given by P_e in Equation 7.7, where ρ is as in Equation 7.8, but now

$$\rho = \cos\phi \qquad (7.10)$$

It is assumed here that the signal carrier frequency is an integral multiple of $1/2T$ Hz or much greater than $1/T$ Hz, or possibly both.

Figure 7.10 shows the variation of error probability with signal/noise ratio for each of the different signals and detection processes considered in Table 7.1. The performance of an FSK signal, with a frequency shift of $0.7/T$ Hz and ideal coherent detection at the receiver, is also shown. The signal/noise ratio, ψ dB, is given by

$$\psi = 10 \log_{10}(E/N_0) \qquad (7.11)$$

It can be seen that, with a binary signal at high signal/noise ratios such that the error probability is less than 10^{-4}, coherent detection gains an advantage of less than about 1 dB in tolerance to additive white Gaussian noise over incoherent detection. This in fact holds for every case other than that of an FSK signal with a frequency shift that is not a multiple of $1/T$ Hz or close to this. The advantage of up to about 1 dB gained by coherent detection in the case of these signals (when the error probability is less than 10^{-4}) is not normally important. However, at a low signal/noise ratio, giving an error probability of around 10^{-1}, the advantage in tolerance to additive white Gaussian noise rises to about 3 dB and clearly becomes significant.

Figure 7.11 shows how the tolerance to additive white Gaussian noise of a binary FSK signal varies with the frequency shift,

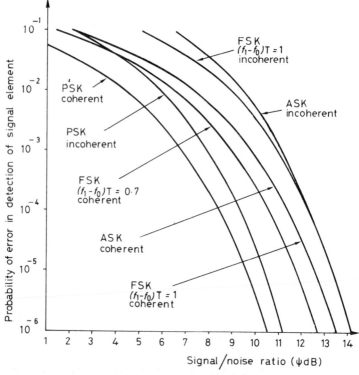

Fig. 7.10   Performances of the different systems

Table 7.1   PROBABILITY OF ERROR IN THE DETECTION OF THE
BINARY ELEMENT VALUE FROM $r(t)$

Data signal	Probability of error	
	Coherent detection	Incoherent detection
ASK	$Q\left(\sqrt{\dfrac{E}{N_0}}\right)$	$\simeq \frac{1}{2}\exp\left(-\dfrac{E}{2N_0}\right)$
FSK	$Q\left(\sqrt{\dfrac{E}{N_0}}\right)$	$\frac{1}{2}\exp\left(-\dfrac{E}{2N_0}\right)$
PSK	$Q\left(\sqrt{\dfrac{2E}{N_0}}\right)$	$\frac{1}{2}\exp\left(-\dfrac{E}{N_0}\right)$

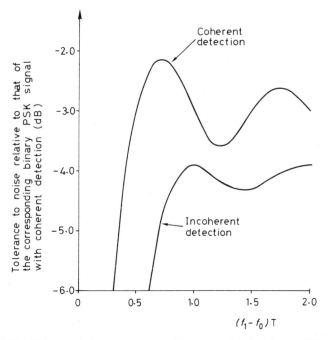

Fig. 7.11 Variation of tolerance to noise with frequency shift for a binary FSK signal

$f_1 - f_0$ Hz, for both ideal coherent and ideal incoherent detection. As before, f_0 and f_1 are the two carrier frequencies of the FSK signal (in Hz), and T seconds is the duration of the signal element. The tolerance to noise is here taken as the signal/noise ratio, E/N_0, measured in dB relative to its value for the corresponding binary PSK signal with ideal coherent detection, where each element is received in the presence of additive white Gaussian noise and the probability of error in the detection of the signal element is again 10^{-4}. It can be seen that, with incoherent detection, the best tolerance to noise of the FSK signal is obtained with a frequency shift of $1/T$ Hz, the tolerance to noise being about 4 dB below that of the corresponding PSK signal with coherent detection and only 0.9 dB below that of the given FSK signal with coherent detection. However, with coherent detection, the best tolerance to noise of the FSK signal is obtained with a frequency shift of $0.715/T$ Hz, the tolerance to noise being now 2.15 dB below that of the corresponding PSK signal with coherent detection. If incoherent detection is used here in place of coherent detection, for the FSK signal, the tolerance to noise is reduced by nearly 3 dB, which is a significant reduction. When the frequency shift of the FSK signal is reduced from $1/T$ Hz to $2/3T$ or $1/2T$ Hz, the tolerance to noise of an incoherent detector is reduced by about 1.5 or 3.5 dB, respectively. Thus, for frequency shifts in the FSK signal well below $1/T$ Hz, incoherent detection becomes substantially inferior to coherent detection, and as the frequency shift decreases below $1/2T$ Hz, the tolerance to additive white Gaussian noise decreases rapidly with the frequency shift for both coherent and incoherent detection.

An important advantage of coherent detection over incoherent detection, for AM, FM and PM signals, is that it gives a much better tolerance to the most general types of attenuation and delay distortions experienced over voice-frequency channels[309]. In the detection of PM signals, a coherent detector gives a better tolerance to a small frequency offset of the received signal than does an incoherent (differentially coherent) detector, provided only that a suitable phase-locked oscillator is used to generate the reference carrier in the coherent detector.

The first important advantage of incoherent detection, for each of the three modulation methods, is that it involves less complex equipment than coherent detection. The advantage is considerable in the case of AM and FM systems, but less important for PM systems. The second important advantage of incoherent detection, again for each of the three modulation methods, is that it gives a much better tolerance to sudden phase changes introduced into the received signal by telephone carrier links.

Two further points are worth mentioning, concerning coherent and differentially coherent detection of PM signals.

In a practical coherent detector for a PM signal, as the effective filtering applied to the reference carrier is made finer, to reduce the level of the phase jitter, so the tolerance to frequency modulation effects on the received signal is reduced, and in practice a compromise must be reached between the two requirements. One result of this is that a practical coherent detector cannot approach so closely to the ideal coherent detector, as a practical differentially coherent detector can approach to its ideal. Thus the advantage in tolerance to additive noise and signal distortion, of a coherent detector over a differentially coherent detector, is not always quite as great as that predicted on theoretical grounds.

In order that the best available tolerance to noise and distortion is achieved by a differentially coherent detector for a binary PM signal, as in Figure 7.9, any two *adjacent* elements of the PM signal should either be the same or else be the negatives of each other. Each element must now contain a whole number of half cycles of the signal carrier, with at least one complete cycle. Where for any reason this cannot be achieved, the value of delay used in the differentially coherent detector should equal the duration of the largest number of half cycles of the signal carrier whose total duration is less than that of one signal-element. Under these conditions the tolerance to noise and distortion will always be less than that of the ideal arrangement, because now only a portion of each signal element is used in the detection process. The reason for this effect is that, in differentially coherent detection, each signal element is compared with the *preceding* element and not with one or other of the two possible noise-free forms of the element itself, as in coherent detection. The two possible forms of the element are, of course, the negatives of each other, and the whole of each received signal-element is always used in a coherent detection process. Thus, when each element does not contain a whole number of half-cycles of the signal carrier, coherent detection achieves a greater advantage in tolerance to additive Gaussian noise over differentially coherent detection, although the improved tolerance would normally be small, not often exceeding 1 dB[197].

Consideration of the various properties of coherent and incoherent detection shows that it is not cost-effective to use coherent detection with either AM or FM signals, largely because of the considerable equipment complexity involved. Thus, incoherent detection is nearly always used for both binary AM signals and binary FM signals, where the latter have a frequency shift of $1/T$ Hz. However, in applications of digital data-transmission at 600 or 1200 bit/s over telephone circuits, where the data signal is an FM signal, the most cost-effective system employs a frequency shift of $2/3T$ Hz in the FM signal and uses a discriminator at the receiver to achieve *noncoherent* detection. As is explained in Section 7.2, the tolerance of such a detector to additive white Gaussian noise can be made to approach quite closely to that of an ideal coherent detector, giving it a useful advantage in tolerance to noise over the corresponding incoherent detector. Since the noncoherent detector can also be quite simple to implement, it is preferred to the incoherent detector. Both coherent and incoherent detection are cost-effective when used with binary PM signals. Clearly, there are four different binary data-transmission systems worthy of further study:

(1) AM with incoherent detection
(2) FM with noncoherent detection
(3) PM with incoherent detection
(4) PM with coherent detection.

8

Transmission rates

8.1 Maximum transmission rate

Nyquist showed in 1928 that the maximum signal-element rate which may be transmitted over a bandwidth B Hz, for no inter-symbol interference, is $2B$ bauds (elements per second), and this is sometimes known as the Nyquist rate[268]. Figure 8.1 shows the shape of a pulse, corresponding to an individual signal element, whose energy-density spectrum (distribution of energy over the different frequencies) is constant from 0 to B Hz and zero over all higher frequencies. The energy-density spectrum is shown in Figure 8.2. Signal elements shaped as in Figure 8.1, when spaced (delayed) relative to each other at time intervals which are multiples of $1/2B$ seconds, will cause no intersymbol interference if sampled at the central positive peaks. That is, at the centre of any one signal element there can be no signal contributed by any other element.

The maximum signal-element rate of any given m-level signal over a given frequency band, for no intersymbol interference, is a good guide as to the efficiency of the signal in the use of bandwidth. The latter is a most important parameter of a signal, since it is nearly always required to achieve the maximum conveniently (or simply) obtainable transmission rate over any given channel. Frequently, in comparing the bandwidth efficiencies of two signals, a comparison is made of the respective power-density spectra[267-284]. This can be very misleading, since the important criterion is not the bandwidth of the *undistorted* signal but rather the minimum bandwidth over which satisfactory operation can be achieved with the given trans-mitted signal, which now has its undistorted form only at the transmitter output. In other words, it is necessary to consider also the degree of bandlimiting that is tolerated by the signal. Quite often a data signal, having a relatively wide bandwidth in its undistorted form, tolerates a considerable degree of bandlimiting, whereas another signal, whose undistorted form has a relatively

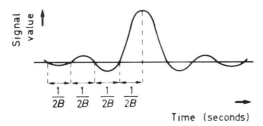

Fig. 8.1   Individual signal element

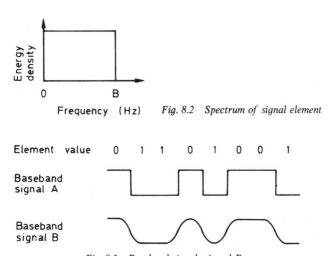

Fig. 8.2   Spectrum of signal element

Fig. 8.3   Baseband signals A and B

narrow bandwidth, tolerates only a small degree of bandlimiting, so that, at a given transmission rate, the former signal can in fact be transmitted satisfactorily over a narrower frequency-band than can the latter.

In order to simplify the following discussion, it will be assumed throughout that binary signals are being used. The various results quoted here therefore apply specifically to such signals.

8.2   Baseband signals

Figure 8.3 shows the waveforms of two different binary polar baseband signals carrying the same sequence of binary values. In each case the element spacing is T seconds, giving an element rate

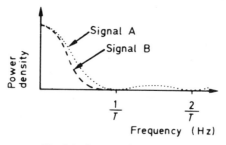

Fig. 8.4 *Spectra of signals A and B*

of $1/T$ bauds. It is assumed that a very long sequence of binary element values is transmitted, the element values being statistically independent and equally likely to be either 0 or 1.

The baseband signal A has the power-density spectrum given by the dotted line in Figure 8.4. Although much of the signal power is concentrated here at the lower frequencies, below $1/T$ Hz, a considerable amount of the signal power is distributed over the higher frequencies, the signal having an infinite bandwidth. If the waveform of the signal A is now rounded to give the signal B, the power density at the higher frequencies is very much reduced and the power-density spectrum is that given by the dashed line in Figure 8.4. The spectrum of signal A has points of zero power density at frequencies which are multiples of $1/T$ Hz, and peaks of power density between the adjacent zeros. The spectrum of signal B has some power over the frequencies above $1/T$ Hz, but at a very much lower level than for signal A, and this power may usually be neglected. As before, only *positive* frequencies are considered.

An individual pulse of the signal A (a signal element of binary value 1 preceded and followed by signal elements of binary value 0, or vice versa) has a total duration of T seconds and is only present over the corresponding element period. On the other hand, an individual pulse of the signal B has a total duration of $2T$ seconds and overlaps into the periods of T seconds allocated to the two immediately adjacent elements. Thus the reduction in the bandwidth of the signal B, relative to that of the signal A, is accompanied by a doubling of the total duration of each individual signal element.

For an element period of T seconds, the element rate is $1/T$ bauds. From Nyquist[267,268], this requires a minimum bandwidth from 0 to $1/2T$ Hz in the transmission path, for the detection of the received signal elements without intersymbol interference. Thus, for both baseband signals A and B, the frequency band from 0 to $1/2T$ Hz contains the essential information carried by the signal, and is

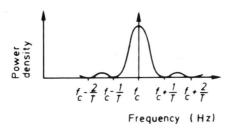

Fig. 8.5 Spectrum of AM signal

necessary for the correct transmission of the data. Any band limiting by the transmission path of the transmitted signal A or B, even if it has no effect on the frequency components below $1/2T$ Hz, will of course change both the signal waveform and the corresponding power density spectrum. It can be seen that the maximum element rate for a baseband signal, originally shaped as signal A or B, is 2 bauds/Hz, although in practice the rate is preferably not very much greater than 1 baud/Hz, say no more than $\frac{4}{3}$ bauds/Hz (over the pass-band of the transmission path bounded by zero frequency and the point at which the attenuation exceeds that at low frequencies by 20 dB).

The baseband signal A or B may be used to modulate a suitable carrier frequency, using amplitude, frequency or phase modulation[94-243].

8.3 AM signals

Figure 8.5 shows the frequency spectrum of an amplitude modulated carrier, using the rectangular baseband signal A as the modulating waveform. The frequency spectrum is symmetrical about the carrier frequency f_c, the lower sideband being inverted with respect to the upper sideband and the upper sideband similar to the spectrum of the baseband signal A, in Figure 8.4, but shifted up in frequency by f_c Hz.

The information carried in each sideband is the same and thus there is 50% redundant information in the two sidebands. The signal carrier itself carries no useful information. Ideally then the information in the signal could be transmitted equally well using only one sideband and thus requiring only half the frequency band. In speech the lowest useful frequency is about 300 Hz, leaving an appreciable margin between the carrier and each sideband in the signal formed by amplitude modulating a carrier with a speech waveform. Thus a practical filter can remove the carrier and one sideband of this signal, to leave only the other sideband, and so give single sideband suppressed carrier transmission. In data transmission, however, the power in the modulating waveform is usually concentrated towards the very low frequencies, including zero frequency or d.c., and giving rise to the characteristic frequency spectra shown in Figure 8.4. Under these conditions it is not practical to use signal sideband suppressed carrier transmission. However, it is possible to remove a good part of one sideband, and this is done in a vestigial sideband AM signal, where one sideband, the carrier and only a vestige of the other sideband are transmitted. The carrier itself can also be suppressed to give a vestigial sideband suppressed carrier AM signal[285-296]. In the case of a binary signal, this is the same as a vestigial sideband PM signal and is considered separately under PM signals.

It is in fact possible to generate a true single sideband suppressed carrier AM signal by first shaping the spectrum of the baseband modulating data signal so that it has the value zero at d.c. Techniques for doing this are considered in Chapter 15. It is now possible to remove the *whole* of one of the two sidebands of the modulated-carrier signal. The resultant signal occupies a significantly smaller bandwidth than the corresponding vestigial sideband suppressed carrier AM signal, but it generally has a lower tolerance to additive noise as well as to attenuation and delay distortions.

One rather unfortunate effect in vestigial-sideband signals is the presence of appreciable signal distortion, resulting from the asymmetry between the two sidebands. The distortion appears as an additional sine wave at the carrier frequency but at $90°$ (in phase quadrature) with the main signal carrier. It is known as a quadrature component. The effect of this distortion can be eliminated by using coherent detection at the receiver, since the coherent detector does not respond to the quadrature component. However, the coherent detector introduces a low tolerance to the rapid phase variations introduced over telephone circuits. The tolerance of the AM system to frequency modulation effects is now similar to that of a PM system using coherent detection, and since the latter system could also, when suitably designed, be used with a vestigial-sideband signal and with the effective elimination of the quadrature component in the detector, it would of course in general be a much better alternative. Another approach which has been used is to reduce the depth of modulation in the vestigial sideband AM signal to somewhat below 100%, which considerably reduces the level of the quadrature component and enables satisfactory detection to be obtained. The reduction in tolerance to additive white Gaussian noise of such an arrangement, resulting from the signal distortion and the means used to reduce it, is, however, typically about 5 or 6 dB. Such a system has therefore a very low tolerance to both the additive noise and the amplitude modulation effects over voice-frequency channels.

Again, in a double-sideband signal, by virtue of the fact that each sideband carries the same information and since the detected signal in the receiver is derived equally from each sideband, any distortion in one sideband will have appreciably less effect on the receiver detected waveform than if only that one sideband were used to transmit the same information. Thus where the required transmission rate can be achieved satisfactorily using double-sideband transmission, this should always be done.

In Figure 8.5, the element rate of the AM signal is $1/T$ bauds. The essential information in each sideband is contained in a frequency band with one boundary at the carrier frequency and having a width of $1/2T$ Hz. Thus the bandwidth containing the essential information in a double-sideband signal is $1/T$ Hz, which is equal to the element rate in bauds. Clearly, the maximum element rate for a double sideband AM system is one baud/Hz of the frequency band. In the case of a vestigial sideband AM system, the maximum element rate approaches 2 bauds/Hz of the frequency band. Practical systems are normally used at appreciably lower element rates.

Practical AM systems of course do not often use a rectangular modulating waveform, but more generally one with a rounded shape, thus restricting the frequency band occupied by this waveform as illustrated in Figure 8.4. The envelope of each signal-element now has a rounded shape and each signal-element overlaps somewhat into the space allocated to the adjacent element on either side[94-102].

8.4 PM signals

Since a binary PM signal is also a suppressed carrier AM signal, the frequency spectrum of a binary PM signal is the same as that of the corresponding AM signal, except that the discrete carrier frequency component is now omitted. The PM signal therefore requires the same bandwidth as the AM signal.

The PM signal can be transmitted either as a double-sideband or as a vestigial-sideband signal. Where vestigial-sideband transmission is used with a binary PM signal, and where the receiver employs differentially coherent detection in place of coherent detection, there may be an unacceptable increase in signal distortion caused by the presence of the quadrature component. This is because coherent detection tends to eliminate the quadrature component in the received vestigial-sideband signal, whereas differentially coherent detection is adversely affected by it.

This advantage of coherent detection is, however, largely offset by the fact that a coherent detector can in general only extract the necessary information from the received signal in order to reconstitute the reference carrier needed for detection, from *both* the upper and lower sidebands, there being of course no discrete carrier frequency component in the received signal. The reference carrier is in fact derived from all *pairs* of frequency components of the received signal that are equally spaced in frequency above and below the carrier frequency[244-266]. Since the vestigial-sideband filter removes the frequency components, corresponding to the higher modulating frequencies, from one of the two sidebands, the reference carrier can only be derived from the lower modulating frequencies. Signal patterns containing only the higher modulating frequencies, such as successive phase reversals, cannot therefore be used for regenerating the reference carrier. Thus a restriction must be placed on the transmitted sequence of element values, in order to limit the periods during which only the higher modulating frequencies are received, and this is a severe limitation to the use of coherent detection with vestigial sideband PM signals.

The need for restricting the transmitted sequence of element values, with vestigial-sideband transmission, can be avoided by adding to the transmitted signal a sine wave at the carrier frequency and suitably phased relative to the signal carrier, whereby the receiver is enabled under all conditions to obtain the reference carrier needed for coherent detection. However, such an arrangement is inevitably more complex, due to the requirement for preventing interference between the transmitted signal and the additional carrier, and it has a lower tolerance to noise. The receiver here is also normally sensitive to sudden signal level changes, thus adding a further and more serious weakness to this method of coherent detection[244-266,285-296]

The maximum element rate for a PM signal is the same as that for an AM signal, in the case of either a double-sideband or vestigial-sideband signal. Thus the ideal maximum element rate for a double-sideband PM system is one baud/Hz of the frequency band, and the ideal maximum element rate for a vestigial-sideband PM system approaches 2 bauds/Hz. Practical systems are normally used at appreciably lower rates.

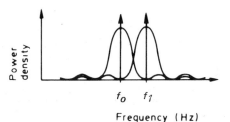

Fig. 8.6   *Spectrum of FM signal*

8.5   FM signals

A binary FM signal, which has a rectangular modulating waveform and one of whose two binary elements has a whole number of carrier cycles more than the other, is the sum of two complementary AM signals as illustrated in Figure 5.3. One of these AM signals has a carrier frequency f_0 Hz and the other a carrier frequency f_1 Hz, where f_0 and f_1 are the two values of the instantaneous frequency of the FM signal, and

$$f_1 = f_0 + n/T$$

where n is a positive integer and T is the element duration. The frequency spectrum of the FM signal is therefore formed by the addition of the spectra of two complementary AM signals. This is shown diagrammatically in Figure 8.6 for the case where $n = 1$. The two spectra do not necessarily add either linearly or on a power basis, since the power density of the FM signal at any frequency is a function of the phase angle between the corresponding frequency components of the two AM signals, and this phase angle may in principle have any value. In practice, when $f_1 - f_0 \leqslant 1/T$, the frequency components of the two AM signals tend to reinforce each other over the central frequency-band of $1/T$ Hz, and to oppose each other (to cancel) outside this frequency band[476].

To obtain the optimum tolerance to additive white Gaussian noise with a binary FM system, assuming a reasonable signal bandwidth and the use of *incoherent* detection at the receiver, it is necessary that

$$f_1 = f_0 + 1/T$$

so that the frequency separation of the two carrier frequencies (measured in Hz) has the same value as the signal-element rate (measured in bauds). Under these conditions, the frequency corresponding to the first zero power point below f_1 Hz for the higher frequency spectrum is equal to f_0 Hz, and the frequency corresponding to the first zero power point above f_0 Hz for the lower frequency spectrum is equal to f_1 Hz. That is, the first inside zero of each spectrum coincides with the carrier frequency of the other, as shown in Figure 8.6.

As is shown in Figure 7.11, the tolerance to additive white Gaussian noise of an ideal coherent detector for a binary FM signal is optimum when the frequency shift in the signal is $0.715/T$ Hz, the tolerance to noise being now 2.15 dB below that of the corresponding PM system with coherent detection. Since the performance of a noncoherent detector employing a discriminator can be made to approach very closely to that of a coherent detector, a frequency shift of $0.715/T$ Hz is, for practical purposes, also optimum for a discriminator detector. Practical FM modems operating at 600 and 1200 bit/s use a frequency shift of $2/3T$ Hz, and the power-density spectrum of such a signal is nearly rectangular, with an effective bandwidth of $1.2/T$ Hz symmetrically placed with respect to the two carrier frequencies and containing about 98% of the signal power. This is much narrower than the bandwidth of the FM signal with a frequency shift of $1/T$ Hz (Figure 8.6), and is also narrower than the bandwidth of a binary AM or PM signal with the same element rate (Figure 8.5)[271-274]. When a good noncoherent detector is used, the frequency shift of $2/3T$ Hz probably achieves the best compromise between tolerance to noise and bandwidth. Any reduction in frequency shift of the FM signal below $2/3T$ Hz produces a significant reduction in tolerance to noise, regardless of whether a coherent, noncoherent or incoherent detector is used, and without a compensating reduction in bandwidth. The maximum practical element rate of a binary FM signal, with a frequency shift of $2/3T$ Hz, is about one baud per Hz of the frequency band, although a much lower rate would normally be used over the telephone network. Unfortunately, the fact that the FM signal has a narrower bandwidth than the corresponding AM or PM signal does not mean that it can be transmitted at a higher rate over the poorer telephone circuits. Indeed, for the reasons to be considered in Section 8.6, a higher transmission rate is in fact likely to be achieved over the poorer telephone circuits with a binary AM or PM signal.

To obtain the best performance from an FM system, the two carrier frequencies should be derived from a single frequency-shift oscillator and not from two independent oscillators. The reason for this is that where the two frequencies are derived from one oscillator, there are no phase discontinuities between adjacent elements, thus narrowing the transmitted signal spectrum and reducing certain distortion effects which otherwise result in transmission[117].

A modulating waveform having a somewhat rounded shape may, if required, be used instead of one with a rectangular shape as shown. The FM signal is *never* now the sum of two complementary AM signals, since the instantaneous carrier frequency is no longer constant over any signal element.

8.6 Comparison of FM and PM systems

An important difference between FM and PM systems lies in the effect on these systems of the input band-pass filter and the post-demodulation low-pass filter of the receiver. In the case of the FM system, the tolerance to additive white Gaussian noise is determined primarily by the bandwidth of the receiver input band-pass filter and only relatively slightly by the post-demodulation low-pass filter, assuming the normal situation where the bandwidth of the input filter (in Hz) is less than twice the signal element rate ($1/T$ bauds). In the case of a PM system with incoherent (differentially coherent) detection, much more of the signal filtering can be carried out in the post-demodulation filter, although a certain amount of filtering of the input signal is still required. In the case of a PM system with coherent detection, optimum tolerance to noise can be achieved with most of the signal filtering carried out in the post-demodulation low-pass filter. Since, for a given degree of filtering, less equipment complexity is generally involved in a low-pass filter than in a band-pass filter, an optimized PM system usually requires less complex filters than an optimized FM system. Furthermore, partly for the reasons mentioned in Sections 9.2 and 9.3, rather more signal processing may be required in an FM system than in the corresponding PM system. Thus an FM modem that achieves its optimum performance tends to be more complex than a PM modem, whether the latter uses coherent or differentially-coherent detection. For this reason, FM modems used in practice are often suboptimum, such that they do not achieve their best available tolerance to noise.

A further weakness of FM systems is the fact that when the attenuation introduced by the telephone circuit increases steadily with frequency, as is often the case, this usually degrades the tolerance to additive noise of the FM system more seriously than that of the corresponding PM system. The effect can be explained by considering the idealised attenuation characteristic of a typical

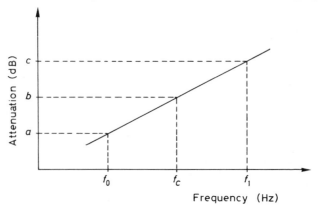

Fig. 8.7   Idealised attenuation characteristic of a typical telephone circuit

telephone circuit, over the frequency band of the data signal, as shown in Figure 8.7. f_0 and f_1 Hz are the two carrier frequencies of the binary FM signal, and f_c Hz is the carrier frequency of the binary PM signal having the same element rate. When the attenuation does not increase too rapidly with frequency, the tolerance of the FM system to additive white Gaussian noise (when the error rate in the detected element-values is around 1 in 10^5) is close to that where a constant attenuation of c dB is applied over the whole signal frequency-band, in fact reducing the tolerance to noise of the FM system by nearly c dB. This is because practically all errors in the detected element-values of the received FM signal now occur when the carrier frequency f_1 Hz is received and the signal is attenuated by c dB. This condition holds for half the time, so that the average error rate is about half that of an FM signal in which both carrier frequencies are attenuated by c dB. At an error rate of 1 in 10^5, halving the error rate corresponds to an increase in signal/noise ratio of only 0.3 dB, which is not very significant here. The tolerance to noise of the PM system is, however, reduced by only about b dB (to a first approximation), giving the PM system a further advantage of nearly $c - b$ dB in tolerance to noise over the FM system.

Suppose now that the attenuation in Figure 8.7 increases rapidly with frequency and that the FM signal has a frequency shift of $2/3T$ Hz and an element rate of $1/T$ bauds, giving it a near-rectangular spectrum with a bandwidth of about $1.2/T$ Hz at the output of the transmitter. The signal elements are here assumed to be statistically independent and equally likely to have either binary value. The resulting power-density spectrum of the FM signal at the

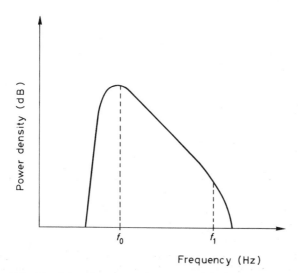

Fig. 8.8   *Power-density spectrum of FM signal at receiver input*

input to the receiver is now approximately as shown in Figure 8.8.

During the receipt of a stream of successive signal-elements with a carrier frequency f_0 Hz, the FM signal is received at a very much higher level than during the receipt of a stream of successive signal-elements with a carrier frequency f_1 Hz. Furthermore, the effective bandlimiting of the FM signal about the frequency f_0 Hz prevents a rapid change in the envelope or carrier frequency of the received signal, when a carrier frequency f_1 Hz is transmitted, immediately following two or three signal-elements all with the carrier frequency f_0 Hz. Because of the relatively low level of the received signal-element with carrier frequency f_1 Hz, the latter signal-element, if followed by another with frequency f_0 Hz, is effectively swamped by the slowly varying edges of its two neighbours, thus preventing its correct detection. An alternative analysis of this effect has been given by B. M. Smith[153].

Since a binary PM signal uses the same carrier frequency for each of the two binary signal-elements, it does not suffer from the effect just described and is in fact much more tolerant than the corresponding FM signal to a steady and rapid increase in attenuation over the signal frequency band. Thus, for a given tolerance to noise, a significantly higher transmission rate can be achieved over such a telephone circuit by means of a PM system than by means of an FM system, even though the FM signal (with a frequency shift of $2/3T$ Hz) occupies a narrower frequency band than does the corresponding PM signal.

9

Binary data-transmission systems for use over telephone circuits

9.1 Comparison of systems

Having considered now the most important parameters and properties of data-transmission systems, and having selected the four systems that are listed at the end of Chapter 7 as being worthy of further study, we are now in a position to select the particular data-transmission system that is most suitable for use over the switched telephone network, at a transmission rate of 600 or 1200 bit/s. We have already seen that this should be a synchronous serial binary system with a double-sideband signal, so that it remains for us to select the most suitable combination of modulation method and detection process. A considerable amount of work has been carried out over the past 30 years in comparing the different modulation methods and detection processes[297–351]. In the selection process it is assumed that the different modulation methods and detection processes, where listed in the order of their tolerances to the additive noise over telephone circuits, remain in the same order when compared on the basis of their tolerances to additive white Gaussian noise. This assumption is well supported by the available theoretical and experimental evidence[297–367]. Bearing in mind that additive white Gaussian noise is the most 'random' or 'unpredictable' of all random processes and is therefore an ideal form of noise, the result is not altogether surprising.

Because of the wide range of attenuations over different telephone circuits, an AM system must use an AGC amplifier at the input of the receiver. Unfortunately, the gain of the AGC amplifier is affected, at least to some degree, both by the transmitted sequence of element values and by the noise level. The gain of the AGC amplifier therefore often differs somewhat from its correct value, resulting in a reduced tolerance of the AM system to noise, since the correct threshold level is not now used in the detection of an element value. Amplifier limiters are not affected in this way and are furthermore less complex than AGC amplifiers. Thus, because FM and PM systems can use amplifier limiters, they gain an advantage over AM systems.

Since FM and PM systems use a continuous transmitted signal, the presence or absence of this signal at any time may with these systems be used to carry an additional piece of information, namely as to whether or not a fault condition causing loss of signal develops in the transmission path or at the transmitter, during the transmission of a message. Transient interruptions on the line exceeding about 10 ms may also conveniently be detected in this way. In AM systems, however, the absence of the signal carrier is one of the two binary elements transmitted. Thus the absence of the signal at the receiver input can here only be taken to imply a true loss of signal, if its duration exceeds the maximum obtainable with the code used for the transmitted signal, and this may often correspond to many signal elements.

The binary FM signal achieving the best compromise between the bandwidth required for satisfactory transmission and the tolerance to additive Gaussian noise, uses a frequency shift of $2/3T$ Hz, where T seconds is the element duration. This is close to the frequency shift of $0.715/T$ Hz for the binary FSK signal giving the best tolerance to additive white Gaussian noise with an ideal coherent detector. When a reasonably well designed noncoherent detector is used, the tolerance to additive white Gaussian noise of the FM system lies in the range 2.5 to 3.5 dB below that of the corresponding binary PM system using coherent detection.

The tolerance of an FM system to both amplitude and frequency modulation effects is much the same as that of the corresponding PM system using incoherent detection. The FM system does, however, have a better tolerance than an AM or PM system to attenuation and delay distortions which are symmetrical about the centre of the signal frequency band. Indeed, if these were the dominant types of distortion, an FM system would be capable of achieving a higher transmission rate over telephone circuits than an AM or PM system. The real weakness of the FM system, that is largely responsible for the lower value of the maximum transmission rate of an FM signal over telephone circuits, is its much lower tolerance to a steadily increasing attenuation over the signal frequency band, which is often experienced over these circuits. The reason for this is explained in Section 8.6.

Three of the four selected data-transmission systems each have a serious weakness, as follows. The FM system has a lower value of the maximum transmission rate than do the AM and PM systems, which means that its performance at 1200 bit/s over the poorer telephone circuits is likely to be significantly inferior to that obtainable with the better of the other systems. The AM system has a much lower tolerance to sudden level changes than the other systems, and the PM system with coherent detection has a much lower tolerance to sudden phase changes.

A comparison of the four systems is given in Table 9.1[328]. Each system here is a synchronous serial binary system, using a double-sideband signal and operating at 600 or 1200 bit/s over the telephone network. The smaller the number against a system in any column of the table, the better the rating of the system for the particular property considered. The term 'maximum transmission rate' in Table 9.1 is taken to be the maximum signal-element rate (which is, of course, not here fixed at 600 or 1200 bauds) for correct operation in the absence of noise over a typical poor telephone circuit whose attenuation and delay characteristics are as in Figures 2.4 and 2.6. The same ratings as those given in Table 9.1 for the maximum transmission rate also apply to the fraction of the total number of different telephone circuits in the public switched telephone network of the U.K. for which satisfactory operation is likely to be achieved at 1200 bit/s. The maximum transmission rate is clearly one of the more important measures of the suitability of any system. Tolerance to symmetric attenuation and delay distortions is considerably less important than tolerance to asymmetric attenuation and delay distortions, and a frequency offset in the received signal carrier does not normally have a significant effect on the performance of any of the systems. It appears therefore that the most cost-effective system for use over telephone circuits is the PM system with incoherent detection.

9.2 Complete synchronous serial systems

In a synchronous serial PM system in which the carrier is synchronized to the modulating waveform at the transmitter, the signal carrier and a timing waveform synchronized to this carrier are usually both generated from the same oscillator in the transmitter of the modem. The timing waveform is fed from the transmitter to the associated equipment, where it is used to synchronize the rectangular data signal which is fed from this equipment to the transmitter.

In a synchronous serial PM system in which the carrier is not synchronized to the modulating waveform in the transmitter, or in a

Table 9.1 COMPARISON OF THE FOUR DATA-TRANSMISSION SYSTEMS

	Complexity	Maximum transmission rate	Tolerance to symmetric attenuation and delay distortions	Tolerance to asymmetric attenuation and delay distortions	Tolerance to additive noise	Tolerance to sudden level changes	Tolerance to sudden phase changes	Tolerance to small frequency offset
AM (incoherent detection)	1	2	2	2	4	2	1	1
FM (noncoherent detection)	3	3	1	3	3	1	2	3
PM (incoherent detection)	2	2	3	2	2	1	2	3
PM (coherent detection)	4	1	2	1	1	1	3	2

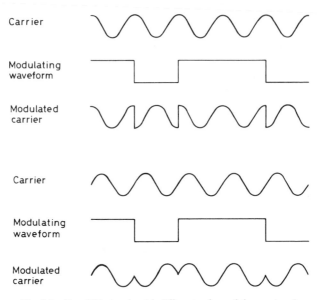

Fig. 9.1   *Two PM signals with different values of the carrier phase*

synchronous serial FM system, the signal carrier is generated by an oscillator in the transmitter, and the rectangular data signal which is fed to the transmitter from the associated equipment, is synchronized to a separate frequency source, located either in the transmitter or in the associated equipment. Two separate oscillators are required here at the transmitting terminal, compared with only the one oscillator in the previous arrangement.

In either arrangement, an element timing signal is generated at the transmitting terminal and used to synchronize the rectangular data signal which is fed to the transmitter.

In order that the highest transmission rate over a given bandwidth may be obtained with a practical PM system, while still maintaining the most economic arrangement for the transmitter, effective use must be made of one or two simple properties of the waveforms involved. In a PM system, the modulating waveform used at the transmitter would normally be either a rectangular or rounded waveform as shown in Figure 8.3, bearing in mind that *suppressed carrier amplitude modulation* is in fact assumed here.

Consider first a PM system where a rectangular modulating waveform is used and where the signal carrier is synchronized to the modulating waveform. Two examples of this are shown in Figure 9.1, with different values of the carrier phase. When the transition from one signal element to the next always occurs at a peak of the signal carrier, the larger part of the power at the modulator output is located at frequencies above the carrier frequency; when the transition from one signal element to the next always occurs at a zero level crossing of the signal carrier, the larger part of the power is located at frequencies below the carrier frequency. When the transition from one signal element to the next occurs midway between these two points, the frequency spectrum is symmetrical about the carrier. This relationship between the phase of the carrier and the frequency spectrum of the signal thus provides a means of achieving an appreciable filtering action without introducing at the same time any distortion into the modulated signal. The filtering effect becomes more important as the element rate of the modulating waveform increases relative to the carrier frequency and for those frequencies further removed from the carrier. It is particularly noticeable when there are not more than two cycles of the carrier per signal element. It occurs whenever the highest frequency component of the modulating waveform exceeds the carrier frequency.

The fact that the phase of the signal carrier relative to the element boundaries may subsequently be changed in transmission, does not in any way affect the filtering action which has *already* been carried out at the transmitter by synchronizing the carrier to the modulating waveform at the selected phase angle. Nor does the subsequent change in carrier phase itself necessarily change the power-density spectrum of the transmitted signal.

When a rectangular modulating waveform is used and there is no phase coherence between the signal carrier and the modulating waveform at the transmitter, each signal element, depending on the particular phase relationship between the carrier and modulating waveform, contributes more energy to the higher or to the lower frequencies. The transmitted frequency spectrum is now wider and correspondingly more filtering is therefore required at the modulator output to limit the transmitted frequency spectrum to the required frequency band. Because more filtering is required, more delay distortion is introduced into the frequency band, unless yet additional delay equalization is used or unless more complex filters having a linear phase characteristic are used.

For this reason, where a rectangular modulating waveform is used, the signal carrier should always where possible by synchronized (phase locked) to the modulating waveform and frequency related to it in such a way that each signal element contains an exact multiple of one half cycle of the carrier with at least one complete cycle. This is of course also a necessary condition for achieving the optimum tolerance to additive Gaussian noise with differentially coherent detection as in Figure 7.9.

The alternative approach is to feed the rectangular baseband data signal through a low-pass filter, to give a rounded modulating waveform, similar to the baseband signal B in Figure 8.3 and with the corresponding spectrum in Figure 8.4. Provided that the low-pass filter effectively removes all the frequency components in the modulating waveform which are higher than the carrier frequency, a fixed, symmetrical and reasonably narrow frequency spectrum is obtained for any phase relationship between the signal carrier and modulating waveform. Thus with this arrangement, a carrier which is not synchronized to the modulating waveform can be used with no widening of the frequency spectrum and therefore no need for further filtering. The arrangement has, however, the disadvantage that a linear double-balanced modulator must be used in place of the simpler balanced gate circuit needed for the other arrangement. Also, in those applications where the carrier is in any case synchronized to the modulating waveform, all the shaping of the transmitted frequency spectrum must now be achieved in the normal manner using filters, and the system loses the versatility of the former arrangement, whereby a simple change in the phase relationship between the carrier and modulating waveform can be used to give an appreciable shift in the frequency location of the transmitted power.

Thus in applications where the carrier is synchronized to the modulating waveform, the former arrangement using a rectangular modulating waveform is the best, whereas in applications where the carrier is not synchronized to the modulating waveform, the latter arrangement using a suitably rounded modulating waveform is to be preferred.

Another important reason for synchronizing the signal carrier to the modulating waveform is that only a single oscillator is now required at the transmitter, thus further reducing the equipment complexity. In the case of an FM system, two separate oscillators are normally always required, one for generating the signal carrier and the other for timing the data signal, whatever technique is used for shaping the transmitted signal. In view of the various useful simplifications which may be achieved at the transmitter of a PM system, when the carrier is synchronized to the modulating waveform, the PM transmitter can be made significantly less complex than the corresponding FM transmitter. Clearly, in a PM system, the signal carrier should whenever possible by synchronized to the modulating waveform.

In any arrangement, the receiver is required to provide at its output, a rectangular data signal and the associated element-timing waveform, without which the information in the data signal cannot be correctly interpreted. The data signal should, of course, be the same as that fed to the transmitter at the other end of the line.

Any transmitter or receiver (of a modem) which does not generate an element timing waveform, is necessarily incomplete, and the required timing signal must always in that case be generated in the associated equipment.

9.3   Asynchronous systems

Where it is required to transmit binary coded data at any one of a number of different rates, using as much common transmission equipment as possible for the different rates, the optimum synchronous serial PM system with differentially coherent detection (Figure 7.9) cannot be used.

The most suitable arrangement here is an FM system in which the element-timing waveform generators are omitted from both the transmitter and receiver, so that the modem performs no element timing. The rectangular data signal fed to the transmitter is here timed by a separate oscillator, which forms part of the data processing equipment associated with the transmitter and is not therefore in the modem itself. The modem accepts a rectangular data signal at the input to the transmitter, converts it to the corresponding FM signal, which at the receiver is converted back again into a rectangular data signal. The latter is ideally the same as the corresponding data signal fed to the transmitter at the other end of the line, but it usually has some distortion. The element timing waveform needed for detection is extracted from the receiver output signal and is then used to sample this signal. The operations of timing and detection are now carried out in the data processing equipment associated with the receiver and not in the modem itself.

The modem just described is sometimes referred to as an asynchronous system, containing as it does only that part of a complete data transmission system which is not involved with element timing. It is clearly not a complete system on its own.

Alternatively a PM system with coherent detection may be used, in which the ambiguity in the binary value associated with the phase of the received signal carrier is overcome by sending at the beginning of each transmission a continuous series of '0's or '1's or some other convenient code, whereby the receiver can determine the carrier phase associated with either a '0' or a '1'. The receiver can then remember by suitable means the phase of the signal carrier which corresponds to either a '0' or a '1' at any point during the rest of the transmission. Such an arrangement can be made to work satisfactorily so long as the phase variations in the signal carrier, introduced by the telephone circuit, are not rapid enough to be confused with transmitted phase changes between adjacent elements. Since such phase variations would in any case always result in errors, this requirement is not a serious limitation of the system. As in the case of the asynchronous FM system, the element-timing waveform generators, at both the transmitting and receiving terminals, are located in the data processing equipment associated with the modem and not in the modem itself. Clearly, no attempt is made at the transmitter to synchronize the signal carrier to the modulating waveform.

A disadvantage of the two asynchronous systems is that the total equipment complexity involved in the generation and detection of the data signals is in each case greater than that in the corresponding complete synchronous serial system. In addition, any asynchronous system must be designed for the highest of the range of element rates over which it will be used, and its tolerance to noise is, therefore, effectively limited to that of the highest rate. Thus, when the modem is used at any lower rate, there is a reduction in tolerance to noise relative to that which would be obtained with the corresponding system specifically designed for that rate. Finally, of course, neither of the two asynchronous systems contains the preferred combination of modulation method and detection process for use over telephone circuits, leading to a further degradation in performance relative to that of the optimum system.

The main use for asynchronous systems is in those applications where it is required to standardize the data-transmission equipment and where the peripheral equipment from which it is required to transmit data, can only work at a fixed rate which differs from one type of equipment to another. For these applications, an asynchronous system of either type outlined above could be used.

In practice, however, a large number of the types of peripheral equipment between which it is required to transmit data are of the type which enable the transmitter to dictate the element rate. With all these types of equipment it is possible and indeed highly desirable to standardize on a fixed rate data-transmission system, which is designed to give both the optimum tolerance to noise and distortion and the maximum element rate for the class of telephone circuits to be used.

9.4   Synchronous serial PM system

For data transmission over telephone circuits at 1200 bit/s, the most cost-effective system is a synchronous serial binary PM system

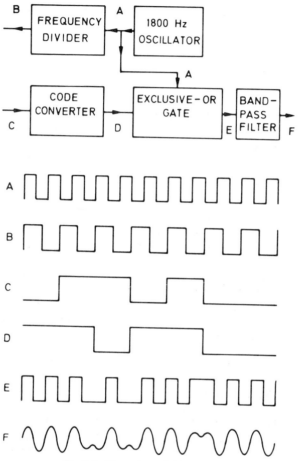

Fig. 9.2   Transmitter of PM system

using differentially coherent detection at the receiver.

The block diagram of the transmitter and the associated wave-forms of a very simple system are shown in Figure 9.2.

The 1800 Hz square wave A at the output of the 1800 Hz oscillator is used as the signal carrier and is also fed to the frequency divider which gives an output square wave of 1200 Hz. This is the element timing waveform B, whose positive-going transitions mark the element boundaries. The timing waveform is fed to the data processing equipment associated with the transmitter, to synchronize the data signal fed from this equipment to the transmitter. A negative level, over an element period of 1/1200 s in the input data signal C, carries the element value 1, and a positive level carries the element value 0. The code converter changes a positive level in the waveform C into a change in level at the end of the corresponding element period in the waveform D, and it changes a negative level into no change in level. When the waveform D at the input to the exclusive-OR gate is negative, the square-wave carrier A is inverted by the exclusive-OR gate, whereas, when the waveform D is positive, the square-wave carrier is passed through unchanged. In the output signal E from the exclusive-OR gate, the binary value 0 is represented by a 180° phase shift at the boundary between two adjacent signal-elements, and the binary value 1 by no change. Notice, however, that two adjacent signal-elements in the waveform E, with a 180° phase change in the carrier at the boundary separating them, have the same waveform, whereas two adjacent elements with no phase change are the negatives of each other. The band-pass filter bandlimits the input rectangular waveform to restrict its spectrum to the available bandwidth of the telephone circuit.

The block diagram of the receiver and the associated waveforms are shown in Figure 9.3.

The band-pass filter removes the noise frequencies outside the signal frequency band to give the filtered signal waveform A. This is, for convenience, assumed to be the same as the transmitted waveform, although in practice it would normally contain both noise and distortion. The amplifier limiter slices the signal waveform A at a level exactly half-way between the positive and negative peaks and amplifies the resultant narrow section of the signal to give the output rectangular waveform B.

The shift register contains 512 bistable circuits connected in cascade and is triggered at 614,400 pulses per second by the output square-wave from the 614,400 Hz oscillator. This is a free running stable oscillator, which is not synchronized in any way to the received signal. At each triggering pulse (positive-going edge of the 614,400 Hz square-wave) the binary signal stored in each of the 512 bistable circuits of the shift register is transferred to the immediately following bistable circuit and a sample value of the signal at the input to the shift register appears at the output after 1/1200 s, which is the duration of one signal-element. The shift register clearly introduces a delay equal to the duration of one signal element, and the waveform B at the output of the amplifier limiter is sampled at a sufficiently rapid rate so that no significant detail in the waveform B is lost in the waveform C.

The original and delayed signal waveforms B and C, from the amplifier limiter, are fed to the exclusive-OR gate. Whenever the

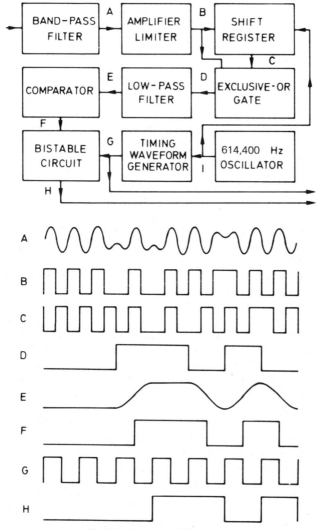

Fig. 9.3 Receiver of PM system

two input signals are different, the output signal D from the exclusive-OR gate is negative, and whenever the two input signals are the same, the output signal D is positive. Although the wave-form D is ideally as shown in Figure 9.2, it often has a number of fine irregularities due to the effects of signal distortion.

The low-pass filter has a linear phase characteristic and removes the fine irregularities in the input signal to give the rounded output waveform E. The output signal from the low-pass filter at any instant is equal to the integral of the input signal over the preceding period of about 1/1200 s (the element duration), assuming that the different portions of this input signal have first been suitably weighted, giving more weight to those parts of the input signal in the middle of the integration period and less weight to those at the beginning and the end.

The comparator compares the waveform E with a fixed threshold level, which is exactly half way between the positive and negative peaks of the waveform E. Whenever the waveform E lies above the threshold level, the comparator gives a positive output signal, and whenever the waveform E lies below the threshold, the comparator gives a negative output signal. The threshold used in the comparator determines the level (value) below which the waveform E represents the binary value 1 and above which it represents the binary value 0.

The 614,400 Hz square-wave signal I is fed to a frequency divider, in the timing waveform generator, and this divides the input frequency by 512 to give an output square-wave of 1200 Hz, which is the element timing waveform G. The following arrangement can be used to hold the element timing waveform correctly synchronized to the received signal. Whenever a positive or negative going transition occurs in the waveform F, the time of occurrence is compared with that of the nearest negative-going transition of the element timing waveform G. If the transition in the square-wave G leads that in the waveform F, then, during the next element period, one of the 512 cycles of the square-wave I is blocked from the input to the frequency divider to delay the waveform G by 1/512 of an element period. On the other hand, whenever the transition in the square-wave G lags that in the waveform F, an additional pulse is fed to the frequency divider to advance the waveform G by 1/512 of an element period. Thus the phase of the element timing waveform G is gradually adjusted to have the required value, such that each signal element in the waveform F is sampled at its mid point by the positive-going edge of the element timing waveform. In practice, more sophisticated arrangements of phase control are sometimes used[46-86]. The integrating or averaging action achieved by introducing only a small phase change in G, at each comparison with F, reduces the jitter introduced into the timing waveform by noise in the received signal, and means that the phase adopted by the timing waveform G is the average value of that dictated by a large number of the immediately preceding transitions in the waveform F. Thus the phase-locked oscillator generating the timing waveform G has a high effective 'Q'.

At the input of the bistable circuit, the waveform F, which is the demodulated and sliced data signal, is sampled at the time instants when the waveform E is equal to the weighted average of the waveform D over the preceding element period. When the two signal elements whose phases are being compared are on average at a phase angle less than 90°, the waveform F is positive at the sampling instant and represents the binary value 0. When the two signal elements are on average at a phase angle greater than 90°, the waveform F is negative at the sampling instant and represents the binary value 1. The output signal H from the bistable circuit adopts the value of the input waveform F at each sampling instant, and holds this value until the next sampling instant. The rectangular waveform H therefore carries the detected binary values of the received PM signal. The system performance is a little suboptimum.

It can be seen that both the transmitter and receiver are almost entirely digital and use only binary signals. The processes of modulation and demodulation have both been reduced to very simple logical operations using standard gate-circuits. The corresponding synchronous serial FM system requires more complex equipment and has, in general, an inferior performance.

In a complete data-transmission system it is customary to use a return signalling channel at 75 or 150 bit/s over the frequency band from about 300 to 500 Hz. An important function of the return channel is to inform the transmitting terminal as to whether or not the transmitted signal is being correctly received at the other end of the telephone line. The modem also performs a number of additional operations, which include the detection of the presence or absence of the received signal carrier, in order to identify loss of signal during a transmission.

9.5 Asynchronous serial FM system

The data-transmission system recommended by CCITT for use over telephone circuits at transmission rates from 600 to 1200 bit/s is an asynchronous serial binary FM system. This is the portion of a serial binary FM system not involved with the generation of element timing signals, so that it is not a complete system.

The block diagram of the transmitter and the associated waveforms of a very simple system are shown in Figure 9.4.

The input binary data signal (waveform A) is generated and timed in the data processing equipment associated with the transmitter. Waveform A controls the frequency of the voltage controlled oscillator, whose output waveform is a frequency modulated rectangular carrier (waveform B). The carrier frequencies, corre-

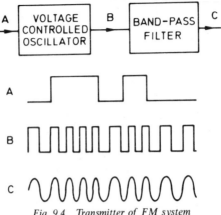

Fig. 9.4   Transmitter of FM system

sponding to the element values 0 and 1, are 2100 Hz and 1300 Hz respectively. The band-pass filter limits the spectrum of the transmitted signal (waveform C) to the available bandwidth of the telephone circuit.

The rectangular waveform A could alternatively be filtered in a low-pass filter, to give a suitably rounded waveform. This would prevent the highest frequency component of the modulating waveform from exceeding the carrier frequency, and so prevent the consequent broadening of the signal spectrum which occurs with the system described here. However, the frequency of the voltage controlled oscillator would now have to vary linearly with the input voltage, resulting in a more complex design of the oscillator. Furthermore, in the case of an FM signal with no phase discontinuities at the element boundaries, the reduction in bandwidth, when a rectangular modulating waveform is replaced by a suitably rounded waveform, is much less than that in the case of an AM or PM signal, and no useful simplification is achieved here in the transmitter band-pass filter, when there is a rounded modulating waveform. The tolerance to noise would, in general, also be reduced.

The block diagram of the receiver and the associated waveforms are shown in Figure 9.5. The receiver uses a zero-crossing detector.

The band-pass filter removes the noise frequencies outside the signal frequency band to give the filtered signal waveform A. The amplifier limiter slices and amplifies the waveform A to give the rectangular waveform B. The differentiator and rectifier generate a short positive-going pulse at each transition of the rectangular waveform B, to give the waveform C. Each positive-going pulse in the waveform C triggers the monostable circuit to give a rec-

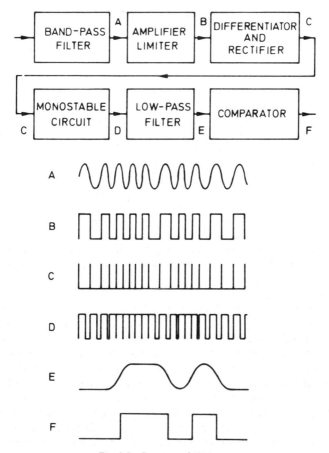

Fig. 9.5   Receiver of FM system

tangular positive pulse whose duration is somewhat less than that of one half cycle of the higher of the two carrier frequencies in B, to give the waveform D. The high-frequency components in this waveform are removed by the low-pass filter, to give the rounded waveform E. During a received signal-element with binary value 0, E moves towards or maintains a fixed positive value, whereas during a received signal-element with binary value 1, E moves towards or maintains a fixed negative value.

The differentiator and rectifier, monostable circuit and low-pass filter, together form an FM discriminator, whose output signal becomes steadily more negative as the instantaneous frequency of the input signal decreases from the higher of the two carrier frequencies used for the FM signal. The discriminator output signal E does not correctly track the input signal frequency, as in an ideal FM discriminator, but with a wider bandwidth input filter, the instantaneous frequency of the FM signal carrier, over the duration of any signal element, is either 1300 Hz or 2100 Hz, and changes rapidly at the boundary between adjacent elements with different binary values thus minimizing the resulting distortion.

The comparator compares the waveform E with a fixed threshold level. Whenever E exceeds this threshold, the comparator gives a positive output signal, and whenever E lies below the threshold, the comparator gives a negative output signal. The threshold used in the comparator determines the level below which E represents the binary value 1 and above which it represents the binary value 0. The output signal F carries the binary values of the received signal but it is not the detected binary signal.

The detection process is completed in the data processing equipment associated with the receiver. The element timing waveform is generated here from the waveform F and is used to sample this waveform, to give the detected data signal.

When the portions of the serial binary FM system, involved in the generation of the element timing waveform at both the transmitter and receiver, are considered together with the asynchronous part of the data-transmission system, just described, it can be seen that the complete FM system is significantly more complex than the corresponding PM system described in Section 9.4.

Whereas a PM system should give reliable operation at 1200 bit/s over the very large majority of private and switched telephone circuits, an FM system does not operate satisfactorily at this transmission rate over the poorest switched telephone circuits, without at least the partial equalization of these circuits[197]. The PM system should have a useful advantage in tolerance to additive white Gaussian noise over the FM system and it should operate significantly better over the poorer telephone circuits with frequency characteristics approaching those in Figures 2.4 and 2.6. The advantage of the asynchronous FM system lies in its flexibility. The modem can be used at any one of a number of different transmission rates, with no change in design or adjustment, so that the same modem may be used for transmitting data between quite different data-processing equipments.

10

Multilevel data-transmission systems for use over telephone circuits

10.1 Double-sideband systems

The simplest method of increasing the transmission (information) rate over a given bandwidth, that is of increasing the bandwidth efficiency, is to use multilevel signals in place of the binary signals assumed so far. This approach, however, is only effective with AM and PM signals. Multilevel AM and PM signals, together with various combinations of these that make an efficient use of band-width, have been widely studied[368-396]. With FM signals no increase in bandwidth efficiency can be achieved by the use of multilevel signal elements, although a greater tolerance to additive Gaussian noise, with no reduction in the bandwidth efficiency, can be achieved by the use of 4-level signals in place of binary signals (Chapter 16). Unfortunately, a 4-level FM system is appreciably more complex than a binary FM system. Any further increase in the number of levels of the FM signal is of no benefit, since it reduces the bandwidth efficiency and further increases the equipment complexity[320].

The 4-level signal achieving the best compromise between band-width efficiency and tolerance to additive Gaussian noise is a 4-level PM signal (Chapter 16). Whereas a double sideband binary PM system can achieve a transmission rate of between $\frac{1}{2}$ and 1 bit/s per Hz of the available bandwidth, a double sideband 4-level PM system can achieve a transmission rate of between 1 and 2 bit/s per Hz. If differentially coherent detection is used for the 4-level PM signal, in place of coherent detection, the tolerance of the system to additive white Gaussian noise at high signal/noise ratios, is reduced by 2.3 dB. For an 8-level PM signal the reduction is approximately

3 dB[320]. Thus for multilevel PM signals, the reduction in tolerance to additive Gaussian noise resulting from the use of incoherent detection in place of coherent detection can no longer be neglected. Since coherent detection furthermore achieves a better tolerance to distortion than does incoherent detection and with 4-level signals this is a significantly more important advantage than it is with binary signals, it follows that coherent detection is now to be preferred to incoherent detection, inspite of its lower tolerance to sudden phase changes.

Where an even higher transmission rate is required than that obtainable with an 8-level PM signal, the arrangement achieving the best tolerance to additive Gaussian noise for a given bandwidth efficiency, uses two m-level double sideband suppressed carrier AM signals in phase quadrature, where $m > 2$. The two AM signals, known as the 'in-phase' and 'quadrature' signals, here have the same carrier frequency, the carriers being at a phase angle of 90°, and two coherent detectors with reference carriers in phase quadrature are used at the receiver. When the in-phase and quadrature signals each take on any of their m possible element-values independently of the other, to give a resulting m^2-level signal, this is referred to as a quadrature amplitude modulated (QAM) signal. The 4-level QAM signal, obtained when $m = 2$ is also a 4-level PM signal. It is, of course, not necessary for the in-phase and quadrature AM signals to be modulated independently (that is, by two independent baseband waveforms) as in a QAM signal, and, by using the appropriate relationship between the two modulating waveforms, a transmitted signal-element may be given any required set of possible combinations of level and carrier phase. Such a signal is referred to as an AM-PM signal.

Any QAM or AM-PM signal can be represented as

$$s(t) = a(t) \cos (2\pi f_c t + \phi) + b(t) \cos (2\pi f_c t + \pi/2 + \phi) \quad (10.1)$$

where $a(t)$ and $b(t)$ are the in-phase and quadrature baseband modulating waveforms, f_c Hz is the carrier frequency and ϕ radians is an arbitrary carrier phase shift. Consider now an individual signal-element of $s(t)$ extending from $t = 0$ to $t = T$ and such that $a(t)$ and $b(t)$ are constant at a and b, respectively, over this time interval, being zero elsewhere. Under these conditions and when $0 < t < T$,

$$s(t) = a \cos (2\pi f_c t + \phi) + b \cos (2\pi f_c t + \pi/2 + \phi) \quad (10.2)$$

which simplifies to

$$s(t) = c \cos (2\pi f_c t + \theta + \phi) \quad (10.3)$$

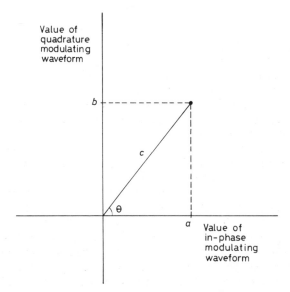

Fig. 10.1   *Representation of QAM or AM-PM signal element*

where

$$c = \sqrt{(a^2 + b^2)} \qquad (10.4)$$

and

$$\theta = \tan^{-1}\left(\frac{b}{a}\right) \qquad (10.5)$$

c being taken as the positive square root. This shows how, for the given values of f_c and ϕ, any required level c and carrier phase θ can be generated by the appropriate choice of a and b. The signal waveform $s(t)$ in Equations 10.2 and 10.3 can conveniently be represented by the diagram in Figure 10.1, the signal being completely defined by a and b or else by c and θ, for the given values of f_c and ϕ.

Using the representation of the signal-element waveform given by Figure 10.1, the possible signal-element waveforms for a typical 16-level QAM signal are as in Figure 10.2(a), whereas the possible signal-element waveforms in a commonly used AM-PM signal are as in Figure 10.2(b). The QAM signal is much the simplest of the two, the parameters a and b here taking on independently any one of four given values $-3k$, $-k$, k and $3k$, where k is a positive constant. The AM-PM signal is, however, the one of the two that is currently used in practice, for applications of data transmission at 9600 bit/s over telephone circuits, since it gives a better tolerance

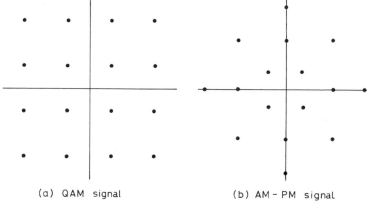

(a) QAM signal   (b) AM – PM signal

Fig. 10.2   Two sets of combinations of possible values of a and b

than the other to phase jitter (random variations in ϕ). However, in the absence of phase jitter, it gives a poorer tolerance to additive white Gaussian noise.

The preferred system (selected from the various techniques studied so far) for a transmission rate of 2400 bit/s over private telephone circuits, is a synchronous serial differentially coded 4-level PM system using coherent detection at the receiver[213,236]. Satisfactory operation is, however, unlikely to be obtained with this system over some of the poorer switched telephone circuits, for which more sophisticated techniques are required at this transmission rate.

10.2   Vestigial-sideband systems

As has been mentioned in Chapter 8, a useful improvement in the transmission rate of binary AM and PM systems can be achieved by replacing a double-sideband signal by the corresponding vestigial-sideband signal[285-296]. The latter achieves the most efficient use of bandwidth for a given modulating waveform (baseband data signal). However, the resulting vestigial-sideband system is appreciably more complex than the original double-sideband system (with a single modulated-carrier signal), partly because precise filtering is now required for the transmitted signal and partly because coherent detection must be used at the receiver, together with special (and sometimes complex) arrangements for extracting from the received signal the reference carrier needed here. Vestigial-sideband signals are not therefore normally used where the required transmission rate can be achieved with a binary double-sideband signal.

Most vestigial-sideband systems use a suppressed carrier AM signal with a low-level pilot carrier inserted into the transmitted signal[285-296]. The pilot carrier enables the reference carrier needed for coherent detection to be extracted at the receiver, regardless of the transmitted sequence of element values.

A vestigial-sideband suppressed carrier AM system, with an m-level signal, achieves nearly the same transmission rate over a given channel as does the corresponding QAM system, with two m-level double sideband suppressed carrier AM signals in phase quadrature and coherent detection at the receiver. The signal element rate in the QAM system is, of course, half that in a vestigial sideband system having the same transmission rate. Although the vestigial-sideband system, in practice, tends to have a lower tolerance to attenuation and delay distortions, than does the double-sideband system, it is less complex since it only transmits the one signal.

10.3 Adaptive systems

Extensive studies have recently been carried out on modems operating at speeds of 4800 and 9600 bit/s over the public switched telephone network[496-510]. A technique that has been employed for the transmission of data at 4800 bit/s over telephone circuits involves the use of an 8-level vestigial sideband suppressed carrier AM signal in a synchronous serial system, with coherent detection and adaptive linear equalization at the receiver. The adaptive equalizer usually operates on the sampled demodulated baseband signal in the receiver and is implemented as a linear feedforward transversal filter whose tap gains are adjusted to make the equalizer appear as the inverse of the channel (which here includes the linear modulator at the transmitter and the linear demodulator at the receiver), so that the channel and equalizer in cascade introduce no significant signal distortion. The equalizer is shown in Figure 10.3. The signals (sample values) at the different points in the transversal filter here are those present at the time instant $t = iT$, each signal being normally held in the form of a binary-coded number with typically 8 to 24 bits. Each square marked T in Figure 10.3 is a storage element that holds the corresponding signal r_{i-h}. The storage elements are triggered at the time instants $\{iT\}$, for all positive integers $\{i\}$, and each time the transversal filter is triggered, the signals $\{r_{i-h}\}$ are shifted one place to the right. Thus the extreme left-hand signal (at the input to the equalizer) is that received

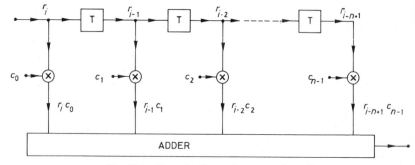

Fig. 10.3   *Linear feedforward transversal equalizer*

at time $t = iT$, the next signal is that received at time $t = (i - 1)T$, and so on, each storage element introducing a delay of T seconds. As before the signal element rate is $1/T$ bauds, so that the de-modulated baseband signal in the receiver (which is here a rounded waveform at the output of a low-pass filter) is sampled once per signal element to give the signals $\{r_i\}$. The output signals from the multipliers, $\{r_{i-h}c_h\}$, are added together to give the equalizer output signal

$$x_i = \sum_{h=0}^{n-1} r_{i-h}c_h \qquad (10.6)$$

at time $t = iT$. A practical linear feedforward transversal equalizer has between 8 and 64 taps and only a single multiplier is normally used, this being shared between the n taps of the equalizer. Under the appropriate conditions the tap gains $\{c_{i-h}\}$ can be adjusted adaptively such that the equalizer removes (or at least greatly reduces) the signal distortion introduced by the voice-frequency channel. Thus, whereas r_i is a linear function of the element values (data symbols) of several different signal elements, so that no one of these can be detected satisfactorily from r_i, x_i is, for practical purposes, a function of only one received element-value, which can therefore be detected by comparing x_i with the appropriate decision thresholds. Further details on the theory and method of adjustment of the linear equalizer are given elsewhere[422]. If the attenuation and delay of characteristics of the channel vary slowly with time, the setting of the equalizer can be adjusted automatically to maintain the correct equalization of the channel. No special training signal (with known element values) need be transmitted (except at the start of a transmission) to enable the equalizer to be correctly adjusted, but the data signal must be scrambled so that it is reasonably random in nature, without repeated sequences.

Although the characteristics of a given telephone circuit do not vary much with time, each new telephone circuit, obtained by dialling a connection between two given subscribers, usually has different attenuation and delay characteristics to the previous circuit, so that the equalizer requires to be reset automatically at the start of each transmission. Furthermore, at a high transmission rate, requiring the use of multilevel elements with say 8 levels, the channel must be equalized very accurately, and significant changes in the channel characteristics do now occur over the typical duration of a transmission.

The weakness of a linear equalizer stems from the fact that it attempts to equalize the gain of the resultant channel at effectively all frequencies over the signal frequency band. Thus, if the channel introduces severe attenuation over a band of frequencies anywhere within this band, the linear equalizer attempts to correct the attenuation distortion by introducing an appropriately high gain over the given band. This results in the corresponding increase in level of the noise frequency components over the band, with a consequent and possibly serious increase in the overall noise level at the equalizer output. A *nonlinear equalizer* does not tend to increase the noise level at its output but instead suffers from error-extension effects, which means that errors tend to occur in bursts. Nevertheless, in the presence of significant attenuation distortion, it gives an appreciably better tolerance to additive white Gaussian noise than the linear equalizer. A nonlinear equalizer (often referred to as a decision-feedback equalizer) comprises a linear feedforward transversal filter, as in Figure 10.3 but with quite different tap gains, feeding the arrangement shown in Figure 15.9, which is studied in Section 15.6. The sampler in Figure 15.9 is omitted here. The combination of the two filters can be made to achieve the accurate equalization of the channel but with no enhancement of the noise. Nonlinear transversal equalizers are studied in detail elsewhere[422].

A potentially more cost-effective technique, than that just described for the transmission of data at 4800 bit/s, is to use, in place of the vestigial sideband suppressed carrier AM signal, a double sideband 8-level PM signal, again with coherent detection and adaptive linear equalization at the receiver. As for the 2400 bit/s PM system mentioned in Section 10.1, differential coding of the PM signal is used at the transmitter, with the corresponding differential decoding of the detected signal at the receiver. In the absence of signal distortion the system gains an advantage of up to nearly 5 dB in tolerance to additive white Gaussian noise over the previous system and it has all the other advantages gained by a PM signal over an AM signal. Its disadvantage is that it uses an appreciably wider frequency band, so that over the poorer telephone circuits its performance is likely to be more seriously degraded than is that of the vestigial sideband AM system.

For a transmission rate of 2400 bit/s over switched telephone circuits a suitable arrangement is a synchronous serial differentially-coded 4-level PM system, with coherent detection and adaptive linear equalization at the receiver.

The preferred arrangement for a transmission rate of 9600 bit/s is a 16-level QAM signal (Figure 10.2) with an adaptive linear or nonlinear equalizer at the receiver, or better still, with a near-maximum-likelihood detection process. The latter, although more complex than an equalizer, can, with the poorest telephone circuits, gain an improvement of up to some 6 dB in tolerance to additive white Gaussian noise over the corresponding nonlinear equalizer[506,510], which, in turn, gives a significantly better tolerance to noise than the corresponding linear equalizer[422].

Modems operating at 14.4 kbit/s and 16 kbit/s have been built and shown to be capable of operating satisfactorily over the better telephone circuits. The highest transmission rate currently under consideration for use over telephone circuits is 19.2 kbit/s. The modem here uses a 64-level QAM signal and a near-maximum-likelihood detection process. The modem includes also an adaptive technique for tracking carrier phase jitter and hence reducing its effects. A maximum-likelihood detector, instead of equalizing the channel, estimates the channel response (strictly speaking the sampled impulse-response of the channel) and then determines the possible sequence of transmitted element values (data symbols) which, with the given channel response and in the absence of noise, gives a received signal approximating most closely (in the mean-square sense) to the signal actually received. The operation just described is approached quite closely by a near-maximum-likelihood detector, which involves far less complex equipment than a true maximum-likelihood detector. Near-maximum-likelihood detectors, when operating over telephone circuits, do, however, require the adaptive partial linear equalization of the channel, such that the group delay distortion is removed, the attenuation distortion being left unchanged[506], and this is one reason why such detectors are always more complex than the corresponding equalizers. Since the transmission rate of 19.2 kbit/s is approaching the Shannon limit for voice-frequency telephone circuits, which is typically around 30 kbit/s, it seems unlikely that much faster transmission rates will be achieved. The major single problem at these very high transmission rates is the accuracy to which the receiver must estimate the channel response in order to achieve a satisfactory tolerance to the additive noise present.

Full duplex transmission over a two-wire line is the simultaneous transmission of data over the line in both directions. Full duplex transmission, with a transmission rate of 2400 bit/s in each direction, can be achieved over telephone circuits as follows. The available bandwidth of the telephone circuit is divided into two equal and non-overlapping frequency bands, each somewhat less than half the total available bandwidth. The spectrum of the signal transmitted in one direction is now confined to one of the two frequency bands and the spectrum of the other signal is confined to the remaining frequency band. Careful filtering of the two signals is required here to avoid interference between them, and 16-level QAM signals can be used for each direction of transmission, with coherent detection and adaptive linear or nonlinear equalization at the receiver. The arrangement just described is one of frequency-division multiplexing but now with the multiplexed signals travelling in opposite directions.

Full duplex transmission over a two-wire line at speeds of up to 9600 bit/s in each direction can be achieved by the use of *echo cancellation*[511]. The portion of the transmitted signal, that reaches the receiver of the modem from which the signal has been transmitted, is here cancelled (removed by subtraction) from the received signal. The sequence of transmitted element-values (data symbols) is, of course, known at the receiver, so that, if the impulse response of the channel formed by the coupling between the transmitter and receiver is known, the interfering signal at the receiver input can be determined and removed. The coupling is introduced both at the input to the telephone circuit, where it can be reduced by using a hybrid transformer (Figure 2.1), and also at points of reflection over the length of the circuit. The required impulse response can be estimated by means of an adaptive linear feedforward transversal filter[511,517].

A combination of the techniques of frequency-division duplex operation and echo cancellation, just mentioned, can be applied to give full duplex operation over a two-wire line, with a transmission rate of 4800 bit/s in each direction. The frequency bands occupied by the 'go' and 'return' signals together occupy the whole of the available bandwidth of the telephone circuit, but they overlap somewhat over the central region of this frequency band. The interfering signal is now partly removed by filtering, the residual interference being removed by echo cancellation.

11

Data-transmission systems for use over HF radio links

11.1 Parallel systems

HF radio links are time-varying channels which can introduce considerable levels of attenuation and delay distortions[32-45]. Thus, where a data-transmission system is required to operate correctly over HF radio links for the greatest possible fraction of the time, it is important that the system be designed for the optimum tolerance to attenuation and delay distortions.

It is well known that for given levels of attenuation and delay distortions in the signal frequency band, the degree of distortion in the demodulated digital signal is inversely proportional to the element duration. In a serial data-transmission system, the transmitted signal comprises a sequential stream of data elements whose frequency spectrum occupies the whole of the available frequency band. Consider now the parallel system in which the total signal frequency band is divided into n separate non-overlapping frequency bands, as in a typical FDM system, to give n parallel data channels. Assume that these n channels are synchronously multiplexed, so that the individual data signals have the same element duration and are in element synchronism. The element duration of an individual data signal is here n times that of an element in the equivalent serial system, and each channel occupies $1/n$th of the total frequency band. It is evident that in this arrangement, not only is the duration of an individual signal element increased, but the attenuation and delay distortions introduced by the transmission path over the frequency band occupied by an individual signal element is reduced. Thus for the optimum tolerance to attenuation and delay distortions introduced in the transmission path, a parallel system, comprising a synchronously multiplexed FDM system, should be used in place of a serial system.

138

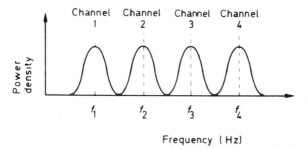

Fig. 11.1   Transmitted-signal spectrum of a parallel FDM system with non-overlapping channels

It is significant that digital data-transmission systems that have in the past been designed for use over HF radio links, are generally parallel systems, even though these are considerably more complex than the equivalent serial systems. In applications over telephone circuits, where the attenuation and delay distortions are less severe and where the cost of the modems is usually the most important single factor to be considered, serial systems are normally used.

11.2   Conventional FDM systems

Where an efficient use of bandwidth is not required, the most effective parallel system is that where the spectra of the different channels do not overlap, there being a sufficient frequency separation between the edges of any two adjacent spectra to enable these to be isolated from each other at the receiver by conventional filters[397-404]. This is the arrangement in conventional FDM telegraph systems. By using a sufficient number of channels such an arrangement can within certain limits be given as great a tolerance to attenuation and delay distortions as may be required. The system is illustrated in Figure 11.1.

It may be shown that for a given total transmission rate and for given attenuation and delay characteristics of the transmission path, the distortion in the demodulated signal of a typical channel is approximately inversely proportional to the square of the number of channels. This follows from the fact that as the number of channels increases, so the element duration of a channel signal increases and at the same time the attenuation and delay distortions, introduced by the transmission path into the channel frequency-band, are reduced. Each of these effects tends to reduce the distortion in the demodulated signal in proportion to the reduction in the bandwidth of the channel, and therefore in proportion to the increase in the number of channels.

The only distortion effect which this parallel system cannot tolerate is the effective loss of the received signal in one or more of the different channels, such as may be produced by severe frequency-selective fading. However, so long as the received signal level in any channel does not fall below a given value, correct detection of the received signals will not be prevented by attenuation and delay distortion effects alone, provided only that a sufficient number of channels are used.

The limit to the number of channels which may be used is determined partly by the maximum permitted cost of the equipment, since the equipment complexity increases linearly with the number of channels, and also by the required tolerance to frequency-modulation effects in the transmission path. The more channels that are used, the smaller is the frequency separation between adjacent channels and so the lower is the tolerance to frequency modulation effects in the transmission path, since a smaller frequency offset in the received signal spectrum can now cause interchannel interference between adjacent channels.

The main weakness of this arrangement is the inefficient use of bandwidth caused by the frequency guard bands between adjacent channels. Since there is a lower limit to the width of the frequency guard band between adjacent channels, the efficiency in the use of bandwidth tends to be reduced as the number of channels increases, the rate of reduction increasing with the number of channels. With an FDM system of the type considered here, it would be difficult to achieve transmission rates as high as 2400 bit/s over a frequency band from 300 to 3000 Hz, while still using a sufficient number of channels to gain an adequate tolerance to attenuation and delay distortions in the transmission path. With the present state of the art, 2400 bit/s does not really make an efficient use of bandwidth over voice-frequency channels using HF radio links.

11.3   Overlapping-spectra FDM systems

A much more efficient use of bandwidth can be obtained with a parallel system, if the spectra of the individual channels are permitted to overlap each other[405-413]. The total element rate over a given bandwidth of B Hz can now approach the ideal Nyquist rate of $2B$ bauds (elements per second), giving a total transmission rate approaching $2B$ bit/s, where binary signals are used.

In the simplest arrangement of such a system, the signals in the

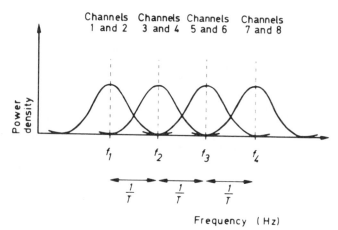

Fig. 11.2   Transmitted-signal spectrum of a parallel FDM system with overlapping channels

different channels are synchronously multiplexed and have an element duration of T seconds. The signal in each channel is a binary antipodal signal, with a carrier whose instantaneous amplitude and frequency remain constant over the duration of an element. This is a double sideband binary PM or suppressed carrier AM signal, with a rectangular modulating waveform and envelope.

The channels are arranged in pairs, so that the two signals in a pair of channels use the same carrier frequency but are in phase quadrature, having a phase angle of 90° between their respective carriers. The different carrier frequencies are spaced at regular intervals of $1/T$ Hz and are themselves multiples of $1/2T$ Hz. Clearly, if enough channels are used, so that the bandwidth occupied by the signal above the highest carrier frequency and below the lowest carrier frequency is small compared with the frequency band between these two carrier frequencies, then there are effectively two channels per $1/T$ Hz of bandwidth, giving a total transmission rate of nearly 2 bit/s per Hz of bandwidth. The system is illustrated in Figure 11.2.

Each binary signal is detected at the receiver by the corresponding coherent detector. The detector multiplies the received signal (comprising the n parallel binary signals) by a reference carrier which has the same frequency and phase as the carrier of the wanted binary signal (the phase having one of the two possible values over any individual signal element). The resulting product is integrated over each element period, and the output signal from the integrator, at the end of the element period, is compared with a threshold level of zero to give the detected element value.

It may readily be shown that, with no signal distortion in transmission, the coherent detector for a signal element in any one channel of the parallel system, gives no output for a received signal-element in any other channel, whether or not this shares the same carrier frequency. The n received signal elements, corresponding to the n channels of the parallel system, are said to be orthogonal, and no further filtering is needed to separate the different channels.

The power density spectrum of the binary PM signal, in any one of the n parallel channels, has a central positive peak at the signal carrier frequency and zeros at all frequencies spaced at intervals of $1/T$ Hz from this frequency. Thus the spectrum has zeros at all other signal carrier frequencies.

With rectangular modulating waveforms and an element duration of T seconds, in a synchronously multiplexed parallel system where each received signal element is detected over the whole of its duration of T seconds, the necessary and sufficient conditions for coincident signal elements (with different carrier frequencies) to be orthogonal, and at the same time for the spectrum of each individual signal to have zeros at all other carrier frequencies, is that the different carrier frequencies are spaced at intervals of $1/T$ Hz and are themselves multiples of $1/2T$ Hz. A constant envelope is assumed for each element.

The individual signals used in the arrangement just described have an infinite bandwidth, although in a practical system the spectrum of the total transmitted signal must of course be limited to the available frequency band. Where $n \gg 1$, the effect of the band limiting on any individual signal is small, so that these signals approximate reasonably well to the ideal signals just described.

The weakness of the above system is that attenuation and delay distortions in the transmission path can now cause not only intersymbol interference in any channel, that is, interference between different signal elements in any one channel, but also interchannel interference, that is, interference between signals in different channels. This follows directly from the fact that the spectra of the different channels are no longer disjoint (non-overlapping), so that the signal in any one channel cannot be isolated from that in any other by simple filtering (employing a bandpass filter). In the detection of a signal element in any one channel, the reference carrier used in the coherent detector tuned to this channel is not now necessarily orthogonal with respect to the coincident signal element received in any other channel using a different carrier frequency. Furthermore, the interchannel interference is in general more serious than the intersymbol interference[407].

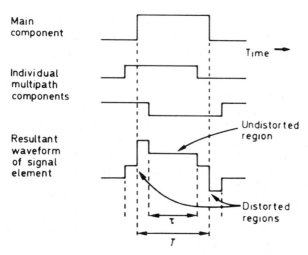

Fig. 11.3   An individual demodulated signal-element that has been distorted by multipath propagation

11.4   Effects of multipath propagation

Since the serious attenuation and delay distortions experienced over HF radio links are caused by multipath propagation, the intersymbol interference effects in any one signal appear as echoes added to each of the received signal-elements. Thus, if the signal in only one channel is transmitted, then any one *demodulated* signal-element appears as a main component, which is a single rectangular positive or negative pulse of duration T seconds and is the demodulated signal-element in the absence of distortion, together with a number of additional pulses (echoes) with the same shape as the main component but different values (both positive and negative) and different delays. So long as the spread in the delays is smaller then the element duration, the central portion of the resultant demodulated signal-element contains the main component of the element together with *all* the echoes, so that it has a constant value (with time). Towards the edges of the demodulated element, however, its waveform may vary considerably with time, due to the different numbers of echoes present at different points in the waveform here. This is illustrated in Figure 11.3. The variation of the element waveform with time represents signal distortion. One of the reasons for using a parallel system is to make the signal-element duration long in comparison with the total time interval between the arrival of the first and last of the components of a transmitted element. Under these conditions the signal distortion due to multipath propagation is concentrated at the boundaries between adjacent elements, the main central portions of the demodulated signal-elements being free from distortion but having of course arbitrary values.

Since a rectangular modulating waveform is used, the central portion of an individual received signal-element (before demodulation) is a sine wave with constant level and constant instantaneous frequency. The carrier phase over this portion of the element has an arbitrary value, having been shifted in transmission over the HF radio link. The phase shift in transmission, although essentially constant over the central portion of any one received signal element, may vary slowly with time. The carrier phase over the central portion of a received signal-element may be either in phase or in anti-phase with the suppressed carrier of the received signal over this period. Thus the receiver must have prior knowledge of the phase of the suppressed carrier of the received signal over each detection period. This prior knowledge must be continuously updated to follow the variations in the received carrier phase, and it is used to adjust the phase of the reference carrier in the coherent detector to have the same value as that of the suppressed carrier in the received signal.

The signal level over the central portion of a received signal-element in any channel (before demodulation), although constant for any one element, will in general vary slowly with time and for any element differ somewhat from its value in the absence of multipath propagation. This can be considered to be the result of amplitude modulation of the transmitted signal in the transmission path, that is, the effect of multiplicative noise. The level change in transmission (measured in decibels) is independent of the element value, so that if the receiver has prior knowledge of the level of the received signal carrier (over the central portion of a received signal-element) for any one element value, then it has prior knowledge of all possible values of the signal level. The prior knowledge must be continuously updated to follow the variations in the received signal level, and it is used to adjust the effective threshold levels used in the detection of the element values, when multilevel signals are transmitted.

It can be seen that if the signal in only *one* channel is transmitted, if the receiver has prior knowledge of the possible values of carrier phase and level over the central portions of the received signal elements, and if each signal element is detected only over the central portion where its level and instantaneous frequency are both constant, then correct detection can be achieved and all intersymbol interference between neighbouring signal-elements eliminated.

11.5   Time guard bands

In a parallel system where a number of synchronously multiplexed signals are transmitted, as the number of channels is increased for a constant total transmission rate, so there is a corresponding increase in the element duration. There is therefore a reduction in the fraction of any individual signal element which is distorted by the effects of multipath propagation, with the result not only that the intersymbol interference between adjacent signal-elements is reduced but also that coincident signal-elements in different channels become more nearly orthogonal, thus reducing the interchannel interference. Unfortunately, a very large number of parallel channels must be used here to obtain an adequate reduction in both intersymbol and interchannel interference.

A simple method of reducing the intersymbol and interchannel interference effects of multipath propagation is to introduce time guard bands between the detection processes for successive signal-elements in a channel. Thus, following the detection of an element, there is a fixed time interval before the start of the detection process for the next element in that channel. Successive signal-elements are transmitted consecutively with no time gaps, as before.

In a parallel system where a number of synchronously multiplexed signals are transmitted, if the detection process for an individual received element only involves the central portion of this element, over which period there is normally no serious distortion either in this or in any of the corresponding elements in the other channels, then both the intersymbol and interchannel interference effects should be largely eliminated.

In order that the signals in the different channels should still be orthogonal, the different carrier frequencies are now spaced at intervals of $1/\tau$ Hz and are themselves multiples of $1/2\tau$ Hz, where τ seconds is the detection (or integration) period used in the coherent detector. If the signal-element duration is T seconds, $\tau < T$. Provided that the amplitude and instantaneous frequency of each individual signal-element at the receiver input are both constant over a detection period and provided this detection period is used for all parallel channels, then coincident received signal-elements having different carrier frequencies must always be orthogonal over a detection period, regardless of their carrier phases. This means that a coherent detector tuned to one of these signals gives no response to the other signals, and thereby completely isolates the wanted signal from the others. The two coincident signal elements in a pair of channels sharing the same carrier frequency, are always orthogonal over a detection period, because their carriers are in phase quadrature (at

90°), having been phase shifted by exactly the same amount in transmission.

The previous discussion suggests that a sufficient number of channels should be used so that the undistorted central portion of an individual signal element occupies a large fraction of the signal-element duration. Only this portion of a signal element is now used in the detection process, and the different carrier frequencies are suitably spaced to maintain the orthogonal relationship between coincident signal elements over an element detection process. By this means the intersymbol and interchannel interference caused by multipath propagation can be largely eliminated, without an excessive reduction in either the bandwidth efficiency or the tolerance to additive noise.

From the various estimates of the spread in the arrival time of a transmitted signal, due to multipath propagation, it appears that this should not often exceed 6 ms and would most often be less than 3 ms[36,37]. A good tolerance to the effects of multipath propagation should therefore be obtained by using a time guard band of 3 to 6 ms between successive element detection processes. Except under extreme conditions this should effectively remove both intersymbol and interchannel interference effects caused by multipath propagation. It is assumed, of course, that rectangular modulating waveforms and envelopes are used, with only the minimum of band limiting of the individual channels.

In order to prevent the time guard bands resulting in an excessive reduction in bandwidth efficiency or in tolerance to additive noise, the detection period τ should be appreciably greater than the duration of the time guard band. Thus with a time guard band of between 3 to 6 ms, the detection period should not be less than about 10 ms.

Where a large number of channels are used, the resultant transmitted signal has a very large ratio of peak to r.m.s. value. This requires the transmitter output and receiver input stages of the modem, as well as the whole of the associated radio equipment, to be capable of handling relatively very high signal levels without overloading or even introducing significant non-linear distortion. On the other hand, in the transmission of digitally-coded speech signals, where error rates of up to around 1 in 10^4 have no noticeable effect on the reconstituted speech signal at the receiver, a useful improvement in tolerance to noise can be achieved by deliberately limiting the transmitted signal (that is, truncating its positive and negative excursions) such that an appropriate low error rate is obtained in the detected signal-elements in the complete absence of additive noise. A useful reduction in the average transmitted signal power level can be achieved in this way for no noticeable degradation in performance of the system, thus improving the tolerance to noise for a given average transmitted signal energy per bit.

11.6 Collins Kineplex system

The practical equipment which has been developed for use over HF radio links and which approximates most closely to the ideal arrangement just outlined, is the Collins Kineplex system[405,406]. This is a parallel system with orthogonal multiplexing, the signals in the different channels being in element synchronism. It uses time guard bands and the minimum of filtering of the individual channels. The signal in each channel is a binary PM signal. The channels are arranged in pairs and the two signals in a pair of channels use the same carrier frequency but are in phase quadrature. Thus the resultant signal of a pair of channels is a 4-level PM signal. The different carrier frequencies are spaced at $1/\tau$ Hz, where τ seconds is the element detection period, which is less than the element duration of T seconds. An individual 4-level PM signal is differentially coded at the transmitter and is detected by a differentially coherent detector at the receiver. To prevent interference from the other channels, the differentially coherent detection of an individual received 4-level PM signal is implemented as follows. During a detection period of τ seconds, the received signal (containing all channels) is fed to an infinite 'Q' tuned circuit whose resonant frequency is equal to the carrier frequency of the wanted PM signal and whose output signal is set to zero at the start of the detection period. At the end of the detection period, the output signal from the tuned circuit is dependent only on the wanted signal (and noise), the unwanted signals giving no response from the tuned circuit at this instant in time. The received signal is now disconnected from the tuned circuit, which continues to oscillate at the same instantaneous frequency and with no subsequent change of phase, until the end of the following detection period. Before the start of the next detection period, the output signal of the tuned circuit is reset to zero, ready to repeat the process just described, over the following two detection periods, and so on. A second tuned circuit with infinite 'Q' operates in exactly the same manner as does the tuned circuit just described, but while the received signal is being fed to the second tuned circuit, the first is storing the phase from the previous detection period, and vice versa. At the end of each detection period, the phase angle between the sine waves at the outputs of the two tuned circuits is measured, to give the phase change between the corresponding pair of received 4-level PM signal elements and hence the corresponding detected element value. This is then decoded to give the detected binary values of the two binary signal elements which make up the 4-level PM signal element.

The Collins Kineplex system corresponds exactly to the design considered in Section 11.5, except that it uses incoherent detection at the receiver, in place of coherent detection[405,406]. The system suffers a loss of 2.3 dB in tolerance to additive white Gaussian noise relative to the corresponding system using coherent detection (assuming that this could be satisfactorily implemented). It also has a lower tolerance to the small frequency offset of the received signal, likely to be introduced by an HF radio link, and it has a lower tolerance to certain attenuation and delay distortions. A well designed receiver can in fact remove not only any constant frequency offset in the received signal but also the effects of flat fading in which both the attenuation and frequency offset of the received signal vary with time. The two conditions that must be satisfied here are that the fading rate is not too rapid and the maximum depth of fade is not too great. Correction of flat fading is possible essentially because the same level and phase changes are introduced into each of the different channels (modulated-carrier signals) of the parallel system, so that the required corrections can be determined from and applied to the received signal without too much difficulty. Unfortunately, in the presence of frequency-selective fading, the level and phase changes introduced into any one channel of the parallel system are no longer in general the same as those in any other, nor even related to them in any very simple manner. It is therefore much more difficult now to correct for these changes, an appropriate correction needing to be applied separately to each channel. Thus in practice, the most that can effectively be achieved in the systems of the type considered here, in the presence of frequency-selective fading, is the removal of any constant frequency offset. Under these conditions, the greater the duration of a signal element, the lower the frequency spread (and hence also the lower the fading rate) that is tolerated by the system. This is essentially because, for a given frequency spread introduced by the HF radio link into the received signal, the resulting change in level and phase of the signal carrier, over the segment of the received signal involved in an element detection process, increases with the duration of a signal element. Of course, a sufficiently large carrier phase change here causes an error in the detection of the corresponding signal-element. Thus the duration of a signal element, and hence the number of channels in the parallel system, are limited by the frequency spreads likely to be experienced. In a typical system of the type being considered, frequency spreads of around 0.5 Hz are generally sufficient to cause an appreciable error rate in the detected element values, even in the complete absence of additive noise (see Figure

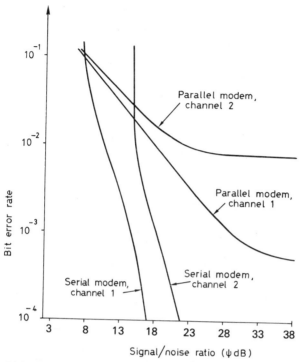

Fig. 11.4   Performances of serial and parallel modems over channels 1 and 2

11.4). The important advantage of the Collins Kineplex system is that by using differentially-coherent detection it completely avoids the serious problem of extracting the reference carriers needed for coherent detection of the received signals. In fact, there does not appear to be any simple means of extracting these reference carriers from the particular signals transmitted here.

At a transmission rate of 2400 bit/s over a voice-frequency channel using an HF radio link, where there is no unusually severe frequency-selective fading, the Collins Kineplex system is in principle the most cost-effective parallel system. At a transmission rate of 4800 bit/s, or under conditions of very severe frequency-selective fading at a transmission rate of 2400 bit/s, the use of coherent detection in place of differentially-coherent detection should produce a significant improvement in performance, even though a less ideal transmitted signal may have to be used in order that coherent detection can be achieved at the receiver. However, the resultant system is probably more complex, so that it is not necessarily more cost effective.

11.7   APR systems

Various proposals have recently been made for the implementation of parallel data-transmission systems that achieve a truly efficient use of bandwidth combined with a good tolerance to frequency-selective fading of the type experienced over HF radio links[405-413]. We shall now consider the basic principles (but no design details) of one possible arrangement that illustrates clearly the fundamental techniques involved in the design of such a system.

The ideal parallel system for very high transmission rates uses rectangular modulating waveforms and two m-level suppressed carrier AM signals in phase quadrature for each pair of channels sharing the same carrier frequency. It uses coherent detection at the receiver. The detection period is τ seconds, which is at least 10 ms and between 3 and 6 ms less than the element duration of T seconds. The carrier frequencies are spaced at regular intervals of $1/\tau$ Hz and are themselves multiples of $1/2\tau$ Hz. This ensures that for multipath propagation effects within the design limits of the system, there is no intersymbol or interchannel interference in the detection of any individual received signal element.

The coherent detector for a received signal-element in one of the n channels of the parallel system must now satisfy two important requirements. Firstly it must have a reference carrier with the correct frequency and phase, and secondly it must use the correct decision-thresholds with which to compare the coherent detector output signal at the end of an element detection process. Unfortunately, without rather complex equipment, it is not always possible to achieve either of these requirements, particularly when the transmission path introduces severe frequency-selective fading.

These problems can be overcome as follows. The transmitter sends with each pair of data signals, that share the same carrier frequency, an unmodulated carrier which is isolated at the receiver and used as a reference for the correct adjustment of the corresponding two coherent detectors. The unmodulated carrier has the same frequency as the data-signal carriers, and its level and phase are in fixed and known relationships with the level and carrier phase, respectively, of each of the two parallel signal-elements when these have any given pair of element values. The phase of the unmodulated carrier is used at the receiver to control the phase of the reference carrier in each of the two coherent detectors, and its amplitude effectively controls the threshold levels with which each coherent detector output signal is compared to determine the element value of the corresponding data signal. The arrangement relies on the fact that over the detection period of a signal element, that is, over its central portion, any changes in the amplitude and phase of the element carrier introduced by the transmission path, are matched by corresponding changes in the amplitude and phase of the reference carrier, so that the effects of these changes may be compensated for in the detection process. The correct operation of each coherent detector is thus ensured. A system employing these techniques is known here as an amplitude-and-phase reference (APR) system [414-421].

In order that the receiver is to be able to isolate the unmodulated carrier, at each of the different carrier frequencies, from the received data signals (and vice versa), using simple linear filtering techniques preferably with phase-locked oscillators, it is necessary that the transmitted data signals in the n parallel channels have no frequency components at any of the different carrier frequencies. Thus, if the system is to be transparent in the sense that it can handle any sequence of data element values, the spectrum of any sequence of the transmitted data-elements in any of the n channels, whether the sequence is repetitive or not, must have a zero at each carrier frequency. This condition can best be satisfied as follows. Each carrier frequency is chosen to be a multiple of $\frac{1}{2}d$ Hz and the different carrier frequencies are spaced at regular intervals of d Hz. The spectrum of the rectangular baseband modulating signal must now have zeros at all integral multiples of d, including zero frequency. This may be achieved by feeding the baseband signal through the appropriate coder, similar to that in Figure 15.17 of Chapter 15. The coder forces zeros into the spectrum of its output baseband signal, at all integral multiples of $1/lT$ Hz (including zero), where l is a selected positive integer and T seconds is the element duration. In Figure 15.17, $l = 2$. Thus a condition that must be satisfied is $d = i/lT$, where i is any positive integer. Since the parallel signal-elements must be orthogonal over the detection period of τ seconds, another condition that must be satisfied is $d = j/\tau$ where j is any positive integer. It is evident that the two conditions can be satisfied through the appropriate choice of l, T and τ.

The element timing signal is transmitted in a separate channel, at the centre of the signal frequency band. It uses a separate carrier frequency, spaced at d Hz from the carriers of the two adjacent data signals.

Each unmodulated-carrier is at the centre of the frequency band of the two associated data signals, so that the amplitude and phase of the received unmodulated carrier should vary in step with the amplitude and phase of each of the data signals. Thus a very good tolerance should be obtained by this arrangement, both to slowly varying signal levels and to small values of frequency offset introduced in the transmission path. In practice, of course, a compromise must be reached at the receiver between the rates of change in the amplitude and phase of the unmodulated carrier, which the receiver can follow in terms of the corresponding changes in the effective threshold levels and in the phase of the reference carrier of the coherent detector, and the amounts of noise which may appear in the effective threshold levels and reference carrier. The greater the rejection of additive noise, the slower the rates of change in amplitude and phase which can be followed by the receiver. On the other hand, the more rapid these rates of change, the smaller the rejection of additive noise.

It can be seen that the receiver in a APR system is *fully adaptive*, in the sense that it is held correctly matched to the slowly time-varying HF radio link. By splitting the transmitted signal into a number of parallel synchronously multiplexed narrow-band signals, and through the use of time guard bands to separate successive detection processes, the attenuation and delay distortions introduced by the radio link appear simply as different values of attenuation and phase shift in the different channels. These are suitably compensated for in the detection process.

11.8 Serial systems

Using recently developed integrated circuits, the Collins Kineplex system can be implemented digitally, the demodulation and modulation processes in the parallel modem being achieved by means of the FFT (fast Fourier transform) and inverse FFT, respectively. By this means a 2400 bit/s parallel modem can be implemented very simply, leading to a most cost-effective system[512-514]. However, an unfortunate effect of frequency-selective fading on a parallel system is that it can, for practical purposes, cause the complete loss of signal in a pair of channels sharing the same carrier frequency. The fact that the parallel system effectively eliminates signal distortion in the individual channels is of no help in detecting the lost signals. Again, when the fading rate or frequency spread introduced by the HF radio link into the data signal exceeds a certain value, errors are introduced into the detected element values even in the complete absence of additive noise. On the other hand, the signal distortion introduced into a *serial* signal by frequency selective fading does not introduce the complete loss of any received signal-element. Nor does a high fading rate or large frequency spread necessarily cause errors in the detected element-values. The transmitted signal in the 2400 bit/s serial modem now to be considered is a 4-level QAM or PM signal, and an adaptive near-maximum-likelihood detection process is used here at the receiver[515-518]. The latter gives a potentially better

Table 11.1 CHANNELS USED IN THE TESTS

Channel	Frequency spread introduced into the data signal (Hz)	Relative transmission delay of the two sky waves (seconds)
1	0.5	1×10^{-3}
2	2	3×10^{-3}

tolerance to additive white Gaussian noise than a conventional adaptive linear or nonlinear equalizer.

Figure 11.4 shows the results of computer simulation tests on the 2400 bit/s serial and parallel modems just described, for the case where the HF radio link has two independent Rayleigh fading sky waves that introduce equal frequency spreads and equal average attenuations into the corresponding received data signals. The characteristics of the channels 1 and 2 are given in Table 11.1, and the signal/noise ratio, ψ dB, is defined to be the ratio of the average transmitted energy per bit to the one-sided power spectral density of the additive white Gaussian noise at the receiver input. (The corresponding value of ψ for a binary signal is given by Equation 7.11.) It is clear from Figure 11.4 that, at bit error rates below 1 in 100 for each channel, the serial modem has a considerably better performance than the parallel modem. The disadvantage of the serial modem is that it is considerably more complex than the parallel modem, much of the complexity of the serial modem being involved in the implementation of the near-maximum-likelihood detector. The serial modem nevertheless appears to be potentially more cost-effective than the parallel modem.

12

Matched-filter detection

Chapters 12 to 16 contain a theoretical analysis of various digital signals that can be used for the transmission of data over baseband and bandpass channels. The main emphasis in this study is on the contribution of the signal waveforms themselves to the properties of the data-transmission system using these signals. Hence, in general, only the 'optimum' detection process is considered. The detection process is optimum in the sense that it minimizes the probability of error in the detection of a received signal-element, when this is detected from the corresponding portion of the received signal, in a separate operation from the detection of the other received elements.

It is assumed that no signal distortion is introduced by the transmission path, so that the signal waveform is shaped entirely at the transmitter and receiver. The transmission path, however, introduces additive white Gaussian noise. A comparison is made of the relative tolerances of the different digital signals to this noise, where the tolerance of a signal to noise is taken as the noise level, for a given signal power level and information rate, and a given average element-error rate of the order of 1 in 10^5 in the optimum detection of the signal. Although the additive noise introduced by many practical transmission paths does not approximate to Gaussian noise, it is well known that a digital signal having a better tolerance to additive white Gaussian noise than another signal, will normally also have a better tolerance to the additive noise obtained in practice. The relative tolerances of different signals to additive white Gaussian noise are therefore usually a good measure of their relative tolerances to the additive noise present over a practical transmission path.

The study of the different digital signals, carried out as just described, brings out some interesting relationships between the different signals, which helps to clarify the true nature of these signals.

Before considering the different waveforms often used for digital signals and the properties that result from the particular waveforms of these signals, it is necessary first to consider in some detail the

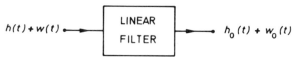

$$h(t) + w(t) \longrightarrow \boxed{\begin{array}{c} \text{LINEAR} \\ \text{FILTER} \end{array}} \longrightarrow h_0(t) + w_0(t)$$

Fig. 12.1   *Linear filtering of r(t)*

optimum detection process for an individual element (digit or symbol) of the signal, where this is received in the presence of additive white Gaussian noise[423,424].

Consider first a signal waveform $h(t)$, with a duration from 0 to T seconds, such that $h(t)$ is zero for $t < 0$ and $t > T$, and where $h(t)$ may have any desired shape over the time interval 0 to T seconds.

The signal waveform is received in the presence of additive white Gaussian noise with zero mean and a two-sided power spectral density $\frac{1}{2}N_0$ over all positive and negative frequencies. Strictly speaking this noise is non-physical (in the sense that it cannot be realised in practice) since the power level of the noise must be infinite. However, if the Gaussian noise has a power spectral density of $\frac{1}{2}N_0$ over a finite bandwidth, wider than that of $h(t)$ and therefore very much wider than $1/T$ Hz, with no power outside the given frequency band, its effect on the detection of the received signal-element $h(t)$ is for practical purposes the same as that which would result if its bandwidth were truly infinite. It is therefore quite reasonable to assume ideal white Gaussian noise and this greatly simplifies the theoretical analysis of the detection process. Assume therefore that a noise waveform $w(t)$ is added to $h(t)$, where $w(t)$ is a Gaussian random process with zero mean and a two-sided power spectral density of $\frac{1}{2}N_0$. Thus the received signal is

$$r(t) = h(t) + w(t) \qquad (12.1)$$

It is assumed here and throughout this book that the data and noise waveforms are statistically independent.

The received signal $r(t)$ is fed to a linear filter whose transfer function is $G(f)$ and impulse response $g(t)$. The signal and noise waveforms at the filter output are $h_0(t)$ and $w_0(t)$, respectively, as shown in Figure 12.1.

The problem is to determine the filter characteristics that *maximize* the signal/noise power ratio at the output of the linear filter at time $t = T$.

It is assumed throughout this and the subsequent analysis that, for any signal, the source or load impedance is one ohm and the signal value is measured in volts or amps. Thus the instantaneous signal power at any given time is the square of the signal value, and the signal energy over any given time interval is simply the integral of the square of the signal over the given interval. All signals are real valued.

The instantaneous signal power at the output of the linear filter, at time $t = T$, is

$$F = h_0^2(T) \tag{12.2}$$

and the expected noise power is

$$N = \overline{w_0^2(T)} \tag{12.3}$$

where $\overline{w_0^2(T)}$ is the expected value of $w_0^2(t)$ at time $t = T$. Thus the output signal/noise power ratio at time $t = T$ is

$$\frac{F}{N} = \frac{h_0^2(T)}{\overline{w_0^2(T)}} \tag{12.4}$$

where this is, of course, the ratio of the instantaneous signal power to the expected noise power.

The spectrum (Fourier transform) of $h(t)$ is

$$H(f) = \int_{-\infty}^{\infty} h(t) \exp(-j2\pi ft)\, dt \tag{12.5}$$

and

$$h(t) = \int_{-\infty}^{\infty} H(f) \exp(j2\pi ft)\, df \tag{12.6}$$

where f is the frequency in Hz and $j = \sqrt{-1}$.

The spectrum of $h_0(t)$ is $G(f)H(f)$, and

$$h_0(t) = \int_{-\infty}^{\infty} G(f)H(f) \exp(j2\pi ft)\, df \tag{12.7}$$

so that the magnitude of the output signal at time $t = T$ is

$$|h_0(T)| = \left| \int_{-\infty}^{\infty} G(f)H(f) \exp(j2\pi fT)\, df \right| \tag{12.8}$$

and the power of the output signal at this time instant is

$$F = |h_0(T)|^2 = \left| \int_{-\infty}^{\infty} G(f)H(f) \exp(j2\pi fT)\, df \right|^2 \tag{12.9}$$

The power spectral density of $w_0(t)$ is

$$\tfrac{1}{2}N_0|G(f)|^2 \tag{12.10}$$

from a well known theorem[425], and the expected power level of $w_0(t)$ is

$$N = \tfrac{1}{2}N_0 \int_{-\infty}^{\infty} |G(f)|^2 \, df \tag{12.11}$$

from another well known theorem[425]. Clearly, N is independent of time.

The ratio of instantaneous signal power to the expected noise power, at the output of the linear filter at time $t = T$, is

$$\frac{F}{N} = \frac{|\int_{-\infty}^{\infty} G(f)H(f) \exp\,(\mathrm{j}2\pi f T)\, df|^2}{\tfrac{1}{2}N_0 \int_{-\infty}^{\infty} |G(f)|^2 \, df} \tag{12.12}$$

It is now required to maximize F/N, which will be referred to as the output signal/noise ratio.

By the Schwarz inequality[426],

$$\left| \int_{-\infty}^{\infty} U(f)V(f) \, df \right|^2 \leqslant \int_{-\infty}^{\infty} |U(f)|^2 \, df \int_{-\infty}^{\infty} |V(f)|^2 \, df \tag{12.13}$$

where $U(f)$ and $V(f)$ are any finite-energy complex functions of f. Equality holds in Equation 12.13 when

$$U(f) = cV^*(f) \tag{12.14}$$

for any positive or negative real constant c. $V^*(f)$ is the complex conjugate of $V(f)$.

In Equation 12.13, substitute $G(f)$ for $U(f)$ and $H(f) \exp\,(\mathrm{j}2\pi f T)$ for $V(f)$, so that

$$\left| \int_{-\infty}^{\infty} G(f)H(f) \exp\,(\mathrm{j}2\pi f T) \, df \right|^2$$

$$\leqslant \int_{-\infty}^{\infty} |G(f)|^2 \, df \int_{-\infty}^{\infty} |H(f) \exp\,(\mathrm{j}2\pi f T)|^2 \, df$$

$$= \int_{-\infty}^{\infty} |G(f)|^2 \, df \int_{-\infty}^{\infty} |H(f)|^2 \, df \qquad (12.15)$$

with equality when

$$G(f) = cH^*(f) \exp(-j2\pi fT) \qquad (12.16)$$

where $H^*(f)$ is the complex conjugate of $H(f)$.

From Parseval's theorem[426],

$$\int_{-\infty}^{\infty} |H(f)|^2 \, df = \int_{-\infty}^{\infty} h^2(t) \, dt = E \qquad (12.17)$$

where E is the energy of the signal waveform $h(t)$. Clearly, E is fixed by the received signal.

From Equations 12.9, 12.15 and 12.17,

$$F \leqslant E \int_{-\infty}^{\infty} |G(f)|^2 \, df \qquad (12.18)$$

and from Equation 12.11,

$$N = \tfrac{1}{2} N_0 \int_{-\infty}^{\infty} |G(f)|^2 \, df \qquad (12.19)$$

Thus the output signal/noise ratio at time $t = T$ is

$$\frac{F}{N} \leqslant \frac{E}{\tfrac{1}{2} N_0} \qquad (12.20)$$

The output signal/noise ratio has its maximum value

$$\left(\frac{F}{N}\right)_{\text{max}} = \frac{E}{\tfrac{1}{2} N_0} \qquad (12.21)$$

when equality holds in Equation 12.15, and the transfer function of the linear filter is now $G(f)$ in Equation 12.16. The impulse response of this linear filter is

$$g(t) = \int_{-\infty}^{\infty} G(f) \exp(j2\pi ft) \, df$$

$$= c \int_{-\infty}^{\infty} H^*(f) \exp \left[j2\pi f(t - T)\right] df$$

$$= c \int_{-\infty}^{\infty} H(-f) \exp \left[j2\pi f(t - T)\right] df$$

$$= c \int_{-\infty}^{\infty} H(f) \exp \left[j2\pi f(T - t)\right] df \qquad (12.22)$$

so that

$$g(t) = ch(T - t) \qquad (12.23)$$

Thus the linear filter with impulse response $ch(T - t)$ maximizes the output signal/noise ratio, at time $t = T$ seconds. The filter is said to be *matched* to the received signal $h(t)$ and is known as a *matched filter*[423,424].

From Equations 12.18, 12.16 and 12.17, the instantaneous signal power at the output of the matched filter, at time $t = T$, is

$$E \int_{-\infty}^{\infty} |cH^*(f) \exp(-j2\pi f T)|^2 df = c^2 E \int_{-\infty}^{\infty} |H(f)|^2 df$$

$$= c^2 E^2 \qquad (12.24)$$

From Equations 12.19, 12.16 and 12.17, the expected noise power at the output of the matched filter, at time $t = T$, is

$$N = \tfrac{1}{2}N_0 \int_{-\infty}^{\infty} |cH^*(f) \exp(-j2\pi f T)|^2 df = \tfrac{1}{2}N_0 c^2 \int_{-\infty}^{\infty} |H(f)|^2 df$$

$$= \tfrac{1}{2}N_0 c^2 E \qquad (12.25)$$

The output signal/noise power ratio is clearly $E/\tfrac{1}{2}N_0$, as before.

The output signal/noise ratio depends only on the energy of the received signal waveform and on the noise power spectral density. It is independent of the shape of $h(t)$.

Since $h(t) = 0$ for $t < 0$ and $t > T$, it follows from Equation 12.23 that, for the matched filter, $g(t) = 0$ for $t < 0$ and $t > T$, so that $g(t)$ is physically realisable.

A practical filter matched to $h(t)$ will often have an impulse response $ch(T + \tau - t)$, where $\tau > 0$. The output signal from this filter is now sampled at the time instant $t = T + \tau$, but is otherwise as previously described. The impulse response of this filter is clearly $g(t - \tau)$, which is $g(t)$ with an added delay of τ seconds. The non-physically realisable matched-filter, whose output signal is sampled at time $t = 0$ instead of at time $t = T + \tau$, has the transfer function $cH^*(f)$ and impulse response $h(-t)$.

If now the additive Gaussian noise at the input to the non-physically realisable matched-filter is not white but coloured, such that its two-sided power spectral density is $N_c(f)$ instead of $\frac{1}{2}N_0$, the received waveform $r(t)$ (Equation 12.1) can first be fed through a noise-whitening filter whose transfer function is $\sqrt{\frac{1}{2}N_0/N_c(f)}$, before feeding it to the appropriate matched-filter. Since the matched filter removes all frequency components of the noise that lie outside the frequency band of the signal-element $h(t)$, it is only necessary for the transfer function of the noise-whitening filter to satisfy the given condition over the frequency band of $h(t)$, which is effectively finite. Thus it is assumed that over this frequency band $N_c(f) \neq 0$. The two-sided noise power spectral density at the output of the noise-whitening filter (over the frequency band of $h(t)$) is

$$N_c(f) \left| \sqrt{\left\{ \frac{\frac{1}{2}N_0}{N_c(f)} \right\}} \right|^2 = \frac{1}{2}N_0 \qquad (12.26)$$

and the Fourier transform of the data signal (signal-element waveform) at the output of the filter is

$$H_w(f) = \sqrt{\left\{ \frac{\frac{1}{2}N_0}{N_c(f)} \right\}} H(f) \qquad (12.27)$$

The transfer function of the matched filter for this signal is

$$G_w(f) = cH_w^*(f) = c \sqrt{\left\{ \frac{\frac{1}{2}N_0}{N_c(f)} \right\}} H^*(f) \qquad (12.28)$$

this being the non-physically realisable matched-filter whose output signal is sampled at time $t = 0$.

In practice, the noise-whitening filter and matched filter would be combined into a single filter, to give the matched filter for the signal-element $h(t)$ received in the presence of coloured Gaussian noise. The transfer function of the latter filter is

$$\begin{aligned} G_c(f) &= \sqrt{\left\{ \frac{\frac{1}{2}N_0}{N_c(f)} \right\}} G_w(f) \\ &= c \frac{\frac{1}{2}N_0}{N_c(f)} H^*(f) \end{aligned} \qquad (12.29)$$

The impulse response of this filter is not simply related to $h(t)$, and to make the matched filter physically realisable a sufficient delay must be introduced into its impulse response, the same delay being introduced into the sampling instant for its output waveform.

Suppose now that the received signal is $sh(t)$, where $h(t)$ is zero for $t < 0$ and $t > T$, as before, and $h(t)$ may have any desired shape over the time interval 0 to T seconds. $h(t)$ is known at the receiver but s is an unknown real number whose value it is required to estimate by means of a matched filter. $sh(t)$ is received in the presence of the white Gaussian noise waveform $w(t)$ previously assumed, so that the received signal is

$$r(t) = sh(t) + w(t) \tag{12.30}$$

If $r(t)$ is fed to a filter matched to $h(t)$ and having an impulse response

$$g(t) = ch(T - t) \tag{12.31}$$

the output signal at time $t = T$ is

$$x = \int_{-\infty}^{\infty} r(t)g(T - t) \, dt$$

$$= \int_{0}^{T} r(t)ch(t) \, dt$$

$$= sc \int_{0}^{T} h^2(t) \, dt + c \int_{0}^{T} w(t)h(t) \, dt$$

$$= scE + v \tag{12.32}$$

where

$$v = c \int_{0}^{T} w(t)h(t) \, dt \tag{12.33}$$

and E is the energy of $h(t)$, but not of $sh(t)$. v is a Gaussian random variable with zero mean.

Equation 12.32 shows that

$$x = \int_{0}^{T} r(t)ch(t) \, dt \tag{12.34}$$

so that x could alternatively be obtained by multiplying $r(t)$ by $ch(t)$ and integrating the product over the time interval 0 to T. This operation gives the *time correlation* of $r(t)$ and $ch(t)$ over the time interval 0 to T. It is evident therefore that in each of Figures 6.1–6.4 and 7.1 a multiplier and the following integrator can be replaced by the corresponding matched filter, whose impulse response is the time reverse of the signal element waveform (or component of this waveform) to which it is matched.

In order to estimate s, assuming a prior knowledge of c and E at the receiver, x is multiplied by $1/cE$ to give

$$\frac{x}{cE} = s + \frac{v}{cE} \tag{12.35}$$

which is the required linear estimate of s. The matched filter maximizes the ratio of instantaneous signal power to average noise power in x, so that it also maximizes this ratio in x/cE.

The expected or mean value of x/cE is

$$\begin{aligned}
\mathrm{E}\left[\frac{x}{cE}\right] &= \mathrm{E}\left[s + \frac{v}{cE}\right] \\
&= \mathrm{E}[s] + \mathrm{E}\left[\frac{v}{cE}\right] \\
&= \mathrm{E}[s] \tag{12.36}
\end{aligned}$$

since v is a Gaussian random variable with zero mean. Equation 12.36 means that x/cE is an *unbiased* estimate of s.

From Equation 12.35, the error in x/cE is clearly v/cE which is introduced by the Gaussian noise. Since the matched filter is linear and since $w(t)$ is a Gaussian random process with zero mean, v is a Gaussian random variable with zero mean. But the mean-square value of v is the expected noise power at the output of the matched filter at time $t = T$ and so (from Equation 12.25) is

$$\mathrm{E}[v^2] = \tfrac{1}{2}N_0 c^2 E \tag{12.37}$$

Thus the mean-square error in x/cE is

$$\begin{aligned}
\mathrm{E}\left[\left(\frac{x}{cE} - s\right)^2\right] &= \mathrm{E}\left[\left(\frac{v}{cE}\right)^2\right] \\
&= \frac{1}{c^2 E^2}\mathrm{E}[v^2] \\
&= \frac{\tfrac{1}{2}N_0 c^2 E}{c^2 E^2} = \frac{\tfrac{1}{2}N_0}{E} \tag{12.38}
\end{aligned}$$

Since x/cE is the unbiased estimate of s with the maximum signal/noise ratio, it is also the unbiased estimate with the minimum mean-square error, which is $\frac{1}{2}N_0/E$. Furthermore, no other estimate of s, whether linear or nonlinear, can give an unbiased estimate with a lower mean-square error.

Suppose now that s is equally likely to have either of two values k_0 and k_1, where $k_1 > k_0$ and where both k_0 and k_1 are known at the receiver. $sh(t)$ is here a binary signal-element whose two possible waveforms are known at the receiver. For convenience assume that the constant c in Equation 12.31 is positive.

As before, the output signal from the matched filter at time $t = T$ is

$$x = cEs + v \qquad (12.39)$$

where v is a Gaussian random variable with zero mean and variance

$$N = \frac{1}{2}N_0 c^2 E \qquad (12.40)$$

To detect the value of s, x is now compared with a threshold level of $\frac{1}{2}cE(k_0 + k_1)$ which lies *half way* between cEk_0 and cEk_1, the two possible values of cEs.

When

$$x < \tfrac{1}{2}cE(k_0 + k_1), \quad s \text{ is detected as } k_0,$$

and when

$$x > \tfrac{1}{2}cE(k_0 + k_1), \quad s \text{ is detected as } k_1.$$

Clearly, s is detected as k_0 or k_1 depending upon whether x is *closer* to cEk_0 or cEk_1, respectively. It can be shown that this arrangement minimizes the probability of error in the detection of s from x, under the assumed conditions[422].

In order to evaluate the probability of error in the detection of s, the *probability density function*, $p(v)$, of the noise component v in Equation 12.39 is required. The function $p(v)$ is such that the integral $\int_a^b p(v)\,dv$ gives the probability that $a < v \leqslant b$, where a and b are constants and $b > a$. In order to simplify the terminology used throughout this analysis, the *same* symbol is used for a *random variable* and its *sample value*, the correct meaning being made clear in the context. A sample value of a random variable is, of course, a fixed quantity. Thus, for example, v in Equations 12.35–12.39 is a random variable, whereas the same symbol in $p(v)$ is a sample value of this random variable. Since v is a Gaussian random variable with zero mean and variance N,

$$p(v) = \frac{1}{\sqrt{(2\pi N)}} \exp\left(-\frac{v^2}{2N}\right) \qquad (12.41)$$

It is evident from Equation 12.39 that, for a *given* value of s, x is a

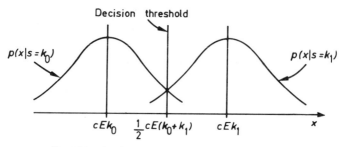

Fig. 12.2 *Conditional probability-density functions of x*

Gaussian random variable with mean value cEs and variance N, so that the probability density function of x is now

$$p(x) = \frac{1}{\sqrt{(2\pi N)}} \exp\left\{-\frac{(x - cEs)^2}{2N}\right\} \qquad (12.42)$$

Thus x has two possible probability-density functions $p(x \mid s = k_0)$ and $p(x \mid s = k_1)$, its probability density depending upon whether $s = k_0$ or k_1. $p(x \mid s = k_0)$ and $p(x \mid s = k_1)$ are the conditional probability densities of x, given that $s = k_0$ and k_1, respectively. The two conditional probability densities are shown in Figure 12.2.

Clearly,

$$p(x \mid s = k_0) = \frac{1}{\sqrt{(2\pi N)}} \exp\left\{-\frac{(x - cEk_0)^2}{2N}\right\} \qquad (12.43)$$

and

$$p(x \mid s = k_1) = \frac{1}{\sqrt{(2\pi N)}} \exp\left\{-\frac{(x - cEk_1)^2}{2N}\right\} \qquad (12.44)$$

The decision threshold used in the detection of x is

$$e = \tfrac{1}{2}cE(k_0 + k_1) \qquad (12.45)$$

If $s = k_0$, an error occurs in the detection of s when $x > e$, so that the probability of error is

$$P_0 = \int_e^\infty \frac{1}{\sqrt{(2\pi N)}} \exp\left\{-\frac{(x - cEk_0)^2}{2N}\right\} dx \qquad (12.46)$$

If $s = k_1$, an error occurs in the detection of s when $x < e$, so that the probability of error is

$$P_1 = \int_{-\infty}^e \frac{1}{\sqrt{(2\pi N)}} \exp\left\{-\frac{(x - cEk_1)^2}{2N}\right\} dx \qquad (12.47)$$

The expressions for P_0 and P_1 may be simplified by replacing the variable x in each integral by the corresponding variable $v = x - cEs$. The same result may, however, be obtained directly, as follows. It can be seen from Figure 12.2 that both cEk_1 and cEk_2 are at a distance

$$d = \tfrac{1}{2}cE(k_1 - k_0) \tag{12.48}$$

from the decision threshold. Thus if $s = k_0$, an error occurs in the detection of s whenever $v > d$. Similarly, if $s = k_1$, an error occurs in the detection of s whenever $v < -d$. Hence P_0 is the probability that the noise component v has a value more positive than d, and P_1 is the probability that v has a value more negative than $-v$. It follows that

$$P_0 = \int_d^\infty \frac{1}{\sqrt{(2\pi N)}} \exp\left(-\frac{v^2}{2N}\right) dv \tag{12.49}$$

and

$$P_1 = \int_{-\infty}^{-d} \frac{1}{\sqrt{(2\pi N)}} \exp\left(-\frac{v^2}{2N}\right) dv \tag{12.50}$$

Use is made here of the assumption that s and v are statistically independent. Since $\exp(-v^2/2N)$ is an even function of v,

$$P_0 = P_1 = \int_d^\infty \frac{1}{\sqrt{(2\pi N)}} \exp\left(-\frac{v^2}{2N}\right) dv$$

$$= \int_{d/\sqrt{N}}^\infty \frac{1}{\sqrt{(2\pi)}} \exp\left(-\tfrac{1}{2}v^2\right) dv = Q\left(\frac{d}{\sqrt{N}}\right) \tag{12.51}$$

where d is given by Equation 12.48 and N is given by Equation 12.40. Also

$$Q(y) = \int_y^\infty \frac{1}{\sqrt{(2\pi)}} \exp\left(-\tfrac{1}{2}v^2\right) dv \tag{12.52}$$

The integral giving $Q(y)$ cannot be evaluated directly, but $Q(y)$ has been tabulated for positive real values of y.

Whether $s = k_0$ or $s = k_1$, the probability of error in the detection of s is

$$Q\left(\frac{d}{\sqrt{N}}\right) = Q\left\{\frac{\frac{1}{2}cE(k_1 - k_0)}{\sqrt{(\frac{1}{2}N_0 c^2 E)}}\right\}$$

$$= Q\left\{\frac{1}{2}(k_1 - k_0)\bigg/\left(\frac{E}{\frac{1}{2}N_0}\right)\right\} \qquad (12.53)$$

where $\frac{1}{2}(k_1 - k_0)$ is half the distance between k_0 and k_1, and E is the energy of $h(t)$.

It can be seen from Equation 12.53 that the error probability is independent of the shape of the signal waveform and is dependent only on $k_1 - k_0$, E and N_0.

The matched filter maximizes the signal/noise power ratio in the output signal x, and the detection of s from x, by comparing x with a decision threshold of $\frac{1}{2}cE(k_0 + k_1)$, minimizes the probability of error in this detection process. Thus the combination of the matched filter and the associated detection process, minimizes the probability of error in the detection of s from the received waveform $r(t)$. This is an arrangement of *matched-filter detection* and is the optimum detection process for the wanted signal under the assumed conditions.

The average energy of the two signal waveforms $k_0 h(t)$ and $k_1 h(t)$ is

$$\frac{1}{2}(k_1^2 + k_0^2)E = \frac{1}{4}(k_1 - k_0)^2 E + \frac{1}{4}(k_1 + k_0)^2 E \qquad (12.54)$$

E is the energy of $h(t)$ and so is always positive, so that both $\frac{1}{4}(k_1 - k_0)^2 E$ and $\frac{1}{4}(k_1 + k_0)^2 E$ are positive for all values of k_0 and k_1. Thus for any given values of $k_1 - k_0$ and E, the average energy of the two signal waveforms has a minimum value of $\frac{1}{4}(k_1 - k_0)^2 E$, and this is obtained when $k_1 = -k_0$. But, from Equation 12.53, the probability of error is dependent only on $k_1 - k_0$, E and N_0, so that for a given probability of error and for given values of $k_1 - k_0$ and E, the noise power spectral density $\frac{1}{2}N_0$ of the white Gaussian noise at the input to the matched filter has a fixed value. Thus, for a given probability of error and for given values of $k_1 - k_0$ and E, the signal/noise ratio $\frac{1}{2}(k_1^2 + k_0^2)E/(\frac{1}{2}N_0)$ at the input to the matched filter has its minimum value when $k_1 = -k_0$. In other words, the tolerance to additive white Gaussian noise is maximized under these conditions.

Suppose now that

$$k_1 = -k_0 = a \qquad (12.55)$$

where $a > 0$. Under these conditions, the decision threshold used for the detection of s from x becomes

$$e = \frac{1}{2}cE(k_0 + k_1) = 0 \qquad (12.56)$$

from Equation 12.45. Thus s is detected as k_0 when $x < 0$, and s is detected as k_1 when $x > 0$.

The energy of the received signal-element is now

$$E_s = a^2 E \tag{12.57}$$

and the probability of error in the detection of s is

$$Q\left\{ a\sqrt{\frac{E}{\frac{1}{2}N_0}} \right\} = Q\left\{ \sqrt{\frac{E_s}{\frac{1}{2}N_0}} \right\} \tag{12.58}$$

from Equation 12.53. The error probability is here a function only of the signal/noise ratio at the input to the matched filter, and has its minimum value for any given signal/noise ratio.

This is clearly the optimum combination of signal design and detection process for a binary signal, where the two binary values are equally likely and the signal is received in the presence of additive white Gaussian noise. Any waveform of duration from 0 to T seconds may be used for the transmitted signal-element, so long as it has the required energy and so long as the waveform corresponding to one of the two binary values is the negative of that corresponding to the other binary value. Such a signal is known as a binary antipodal signal-element.

Since a decision threshold of zero is used for the detection of the binary value, the receiver requires no prior knowledge of the values of k_0 and k_1 other than that k_0 is negative and k_1 is positive. In other words, the receiver requires no prior knowledge of the received signal level in order to achieve the optimum detection of the element binary value.

If the received signal-element is m-level instead of binary, such that s now has any one of m different values, the detection process that minimizes the probability of error is a combination of a linear filter matched to $h(t)$ and a detector that compares the output signal from the matched filter with the appropriate $m - 1$ decision thresholds, to give the detected value of s.

In a practical data-transmission system, the received signal is normally a sequential stream of similarly shaped signal-elements with no time gaps between adjacent elements, so that the start of any one signal element may overlap the end of the preceding element. The signal elements are often, for practical purposes, statistically independent. A matched-filter detector, matched to each individual received signal-element and detecting each element value in a separate process, is now the optimum detector for the received signal, only if the sample value x at the output of the matched filter, corresponding to any individual received element, is unaffected by the neighbouring elements. In other words, the matched-filter detector is only optimum in the absence of intersymbol interference between neighbouring signal elements. In the presence of intersymbol interference, a more sophisticated detection process must be used to minimize the error probability.

13

Rectangular baseband signals

13.1 Binary signals

The simplest digital signals are serial binary baseband signals in which each signal element has a duration of T seconds and has one of two fixed values over this period. The two most common of such signals are shown in Figure 13.1 where k is an appropriate positive constant.

It is assumed that the signal elements are statistically independent and equally likely to have either binary value. Thus each element carries one bit of information. Clearly the signal element rate is $1/T$ elements per second and the information rate is $1/T$ bits per second.

The mean power level of the binary unipolar signal is $\frac{1}{2}(4k^2 + 0^2)$ $= 2k^2$, whereas the power level of the binary polar signal is k^2. However, both signals have the same basic shape for each element, with a difference of $2k$ between the two element values in either case. It is therefore reasonable to assume that each signal has the same tolerance to additive white Gaussian noise, since, for a given basic detection process, an additive noise waveform that produces an error in the detection of a received element in the binary polar signal will always produce an error in the detection of the corresponding element of the binary unipolar signal, and vice versa.

For the same average signal power, the value of k for the binary unipolar signal must clearly be $1/\sqrt{2}$ times that for the binary polar signal. Thus for a given average signal power and a given error rate in the detection of the received signal elements, it is reasonable to assume that the noise power in the case of the binary polar signal is twice that in the case of the binary unipolar signal. In other words, the binary polar signal has an advantage of 3 dB, in tolerance to additive white Gaussian noise, over the binary unipolar signal.

This may be seen alternatively as follows. If a d.c. component of value k is added to the binary polar signal, the binary unipolar signal is obtained. The power level of the d.c. component is k^2. The d.c.

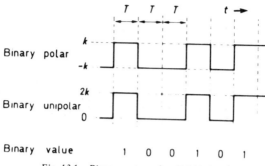

Fig. 13.1   Binary rectangular digital signals

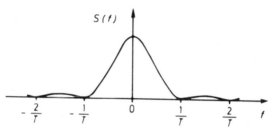

Fig. 13.2   Power-density spectrum of binary polar signal

component, however, carries no useful information, that is, it does not assist in any way in the detection of the values of the received signal elements. Thus the binary unipolar signal is the sum of the binary polar signal and a d.c. component, each of power level k^2, so that only half the power and therefore only half the energy of the unipolar signal is used in the detection process.

The power-density spectrum of the binary polar signal is shown in Figure 13.2. The binary unipolar signal has the same spectrum except that it has in addition a positive impulse at the origin, due to the d.c. component in the signal. Evidently both signals have infinite bandwidth and can only be transmitted satisfactorily (without excessive distortion) over channels whose bandwidth (in positive frequencies) is much wider than $1/T$ Hz and which include zero frequency (d.c.).

Since the least efficient use of bandwidth normally considered acceptable in a serial system is 1 element-per-second per Hz of bandwidth, it is clear that the simple rectangular signals will not often be used in serial systems. They may, however, be used as the modulating waveforms in a parallel system, where the total band-

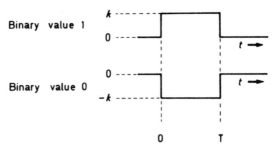

Binary value 1

Binary value 0

Fig. 13.3 *Two possible waveforms of s(t)*

width is large compared with the signal-element rate of any individual signal.

13.2 Detection of a binary polar signal-element

Consider now the detection of an element $s(t)$ of a binary polar signal received in the presence of additive white Gaussian noise $w(t)$. The received waveform is

$$r(t) = s(t) + w(t) \tag{13.1}$$

and the binary value of $s(t)$ is detected from $r(t)$, assuming a prior knowledge of the two possible signal waveforms $s(t)$ but no prior knowledge of the noise waveform $w(t)$.

Suppose that the signal element $s(t)$ is equally likely to have one of the two values

$$s = \pm k \tag{13.2}$$

over the period 0 to T seconds, and has the value zero elsewhere. The signal element $s(t)$ therefore has the two possible waveforms shown in Figure 13.3.

s will for convenience be assumed to be the value of $s(t)$ during the time interval 0 to T seconds. Furthermore, $s = k$ will be taken to represent the binary value 1, and $s = -k$ will be taken to represent the binary value 0.

The Gaussian noise waveform $w(t)$ is a Gaussian random process with zero mean and a two-sided power spectral density of $\frac{1}{2}N_0$. In other words, the Gaussian noise is white, with a power spectral density of $\frac{1}{2}N_0$ over all positive and negative frequencies.

The detection process that minimizes the probability of error, under the assumed conditions, is shown in Figure 13.4. The received waveform $r(t)$ is fed to a linear filter matched to $s(t)$. For any

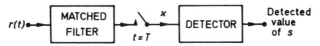

Fig. 13.4   Matched-filter detection of s(t)

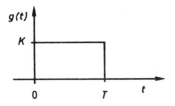

Fig. 13.5   Impulse response of matched filter

waveform $s(t)$, that is non-zero only over the time interval 0 to T seconds, the impulse response of the matched filter is

$$g(t) = cs(T - t) \qquad (13.3)$$

where c is any positive or negative constant. The output signal from the matched filter is sampled at time T seconds and the sample value x is fed to the detector. The detector compares x with the appropriate threshold level (decision threshold) to give the detected value of s and hence the detected binary value of the received signal element.

For the assumed signal waveform $s(t)$, the impulse response of the matched filter is shown in Figure 13.5. It has the positive value K over the time interval 0 to T seconds and the value zero elsewhere. Thus the filter impulse-response is

$$g(t) = cs(T - t) = cs(t) \qquad (13.4)$$

where $c = K/k$ or $-K/k$, depending upon whether $s = k$ or $-k$, respectively. The filter is clearly matched to $s(t)$.

The output signal from the matched filter at time $t = T$ is

$$x = \int_{-\infty}^{\infty} r(t)g(T - t)\, dt = \int_{0}^{T} Kr(t)\, dt$$

$$= K \int_{0}^{T} [s(t) + w(t)]\, dt = KTs + v \qquad (13.5)$$

where

$$v = K \int_{0}^{T} w(t)\, dt \qquad (13.6)$$

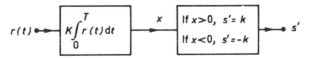

Fig. 13.6   *Matched-filter detection of a binary polar signal*

Thus x is the sum of a signal component KTs and a noise component v.

In practice the matched filter is often implemented as an integrator that multiplies the received signal $r(t)$ by a positive constant K and integrates the resultant signal over the time interval 0 to T seconds, to give the output signal

$$x = KTs + v \qquad (13.7)$$

at the time instant $t = T$.

The signal x is fed to the detector where it is stored and compared with a threshold value of zero, which is half way between the two possible values of KTs. When $x > 0$, s is detected as k, and when $x < 0$, s is detected as $-k$. It can be seen that s is detected as the one of its two possible values for which $|x - KTs|$ is minimum, where $|x - KTs|$ is the magnitude of $x - KTs$. s is therefore detected as its possible value for which KTs is *nearest* to x. The detected value of s is designated s'.

The operation of the matched-filter detector is illustrated in Figure 13.6. It can be seen that the matched filter itself performs a linear operation on the received waveform $r(t)$ to give the output signal x, where x is a *linear* estimate of KTs. The detector performs a decision process on x to give the detected value of s. This is, of course, a *nonlinear* operation.

13.3   Error probability in the detection of a binary polar signal-element

The integrator in Figure 13.6 operates on $r(t)$ as though the integrator were a linear filter with the impulse response $g(t)$ shown in Figure 13.5. Thus, at time $t = T$, the integrator can be considered to be a linear filter with the transfer function

$$G(f) = \int_{-\infty}^{\infty} g(t) \exp(-j2\pi ft) \, dt \qquad (13.8)$$

The two-sided power spectral density of the Gaussian noise

waveform $w(t)$ at the input to the integrator is $\frac{1}{2}N_0$, so that at time $t = T$ at the output of the integrator, the noise power spectral density is

$$\frac{1}{2}N_0|G(f)|^2 \tag{13.9}$$

and the average (or expected) noise power is

$$\frac{1}{2}N_0 \int_{-\infty}^{\infty} |G(f)|^2 \, df = \frac{1}{2}N_0 \int_{-\infty}^{\infty} g^2(t) \, dt$$

$$= \frac{1}{2}N_0 K^2 T \tag{13.10}$$

Since the noise waveform $w(t)$ is a Gaussian random process with zero mean and since the integrator acts as a linear filter with impulse response $g(t)$, it follows that the noise component v in the signal x at the output of the integrator at time $t = T$ (Equation 13.7), is a Gaussian random variable with zero mean and variance

$$N = \frac{1}{2}N_0 K^2 T \tag{13.11}$$

The probability density function of the noise component v in Equation 13.7 is

$$p(v) = \frac{1}{\sqrt{2\pi N}} \exp\left(-\frac{v^2}{2N}\right) \tag{13.12}$$

It can be seen from Equation 13.7 that if $s = -k$, an error occurs in the detection of s when $v > KTk$. Similarly, if $s = k$, an error occurs in the detection of s when $v < -KTk$. Thus, whether $s = -k$ or k, the probability of error in the detection of s is

$$P_e = \int_{KTk}^{\infty} \frac{1}{\sqrt{(2\pi N)}} \exp\left(-\frac{v^2}{2N}\right) dv$$

$$= \int_{KTk/\sqrt{N}}^{\infty} \frac{1}{\sqrt{(2\pi)}} \exp\left(-\frac{1}{2}v^2\right) dv = Q\left(\frac{KTk}{\sqrt{N}}\right) \tag{13.13}$$

It is assumed that the signal element with a duration from 0 to T seconds is one of a sequential stream of elements, each of duration T seconds and with a value $\pm k$ over its duration. The immediately preceding element has a duration from $-T$ to 0 seconds and the immediately following element has a duration from T to $2T$ seconds, and so on. The resultant signal is similar to the binary polar signal in Figure 13.1. The signal elements are statistically independent and equally likely to have either binary value. Each element therefore carries one bit of information.

Since $s(t) = \pm k$, for $0 < t < T$, the average energy per signal element is

$$E = \int_0^T s^2(t)\, dt = k^2 T \qquad (13.14)$$

and the average energy per bit of information is

$$E_b = k^2 T \qquad (13.15)$$

since, of course, $E_b = E$. From Equations 13.11 and 13.13, the probability of error in the detection of s is

$$P_e = Q\left\{\sqrt{\left(\frac{2k^2 T}{N_0}\right)}\right\} = Q\left\{\sqrt{\left(\frac{2E}{N_0}\right)}\right\} = Q\left\{\sqrt{\left(\frac{2E_b}{N_0}\right)}\right\} \qquad (13.16)$$

13.4   Detection of a binary unipolar signal element

Consider now the detection of an element $s(t)$ of a binary unipolar signal received in the presence of additive white Gaussian noise $w(t)$. As before, the received waveform is

$$r(t) = s(t) + w(t) \qquad (13.17)$$

and the binary value of $s(t)$ is detected from $r(t)$, assuming a prior knowledge of the two possible signal waveforms $s(t)$ but no prior knowledge of the noise waveform $w(t)$.

Suppose that the signal element $s(t)$ is equally likely to have one of the two values

$$s = 0 \quad \text{or} \quad 2k \qquad (13.18)$$

over the period 0 to T seconds, and has the value zero elsewhere. The signal element $s(t)$ therefore has the two possible waveforms shown in Figure 13.7.

As before, the Gaussian noise waveform $w(t)$ is a Gaussian random process with zero mean and a two-sided power spectral density of $\frac{1}{2}N_0$.

The detection process that minimizes the probability of error in the detection of s from $r(t)$ is as shown in Figure 13.6, but now the decision threshold with which x is compared in the detector is not zero but KTk.

From Equation 13.7, the sample value fed to the detector at time $t = T$ is

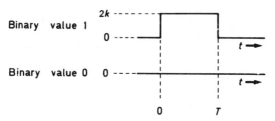

Binary value 1

Binary value 0

Fig. 13.7   Two possible waveforms of $s(t)$

$$x = KTs + v \tag{13.19}$$

where v is a Gaussian random variable with zero mean and variance N (Equation 13.11).

Clearly, the decision threshold, used in the detection of s from x, lies half way between the two possible values of KTs and at a distance of KTk from each of the two values, just as for the binary polar signal. Thus s is detected as its possible value for which $|x - KTs|$ is the smaller and therefore as its value for which KTs is nearer to x.

An error occurs in the detection of s when v has a magnitude greater than KTk and a sign such as to carry x nearer to the incorrect value of KTs. Thus, if $s = 0$, an error occurs when $v > KTk$, and if $s = 2k$, an error occurs when $v < -KTk$. Clearly, whether $s = 0$ or $2k$, the probability of error in the detection of s is

$$P_e = \int_{KTk}^{\infty} \frac{1}{\sqrt{(2\pi N)}} \exp\left(-\frac{v^2}{2N}\right) dv$$

$$= Q\left(\frac{KTk}{\sqrt{N}}\right) \tag{13.20}$$

which, for a given value of k, is the same as that for the binary polar signal, as given by P_e in Equation 13.13.

Again, the signal element with a duration from 0 to T seconds is assumed to be one of a sequential stream of such elements, as in Figure 13.1, the signal elements being statistically independent and equally likely to have either binary value. Each signal element carries one bit of information. Thus the average energy per signal element is

$$E = \tfrac{1}{2}(0 + 4k^2 T) = 2k^2 T \tag{13.21}$$

and the average energy per bit of information is

$$E_b = 2k^2 T \tag{13.22}$$

since, of course, $E_b = E$.

From Equations 13.11 and 13.20, the probability of error in the detection of s is

$$P_e = Q\left\{\sqrt{\left(\frac{2k^2T}{N_0}\right)}\right\} = Q\left\{\sqrt{\left(\frac{E}{N_0}\right)}\right\} = Q\left\{\sqrt{\left(\frac{E_b}{N_0}\right)}\right\} \quad (13.23)$$

If two signals have the same average power level and the same element rate, they also have the same average signal energy per element. Similarly, if the two signals have the same average power level and the same information rate, they also have the same average signal energy per bit. The most useful comparison of the tolerances of two signals to additive white Gaussian noise, is to adjust both signals to the same average signal energy per bit, and then to adjust the noise level so that each signal has the same error probability and therefore the same average error rate. The relative noise levels now give the relative tolerances of the two signals to the additive white Gaussian noise, when the signals are transmitted at the same average power level and the same information rate.

Comparing Equations 13.16 and 13.23, it can be seen that, for a given error probability and a given average signal energy per bit, the noise power spectral density in the case of the binary polar signal is twice that for the binary unipolar signal, so that the binary polar signal has an advantage of 3 dB, in tolerance to additive white Gaussian noise, over the binary unipolar signal.

13.5   Quaternary polar signals

An element $s(t)$ of a quaternary polar signal, corresponding to the binary polar signal previously considered, has one of the four values $-3k$, $-k$, k and $3k$, over the period 0 to T seconds, and has the value zero elsewhere. Suppose that it is equally likely to have any one of the four values, and is received in the presence of the noise waveform $w(t)$, which is additive white Gaussian noise with zero mean and a two-sided power spectral density of $\frac{1}{2}N_0$. The received waveform is

$$r(t) = s(t) + w(t) \quad (13.24)$$

and the quaternary value of $s(t)$ is detected from $r(t)$, assuming a prior knowledge of the four possible signal waveforms for $s(t)$ but no prior knowledge of the noise waveform $w(t)$.

The detection process that minimizes the probability of error, under the assumed conditions, is shown in Figure 13.8.

From Equation 13.7, the output signal from the integrator, at time $t = T$, is

$$x = KTs + v \quad (13.25)$$

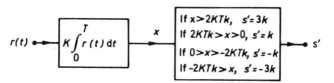

Fig. 13.8 Matched-filter detection of a quaternary polar signal

where v is a Gaussian random variable with zero mean and variance

$$N = \tfrac{1}{2}N_0K^2T \qquad (13.26)$$

The signal x is fed to the detector where it is stored and compared with the three threshold values $-2KTk$, 0 and $2KTk$. It can be seen that these are placed half way between adjacent possible values of KTs, each being at a distance of KTk from the two nearest values of KTs. If $x > 2KTk$, s is detected as $3k$; if $2KTk > x > 0$, s is detected as k; if $0 > x > -2KTk$, s is detected as $-k$; and if $-2KTk > x$, s is detected as $-3k$. Thus s is detected as the one of its four possible values for which $|x - KTs|$ is minimum and therefore as the value for which KTs is nearest to x.

When $s = \pm 3k$, an error occurs in the detection of s when the magnitude of the noise component v exceeds KTk and has a sign opposite to that of s. Thus the probability of error in the detection of s is

$$\int_{KTk}^{\infty} \frac{1}{\sqrt{(2\pi N)}} \exp\left(-\frac{v^2}{2N}\right) dv = Q\left(\frac{KTk}{\sqrt{N}}\right) \qquad (13.27)$$

When $s = \pm k$, an error occurs in the detection of s when the magnitude of the noise component v exceeds KTk, whether v is positive or negative. Thus the probability of error in the detection of s is now

$$\int_{-\infty}^{-KTk} \frac{1}{\sqrt{(2\pi N)}} \exp\left(-\frac{v^2}{2N}\right) dv + \int_{KTk}^{\infty} \frac{1}{\sqrt{(2\pi N)}} \exp\left(-\frac{v^2}{2N}\right) dv$$

$$= 2 \int_{KTk}^{\infty} \frac{1}{\sqrt{(2\pi N)}} \exp\left(-\frac{v^2}{2N}\right) dv = 2Q\left(\frac{KTk}{\sqrt{N}}\right) \qquad (13.28)$$

Since s is equally likely to have any one of the four possible values, it follows that the average probability of error is

$$P = 1.5Q\left(\frac{KTk}{\sqrt{N}}\right) \qquad (13.29)$$

At high signal/noise ratios, such that the probability of error is around 1 in 10^5 or 1 in 10^6, a change of ten times in the probability of error corresponds to a change of only about 1 dB in the signal/noise ratio. Thus no significant inaccuracy is introduced by taking the average probability of error as

$$P_e = Q\left(\frac{KTk}{\sqrt{N}}\right) \qquad (13.30)$$

As before, the signal element with a duration from 0 to T seconds is assumed to be one of a sequential stream of such elements, the signal elements being statistically independent and equally likely to have any of the possible element values. Each element of the quaternary signal carries two bits of information so that its information content is equal to that of two binary elements. Thus, for a given signal element rate, the quaternary signal has twice the information rate of the corresponding binary signal. If both signals now have the same average power level, they have the same average energy per signal element. Clearly, if the tolerances of the two signals to additive white Gaussian noise are compared for a given average energy per signal element, then at a given element rate the two signals have the same average power level, but the quaternary signal has twice the information rate of the binary signal, so that the two signals are not being compared under equivalent conditions.

In order to compare the tolerance to noise of a quaternary signal with that of a binary signal, these must be considered at the same information rate and at the same average power level. For a given information rate, the signal element rate of a quaternary signal is half that of the corresponding binary signal. If now both signals have the same average power level, the average energy per element of the quaternary signal is twice that of the binary signal, whereas the average energy per bit is the same for the two signals. Clearly, if the tolerances of the two signals to additive white Gaussian noise are compared for a given average energy per bit, then the two signals are being compared both at the same information rate and at the same average power level. This gives the most useful comparison of the two signals.

Since the energy of an individual quaternary polar signal-element is $s^2 T$, where $s = -3k, -k, k$ or $3k$, the average energy per element of the received sequential stream of quaternary elements is

$$E = \tfrac{1}{4}(9k^2 + k^2 + k^2 + 9k^2)T = 5k^2 T \qquad (13.31)$$

and the average energy per bit is

$$E_b = \tfrac{1}{2}E = \tfrac{5}{2}k^2 T \tag{13.32}$$

Thus, from Equations 13.26 and 13.30, the probability of error in the detection of s, at high signal/noise ratios, can be taken to be

$$P_e = Q\left\{ \sqrt{\left(\frac{2k^2 T}{N_0}\right)} \right\} = Q\left\{ \sqrt{\left(\frac{2E}{5N_0}\right)} \right\} = Q\left\{ \sqrt{\left(\frac{4E_b}{5N_0}\right)} \right\} \tag{13.33}$$

Comparing Equations 13.16 and 13.33, it can be seen that for a given element error probability and a given average signal energy per bit, the noise power spectral density in the case of the binary polar signal is 4 dB above that for the quaternary polar signal, so that the binary polar signal has an advantage of 4 dB in tolerance to additive white Gaussian noise over the quaternary polar signal.

13.6 Quaternary unipolar signals

An element $s(t)$ of a quaternary unipolar signal, corresponding to the quaternary polar signal considered in Section 13.5, has one of the four values 0, $2k$, $4k$ and $6k$ over the period 0 to T seconds, and has the value zero elsewhere.

With the received signal $r(t)$ otherwise as assumed in Section 13.5, the optimum detection process for an individual received signal-element is as shown in Figure 13.8, except that the decision thresholds are now set at KTk, $3KTk$ and $5KTk$.

The output signal x from the integrator is given by Equation 13.25, where now $s = 0$, $2k$, $4k$ or $6k$. In the detector, s is detected as its possible value for which KTs is nearest to x, as before.

The average probability of error in the detection of s is given by Equation 13.29, so that, at high signal/noise ratios, the average probability of error can be taken to be

$$P_e = Q\left(\frac{KTk}{\sqrt{N}}\right) \tag{13.34}$$

The average energy per element of the received sequential stream of quaternary unipolar signal-elements is

$$E = \tfrac{1}{4}(0^2 + 4k^2 + 16k^2 + 36k^2)T = 14k^2 T \tag{13.35}$$

and the average energy per bit is

$$E_b = \tfrac{1}{2}E = 7k^2 T \tag{13.36}$$

From Equations 13.26 and 13.34, the average probability of error in the detection of s, at high signal/noise ratios, can be taken to be

$$P_e = Q\left\{\sqrt{\left(\frac{2k^2T}{N_0}\right)}\right\} = Q\left\{\sqrt{\left(\frac{E}{7N_0}\right)}\right\} = Q\left\{\sqrt{\left(\frac{2E_b}{7N_0}\right)}\right\} \quad (13.37)$$

Comparing Equations 13.16 and 13.37, it can be seen that, at a given average signal energy per bit, the binary polar signal has an advantage of 8.5 dB in tolerance to additive white Gaussian noise over the quaternary unipolar signal.

13.7   The Gray code

When the original data to be transmitted is stored in binary form and a transmitted signal-element is quaternary coded, the relationship between the binary and quaternary signals must be such that the most likely errors in the detection of a quaternary signal-element correspond to only one error in the two binary elements derived from that element. With additive Gaussian noise, by far the most likely error in the detection of a quaternary element is that which involves the crossing of the *nearest* decision threshold. Thus the two binary pairs which correspond to any two adjacent quaternary element values, must differ in only *one* of the two binary values. This coding system for the binary signal is known as the Gray code. When the Gray code is used and the signal/noise ratio is high, the element error probability in the binary signal is approximately half that of the quaternary signal from which it is derived. The halving of the error probability is partly offset by the increase of 1.5 times in the error probability of the quaternary signal, which results from the fact that there are two decision boundaries associated with each of the two central element values of this signal. The latter increase in error probability has been neglected in Equations 13.30 and 13.34. Clearly, the element error probability of the binary signal is approximately three-quarters of that given by Equations 13.30 and 13.34, and represents a negligibly small increase in tolerance to noise.

13.8   Comparison of signals

It will be useful now to summarise some of the more important results obtained in this chapter.

The four different baseband signals can be compared on the basis of their relative tolerances to additive white Gaussian noise, at high signal/noise ratios, by assuming that the different signals have the

Table 13.1 RELATIVE TOLERANCES TO ADDITIVE WHITE GAUSSIAN NOISE, EXPRESSED IN dB, FOR A GIVEN AVERAGE SIGNAL POWER LEVEL

Baseband signal	Given element rate	Given information rate
Binary polar	0	0
Binary unipolar	−3	−3
Quaternary polar	−7	−4
Quaternary unipolar	−11.5	−8.5

same average power level and the same error probability in the detection process.

If the different signals have the same *element rate*, then they must also have the same average energy per element, E. Under these conditions all signals have the same bandwidth but the quaternary signals have twice the information rate of the binary signals. The relative tolerances to noise of these signals are determined by equating the given error probability to the appropriate Q-functions of E and N_0, and setting E to the given average element energy. The relative values of the noise power spectral density N_0 now give the relative tolerances to the Gaussian noise.

If the different signals have the same average power level, the same error probability and the same *information rate*, they must also have the same average energy per bit, E_b. Under these conditions the quaternary signals have half the element rate of the binary signals and therefore occupy half the bandwidth. The relative tolerances to noise of these signals are determined by equating the given error probability to the appropriate Q-functions of E_b and N_0, and setting E_b to the given average energy per bit. The relative values of the noise power spectral density again give the relative tolerances to the Gaussian noise.

The relative tolerances of the four baseband signals to additive white Gaussian noise are shown in Table 13.1, both for a given element rate, that is, for a given average element energy E, and for a given information rate, that is, for a given average energy per bit E_b. The tolerances to noise are expressed in dB relative to that of the binary polar signal. It is clear from this comparison that the quaternary signals would only be used in place of the binary signals if the required information rate could not be achieved with the binary signals over the available bandwidth.

14

Rounded baseband signals

14.1 Introduction

The system to be studied here is a synchronous serial baseband data-transmission system in which a sequential stream of baseband digital signal-elements is fed over a transmission path and the spectrum of the transmitted signal occupies the whole of that portion of the bandwidth of the transmission path over which there are no significant attenuation and delay distortions. In the design of a serial system it is normally required to achieve the highest available signal element rate over the given transmission path. It is not usually possible to change the response or characteristics of the transmission path itself.

Rectangular signal elements of the type studied in Chapter 13 are not suitable for the application considered here, because they require relatively wide bandwidths for distortionless transmission. It is not efficient to transmit rectangular signals over a transmission path that significantly reduces the bandwidth of these signals and therefore causes appreciable rounding of the waveforms, since a portion of the signal energy is now lost in transmission and so cannot contribute to the detection of the received signal-elements. Because there is normally an upper limit to the average signal power that may be fed to any practical transmission path, it is important to minimize the signal power lost in transmission. This maximizes the signal/noise power ratio at the receiver input. Clearly, a rectangular signal waveform at the transmitter must first be filtered through a suitable low-pass filter, before feeding the signal to the transmission path.

The transmission path may distort the transmitted signal and may also introduce noise. In this discussion it is assumed that the signal fed to the transmission path has been sufficiently bandlimited (restricted in bandwidth) so that it experiences no further bandlimiting in transmission. Furthermore, the transmission path is taken to introduce no attenuation (that is, no change in signal level), no delay, no

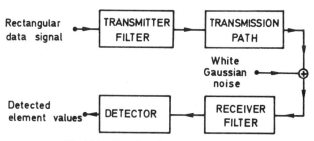

Fig. 14.1   Complete data-transmission system

amplitude distortion, and no phase distortion, over the signal frequency band, so that the signal experiences no attenuation, delay or distortion in transmission. Thus the signal reaches the receiver with exactly the same waveform as that transmitted. It is assumed that the transmission path introduces no multiplicative noise, that is, no amplitude or frequency modulation effects. It introduces only white Gaussian noise with zero mean and a two-sided power spectral density of $\frac{1}{2}N_0$, which is for convenience considered to be added to the data signal at the output of the transmission path.

The resultant signal-plus-noise waveform at the receiver input is first filtered through a suitable low-pass filter. This removes the noise frequencies outside the signal band. The filtered waveform is then fed to the detector, which detects the received signal element values from this waveform.

The model of the complete data-transmission system is shown in Figure 14.1, where the transfer functions of the transmitter and receiver filters are taken to be $C(f)$ and $B(f)$, respectively.

A rectangular data signal of the type shown in Figure 13.1 can be represented as

$$\sum_i s_i d(t - iT) \tag{14.1}$$

where the integer i takes on all positive and negative values, and

$$d(t) = \begin{cases} 1, & \text{for } 0 < t < T \\ 0, & \text{elsewhere} \end{cases} \tag{14.2}$$

as shown in Figure 14.2.

In the general case, where s_i is the value of an m-level signal element, s_i has m possible values given by $k_0 + 2lk$, for $l = 0, 1, \ldots, m - 1$. When $k_0 = 0$, the signal is an m-level unipolar signal, and when $k_0 = -(m - 1)k$, the signal is an m-level polar signal. Adjacent values of s_i differ always by $2k$. It can be seen that for $m = 2$ and $m = 4$, the

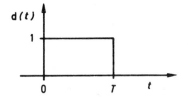

Fig. 14.2   Unit rectangular pulse d(t)

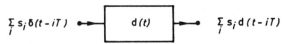

Fig. 14.3   Generation of a rectangular waveform from a sequence of impulses

possible values of s_i correspond to the possible values of s, assumed in Chapter 13 for binary and quaternary signal-elements, respectively.

It follows from Equation 14.1 that a rectangular digital signal may (in principle) be generated by feeding a sequence of impulses, with the appropriate values (areas) and regularly spaced at intervals of T seconds, through a linear filter with impulse response $d(t)$, as shown in Figure 14.3. $\delta(t)$ is here a unit impulse at time $t = 0$.

Let $D(f)$ be the transfer function of the linear filter with impulse response $d(t)$. Then

$$D(f) = \int_{-\infty}^{\infty} d(t) \exp(-j2\pi ft)\, dt = \int_{0}^{T} \exp(-j2\pi ft)\, dt$$

$$= \left[\frac{\exp(-j2\pi ft)}{-j2\pi f}\right]_{0}^{T} = \frac{1 - \exp(-j2\pi fT)}{j2\pi f}$$

$$= T \exp(-j\pi fT)\left(\frac{\exp(j\pi fT) - \exp(-j\pi fT)}{2j\pi fT}\right)$$

$$= T \exp(-j\pi fT)\frac{\sin \pi fT}{\pi fT} \tag{14.3}$$

The modulus of the transfer function $D(f)$ is shown in Figure 14.4.

Clearly, the rectangular data signal may be replaced by the corresponding sequence of impulses feeding a filter of transfer function $D(f)$, so that the transmitter filter is now the original transmitter filter with transfer function $C(f)$ in cascade with the filter of transfer function $D(f)$. The two filters may of course be replaced by a single filter with transfer function

$$A(f) = C(f)D(f) \tag{14.4}$$

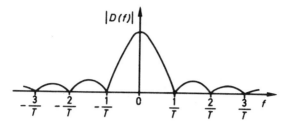

Fig. 14.4   *Frequency response of the filter with impulse response* d(t)

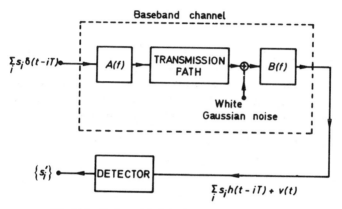

Fig. 14.5   *Basic model of the data-transmission system*

Thus the model of the data-transmission system in Figure 14.1 may be replaced by that in Figure 14.5.

In practice, of course, a rectangular waveform would nearly always be used in preference to a sequence of impulses, at the input to the transmitter filter. However, the theoretical analysis of the system is greatly simplified by using the arrangement of Figure 14.5, and this will be taken as the basic model of the data-transmission system throughout the following discussions. The corresponding system with a rectangular waveform at the transmitter may readily be obtained from Figure 14.5 by noting that

$$C(f) = A(f)D^{-1}(f) \tag{14.5}$$

Since the spectrum of the rectangular signal-waveform is zero at each frequency i/T Hz, where i takes on all positive and negative integer values, $D^{-1}(i/T)$ may be assumed to have any convenient value in Equation 14.5.

14.2 Optimum design of transmitter and receiver filters

It is required to determine the transfer functions $A(f)$ and $B(f)$ of the transmitter and receiver filters, that maximize the signal/noise power ratio at the input to the detector in Figure 14.5.

An m-level signal is assumed, the transmitted signal-elements being statistically independent and equally likely to have any of the m element values. In the regular sequence of impulses carrying the element values $\{s_i\}$, at the input to the baseband channel, $s_i = k_0 + 2lk$ for $l = 0, 1, \ldots, m - 1$, where $k_0 = -(m - 1)k$, so that *polar* signals are assumed throughout the following discussion.

Since a limit is always set on the signal power fed to any practical transmission path, a measure of the transmitted signal level must be obtained. A single transmitted signal-element at the input to the transmission path has the waveform

$$s_i a(t - iT)$$

where $a(t)$ is the impulse response of the transmitter filter. The Fourier transform (frequency spectrum) of the signal element is

$$s_i \exp(-j2\pi f iT)A(f)$$

Thus the energy spectral density of an individual transmitted signal-element, at the input to the transmission path, is

$$|s_i \exp(-j2\pi f iT)A(f)|^2 = s_i^2 |A(f)|^2 \tag{14.6}$$

and its energy is

$$E_i = s_i^2 \int_{-\infty}^{\infty} |A(f)|^2 \, df \tag{14.7}$$

Since the signal elements are statistically independent and have zero means, making them statistically *orthogonal*, the average transmitted energy per signal element, at the input to the transmission path, is the average of expected value of E_i and so is

$$E = \overline{s_i^2} \int_{-\infty}^{\infty} |A(f)|^2 \, df \tag{14.8}$$

where $\overline{s_i^2}$ is the mean-square value of s_i. It is shown elsewhere that for the unipolar signals to be studied here, the waveforms $\{s_i a(t - iT)\}$ of any two transmitted signal-elements are mutually *orthogonal*, which means that the energy of any sequence of signal-elements is the sum of the energies of the individual signal-elements, regardless of the element values[422]. It follows that, in the finally optimized system, Equation 14.8 holds also for the unipolar signals to be studied here. Clearly, at a given element rate, E is a measure of the transmitted signal power level.

The transmitter filter, transmission path and receiver filter, in Figure 14.5, together form a baseband channel with transfer function

$$H(f) = A(f)B(f) \tag{14.9}$$

bearing in mind that the transmission path introduces no attenuation, delay or distortion.

It will, for convenience, be assumed that the gain or attenuation introduced by the transmitter and receiver filters over all frequencies is appropriately adjusted so that

$$\int_{-\infty}^{\infty} |H(f)| \, df = 1 \tag{14.10}$$

This does not in fact restrict the possible combinations of transmitter and receiver filters, other than by adjusting the response of one of these by a constant multiplier. The transmitted signal level may be adjusted as required by changing the value of k.

The impulse response of the baseband channel is

$$h(t) = \int_{-\infty}^{\infty} H(f) \exp(j2\pi ft) \, df \tag{14.11}$$

so that a single received signal-element at the detector input has the waveform

$$s_i h(t - iT)$$

with the Fourier transform

$$s_i \exp(-j2\pi fiT) H(f)$$

Thus the energy spectral density of an individual received signal-element, at the detector input, is

$$|s_i \exp(-j2\pi fiT) H(f)|^2 = s_i^2 |H(f)|^2 \tag{14.12}$$

and its energy is

$$F_i = s_i^2 \int_{-\infty}^{\infty} |H(f)|^2 \, df \tag{14.13}$$

Clearly, the average energy per element of the signal at the detector input is the average or expected value of F_i and is

$$F = \overline{s_i^2} \int_{-\infty}^{\infty} |H(f)|^2 \, df \qquad (14.14)$$

The signal waveform at the input to the detector (in the absence of noise) is

$$\sum_i s_i h(t - iT)$$

so that the resultant waveform at the detector input is

$$r(t) = \sum_i s_i h(t - iT) + v(t) \qquad (14.15)$$

where $v(t)$ is the noise waveform.

Since the noise input to the receiver filter is white Gaussian noise with zero mean and a two-sided power spectral density of $\frac{1}{2}N_0$, $v(t)$ is a Gaussian random process with zero mean and a power spectral density

$$\frac{1}{2}N_0 |B(f)|^2$$

where, of course, $B(f)$ is the transfer function of the receiver filter[425]. Thus, the average power or mean-square value of the noise waveform $v(t)$ is

$$N = \frac{1}{2}N_0 \int_{-\infty}^{\infty} |B(f)|^2 \, df \qquad (14.16)$$

The signal/noise power ratio at the detector input, expressed as the average energy per element of the signal divided by the average noise power, is

$$\frac{F}{N} = \frac{\overline{s_i^2} \displaystyle\int_{-\infty}^{\infty} |H(f)|^2 \, df}{\frac{1}{2}N_0 \displaystyle\int_{-\infty}^{\infty} |B(f)|^2 \, df} \qquad (14.17)$$

Consider now any given transfer-function $H(f)$ of the baseband channel, where $H(f)$ satisfies Equations 14.9 and 14.10. From

Equation 14.8,

$$\overline{s_i^2} = \frac{E}{\int\limits_{-\infty}^{\infty} |A(f)|^2 \, df} \tag{14.18}$$

so that, from Equation 14.17,

$$\frac{F}{N} = \frac{E}{\frac{1}{2}N_0} \frac{\int\limits_{-\infty}^{\infty} |H(f)|^2 \, df}{\int\limits_{-\infty}^{\infty} |A(f)|^2 \, df \int\limits_{-\infty}^{\infty} |B(f)|^2 \, df} \tag{14.19}$$

Replacing $U(f)$ and $V(f)$ in Equation 12.13 by $|A(f)|$ and $|B(f)|$, respectively, gives

$$\int\limits_{-\infty}^{\infty} |A(f)|^2 \, df \int\limits_{-\infty}^{\infty} |B(f)|^2 \, df \geqslant \left(\int\limits_{-\infty}^{\infty} |A(f)||B(f)| \, df \right)^2 \tag{14.20}$$

with equality when

$$|B(f)| = b|A(f)| \tag{14.21}$$

where b is any positive real constant. But, from Equation 14.9,

$$|H(f)| = |A(f)||B(f)| \tag{14.22}$$

so that, from Equation 14.10,

$$\int\limits_{-\infty}^{\infty} |A(f)||B(f)| \, df = 1 \tag{14.23}$$

and, from Equation 14.20

$$\int\limits_{-\infty}^{\infty} |A(f)|^2 \, df \int\limits_{-\infty}^{\infty} |B(f)|^2 \, df \geqslant 1 \tag{14.24}$$

It now follows from Equation 14.19 that

$$\frac{F}{N} \leqslant \frac{E}{\frac{1}{2}N_0} \int\limits_{-\infty}^{\infty} |H(f)|^2 \, df \tag{14.25}$$

with equality when Equation 14.21 holds. Equation 14.21 therefore gives the condition that must be satisfied by the transmitter and receiver filters, in order to maximize the signal/noise power ratio at the detector input. The signal/noise power ratio is here defined as the ratio of the average energy per signal element to the average noise power. This is, of course, not the same as the definition of signal/noise ratio used for the matched filter in Chapter 12, which is the ratio of the *instantaneous* signal power, at the time instant $t = T$, to the average noise power.

Equation 14.21 means that for the maximum signal/noise power ratio at the detector input, the amplitude response $|B(f)|$ of the receiver filter must be in a constant ratio b to the amplitude response $|A(f)|$ of the transmitter filter, over all values of the frequency f. Since $|A(f)|$ and $|B(f)|$ are the moduli of $A(f)$ and $B(f)$, respectively, their values are always positive. $A(f)$ and $B(f)$ are, however, often complex, so that their values at any frequency can be represented by the appropriate vectors in the complex number plane, where the angles made by these vectors with the real number axis give the corresponding phase angles. The values of $|A(f)|$ and $|B(f)|$ are clearly independent of the respective phase angles. Each filter may therefore introduce any degree of phase distortion and therefore any degree of group delay distortion, so long as Equations 14.9 and 14.21 are satisfied, without affecting the signal/noise ratio at the detector input.

The linear filter matched to any given signal-element, $s_0 a(t)$, where s_0 carries the element value and where $a(t)$ is nonzero only over the time interval 0 to T seconds, has an impulse response

$$g(t) = ca(T - t) \tag{14.26}$$

where c is any positive or negative real constant. The transfer function of the linear filter is

$$G(f) = c \exp(-j2\pi fT)A^*(f) \tag{14.27}$$

where $A(f)$ is the Fourier transform of $a(t)$ and $A^*(f)$ is the complex conjugate of $A(f)$. $a(t)$ is here taken to be the impulse response of the transmitter filter in Figure 14.5, so that $s_0 a(t)$ is the received signal waveform at the input to the receiver filter, corresponding to an individual signal-element received in the absence of noise. When the signal element $s_0 a(t)$ is received in the presence of additive white Gaussian noise, the matched filter maximizes the output signal/noise power ratio at the time instant $t = T$, as shown in Chapter 12. The received element value is detected by sampling the output signal from the matched filter at time $t = T$ seconds, and comparing the sample value with the appropriate threshold levels.

The term $\exp(-j2\pi fT)$ in Equation 14.27 is the Fourier transform of a delay of T seconds. This delay can be neglected without affecting the significant points in the present discussion. Thus the transfer function of the matched filter can be taken to be

$$G(f) = cA^*(f) \tag{14.28}$$

and the received element value is detected here by sampling the output signal from the matched filter at the time instant $t = 0$. This is a non-physical system in the sense that it cannot be implemented as such in practice. The implications of this are considered further in Section 14.4. The important point is, of course, that the system can always be made physically realisable again by re-introducing the appropriate delay of T seconds.

From Equation 14.28,

$$|G(f)| = b|A(f)| \tag{14.29}$$

where $b = |c|$. If the matched filter is now used for the receiver filter in Figure 14.5, $B(f) = G(f)$ so that Equation 14.21 is satisfied and the signal/noise power ratio at the output of the filter is maximized. Under these conditions,

$$B(f) = cA^*(f) \tag{14.30}$$

and

$$H(f) = cA(f)A^*(f) \tag{14.31}$$

so that $H(f)$ is real and even (symmetrical about zero frequency), and the impulse response $h(t)$ of the baseband channel is symmetrical about its central point. It can be seen from Equation 14.9 that if $H(f)$ is real and even, and if the receiver filter is matched to the received signal and so satisfies Equation 14.30, then the receiver filter also satisfies Equation 14.21 and so maximizes the signal/noise power ratio at the detector input. However, Equation 14.21 can be satisfied for *any* value of $H(f)$, which means that $H(f)$ need not be real or even. When Equation 14.21 is satisfied and $H(f)$ is not real or even, Equation 14.30 cannot be satisfied, so that the receiver filter cannot now be matched to the received signal.

It is clear from the preceding discussion that when $A(f)$ and $B(f)$ satisfy Equation 14.21, $B(f)$ is not necessarily the complex conjugate of $A(f)$ (or at least proportional to it), so that the receiver filter is not necessarily matched to the received signal. However, when it is matched, Equation 14.21 is necessarily satisfied, so that the matched filter is a particular case for which Equation 14.21 is satisfied.

An important case for which Equation 14.21 is satisfied is that where

$$B(f) = cA(f) \tag{14.32}$$

where c is any positive or negative real constant and $A(f)B(f) = H(f)$. The arrangement satisfying Equation 14.32 is more general than the case where $B(f) = cA^*(f)$, since Equation 14.32 can be satisfied for *any* value of $H(f)$. Furthermore, in the frequently occurring case where $H(f)$ is real, non-negative and even, and Equation 14.32 is satisfied, both $A(f)$ and $B(f)$ are real, non-negative and even, and $B(f) = cA^*(f)$ with c positive, so that the receiver filter is now matched to the received signal. Thus the condition given by Equation 14.32 ensures that the receiver filter is matched to the received signal, whenever $H(f)$ is real, non-negative and even.

14.3   Model of the data-transmission system

Since the constant b in Equation 14.21 may be taken to have any positive real value without affecting the signal/noise power ratio at the detector input and indeed without affecting any other important parameter in the data-transmission system of Figure 14.5, it is convenient to set $b = 1$. Under these conditions, the signal/noise power ratio at the detector input is maximum when

$$|B(f)| = |A(f)| \tag{14.33}$$

It will in fact be assumed that

$$B(f) = \pm A(f) \tag{14.34}$$

which are the simplest and most important combinations of transmitter and receiver filters that satisfy Equation 14.33. As before, $A(f)B(f) = H(f)$. Under these conditions,

$$\int_{-\infty}^{\infty} |A(f)|^2 \, df = \int_{-\infty}^{\infty} |B(f)|^2 \, df = \int_{-\infty}^{\infty} |H(f)| \, df = 1 \tag{14.35}$$

as can readily be seen from Equation 14.10.

Furthermore, the signal/noise power ratio at the input to the detector (Figure 14.5) is now

$$\frac{F}{N} = \frac{E}{\frac{1}{2}N_0} \int_{-\infty}^{\infty} |H(f)|^2 \, df \tag{14.36}$$

as can be seen from Equation 14.25. From Equations 14.8 and 14.35, the average transmitted energy per signal element, at the input to the transmission path, is

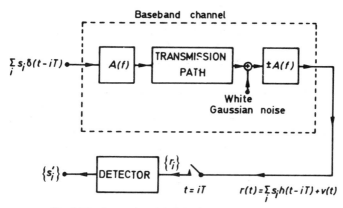

Fig. 14.6 *Assumed model of the data-transmission system*

$$E = \overline{s_i^2} \tag{14.37}$$

bearing in mind that the $\{s_i\}$ are statistically independent and have zero mean, making them statistically orthogonal. From Equations 14.16 and 14.35, the Gaussian random process $v(t)$ at the output of the baseband channel has, at any time, zero mean and variance

$$N = \tfrac{1}{2}N_0 \tag{14.38}$$

Whatever the shape (variation with frequency) of the channel transfer function $H(f)$, this is always normalised (adjusted by the appropriate real multiplier) so that Equation 14.35 is satisfied, and this ensures that both Equations 14.37 and 14.38 are satisfied.

The data-transmission system is now as shown in Figure 14.6, which is a particular arrangement of Figure 14.5, with $B(f) = \pm A(f)$. Clearly, $\pm A^2(f) = H(f)$. A further change in Figure 14.6 is that a sampler is included at the input to the detector. This samples the received waveform $r(t)$ at the time instants $\{iT\}$, for all integer values of i, and feeds the resulting sample values $\{r(iT)\}$ to the detector.

The regular sequence of impulses, at the input to the baseband channel is as previously assumed, the transmitted m-level signal elements being statistically independent and equally likely to have any of the m element values. Both *polar* and *unipolar* signals will, however, now be studied.

The average energy per signal element at the input to the transmission path is $\overline{s_i^2}$, for both polar and unipolar signals s_i. The transmission path introduces no signal distortion, attenuation or delay. White Gaussian noise with zero mean and a two-sided power spectral density of $\tfrac{1}{2}N_0$ is added to the data signal at the output of the

Table 14.1   VALUES OF s_i, E AND E_b FOR THE DIFFERENT SIGNALS

Signal	s_i	E	E_b
Binary polar	$-k$ or k	k^2	k^2
Binary unipolar	0 or $2k$	$2k^2$	$2k^2$
Quaternary polar	$-3k$, $-k$, k or $3k$	$5k^2$	$\frac{5}{2}k^2$
Quaternary unipolar	0, $2k$, $4k$ or $6k$	$14k^2$	$7k^2$

transmission path. The baseband channel has a transfer function $H(f)$ and an impulse response $h(t)$. The noise waveform $v(t)$ at the output of the baseband channel is a Gaussian random process with zero mean and variance $\frac{1}{2}N_0$. Thus the received waveform at the output of the baseband channel is

$$r(t) = \sum_i s_i h(t - iT) + v(t) \tag{14.39}$$

$r(t)$ is sampled once per signal element, and the detector operates *entirely* on the sample values $\{r(iT)\}$ to give the detected element values $\{s_i'\}$. Clearly, the noise component in any sample $r(iT)$ at the detector input, is a Gaussian random variable with zero mean and variance $\frac{1}{2}N_0$. The presence of the noise components in the $\{r(iT)\}$ will, of course, result in occasional errors in the $\{s_i'\}$.

As in Chapter 13, particular emphasis will be given to the following four transmitted signals: binary polar, binary unipolar, quaternary polar and quaternary unipolar. Table 14.1 shows, for each of these signals, the possible values of s_i, the average transmitted energy per signal element, E, and the average transmitted energy per bit, E_b. E and E_b are computed from Equation 14.37.

Having determined the best way of sharing the linear filtering of the signal between the transmitter and receiver, when the transmission path introduces no signal distortion, it is necessary now to study the effect of the overall transfer function $H(f)$, of the transmitter and receiver filters, on the tolerance of the data-transmission system to white Gaussian noise. Several different values of $H(f)$ will be studied and, of course, each of these corresponds to a different transmitted signal waveform. In Figure 14.6, $H(f)$ is the transfer function of the *baseband channel*.

The spectrum (Fourier transform) of the individual received signal-element at the output of the baseband channel in Figure 14.6, resulting from the signal-element $s_i\delta(t)$ at the input to the baseband channel, is clearly $s_i H(f)$. To avoid undue repetition, the term 'signal

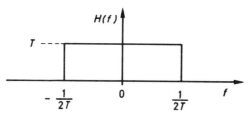

Fig. 14.7 *Channel transfer-function giving a rectangular signal-spectrum*

spectrum' is taken to mean the spectrum of this individual signal-element. Furthermore, in describing the *shape* of the signal spectrum $s_i H(f)$, it is assumed for convenience that $s_i = 1$, so that the signal spectrum is equated to the transfer function of the baseband channel. The reason for considering the signal spectrum in this way is that the different signal spectra to be studied can now be described very simply. The signal spectrum is not therefore to be confused with the energy-density spectrum of any finite sequence of elements, or with the power-density spectrum of an infinite sequence, nor indeed with the spectrum (Fourier transform) of any given finite sequence of elements. However, it is important to note that there is a close relationship between these different spectra, and in particular, if $H(f)$ = 0 for any value of f, then the corresponding power- or energy-density spectrum of the respective infinite or finite sequence of signal elements must itself be zero at this value of f.

14.4 Rectangular spectrum

The simplest design of transmitter and receiver filters in Figure 14.6 is (in principle) that giving a rectangular spectrum for an individual received signal-element at the output of the receiver filter. The transfer function of the baseband channel, and therefore of the transmitter and receiver filters in cascade, is now

$$H(f) = \begin{cases} T, & -\dfrac{1}{2T} < f < \dfrac{1}{2T} \\ 0, & \text{elsewhere} \end{cases} \tag{14.40}$$

as shown in Figure 14.7.

The transfer function of both the transmitter and receiver filter is

$$H^{1/2}(f) = \begin{cases} T^{1/2}, & -\dfrac{1}{2T} < f < \dfrac{1}{2T} \\ 0, & \text{elsewhere} \end{cases} \tag{14.41}$$

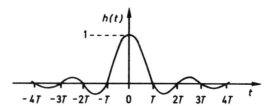

Fig. 14.8   *Impulse response of baseband channel*

The impulse response of the baseband channel is

$$h(t) = \int_{-\infty}^{\infty} H(f) \exp{(j2\pi ft)} \, df = \int_{-1/(2T)}^{1/(2T)} T \exp{(j2\pi ft)} \, df$$

$$= T \left[\frac{\exp{(j2\pi ft)}}{j2\pi t} \right]_{-1/(2T)}^{1/(2T)} = \frac{\exp{\left(j\pi \dfrac{t}{T}\right)} - \exp{\left(-j\pi \dfrac{t}{T}\right)}}{2j\pi \dfrac{t}{T}}$$

$$= \frac{\sin \pi \dfrac{t}{T}}{\pi \dfrac{t}{T}} \tag{14.42}$$

as shown in Figure 14.8.

Since $h(t) \neq 0$ for $t < 0$, $h(t)$ is not physically realisable. This is for the obvious reason that it is not possible to obtain an output from a filter in response to an impulse at its input, *before* the occurrence of the impulse. However, if a large delay of τ seconds is included in the filter characteristics without otherwise changing them, so that $h(t) \simeq 0$ for $t < 0$, the filter then becomes physically realisable, for practical purposes, and has an impulse response approximately equal to $h(t - \tau)$, as shown in Figure 14.9. The error caused in $h(t - \tau)$ by setting this accurately to zero for $t < 0$, is negligible so long as $\tau \gg T$, and under these conditions a practical filter can be made to approximate closely to the theoretical ideal, the approximation getting better as τ increases. Of course, for the practical filter to have an impulse response exactly equal to $h(t - \tau)$, it is necessary that τ tends to infinity.

The fixed delay of τ seconds introduced into the impulse response $h(t)$ of the baseband channel, to make this physically realisable, will be neglected throughout the rest of Chapter 14, since the introduction

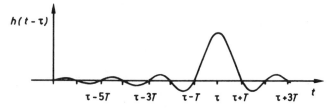

Fig. 14.9   Physically realisable impulse response

of the delay does not affect any of the parameters to be calculated here
and only complicates the mathematics. Thus all the filters now to be
considered are not physically realisable but may be made so by
including a sufficiently large delay in the impulse response. Clearly, if
$h(t)$ is changed to $h(t - \tau)$, $H(f)$ is changed to $\exp(-j2\pi f\tau)H(f)$, so
that to make the response of the baseband channel physically
realisable, its transfer function $H(f)$ must be multiplied by
$\exp(-j2\pi f\tau)$ where $\tau \gg T$.

The signal at the output of the baseband channel in Figure 14.6 is
the continuous waveform

$$r(t) = \sum_i s_i h(t - iT) + v(t) \tag{14.43}$$

where

$$h(t) = \frac{\sin \pi \dfrac{t}{T}}{\pi \dfrac{t}{T}} \tag{14.44}$$

from Equation 14.42.

As can be seen from Figure 14.8,

$$h(0) = 1 \quad \text{and} \quad h(iT) = 0$$

for all values of the integer i other than $i = 0$. Thus the ith received
signal-element $s_i h(t - iT)$ may be detected from the sample value of
the received waveform $r(t)$, at the time instant $t = iT$. The sample
value is

$$r(iT) = s_i + v(iT) \tag{14.45}$$

This may be written more simply as

$$r_i = s_i + v_i \tag{14.46}$$

where $r_i = r(iT)$ and $v_i = v(iT)$. Clearly, r_i is independent of the received signal-elements other than the ith element, so that there is no intersymbol interference.

It is assumed that $s_i = k_0 + 2lk$ where $l = 0, 1, \ldots, m - 1$, the m possible values of s_i being equally spaced at intervals of $2k$. The detection process that minimizes the probability of error in the detection of s_i from r_i, under the assumed conditions, selects the possible value of s_i closest to r_i. This is achieved by comparing r_i with $m - 1$ threshold levels (decision thresholds) whose values are $k_0 + (2l - 1)k$, for $l = 1, 2, \ldots, m - 1$, and then selecting as the detected value of s_i its possible value between the same pair of threshold levels as r_i. When $r_i < k_0 + k$, s_i is detected as k_0, and when $r_i > k_0 + (2m - 3)k$, s_i is detected as $k_0 + 2(m - 1)k$.

An error occurs in the detection of s_i whenever the noise component v_i is such that r_i is closer to a possible value of s_i different from its correct value, that is, whenever the noise component v_i carries r_i onto the opposite side of a decision threshold with respect to the transmitted s_i.

When $s_i = k_0$ or $k_0 + 2(m - 1)k$, an error occurs in the detection of s_i if v_i has a magnitude greater than k and the appropriate sign so that it carries r_i across a decision threshold. Since v_i is a Gaussian random variable with zero mean and variance $\frac{1}{2}N_0$, the probability of an error in the detection of s_i is now

$$\int_k^\infty \frac{1}{\sqrt{(\pi N_0)}} \exp\left(-\frac{v^2}{N_0}\right) dv = \int_{k\sqrt{(N_0/2)}}^\infty \frac{1}{\sqrt{(2\pi)}} \exp\left(-\tfrac{1}{2}v^2\right) dv$$

$$= Q\left\{\frac{k}{\sqrt{(\frac{1}{2}N_0)}}\right\} \qquad (14.47)$$

When s_i has one of its possible values other than k_0 or $k_0 + 2(m - 1)k$, an error occurs in the detection of s_i when the magnitude of the noise component v_i exceeds k, whether v_i is positive or negative. Thus the probability of an error in the detection of s_i is now

$$2\int_k^\infty \frac{1}{\sqrt{(\pi N_0)}} \exp\left(-\frac{v^2}{N_0}\right) dv = 2Q\left\{\frac{k}{\sqrt{(\frac{1}{2}N_0)}}\right\} \qquad (14.48)$$

Since s_i is equally likely to have any of its m possible values, the average probability of error in the detection of s_i is

$$\frac{2(m - 1)}{m} Q\left\{\frac{k}{\sqrt{(\frac{1}{2}N_0)}}\right\}$$

But at high signal/noise ratios, a change of less than two times in the

Table 14.2 RELATIVE TOLERANCES TO ADDITIVE WHITE GAUSSIAN NOISE AT A GIVEN AVERAGE TRANSMITTED SIGNAL ENERGY PER BIT

Signal	Probability of error	Relative tolerance to noise (dB)
Binary polar	$Q\left(\sqrt{\dfrac{2E_b}{N_0}}\right)$	0
Binary unipolar	$Q\left(\sqrt{\dfrac{E_b}{N_0}}\right)$	-3
Quaternary polar	$Q\left(\sqrt{\dfrac{4E_b}{5N_0}}\right)$	-4
Quaternary unipolar	$Q\left(\sqrt{\dfrac{2E_b}{7N_0}}\right)$	-8.5

probability of an error corresponds to a change of only a small fraction of 1 dB in the signal/noise ratio, and for our purposes this can be neglected. Thus the probability of an error in the detection of s_i can be taken to be

$$P_e = Q\left\{\frac{k}{\sqrt{(\frac{1}{2}N_0)}}\right\} \tag{14.49}$$

and this applies for $m = 2, 3, 4, \ldots$.

It can be seen from Equation 14.49 that k is the distance, d, from each possible value of s_i to the nearest decision threshold in the detection process, and $\sqrt{(\frac{1}{2}N_0)}$ is the standard deviation, σ, of the noise component v_i, such that $\sigma^2 = \frac{1}{2}N_0$. Equation 14.49 can now be rewritten

$$P_e = Q\left(\frac{d}{\sigma}\right) \tag{14.50}$$

In all applications considered in Chapters 12–16, this approximation can be applied at sufficiently high signal/noise ratios.

Table 14.1 gives the relationships between k and the average transmitted signal energy per bit, E_b, for the four different signals studied here. Using these results and Equation 14.49, the error probability for each signal can be expressed in terms of E_b and N_0, and hence a comparison can be made of the relative tolerances of the four signals to additive white Gaussian noise, for a given average transmitted signal energy per bit. The results are shown in Table 14.2. The last column of this table shows the values of the noise power spectral density, $\frac{1}{2}N_0$, for the four different signals, expressed in dB relative to that for the binary polar signal, when every signal has the same error probability and every signal has the same average transmitted energy per bit, E_b. The different signals are therefore compared at the same average transmitted power level and the same information rate.

It can be seen from Equations 13.16, 13.23, 13.33, 13.37 and Table 14.2 that the tolerance of any one of the four signals to additive white Gaussian noise is the same, whether the signal is rectangular in shape as in Chapter 13 or whether it is rounded in shape with a rectangular spectrum, as in this section.

14.5   Spectrum with a sinusoidal roll-off

The disadvantage of the rectangular spectrum, just assumed for a signal element at the output of the receiver filter, is that an individual received signal-element at the output of the receiver filter is shaped as $h(t)$ in Figure 14.8, so that a small error in the phase of the sampling instants at the detector input (Figure 14.6) can introduce considerable intersymbol interference. The sample value r_i of the received waveform will now depend not only on s_i and v_i, as in Equation 14.46, but also on the $\{s_l\}$ where l has integer values in the neighbourhood of i. This is because, at the points $\{(i + \frac{1}{2})T\}$, the impulse response $h(t)$ in Figure 14.8 decays very slowly as the integer i becomes more positive or more negative. The received signal waveform

$$\sum_i s_i h(t - iT)$$

at the output of the baseband channel in Figure 14.6 is in fact not bounded at $t = (i + \frac{1}{2})T$ and so may become extremely large at these points for particular sets of values of the $\{s_l\}$.

The situation may be greatly improved by rounding off or smoothing the abrupt change in $H(f)$ at $f = \pm 1/2T$. In general, for a given bandwidth, the more smooth or gradual the variation of $H(f)$ with f, over the whole range of values of f for which $H(f) \neq 0$, the shorter the effective duration of $h(t)$.

Nyquist's vestigial-symmetry theorem states that if $H(f)$ is real and has odd symmetry about the nominal cut-off frequencies $\pm 1/2T$ Hz, then the corresponding impulse-response $h(t)$ is an even time-function (which means that it is symmetrical about $t = 0$), and $h(iT) = 0$ for all nonzero integer values of i[268,328]. Under these conditions it is possible to transmit data at $1/T$ elements per second without intersymbol interference.

The class of signal spectra most often used is that where $H(f)$ is real

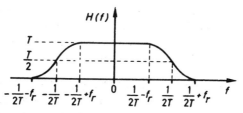

Fig. 14.10 Channel transfer-function giving a signal spectrum with a sinusoidal roll-off

and has a sinusoidal roll-off centered at $\pm 1/2T$ Hz, as shown in Figure 14.10[328].

The transfer function of the baseband channel is now

$$H(f) = \begin{cases} T, & -\dfrac{1}{2T} + f_r < f < \dfrac{1}{2T} - f_r \\[2ex] \tfrac{1}{2}T\left\{1 - \sin\dfrac{\pi\left(|f| - \dfrac{1}{2T}\right)}{2f_r}\right\}, & \dfrac{1}{2T} - f_r \leqslant |f| \leqslant \dfrac{1}{2T} + f_r \\[2ex] 0, & \text{elsewhere} \end{cases}$$

(14.51)

where $f_r \leqslant 1/2T$ and the total bandwidth over positive frequencies is $1/2T + f_r$.

Since $H(f)$ satisfies Nyquist's vestigial-symmetry theorem, $h(iT) = 0$ for all non-zero integer values of i, so that it is possible to transmit data at $1/T$ elements per second without intersymbol interference.

When $f_r = 0$, $H(f)$ becomes the rectangular spectrum previously considered. As f_r increases to $1/2T$, the effective duration of $h(t)$ decreases steadily. When $f_r = 1/2T$, the spectrum has the shape of one cycle of a cosine wave, between adjacent negative peaks, the latter being raised to zero. It is therefore often known as a "raised-cosine" spectrum. This is probably the most important of all particular signal spectra and will now be considered in some detail.

14.6 Raised-cosine spectrum

The transfer function of the baseband channel is

$$H(f) = \begin{cases} \tfrac{1}{2}T(1 + \cos \pi fT), & -\dfrac{1}{T} < f < \dfrac{1}{T} \\[2ex] 0, & \text{elsewhere} \end{cases}$$

(14.52)

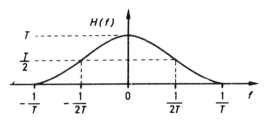

Fig. 14.11   Channel transfer-function giving a raised cosine signal-spectrum

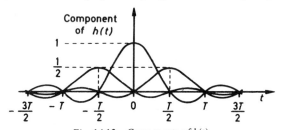

Fig. 14.12   Components of h(t)

as shown in Figure 14.11. The transfer function of both the transmitter and receiver filter in Figure 14.6 is $H^{1/2}(f)$.

The impulse response of the baseband channel is

$$h(t) = \int_{-\infty}^{\infty} H(f) \exp{(j2\pi ft)} \, df$$

$$= \tfrac{1}{2}T \int_{-(1/T)}^{1/T} (1 + \cos{\pi fT}) \exp{(j2\pi ft)} \, df$$

$$= \tfrac{1}{2}T \int_{-(1/T)}^{1/T} \{1 + \tfrac{1}{2}\exp{(j\pi fT)} + \tfrac{1}{2}\exp{(-j\pi fT)}\} \exp{(j2\pi ft)} \, df$$

$$= \tfrac{1}{2}T \int_{-(1/T)}^{1/T} \left[\exp{(j\pi f2t)} + \tfrac{1}{2}\exp{\{j\pi f(2t + T)\}} \right.$$
$$\left. + \tfrac{1}{2}\exp{\{j\pi f(2t - T)\}}\right] \, df$$

$$= \tfrac{1}{2}T\left[\frac{\exp{(j\pi f2t)}}{j\pi 2t} + \frac{1}{2}\frac{\exp{\{j\pi f(2t + T)\}}}{j\pi(2t + T)} \right.$$
$$\left. + \frac{1}{2}\frac{\exp{\{j\pi f(2t - T)\}}}{j\pi(2t - T)}\right]_{-(1/T)}^{1/T}$$

$$= \frac{\exp\left(j\pi\,\frac{2t}{T}\right) - \exp\left(-j\pi\,\frac{2t}{T}\right)}{2j\pi\,\frac{2t}{T}}$$

$$+ \frac{1}{2}\,\frac{\exp\left\{j\pi\left(\frac{2t}{T}+1\right)\right\} - \exp\left\{-j\pi\left(\frac{2t}{T}+1\right)\right\}}{2j\pi\left(\frac{2t}{T}+1\right)}$$

$$+ \frac{1}{2}\,\frac{\exp\left\{j\pi\left(\frac{2t}{T}-1\right)\right\} - \exp\left\{-j\pi\left(\frac{2t}{T}-1\right)\right\}}{2j\pi\left(\frac{2t}{T}-1\right)}$$

$$= \frac{\sin\pi\,\frac{2t}{T}}{\pi\,\frac{2t}{T}} + \frac{1}{2}\,\frac{\sin\pi\left(\frac{2t}{T}+1\right)}{\pi\left(\frac{2t}{T}+1\right)} + \frac{1}{2}\,\frac{\sin\pi\left(\frac{2t}{T}-1\right)}{\pi\left(\frac{2t}{T}-1\right)} \tag{14.53}$$

The three components of $h(t)$, given by Equation 14.53, are shown in Figure 14.12.

The impulse response of the baseband channel simplifies to

$$h(t) = \frac{\sin\pi\,\frac{2t}{T}}{\pi\,\frac{2t}{T}\left\{1 - \left(\frac{2t}{T}\right)^2\right\}} \tag{14.54}$$

which is shown in Figure 14.13.

For practical purposes, $h(t)$ is negligibly small when $|t| > T$. Furthermore,

$$h(0) = 1$$
$$h(\pm\tfrac{1}{2}T) = \tfrac{1}{2}$$

and
$$h(\tfrac{1}{2}iT) = 0$$

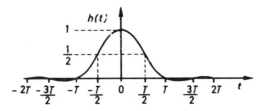

Fig. 14.13 *Impulse response of baseband channel*

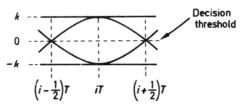

Fig. 14.14 *Eye pattern of a binary polar signal with a raised cosine spectrum*

for all values of the integer i other than $i = 0$ or ± 1. Not only is it possible to transmit data at $1/T$ elements per second without intersymbol interference, but in the resultant signal waveform

$$\sum_i s_i h(t - iT) \tag{14.55}$$

at the sampler input (Figure 14.6), the sample value at time $t = (i + \frac{1}{2})T$ is the arithmetic mean of the sample values at times $t = iT$ and $t = (i + 1)T$, there being no components here from any but the two immediately adjacent signal elements. Thus for a binary polar signal, where $s_i = \pm k$, the eye pattern of the signal waveform given by Expression 14.55 is as shown in Figure 14.14. The eye pattern is the locus of all possible values of the waveform given by Expression 14.55, over a time interval a little wider than $(i - \frac{1}{2})T$ to $(i + \frac{1}{2})T$.

If the binary polar signal is sliced at the decision threshold and the resultant waveform suitably amplified, its eye pattern becomes as shown in Figure 14.15.

The transitions from k to $-k$ and vice versa, in Figure 14.15, occur only at the time instants $\{(i + \frac{1}{2})T\}$, for all integer values of i, so that the transitions occur half way between the adjacent sampling instants $\{iT\}$. Clearly, the sliced signal can be used to determine the time instants $\{iT\}$ at which the received waveform $r(t)$ is sampled in Figure 14.6, without there being an error in these time instants due to

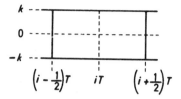

Fig. 14.15   Eye pattern of sliced signal

the signal waveform itself. A signal whose transitions occur only at the instants half way between the sampling instants is said to have no telegraph distortion. The raised-cosine signal spectrum given by Equation 14.52 is the only one considered here which has this desirable property, which means that it is the only one for which the element timing waveform may be derived accurately at the receiver, from the received data signal itself, without the transmission of a special timing signal or the use of other special techniques. Furthermore, it is clear from the shape of $h(t)$ that an appreciable error in the sampling instants can now be tolerated before an unacceptable level of intersymbol interference is introduced.

The signal at the output of the baseband channel in Figure 14.6 is

$$r(t) = \sum_i s_i h(t - iT) + v(t) \tag{14.56}$$

where $h(t)$ is given by Equation 14.54 and shown in Figure 14.13. Thus the sample value of the received waveform $r(t)$, at the time instant $t = iT$, is

$$r_i = s_i + v_i \tag{14.57}$$

which is identical to Equation 14.46 for the signal with a rectangular spectrum. In each case, the noise component v_i is a Gaussian random variable with zero mean and variance $\frac{1}{2}N_0$. Clearly, s_i is detected from r_i exactly as described in Section 14.4 for the signal with a rectangular spectrum, and a signal with a raised-cosine spectrum has the same tolerance to additive white Gaussian noise as the corresponding signal with a rectangular spectrum.

The probability of an error in the detection of s_i from r_i, when s_i has one of the m possible values $k_0 + 2lk$, for $l = 0, 1, \ldots, m - 1$, is given approximately by P_e in Equation 14.49, and the relative tolerances to additive white Gaussian noise of the four signals of greatest interest, at a given average transmitted signal energy per bit, are shown in Table 14.2.

There is a further important property that holds for the noise samples $\{v_i\}$ obtained with any of the different values of $H(f)$ so far considered in Chapter 14.

The noise power spectral density at the output of the receiver filter is[425]

$$\tfrac{1}{2}N_0|H^{1/2}(f)|^2$$

and from the Wiener–Kinchine theorem, the autocorrelation function of the noise waveform $v(t)$ at the output of the receiver filter is[425]

$$R_v(\tau) = \int\limits_{-\infty}^{\infty} \tfrac{1}{2}N_0|H^{1/2}(f)|^2 \exp(j2\pi f\tau)\, df$$

$$= \tfrac{1}{2}N_0 \int\limits_{-\infty}^{\infty} H(f) \exp(j2\pi f\tau)\, df$$

$$= \tfrac{1}{2}N_0 h(\tau) \tag{14.58}$$

since $H(f)$ and $H^{1/2}(f)$ are real and nonnegative for the different cases studied.

The variance of any noise sample v_i is

$$R_v(0) = \tfrac{1}{2}N_0 h(0) = \tfrac{1}{2}N_0 \tag{14.59}$$

as shown before. Furthermore, for any nonzero integer i,

$$R_v(iT) = \tfrac{1}{2}N_0 h(iT) = 0 \tag{14.60}$$

But the sampling instants for any two noise samples v_i and v_l are separated by a multiple of T seconds, and the noise samples have zero mean. Thus any two noise samples v_i and v_l are uncorrelated and therefore statistically independent Gaussian random variables.

15

Partial-response channels

15.1 Introduction

For all the baseband channels studied so far, the impulse response $h(t)$ is such that

$$h(0) = 1 \qquad (15.1)$$

and
$$h(iT) = 0 \qquad (15.2)$$

for all nonzero values of the integer i, which means that the sample value of the received waveform $r(t)$, at the time instant $t = iT$, is

$$r_i = s_i + v_i \qquad (15.3)$$

and there is no intersymbol interference between the different received signal-elements in the samples $\{r_i\}$. As before, $\{\cdot\}$ designates a set.

Unfortunately, in order to satisfy Equations 15.1, 15.2 and 15.3 reasonably accurately, with no significant intersymbol interference and without the need for extreme precision in the timing of the sampling instants, the bandwidth of the baseband channel must be somewhat wider than its minimum possible value of $1/2T$ Hz (for positive frequencies). The data signal at the output of the baseband channel in Figure 14.6 should ideally have a raised-cosine spectrum and a bandwidth of $1/T$ Hz. However, this is twice the bandwidth of the corresponding signal with a rectangular spectrum. For some applications, a more efficient use of bandwidth must be achieved than is possible with a binary signal having a raised-cosine spectrum. One approach, of course, is to use a quaternary signal with a raised-cosine spectrum. However, it can be seen from Table 14.2 that at a given information rate and a given transmitted signal power level, the tolerance to additive white Gaussian noise of the quaternary polar signal is 4 dB below that of the binary polar signal, which is an appreciable reduction in tolerance to noise.

The alternative approach is to use a *partial-response channel*. This

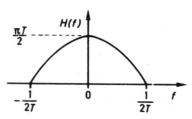

Fig. 15.1   *Channel transfer-function giving a cosine signal-spectrum*

is a baseband channel whose impulse response is such that there is significant intersymbol interference in the samples $\{r_i\}$ of the received waveform $r(t)$ at the output of the baseband channel. A useful reduction in bandwidth can be achieved by allowing considerable but well-defined levels of intersymbol interference between neighbouring signal-elements and by using suitable techniques to eliminate the effects of this interference[429-474].

The best-known partial response channels will now be studied to determine the corresponding tolerances to additive white Gaussian noise[438]. The data-transmission system is again assumed to be as shown in Figure 14.6 and described in Section 14.3, and the Equations 14.37 and 14.38 apply in every case. A polar signal is assumed here.

15.2   Cosine spectrum

The transfer function of the baseband channel is

$$H(f) = \begin{cases} \frac{1}{2}\pi T \cos \pi f T, & -\frac{1}{2T} < f < \frac{1}{2T} \\ 0, & \text{elsewhere} \end{cases} \tag{15.4}$$

as shown in Figure 15.1

The impulse response of the baseband channel is

$$h(t) = \frac{\pi}{4} \left\{ \frac{\sin \pi \left(\frac{t}{T} + \frac{1}{2} \right)}{\pi \left(\frac{t}{T} + \frac{1}{2} \right)} + \frac{\sin \pi \left(\frac{t}{T} - \frac{1}{2} \right)}{\pi \left(\frac{t}{T} - \frac{1}{2} \right)} \right\} \tag{15.5}$$

The two components of $h(t)$, given by Equation 15.5, are shown in Figure 15.2.

As can be seen from Figure 15.2:

$$h(\pm \tfrac{1}{2}T) = \frac{\pi}{4}$$

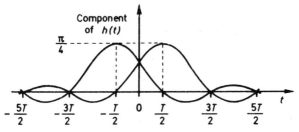

Fig. 15.2   Components of h(t)

and $$h\{(i - \tfrac{1}{2})T\} = 0$$

for all values of the integer i other than $i = 0$ or 1. The received waveform $r(t)$, in Figure 14.6, is now sampled at the time instants $\{(i - \tfrac{1}{2})T\}$ instead of at $\{iT\}$ as shown in Figure 14.6.

If the ith transmitted signal-element at the input to the baseband channel in Figure 14.6 is the impulse $s_i\delta(t - iT)$, the ith received signal element at the output of the baseband channel is the waveform $s_i h(t - iT)$, where $h(t)$ is given by Equation 15.5. The sample values of this signal, at the detector input, are $\frac{\pi}{4}s_i$ at the time instants $(i - \tfrac{1}{2})T$ and $(i + \tfrac{1}{2})T$ and zero elsewhere. Thus the sample value of the received waveform $r(t)$, at the time instant $t = (i - \tfrac{1}{2})T$, is

$$r_i = \tfrac{\pi}{4}s_i + \tfrac{\pi}{4}s_{i-1} + v_i \tag{15.6}$$

where r_i and v_i are now, for convenience, taken to be the sample values of $r(t)$ and $v(t)$, respectively, at the time instant $t = (i - \tfrac{1}{2})T$.

Suppose that, at time $t = (i - \tfrac{1}{2})T$, s_{i-1} has already been correctly detected. The detector therefore knows $\frac{\pi}{4}s_{i-1}$ and it now removes this term by subtraction from r_i, to give

$$x_i = r_i - \tfrac{\pi}{4}s_{i-1} = \tfrac{\pi}{4}s_i + v_i \tag{15.7}$$

The process of subtraction of $\frac{\pi}{4}s_{i-1}$ from r_i eliminates the intersymbol interference of the $(i-1)$th element from r_i, so that x_i depends only on the wanted signal component s_i and the noise component v_i. This is a process of decision-directed cancellation of intersymbol interference. s_i is then detected from x_i.

The signal is assumed to be m-level and such that s_i has one of the values $(2l - m + 1)k$, for $l = 0, 1, \ldots, m - 1$. s_i is detected as its possible value for which $\frac{\pi}{4}s_i$ lies nearest to x_i. Thus x_i is compared with $m - 1$ decision thresholds which lie half way between adjacent possible values of $\frac{\pi}{4}s_i$ and have the values $\frac{\pi}{4}k(2l - m)$, for $l = 1, 2, \ldots,$ $m - 1$. The detected value of s_i is its possible value for which $\frac{\pi}{4}s_i$ lies between the same decision thresholds as x_i.

Following the correct detection of s_i, the detector knows $\frac{\pi}{4}s_i$ which is then subtracted from the next received sample

$$r_{i+1} = \tfrac{\pi}{4}s_{i+1} + \tfrac{\pi}{4}s_i + v_{i+1} \tag{15.8}$$

at time $t = (i + \tfrac{1}{2})T$, to give

$$x_{i+1} = r_{i+1} - \tfrac{\pi}{4}s_i = \tfrac{\pi}{4}s_{i+1} + v_{i+1} \tag{15.9}$$

and s_{i+1} is detected from x_{i+1}. So long as each signal element is correctly detected, the process continues in this way.

To start the detection process, a small group of signal elements with known element values $\{s_i\}$ are first transmitted. During the reception of these elements, the known value of one of the $\{s_i\}$, say s_{i-1}, is used to form $\frac{\pi}{4}s_{i-1}$, without the detection of s_{i-1} from the received signal. $\frac{\pi}{4}s_{i-1}$ is then subtracted from the following received sample r_i, thus removing the intersymbol interference in this sample and enabling the process of detection and signal cancellation to proceed as previously described.

The disadvantage of the arrangement is that the incorrect detection of an element prevents the elimination of the intersymbol interference of the element in the sample value used for the detection of the following element. This tends to cause a group of consecutive errors (an error burst) in the detection of the following elements and so introduces an error extension effect. Fortunately, when $m = 2$ or 4 and under the conditions assumed throughout this analysis, where the $\{s_i\}$ are statistically independent and equally likely to have any of their m possible values, the effect is not as serious as might be imagined. In fact, when $m = 2$ or 4, the average number of errors in an error burst is 2 or 4, respectively[519], thus increasing the average error probability (and hence the error rate) by 2 or 4 times. At high signal/noise ratios this represents a reduction in tolerance to additive white Gaussian noise of only a fraction of 1 dB, and so for our purposes it can be neglected. Thus the tolerance of the system to additive white Gaussian noise, assuming the correct elimination of intersymbol interference, is a good measure of its actual tolerance to the noise.

In the detection of s_i from x_i, in Equation 15.7, the noise component v_i is a Gaussian random variable with zero mean and variance $\tfrac{1}{2}N_0$. An error occurs in the detection of s_i when v_i has a magnitude greater than $\frac{\pi}{4}k$ and a sign such that x_i is closer to another of the possible values of $\frac{\pi}{4}s_i$. More simply, it can be seen that the distance from each possible value of $\frac{\pi}{4}s_i$ to the nearest decision threshold is $\frac{\pi}{4}k$. Thus, at high signal/noise ratios and following the correct detection of s_{i-1}, the probability of an error in the detection of s_i from x_i is approximately

$$\int_{(\pi/4)k}^{\infty} \frac{1}{\sqrt{(\pi N_0)}} \exp\left(-\frac{v^2}{N_0}\right) dv = Q\left\{\frac{\frac{\pi}{4}k}{\sqrt{(\frac{1}{2}N_0)}}\right\} \tag{15.10}$$

so that the average (or actual) error probability can be taken to be

$$P_e = Q\left\{\frac{\frac{\pi}{4}k}{\sqrt{(\frac{1}{2}N_0)}}\right\} \tag{15.11}$$

From Equation 14.49, this compares with an error probability of

$$P_e = Q\left\{\frac{k}{\sqrt{(\frac{1}{2}N_0)}}\right\} \tag{15.12}$$

in the detection of an m-level signal with a rectangular or raised-cosine spectrum.

At a given error probability, with a particular value of m and at a given average transmitted signal energy per bit, P_e and k are fixed. Under these conditions, an m-level signal with a rectangular or raised-cosine spectrum tolerates additive white Gaussian noise with a power spectral density $(4/\pi)^2$ times that tolerated by the corresponding m-level signal with a cosine spectrum. Thus, at a given average transmitted energy per bit, an m-level signal with a rectangular or raised-cosine spectrum has an advantage of 2.1 dB in tolerance to additive white Gaussian noise over the corresponding m-level signal with a cosine spectrum. Polar signals are assumed here.

15.3 Sine spectrum

The transfer function of the baseband channel is

$$H(f) = \begin{cases} \frac{1}{2}j\pi T \sin 2\pi f T, & -\frac{1}{2T} < f < \frac{1}{2T} \\ 0, & \text{elsewhere} \end{cases} \tag{15.13}$$

as shown in Figure 15.3.

The impulse response of the baseband channel is

$$h(t) = \frac{\pi}{4}\left\{\frac{\sin \pi\left(\frac{t}{T}+1\right)}{\pi\left(\frac{t}{T}+1\right)} - \frac{\sin \pi\left(\frac{t}{T}-1\right)}{\pi\left(\frac{t}{T}-1\right)}\right\} \tag{15.14}$$

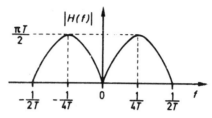

Fig. 15.3   *Channel transfer-function giving a sine signal-spectrum*

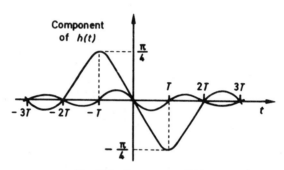

Fig. 15.4   *Components of h(t)*

The two components of $h(t)$, given by Equation 15.14, are shown in Figure 15.4.

As can be seen from Figure 15.4,

$$h(-T) = \tfrac{\pi}{4}$$

$$h(T) = -\tfrac{\pi}{4}$$

and

$$h(iT) = 0$$

for all values of the integer i other than $i = \pm 1$. The received waveform $r(t)$, in Figure 14.6, is now sampled at the time instants $\{iT\}$, as shown.

The sample value of the received waveform $r(t)$, at the time instant $t = (i-1)T$, is

$$r_i = \tfrac{\pi}{4}s_i - \tfrac{\pi}{4}s_{i-2} + v_i \tag{15.15}$$

where r_i and v_i are, for convenience, taken to be the samples of $r(t)$ and $v(t)$, respectively, at the time instant $t = (i-1)T$. This has been done to relate more clearly the received sample value and the corresponding noise component, to the wanted signal component $\tfrac{\pi}{4}s_i$.

Suppose that, at time $t = (i-1)T$, s_{i-2} has already been correctly detected. The detector therefore knows $-\frac{\pi}{4}s_{i-2}$ and it now removes this term by subtraction from r_i, to give

$$x_i = r_i + \frac{\pi}{4}s_{i-2} = \frac{\pi}{4}s_i + v_i \qquad (15.16)$$

s_i is then detected from x_i, as previously described for the signal with a cosine spectrum.

Suppose that at time $t = iT$, s_{i-1} has already been correctly detected. The detector therefore knows $-\frac{\pi}{4}s_{i-1}$ and it now removes this term by subtraction from r_{i+1}, to give

$$x_{i+1} = r_{i+1} + \frac{\pi}{4}s_{i-1} = \frac{\pi}{4}s_{i+1} + v_{i+1} \qquad (15.17)$$

s_{i+1} is then detected from x_{i+1}.

So long as each signal element is correctly detected, the process continues in this way. It is clearly an arrangement of detection and signal cancellation similar to that previously described for the signal with a cosine spectrum.

The incorrect detection of a signal element prevents the elimination of the intersymbol interference of the element in the sample value used for the detection of the next but one element, so that the arrangement is subject to error-extension effects. An error burst, resulting from a wrongly detected signal element, is not now a group of consecutive errors but has every second detected signal-element in error. As before, when $m = 2$ or 4, the average number of errors in an error burst is 2 or 4, respectively, thus increasing the average error probability to 2 or 4 times the error probability with the correct cancellation of the preceding elements.

At high signal/noise ratios and for an m-level signal such that s_i has one of the values $(2l - m + 1)k$, for $l = 0, 1, \ldots, m - 1$, the probability of error in the detection of s_i from x_i, given the correct cancellation of $-\frac{\pi}{4}s_{i-2}$, is approximately

$$\int_{(\pi/4)k}^{\infty} \frac{1}{\sqrt{\pi N_0}} \exp\left(-\frac{v^2}{N_0}\right) dv = Q\left\{\frac{\frac{\pi}{4}k}{\sqrt{(\frac{1}{2}N_0)}}\right\} \qquad (15.18)$$

Thus the average (or actual) error probability can be taken to be

$$P_e = Q\left\{\frac{\frac{\pi}{4}k}{\sqrt{(\frac{1}{2}N_0)}}\right\} \qquad (15.19)$$

For a given value of k, this is the same as that for the signal with a cosine spectrum. Thus the tolerance of a signal with a sine spectrum to additive white Gaussian noise is 2.1 dB below that for the corresponding signal with a rectangular or raised-cosine spectrum.

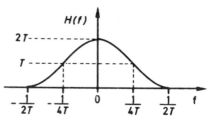

Fig. 15.5   Channel transfer-function giving a cosine² signal-spectrum

15.4   Cosine² spectrum

The transfer function of the baseband channel is

$$H(f) = \begin{cases} 2T \cos^2 \pi f T, & -\dfrac{1}{2T} < f < \dfrac{1}{2T} \\ 0, & \text{elsewhere} \end{cases}$$

$$= \begin{cases} T(1 + \cos 2\pi f T), & -\dfrac{1}{2T} < f < \dfrac{1}{2T} \\ 0, & \text{elsewhere} \end{cases} \tag{15.20}$$

as shown in Figure 15.5.

The impulse response of the baseband channel is

$$h(t) = \frac{\sin \pi \dfrac{t}{T}}{\pi \dfrac{t}{T}} + \frac{1}{2} \frac{\sin \pi \left(\dfrac{t}{T} + 1 \right)}{\pi \left(\dfrac{t}{T} + 1 \right)} + \frac{1}{2} \frac{\sin \pi \left(\dfrac{t}{T} - 1 \right)}{\pi \left(\dfrac{t}{T} - 1 \right)}$$

$$\tag{15.21}$$

The three components of $h(t)$, given by Equation 15.21, are shown in Figure 15.6.

As can be seen from Figure 15.6,

$$h(0) = 1$$
$$h(\pm T) = \tfrac{1}{2}$$
and
$$h(iT) = 0$$

for all values of the integer i other than $i = 0$ or ± 1. The received waveform $r(t)$, in Figure 14.6, is sampled at the time instants $\{iT\}$, as shown.

The ith received signal element has the waveform $s_i h(t - iT)$ at the input to the sampler. The sample values of the ith signal element, at

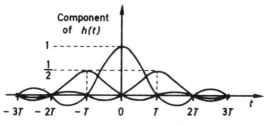

Fig. 15.6   Components of h(t)

the input to the detector, are $\frac{1}{2}s_i$, s_i and $\frac{1}{2}s_i$, at the time instants $(i-1)T$, iT and $(i+1)T$, respectively. Thus the sample value of the received waveform $r(t)$, at the time instant $t = (i-1)T$, is

$$r_i = \tfrac{1}{2}s_i + s_{i-1} + \tfrac{1}{2}s_{i-2} + v_i \tag{15.22}$$

where r_i and v_i are, for convenience, taken to be the samples of $r(t)$ and $v(t)$ at the time instant $t = (i-1)T$.

Suppose that the detector uses an arrangement of decision-directed cancellation of intersymbol interference, as previously described, and that at time $t = (i-1)T$ both s_{i-1} and s_{i-2} have been correctly detected. The detector therefore knows s_{i-1} and $\frac{1}{2}s_{i-2}$ and removes these terms by subtraction from r_i to give

$$x_i = r_i - s_{i-1} - \tfrac{1}{2}s_{i-2} = \tfrac{1}{2}s_i + v_i \tag{15.23}$$

As before, the signal is assumed to be m-level and such that s_i has one of the values $(2l - m + 1)k$, for $l = 0, 1, \ldots, m-1$. s_i is now detected as its possible value for which $\frac{1}{2}s_i$ lies nearest to x_i. Thus x_i is compared with $m-1$ decision thresholds which lie half way between adjacent possible values of $\frac{1}{2}s_i$ and have the values $\frac{1}{2}k(2l - m)$, for $l = 1, 2, \ldots, m-1$. The detected value of s_i is its possible value for which $\frac{1}{2}s_i$ lies between the same decision thresholds as x_i.

The error extension effects here are rather more serious than those for signals with a cosine or sine spectrum, the average error probability, when $m = 2$ or 4, being, respectively, 4 or 13 times that with the correct detection of the immediately preceding elements[517]. It is assumed here, as before, that the $\{s_i\}$ are statistically independent and equally likely to have any of their m possible values. At error rates near 1 in 10^5, the reduction in tolerance to additive white Gaussian noise is around $\frac{1}{2}$ dB for $m = 2$ and around 1 dB for $m = 4$, the reduction becoming steadily smaller as the error rate is reduced. Thus, at sufficiently low error rates, the reduction in tolerance to noise can, for our purposes, be neglected. However, at error rates greater than 1 in 10^5, due account must be taken of the effect of error bursts.

In Equation 15.23, the noise component v_i is again a Gaussian random variable with zero mean and variance $\frac{1}{2}N_0$. An error occurs in the detection of s_i when v_i (in Equation 15.23) carries x_i across one or more decision thresholds from $\frac{1}{2}s_i$. The distance from each possible value of $\frac{1}{2}s_i$ to the nearest decision threshold is $\frac{1}{2}k$. Thus, at high signal/noise ratios and following the correct detection of s_{i-1} and s_{i-2}, the probability of an error in the detection of s_i from x_i is approximately

$$\int_{(1/2)k}^{\infty} \frac{1}{\sqrt{\pi N_0}} \exp\left(-\frac{v^2}{N_0}\right) dv = Q\left\{\frac{\frac{1}{2}k}{\sqrt{(\frac{1}{2}N_0)}}\right\} \tag{15.24}$$

so that the average (or actual) error probability can be taken to be

$$P_e = Q\left\{\frac{\frac{1}{2}k}{\sqrt{(\frac{1}{2}N_0)}}\right\} \tag{15.25}$$

Since k has a fixed value for a given m-level signal at a given average transmitted signal energy per bit, it can be seen from Equation 14.49 that at a given error probability and at a given average transmitted signal energy per bit, an m-level signal with a rectangular or raised-cosine spectrum tolerates additive white Gaussian noise with a power spectral density four times that tolerated by the corresponding m-level signal with a cosine^2 spectrum. Thus, at a given average transmitted energy per bit, an m-level signal with a rectangular or raised-cosine spectrum has an advantage of 6 dB in tolerance to additive white Gaussian noise over the corresponding m-level signal with a cosine^2 spectrum.

15.5 Sine^2 spectrum

The transfer function of the baseband channel is

$$H(f) = \begin{cases} 2T \sin^2 2\pi fT, & -\dfrac{1}{2T} < f < \dfrac{1}{2T} \\ 0, & \text{elsewhere} \end{cases}$$

$$= \begin{cases} T(1 - \cos 4\pi fT), & -\dfrac{1}{2T} < f < \dfrac{1}{2T} \\ 0, & \text{elsewhere} \end{cases} \tag{15.26}$$

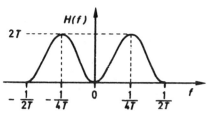

Fig. 15.7   Channel transfer-function giving a sine² signal-spectrum

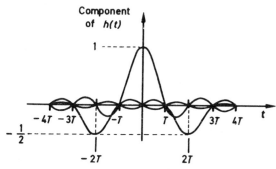

Fig. 15.8   Components of h(t)

as shown in Figure 15.7. The transfer function of the receiver filter
(Figure 14.6) is now $-A(f) = -(-H(f))^{1/2}$, whereas in all the other
cases it is $A(f) = H^{1/2}(f)$.

The impulse response of the baseband channel is

$$h(t) = \frac{\sin \pi \dfrac{t}{T}}{\pi \dfrac{t}{T}} - \frac{1}{2}\frac{\sin \pi\left(\dfrac{t}{T} + 2\right)}{\pi\left(\dfrac{t}{T} + 2\right)} - \frac{1}{2}\frac{\sin \pi\left(\dfrac{t}{T} - 2\right)}{\pi\left(\dfrac{t}{T} - 2\right)}$$

(15.27)

The three components of $h(t)$, given by Equation 15.27, are shown in
Figure 15.8.

As can be seen from Figure 15.8,

$$h(0) = 1$$

$$h(\pm 2T) = -\tfrac{1}{2}$$

and $$h(iT) = 0$$

for all values of the integer i other than $i = 0$ or ± 2. The received waveform $r(t)$, in Figure 14.6, is sampled at the time instants $\{iT\}$, as shown.

The sample values of the ith received signal-element, at the input to the detector, are $-\frac{1}{2}s_i$, s_i and $-\frac{1}{2}s_i$, at the time instants $(i - 2)T$, iT and $(i + 2)T$, respectively. Thus the sample value of the received waveform $r(t)$, at the time instant $t = (i - 2)T$, is

$$r_i = -\tfrac{1}{2}s_i + s_{i-2} - \tfrac{1}{2}s_{i-4} + v_i \qquad (15.28)$$

where r_i and v_i are taken to be the samples of $r(t)$ and $v(t)$ at the time instant $t = (i - 2)T$.

With the correct detection of s_{i-2} and s_{i-4}, the detector knows the components s_{i-2} and $-\frac{1}{2}s_{i-4}$ in r_i and removes these terms by subtraction to give

$$x_i = r_i - s_{i-2} + \tfrac{1}{2}s_{i-4} = -\tfrac{1}{2}s_i + v_i \qquad (15.29)$$

s_i is now detected from x_i by comparing x_i with decision thresholds that lie half way between adjacent possible values of $-\frac{1}{2}s_i$ and have the values $-\frac{1}{2}k(2l - m)$, for $l = 1, 2, \ldots, m - 1$. The intersymbol interference of the ith element is then removed from the following $\{r_i\}$, and so on.

The error extension effects here are similar to those for signals with a cosine^2 spectrum. Thus, at sufficiently high signal/noise ratios, they can, for our purposes be neglected.

At high signal/noise ratios, the probability of an error in the detection of s_i from x_i, assuming the correct detection of s_{i-2} and s_{i-4}, is approximately given by Equation 15.24, so that the average (or actual) error probability can again be taken to be

$$P_e = Q\left\{\frac{\tfrac{1}{2}k}{\sqrt{(\tfrac{1}{2}N_0)}}\right\} \qquad (15.30)$$

For a given value of k, this is the same as that for the signal with a cosine^2 spectrum. Thus the tolerance of a signal with a sine^2 spectrum to additive white Gaussian noise is 6 dB below that for the corresponding signal with a rectangular or raised-cosine spectrum.

15.6 Cancellation of intersymbol interference

The method normally used to achieve decision-directed cancellation of intersymbol interference is best explained by considering an arbitrary baseband channel in Figure 14.6. This is such that the sample values of the ith received signal-element, at the detector input, are y_0s_i, y_1s_i, $\ldots$, y_gs_i at the time instants iT, $(i + 1)T$, $\ldots$, $(i + g)T$, respectively, and zero elsewhere. Thus the sample value of the

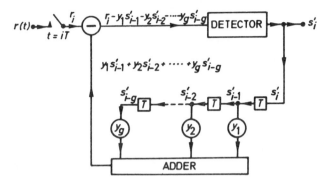

Fig. 15.9   Decision-directed cancellation of intersymbol interference

received waveform $r(t)$, at the time instant $t = iT$, is

$$r_i = y_0 s_i + y_1 s_{i-1} + \cdots + y_g s_{i-g} + v_i \qquad (15.31)$$

where v_i is the Gaussian noise component, as before.

The arrangement of decision-directed cancellation of intersymbol interference, for the signal given by Equation 15.31, is shown in Figure 15.9. The signals marked here are those present at the time instant $t = iT$.

The detected element values $\{s_i'\}$ are fed to the transversal filter containing g stores. Each store is represented in Figure 15.9 as introducing a delay of T seconds, since, if its input signal is s_{i-l+1}', its output signal is s_{i-l}'. Associated with each store is a multiplier, which multiplies the output signal s_{i-l}' from the store by y_l, so that the output signal from the transversal filter, at time $t = iT$, is

$$y_1 s_{i-1}' + y_2 s_{i-2}' + \cdots + y_g s_{i-g}'$$

With the correct detection of these signal elements, the output signal becomes

$$y_1 s_{i-1} + y_2 s_{i-2} + \cdots + y_g s_{i-g}$$

and the input signal to the detector is

$$x_i = r_i - y_1 s_{i-1} - y_2 s_{i-2} - \cdots - y_g s_{i-g}$$
$$= y_0 s_i + v_i \qquad (15.32)$$

from Equation 15.31. Thus the intersymbol interference in r_i has been eliminated at the detector input, and s_i is detected from x_i with no interference from the other received signal-elements[438].

The detected value of s_i is its possible value for which $y_0 s_i$ is closest to x_i. It is assumed, as before, that the $\{s_i\}$ are statistically independent and equally likely to have any of their m possible values, which are regularly spaced at intervals of $2k$. Under these conditions, the average probability of error in the detection of s_i, given the correct detection of $s_{i-1}, s_{i-2}, \ldots, s_{i-g}$, is

$$\frac{2(m-1)}{m} Q\left\{\frac{k|y_0|}{\sqrt{(\frac{1}{2}N_0)}}\right\}$$

(the *average* being, of course, taken over the possible values of s_i). An error burst is now defined to be the group of errors in the $\{s_i'\}$, such that in the first of these, as well as in the first error following the group, all intersymbol-interference components in x_i are correctly cancelled, whereas in each of the remainder there is at least one intersymbol-inference component incorrectly cancelled. If the average number of errors in a burst is b, then the average error rate in the $\{s_i'\}$ is

$$P_e = \frac{2(m-1)b}{m} Q\left\{\frac{k|y_0|}{\sqrt{(\frac{1}{2}N_0)}}\right\} \tag{15.33}$$

As the error rate becomes smaller, so there is a steady reduction in the inaccuracy introduced into the signal/noise ratio, $k|y_0|/\sqrt{(\frac{1}{2}N_0)}$, as a result of taking the error rate to be

$$Q\left\{\frac{k|y_0|}{\sqrt{(\frac{1}{2}N_0)}}\right\}$$

instead of P_e in Equation 15.33. (N_0 is here adjusted to maintain the error rate at the given value.) At a sufficiently small error rate, the inaccuracy in the signal/noise ratio becomes negligible, whatever the value of b. Thus, at sufficiently high signal/noise ratios, the error rate can be taken to be

$$P_e = Q\left(\frac{d}{\sigma}\right) \tag{15.34}$$

as in Equation 14.50, where now $d = k|y_0|$ is the distance from each possible value of $y_0 s_i$ to the nearest decision threshold and $\sigma = \sqrt{(\frac{1}{2}N_0)}$ is the standard deviation of the noise component v_i. The decision thresholds are placed half way between adjacent possible values of $y_0 s_i$. The approximation given by Equation 14.50 is used throughout the Chapters 12–16, such that all the results given for tolerance to additive white Gaussian noise (for which a specific error rate is not quoted) apply accurately at vanishingly small error rates. At error rates much above 1 in 10^5 or at error rates around 1 in 10^5 and with $b > 4$, a useful improvement in the accuracy of the result is obtained by using Equation 15.33 in place of Equation 15.34.

The arrangement in Figure 15.9 is a pure nonlinear (decision

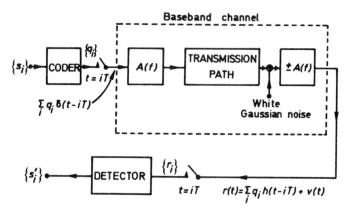

Fig. 15.10   Data-transmission system with precoding

feedback) equalizer, and the signal x_i at the detector input is the equalized signal. It is evident that, for the satisfactory operation of the system, $|y_0|$ must not be too small relative to the largest of the $\{|y_i|\}$, for $i = 1, 2, \ldots, g$, and g must not be too large.

A potentially serious weakness of the technique of decision-directed cancellation of intersymbol interference, which is studied in Sections 15.2–15.6, is that it relies strongly on the assumptions that the $\{s_i\}$ are statistically independent and equally likely to have any of their m possible values. If these conditions are not satisfied, the error-extension effects in any of the systems studied can become serious, leading to prolonged error bursts and a consequent reduction in tolerance to noise that can no longer be neglected. This weakness is avoided by the technique now to be described.

15.7   Precoding

An alternative technique for eliminating the effects of intersymbol interference in digital signals is through the use of precoding at the transmitter. The signal is coded in such a way that each received signal-element is detected from the corresponding received sample value, by comparing this with the appropriate set of decision thresholds, without the need for any cancellation of intersymbol interference[431–442].

The technique will be described by considering some particular applications with the signal spectra previously considered. The data transmission system is now as shown in Figure 15.10.

The sequence of element values $\{s_i\}$ at the input to the transmitter in Figure 15.10 are now such that s_i has one of the values $0, 1, \ldots,$ $m - 1$, the $\{s_i\}$ being statistically independent and equally likely to have any of the m possible values, as before. The coder replaces the $\{s_i\}$ by the corresponding sequence of values $\{q_i\}$, which are sampled at the time instants $\{iT\}$ to give the corresponding sequence of impulses $\{q_i\delta(t - iT)\}$ at the input to the transmitter filter. q_i has one of the values $(2l - m + 1)k$, for $l = 0, 1, \ldots, m - 1$, so that the signal fed to the transmitter filter is an m-level polar signal. The coding process is such that any one q_i is a function of the present and preceding $\{s_i\}$, giving an arrangement of precoding. In every case studied here it can readily be shown that the $\{q_i\}$ are statistically independent and equally likely to have any of the m possible values.

The baseband channel, which contains the transmitter filter, the transmission path and the receiver filter, is identical to the baseband channel assumed earlier in the chapter. Thus the average signal energy per element at the input to the transmission path is $\overline{q_i^2}$, the mean square value of q_i, and the noise component v_i in a received sample r_i at the detector input, is a Gaussian random variable with zero mean and variance $\frac{1}{2}N_0$.

The detected value of s_i is determined in the detector by comparing r_i with the appropriate set of decision thresholds. There is no cancellation of intersymbol interference.

15.8   Cosine and sine spectra

The transfer function $H(f)$ of the baseband channel in Figure 15.10 is assumed here to be given by Equation 15.4 or 15.13, so that the data signal at the output of the baseband channel has either a cosine or sine spectrum. Consider first a binary signal, such that $s_i = 0$ or 1 and $q_i = \pm k$. Clearly the transmitted signal, at the input to the baseband channel, is a binary polar signal.

With a cosine signal-spectrum at the output of the baseband channel, the sample value at the detector input, at the time instant $t = (i - \frac{1}{2})T$, is

$$r_i = p_i + v_i \tag{15.35}$$

where
$$p_i = \tfrac{\pi}{4}q_i + \tfrac{\pi}{4}q_{i-1} \tag{15.36}$$

This can be seen from Equation 15.6, bearing in mind that the impulse at the input to the baseband channel at time $t = iT$ now has the value (area) q_i and not s_i.

With a sine signal-spectrum, the sample value at the detector input, at the time instant $t = (i - 1)T$, is r_i in Equation 15.35 where now

Table 15.1 PRECODING OF BINARY SIGNALS

s_i	0	1
Cosine spectrum	$q_i = -q_{i-1}$	$q_i = q_{i-1}$
Sine spectrum	$q_i = q_{i-2}$	$q_i = -q_{i-2}$
p_i	0	$\pm\frac{\pi}{2}k$

$$p_i = \tfrac{\pi}{4}q_i - \tfrac{\pi}{4}q_{i-2} \tag{15.37}$$

as can be seen from Equation 15.15.

For both cosine and sine signal-spectra, p_i in Equation 15.35 is the received sample in the absence of noise and has the value $-\frac{\pi}{2}k$, 0 or $\frac{\pi}{2}k$. When $s_i = 0$, the coder in Figure 15.10 chooses q_i so that $p_i = 0$. When $s_i = 1$, the coder chooses q_i so that $p_i = \pm\frac{\pi}{2}k$. Under these conditions, s_i is uniquely determined by p_i. The actual method of selecting q_i, so that p_i has the required value, will shortly be considered in some detail. The detector in Figure 15.10 detects p_i from r_i and then determines s_i' from p_i, where s_i' is the detected value of s_i and has the value 0 or 1.

It can be seen from Equations 15.36 and 15.37 that for p_i to have the value 0, $q_i = -q_{i-1}$, in the case of the cosine spectrum, and $q_i = q_{i-2}$, in the case of the sine spectrum. Similarly, for p_i to have the value $\pm\frac{\pi}{2}k$, $q_i = q_{i-1}$, in the case of the cosine spectrum, and $q_i = -q_{i-2}$, in the case of the sine spectrum. The rules for coding the transmitted signal are summarised in Table 15.1.

The relationship between s_i and p_i is clearly shown in Table 15.1. The detector detects s_i as 0 or 1, depending upon whether r_i is closer to 0 or $\pm\frac{\pi}{2}k$, respectively. Thus r_i is compared with two decision thresholds, one at $\frac{\pi}{4}k$ and the other at $-\frac{\pi}{4}k$.

The arrangement of precoding used with a cosine signal-spectrum, as shown in Table 15.1, is known as the duobinary system[431,432]. The corresponding arrangement with a sine spectrum is known as the modified duobinary system[446].

In both Equations 15.36 and 15.37 the wanted signal component $\frac{\pi}{4}q_i$ is added to an intersymbol interference component from a previous signal element. Furthermore, the *magnitude* of the resultant signal component p_i is $\frac{\pi}{2}k$ when $s_i = 1$ and is 0 when $s_i = 0$. The signal coding at the transmitter can therefore be considered as a process of amplitude modulation in which the intersymbol interference component acts as the carrier. If the received signal is full-wave rectified (either before or after sampling), so that the received sample value r_i is converted to its modulus (absolute value)

$$|r_i| = |p_i + v_i| \tag{15.38}$$

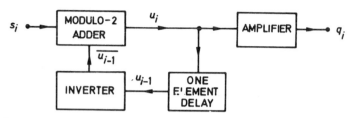

Fig. 15.11   Coder for a binary signal and a channel with a cosine transfer-function

then s_i is detected as 0 or 1, depending upon whether $|r_i|$ is closer to 0 or $\frac{\pi}{2}k$, respectively. Thus $|r_i|$ is compared with a single decision threshold at $\frac{\pi}{4}k$.

When $s_i = 0$ or 1 in the data-transmission system of Figure 15.10 as previously described, where p_i is now detected from r_i in Equation 15.35, each received signal-element is a ternary (3-level) signal and is detected as such. These arrangements are therefore often referred to as pseudo-ternary systems[457]. A method of coding the transmitted signals, to give the received pseudo-ternary signals, and the corresponding detection process for these signals, will now be described in some detail for each of the two baseband channels studied here.

When the baseband channel in Figure 15.10 has a cosine transfer function (Section 15.2), the coder at the transmitter is as shown in Figure 15.11.

The signals s_i, u_i, u_{i-1} and $\overline{u_{i-1}}$ in Figure 15.11 have the possible values 0 and 1, whereas $q_i = \pm k$. The amplifier sets q_i to $-k$ when $u_i = 0$, and to k when $u_i = 1$. The inverter inverts the input signal with respect to a value of $\frac{1}{2}$. Thus, when $u_{i-1} = 0, \overline{u_{i-1}} = 1$, and when $u_{i-1} = 1, \overline{u_{i-1}} = 0$, so that $\overline{u_{i-1}}$ is the binary complement of u_{i-1}. u_i is the modulo-2 sum of s_i and $\overline{u_{i-1}}$, which means that when s_i and $\overline{u_{i-1}}$ have the same binary value, $u_i = 0$, and when s_i and $\overline{u_{i-1}}$ have different binary values, $u_i = 1$. The modulo-2 adder is therefore an exclusive-OR gate.

The truth table for the possible values of s_i, u_i and $\overline{u_{i-1}}$, in the coder of Figure 15.11, is shown in Table 15.2. p_i is here given by Equation 15.36.

When the baseband channel in Figure 15.10 has a sine transfer function (Section 15.3), the coder at the transmitter is as shown in Figure 15.12.

The truth table for the possible values of s_i, u_i and u_{i-2} is shown in Table 15.3. p_i is here given by Equation 15.37.

It can be seen from Tables 15.2 and 15.3 that there is here the same

Table 15.2 TRUTH TABLE FOR CODER IN FIGURE 15.11

s_i	u_{i-1}	u_i	q_{i-1}	q_i	p_i
0	0	0	k	$-k$	0
0	1	1	$-k$	k	0
1	0	1	k	k	$\frac{\pi}{2}k$
1	1	0	$-k$	$-k$	$-\frac{\pi}{2}k$

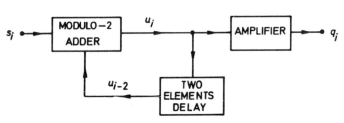

Fig. 15.12 *Coder for a binary signal and a channel with a sine transfer-function*

Table 15.3 TRUTH TABLE FOR CODER IN FIGURE 15.12

s_i	u_{i-2}	u_i	q_{i-2}	q_i	p_i
0	0	0	$-k$	$-k$	0
0	1	1	k	k	0
1	0	1	$-k$	k	$\frac{\pi}{2}k$
1	1	0	k	$-k$	$-\frac{\pi}{2}k$

relationship between s_i and p_i as that shown in Table 15.1, so that in each case s_i is uniquely determined by p_i.

For the precoding of binary polar signals transmitted over a channel with either a cosine or sine transfer function, the sample value r_i at the detector input, used for the detection of s_i, is given by

$$r_i = p_i + v_i \qquad (15.39)$$

where $p_i = 0$ or $\pm\frac{\pi}{2}k$, and v_i is a Gaussian random variable with zero mean and variance $\frac{1}{2}N_0$. When $p_i = 0$, $s_i = 0$, and when $p_i = \pm\frac{\pi}{2}k$, $s_i = 1$. p_i is first detected from r_i by selecting the possible value of p_i closest to r_i. This is achieved by comparing r_i with decision thresholds at $\frac{\pi}{4}k$ and $-\frac{\pi}{4}k$, and selecting the value of p_i between the same thresholds as r_i. s_i' is then determined from the detected value of p_i.

Strictly speaking, the decision thresholds at $\pm\frac{\pi}{4}k$ are not exactly at the correct values for the minimum probability of error in the detection of p_i from r_i. This is because p_i is not equally likely to have any one of its three possible values, but has probabilities of $\frac{1}{2}, \frac{1}{4}$ and $\frac{1}{4}$ of having the values 0, $\frac{\pi}{2}k$ and $-\frac{\pi}{2}k$, respectively. However, at high signal/noise ratios there is a negligible difference between the assumed decision thresholds and their correct values, and there is no significant difference between the respective error probabilities[422].

An error occurs in the detection of s_i when v_i has a magnitude greater than $\frac{\pi}{4}k$ and is such that r_i is closer to an adjacent one of the possible values of p_i than to the correct value. When $p_i = \pm\frac{\pi}{2}k$, no error occurs in the detection of s_i from r_i, if

$$|v_i| > \frac{3\pi}{4}k$$

and v_i has the opposite sign to p_i. However, at high signal/noise ratios, the probability of this occurring is completely negligible in comparison to the probability that

$$\frac{3\pi}{4}k > |v_i| > \frac{\pi}{4}k$$

and v_i has at the same time the opposite sign to p_i. The latter probability is therefore very close to the probability that $|v_i| > \frac{\pi}{4}k$, with v_i having the opposite sign to p_i. Clearly, when $p_i = \pm\frac{\pi}{2}k$, the probability of error is approximately

$$\int_{(\pi/4)k}^{\infty} \frac{1}{\sqrt{(\pi N_0)}} \exp\left(-\frac{v^2}{N_0}\right) dv = Q\left\{\frac{\frac{\pi}{4}k}{\sqrt{(\frac{1}{2}N_0)}}\right\} \quad (15.40)$$

and when $p_i = 0$, the probability of error is

$$2\int_{(\pi/4)k}^{\infty} \frac{1}{\sqrt{(\pi N_0)}} \exp\left(-\frac{v^2}{N_0}\right) dv = 2Q\left\{\frac{\frac{\pi}{4}k}{\sqrt{(\frac{1}{2}N_0)}}\right\} \quad (15.41)$$

Since p_i is equally likely to be either $\pm\frac{\pi}{2}k$ or 0, the average probability of error is

$$1.5Q\left\{\frac{\frac{\pi}{4}k}{\sqrt{(\frac{1}{2}N_0)}}\right\}$$

which at high signal/noise ratios can be taken to be

$$P_e = Q\left\{\frac{\frac{\pi}{4}k}{\sqrt{(\frac{1}{2}N_0)}}\right\} \quad (15.42)$$

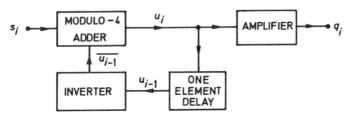

Fig. 15.13   Coder for a quaternary signal and a channel with a cosine transfer-function

This is the same as the average probability of error in the corresponding arrangements with cosine or sine signal-spectra, where no coding is used at the transmitter and decision-directed cancellation of intersymbol interference is used at the detector. However, the arrangements of precoding do not suffer from error extension effects, which gives them a certain advantage over the arrangements of intersymbol-interference cancellation, in that the errors do not now occur in bursts and the error rate is correspondingly reduced. Nevertheless, when $m = 2$ or 4, when the $\{s_i\}$ are statistically independent and equally likely to have any of their possible values, and when the signal/noise ratio is sufficiently high, the tolerances of the different systems to additive white Gaussian noise are, for practical purposes, the same.

Precoding can, of course, be used with multilevel signals as well as with binary signals. The most important of these various systems, other than the two binary systems just considered, are those where the transmitted signal at the input to the baseband channel is a quaternary polar signal. These systems will now be studied in some detail.

When the baseband channel in Figure 15.10 has a cosine transfer-function (Section 15.2), the coder at the transmitter is as shown in Figure 15.13.

The signals s_i, u_i, u_{i-1} and $\overline{u_{i-1}}$ in Figure 15.13 have the possible values 0, 1, 2 and 3, whereas q_i has one of the values $-3k$, $-k$, k and $3k$. The amplifier sets q_i to $-3k$, $-k$, k or $3k$, depending upon whether u_i is 0, 1, 2 or 3, respectively. The inverter inverts the input signal with respect to a value of $1\frac{1}{2}$, so that when u_{i-1} is 0, 1, 2 or 3, $\overline{u_{i-1}}$ is 3, 2, 1 or 0, respectively. Thus $\overline{u_{i-1}}$ is the quaternary complement of u_{i-1}, which means that $\overline{u_{i-1}} = 3 - u_{i-1}$. u_i is the modulo-4 sum of s_i and $\overline{u_{i-1}}$. When

$$s_i + \overline{u_{i-1}} < 4$$
$$u_i = s_i + \overline{u_{i-1}}$$

Table 15.4   TRUTH TABLE FOR CODER IN FIGURE 15.13

s_i	$\overline{u_{i-1}}$	u_i	q_{i-1}	q_i	p_i
0	0	0	$3k$	$-3k$	0
0	1	1	k	$-k$	0
0	2	2	$-k$	k	0
0	3	3	$-3k$	$3k$	0
1	0	1	$3k$	$-k$	$\frac{\pi}{2}k$
1	1	2	k	k	$\frac{\pi}{2}k$
1	2	3	$-k$	$3k$	$\frac{\pi}{2}k$
1	3	0	$-3k$	$-3k$	$-\frac{3\pi}{2}k$
2	0	2	$3k$	k	πk
2	1	3	k	$3k$	πk
2	2	0	$-k$	$-3k$	$-\pi k$
2	3	1	$-3k$	$-k$	$-\pi k$
3	0	3	$3k$	$3k$	$\frac{3\pi}{2}k$
3	1	0	k	$-3k$	$-\frac{\pi}{2}k$
3	2	1	$-k$	$-k$	$-\frac{\pi}{2}k$
3	3	2	$-3k$	k	$-\frac{\pi}{2}k$

and when

$$s_i + \overline{u_{i-1}} \geqslant 4$$

$$u_i = s_i + \overline{u_{i-1}} - 4$$

The truth table for the possible values of s_i, u_i and $\overline{u_{i-1}}$, in the coder of Figure 15.13, is shown in Table 15.4. p_i is here given by Equation 15.36.

Where quaternary polar signals are transmitted over a baseband channel with a sine transfer-function (Section 15.3), the coder at the transmitter is as shown in Figure 15.14.

The truth table for the possible values of s_i, u_{i-2} and u_i is shown in Table 15.5. p_i is here given by Equation 15.37.

It can be seen from Tables 15.4 and 15.5 that in each case the relationship between s_i and p_i is as shown in Table 15.6. Thus in both cases s_i is uniquely determined by p_i.

When precoding is used with a quaternary signal transmitted over a channel with either a cosine or sine transfer-function, the sample value r_i at the detector input, used for the detection of s_i, is given by

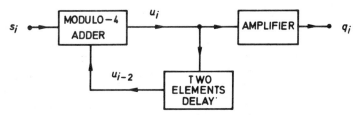

Fig. 15.14   Coder for a quaternary signal and a channel with a sine transfer-function

Table 15.5   TRUTH TABLE FOR CODER IN FIGURE 15.14

s_i	u_{i-2}	u_i	q_{i-2}	q_i	p_i
0	0	0	$-3k$	$-3k$	0
0	1	1	$-k$	$-k$	0
0	2	2	k	k	0
0	3	3	$3k$	$3k$	0
1	0	1	$-3k$	$-k$	$\frac{\pi}{2}k$
1	1	2	$-k$	k	$\frac{\pi}{2}k$
1	2	3	k	$3k$	$\frac{\pi}{2}k$
1	3	0	$3k$	$-3k$	$-\frac{3\pi}{2}k$
2	0	2	$-3k$	k	πk
2	1	3	$-k$	$3k$	πk
2	2	0	k	$-3k$	$-\pi k$
2	3	1	$3k$	$-k$	$-\pi k$
3	0	3	$-3k$	$3k$	$\frac{3\pi}{2}k$
3	1	0	$-k$	$-3k$	$-\frac{\pi}{2}k$
3	2	1	k	$-k$	$-\frac{\pi}{2}k$
3	3	2	$3k$	k	$-\frac{\pi}{2}k$

Table 15.6   RELATIONSHIP BETWEEN s_i AND p_i

s_i	p_i
0	0
1	$\frac{\pi}{2}k$ or $-\frac{3\pi}{2}k$
2	πk or $-\pi k$
3	$\frac{3\pi}{2}k$ or $-\frac{\pi}{2}k$

Equation 15.39, where now p_i has one of the seven possible values $-\frac{3\pi}{2}k$, $-\pi k$, $-\frac{\pi}{2}k$, 0, $\frac{\pi}{2}k$, πk, and $\frac{3\pi}{2}k$. The detector detects p_i by comparing r_i with decision thresholds at $-\frac{5\pi}{4}k$, $-\frac{3\pi}{4}k$, $-\frac{\pi}{4}k$, $\frac{\pi}{4}k$, $\frac{3\pi}{4}k$ and $\frac{5\pi}{4}k$, and selecting the value of p_i between the same thresholds as r_i. s_i' is then determined from the detected value of p_i, according to Table 15.6.

An error occurs in the detection of s_i when the noise component v_i, in Equation 15.39, has a magnitude greater than $\frac{\pi}{4}k$ and is such that r_i is closer to an adjacent one of the possible values of p_i than to the correct value. It can be seen from Tables 15.4 and 15.5 that p_i has a probability of only $\frac{1}{8}$ of having one of its two extreme values $\pm\frac{3\pi}{2}k$, so that the average probability of error is nearly

$$2Q\left\{\frac{\frac{\pi}{4}k}{\sqrt{(\frac{1}{2}N_0)}}\right\}$$

which at high signal/noise ratios can be taken to be

$$P_e = Q\left\{\frac{\frac{\pi}{4}k}{\sqrt{(\frac{1}{2}N_0)}}\right\} \tag{15.43}$$

For a given value of k, this is the same as the error probability for precoding with binary polar signals, and for decision-directed cancellation of intersymbol interference with either binary or multi-level signals, so long as the baseband channel has a cosine or sine transfer-function and the signal/noise ratio is high. However, at a given average transmitted signal energy per bit, k differs as m changes from one value to another, leading to the corresponding change in the error probability. This is considered further in Section 15.10.

15.9 Cosine² and sine² spectra

The transfer function $H(f)$ of the baseband channel in Figure 15.10 is assumed here to be given by Equation 15.20 or 15.26, so that the signal at the output of the baseband channel has either a cosine² or sine² spectrum. Consider a binary signal, such that $s_i = 0$ or 1 and $q_i = \pm k$.

With a cosine² signal-spectrum at the output of the baseband channel, the sample value at the detector input, at the time instant $t = (i-1)T$, is

$$r_i = p_i + v_i \tag{15.44}$$

where

$$p_i = \frac{1}{2}q_i + q_{i-1} + \frac{1}{2}q_{i-2} \tag{15.45}$$

Table 15.7 PRECODING OF BINARY SIGNALS

s_i	0	1
Cosine² spectrum	$q_i = q_{i-2}$	$q_i = -q_{i-2}$
Sine² spectrum	$q_i = q_{i-4}$	$q_i = -q_{i-4}$
p_i	0 or $\pm 2k$	$\pm k$

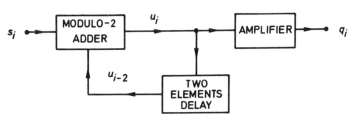

Fig. 15.15   Coder for a binary signal and a channel with a cosine² transfer-function

This can be seen from Equation 15.22, bearing in mind that the impulse at the input to the baseband channel at time $t = iT$ now has the value (area) q_i and not s_i.

With a sine² signal-spectrum, the sample value at the detector input, at the time instant $t = (i - 2)T$, is r_i in Equation 15.44 where now

$$p_i = -\tfrac{1}{2}q_i + q_{i-2} - \tfrac{1}{2}q_{i-4} \qquad (15.46)$$

as can be seen from Equation 15.28.

For both cosine² and sine² signal-spectra, p_i in Equation 15.44 is the received sample in the absence of noise and has one of the five values $-2k$, $-k$, 0, k and $2k$. When $s_i = 0$, the coder in Figure 15.10 chooses q_i so that $p_i = -2k$, 0 or $2k$. When $s_i = 1$, the coder chooses q_i so that $p_i = \pm k$. Under these conditions, s_i may be uniquely determined from p_i. The detector in Figure 15.10 detects p_i from r_i and then determines s_i', the detected value of s_i, from p_i.

It can be seen from Equations 15.45 and 15.46 that q_i must be selected as shown in Table 15.7.

When the baseband channel in Figure 15.10 has a cosine² transfer-function (Section 15.4), the coder at the transmitter is as shown in Figure 15.15.

The signals s_i, u_i and u_{i-2} have the possible values 0 and 1, and $q_i = \pm k$. The truth table for the possible values of s_i, u_i and u_{i-2}, in the coder of Figure 15.15, is shown in Table 15.8. p_i is here given by Equation 15.45.

Table 15.8   TRUTH TABLE FOR CODER IN FIGURE 15.15

s_i	u_{i-2}	u_i	q_{i-2}	q_{i-1}	q_i	p_i
0	0	0	$-k$	$-k$	$-k$	$-2k$
0	0	0	$-k$	k	$-k$	0
0	1	1	k	$-k$	k	0
0	1	1	k	k	k	$2k$
1	0	1	$-k$	$-k$	k	$-k$
1	0	1	$-k$	k	k	k
1	1	0	k	$-k$	$-k$	$-k$
1	1	0	k	k	$-k$	k

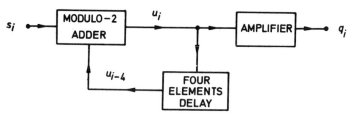

Fig. 15.16   Coder for a binary signal and a channel with a sine² transfer-function

When the baseband channel in Figure 15.10 has a sine² transfer-function (Section 15.5), the coder at the transmitter is as shown in Figure 15.16.

The truth table for the possible values of s_i, u_i and u_{i-4} is shown in Table 15.9. p_i is here given by Equation 15.46.

It can be seen from Tables 15.8 and 15.9 that in each case the relationship between s_i and p_i is as shown in Table 15.10. Thus in both cases s_i is uniquely determined by p_i.

When precoding is used with a binary signal transmitted over a channel with either a cosine² or sine² transfer-function, the sample value r_i at the detector input, used for the detection of s_i, is given by Equation 15.44, where p_i has one of the five possible values $-2k$, $-k$, 0, k and $2k$. The detector detects p_i by comparing r_i with decision thresholds at $-\frac{3}{2}k$, $-\frac{1}{2}k$, $\frac{1}{2}k$ and $\frac{3}{2}k$, and selecting the possible value of p_i between the same thresholds as r_i. s_i is then determined from the detected value of p_i, according to Table 15.10.

An error occurs in the detection of s_i when the noise component v_i in Equation 15.44 has a magnitude greater than $\frac{1}{2}k$ and is such that r_i

Table 15.9 TRUTH TABLE FOR CODER IN FIGURE 15.16

s_i	u_{i-4}	u_i	q_{i-4}	q_{i-2}	q_i	p_i
0	0	0	$-k$	$-k$	$-k$	0
0	0	0	$-k$	k	$-k$	$2k$
0	1	1	k	$-k$	k	$-2k$
0	1	1	k	k	k	0
1	0	1	$-k$	$-k$	k	$-k$
1	0	1	$-k$	k	k	k
1	1	0	k	$-k$	$-k$	$-k$
1	1	0	k	k	$-k$	k

Table 15.10 RELATIONSHIP BETWEEN s_i AND p_i

s_i	p_i
0	0 or $\pm 2k$
1	$\pm k$

is closer to an adjacent one of the possible values of p_i than to the correct value. Thus, at high signal/noise ratios the average probability of error can be taken to be

$$P_e = Q\left\{\frac{\frac{1}{2}k}{\sqrt{(\frac{1}{2}N_0)}}\right\} \qquad (15.47)$$

This is the same as the average probability of error in the corresponding arrangements with cosine^2 or sine^2 signal-spectra, where no coding is used at the transmitter and decision-directed cancellation of intersymbol interference is used at the detector.

15.10 Assessment of systems

When $m = 2$ or 4, when the $\{s_i\}$ are statistically independent and equally likely to have any of their possible values, and when the signal/noise ratio is sufficiently high, there is no great difference in tolerance to additive white Gaussian noise between any one of the arrangements of precoding and the corresponding system employing decision-directed cancellation of intersymbol interference. Further-

Table 15.11 RELATIVE TOLERANCES TO ADDITIVE WHITE GAUSSIAN NOISE OF RECEIVED SIGNALS WITH DIFFERENT SPECTRA, FOR THE SAME TRANSMITTED SIGNAL

Signal spectrum	Probability of error	Relative tolerance to noise (dB)
Rectangular or raised cosine	$Q\left\{\dfrac{k}{\sqrt{(\frac{1}{2}N_0)}}\right\}$	0
Cosine or sine	$Q\left\{\dfrac{\frac{\pi}{4}k}{\sqrt{(\frac{1}{2}N_0)}}\right\}$	-2.1
Cosine^2 or sine^2	$Q\left\{\dfrac{\frac{1}{2}k}{\sqrt{(\frac{1}{2}N_0)}}\right\}$	-6.0

more, both techniques involve much the same equipment complexity, so that, under the assumed conditions, there is not very much to choose between them. However, since the arrangements of precoding do not suffer from error-extension effects, they do not rely on the assumptions made here to achieve satisfactory operation. Thus they can be used over a very much wider range of conditions and are therefore normally preferred in practice.

Consider now a given m-level polar signal at the input to the baseband channel in Figure 14.6 or 15.10, such that the value (area) of an impulse is given by one of the values $(2l - m + 1)k$, for $l = 0, 1, \ldots, m - 1$, and $m = 2$ or 4. The baseband channel may have any of the different transfer functions studied in Chapters 14 and 15. The probability of error in the detection of a received signal-element, at high signal/noise ratios, is approximately as shown in Table 15.11, for the appropriate signal spectrum at the output of the baseband channel. Since the *same* signal is used at the *input* to the baseband channel in every case, k has a fixed value here.

For a given m-level signal at the input to each of the different baseband channels, the average transmitted power level at the input to the transmission path (in Figure 14.6 or 15.10) is fixed, as is the information rate. Thus the average transmitted energy per bit is the same in every case. The relative tolerances to additive white Gaussian noise, for the different channels and therefore the different signal spectra, are now given by the relative values of the noise power spectral density, $\frac{1}{2}N_0$, for a given probability of error. The tolerances to noise, expressed in dB relative to that for a rectangular or raised-cosine signal spectrum, are shown in Table 15.11.

With a binary polar signal at the input to the baseband channel, in Figure 14.6 or 15.10, the average transmitted energy per bit is in every case

Table 15.12 RELATIVE TOLERANCES TO ADDITIVE WHITE GAUSSIAN NOISE AT A GIVEN AVERAGE TRANSMITTED SIGNAL ENERGY PER BIT

Signal spectrum	Probability of error		Relative tolerance to noise (dB)	
	Binary polar signal	Quaternary polar signal	Binary polar signal	Quaternary polar signal
Rectangular or raised cosine	$Q\left\{\sqrt{\left(\dfrac{2E_b}{N_0}\right)}\right\}$	$Q\left\{\sqrt{\left(\dfrac{4E_b}{5N_0}\right)}\right\}$	0	−4.0
Cosine or sine	$Q\left\{\sqrt{\left(\dfrac{\pi^2 E_b}{8N_0}\right)}\right\}$	$Q\left\{\sqrt{\left(\dfrac{\pi^2 E_b}{20N_0}\right)}\right\}$	−2.1	−6.1
Cosine^2 or sine^2	$Q\left\{\sqrt{\left(\dfrac{E_b}{2N_0}\right)}\right\}$	$Q\left\{\sqrt{\left(\dfrac{E_b}{5N_0}\right)}\right\}$	−6.0	−10.0

$$E_b = k^2 \tag{15.48}$$

and with a quaternary polar signal, the average transmitted energy per bit is

$$E_b = \tfrac{5}{2}k^2 \tag{15.49}$$

as can be seen from Table 14.1.

The error probabilities and relative tolerances to additive white Gaussian noise, of binary and quaternary polar signals transmitted over the different channels, are shown in Table 15.12. High signal/noise ratios are assumed here. The error probabilities are derived from Table 15.11, using Equations 15.48 and 15.49. The relative tolerances to noise are the values of the noise power spectral density, $\tfrac{1}{2}N_0$, expressed in dB relative to that for a binary polar signal with a rectangular or raised-cosine spectrum, assuming a given probability of error and a given average transmitted signal energy per bit. It can be seen that the tolerance to noise of the quaternary polar signal is in every case 4 dB below that of the corresponding binary polar signal.

Consider now a binary polar signal with a raised-cosine spectrum, that has a given information rate and a given average transmitted power level. If this signal is replaced by a quaternary polar signal with a raised-cosine spectrum, that has the same information rate and the same average transmitted power level, then the quaternary signal has half the bandwidth. Both signals, however, have the same average transmitted signal energy per bit, so that, from Table 15.12, the quaternary signal has a tolerance to additive white Gaussian noise

4 dB below that of the binary signal. However, if the binary signal is replaced by a binary signal with either a cosine or sine spectrum, that again has the same information rate and the same average transmitted power level, then the new binary signal has half the bandwidth of the original binary signal, but its tolerance to additive white Gaussian noise is only 2.1 dB below that of the original signal. Clearly the binary signal with a cosine or sine spectrum occupies the same bandwidth as the quaternary signal but has an advantage of 1.9 dB in tolerance to additive white Gaussian noise, at a given average transmitted signal energy per bit.

The important advantage of the signals with a cosine or sine spectrum over those with a raised-cosine spectrum, is that, at a given average transmitted power level and at a given information rate, the former use only half the bandwidth of the latter in return for a reduction of only 2.1 dB in tolerance to additive white Gaussian noise.

Another important property of signals with a cosine or sine spectrum is that they have no frequency component at $1/2T$ Hz, regardless of the sequence of data element values. This means that a sine wave of frequency $1/2T$ Hz may be transmitted together with the data signal and used to carry the element timing information that is needed at the receiver to sample the received waveform at the correct time instants. The two signals can be separated from each other without significant interference at the receiver. Thus the sampling instants need not now be determined from the received data signal itself, which is not always an easy thing to do.

The particular advantage of the signal with a sine spectrum over signals with a cosine or raised-cosine spectrum, is that it has no frequency component at zero frequency (d.c.). Thus the signal can be transmitted satisfactorily over a transmission path that does not pass d.c. This is not in general possible with the other signals unless they can be suitably scrambled to remove the d.c. component from the signal spectrum.

At a given information rate and a given average transmitted power level, a binary polar signal with a $\cos^2$ or $\sin^2$ spectrum occupies the same bandwidth as a quaternary polar signal with a raised-cosine spectrum. However, the binary signal has a tolerance to additive white Gaussian noise 2 dB below that of the quaternary signal, since the quaternary signal loses 4 dB, in tolerance to noise, relative to a binary polar signal with a raised-cosine spectrum, whereas the binary signal with a $\cos^2$ or $\sin^2$ spectrum loses 6 dB.

A signal with a $\cos^2$ or $\sin^2$ spectrum has the advantage over the corresponding signal with a cosine or sine spectrum that it has much less signal power in the neighbourhood of $1/2T$ Hz. This makes it easier to transmit the element timing information via a $1/2T$ Hz sine wave, since the data and timing signals are now more easily separated at the receiver.

A signal with a sine^2 spectrum has the advantage over the corresponding signal with a sine spectrum that it has much less signal power in the neighbourhood of zero frequency or d.c. The signal can therefore be transmitted successfully over a transmission path having a significantly greater attenuation at very low frequencies than can be tolerated by the signal with a sine spectrum.

It seems that for many applications a quaternary signal with a raised-cosine spectrum can with advantage be replaced by the corresponding binary signal with a cosine or sine spectrum. On the other hand, the quaternary signal cannot often with advantage be replaced by the corresponding binary signal with a cosine^2 or sine^2 spectrum, mainly because of the relatively low tolerance to additive white Gaussian noise of the latter signal.

A baseband data signal with a sine or sine^2 spectrum can be used to amplitude modulate a carrier, such that after the removal of the carrier and one of the two sidebands of the resultant double-sideband AM signal, a single sideband suppressed carrier AM signal is obtained. This occupies a significantly smaller bandwidth than the corresponding vestigial sideband suppressed carrier AM signal that is generated by a baseband data signal whose spectrum is not zero at d.c.

Many other partial-response channels have been studied[470], but those described here are probably of the greatest practical importance.

15.11 Partial-response channels formed by correlative-level coding

It is evident from Equations 15.5, 15.14, 15.21 and 15.27 that any of the different partial-response channels has an impulse response which is a linear combination of two or three $(\sin x)/x$ waveforms suitably spaced at multiples of T seconds. Thus, for any given partial-response channel, if each impulse of area s_i at the input to the baseband channel is replaced by the sequence of two or three impulses corresponding to these $(\sin x)/x$ waveforms, and if the impulses for the different $\{s_i\}$ are added together linearly and fed over a baseband channel whose impulse response is given by Equation 14.42, then the resultant impulse-response is that of the given partial-response channel. Clearly, any of the different partial-response channels can be implemented by using transmitter and receiver filters which together have the $(\sin x)/x$ impulse response given by Equation 14.42, and by

Table 15.13   VALUES OF q_i FOR THE DIFFERENT CHANNELS

Signal spectrum at output of baseband channel	Value of q_i expressed in terms of the $\{s_i\}$
Rectangular	s_i
Cosine	$s_i + s_{i-1}$
Sine	$s_i - s_{i-2}$
Cosine²	$s_i + 2s_{i-1} + s_{i-2}$
Sine²	$-s_i + 2s_{i-2} - s_{i-4}$

using linear signal coding at the transmitter to give the appropriate impulse-response. Without the signal coding at the transmitter, the signal at the output of the baseband channel has a rectangular spectrum proportional to $H(f)$ in Equation 14.40. The signal coding at the transmitter is known as *correlative-level coding* and is equivalent to an additional filter that converts the rectangular signal-spectrum to the required shape[439].

For example, to obtain a cosine signal spectrum at the output of the baseband channel, the ith signal-element at the input to the channel becomes

$$s_i\delta(t - iT) + s_i\delta(t - (i + 1)T)$$

for each i. With the given baseband channel (Equation 14.42), this gives a signal-element waveform at the output of the channel which is a suitably scaled and delayed version of the waveform in Figure 15.2. Clearly, the resultant signal now fed to the channel, at time $t = iT$, is

$$(s_i + s_{i-1})\delta(t - iT)$$

The arrangement of the data-transmission system is as shown in Figure 15.10, where the transfer function of both the transmitter and receiver filter is $H^{1/2}(f)$, and $H(f)$ is given by Equation 14.40. The coder at the transmitter becomes a part of the baseband channel and now performs a *linear* operation on the input signals $\{s_i\}$, such that each of its output signals $\{q_i\}$ is a linear combination of two or more of the $\{s_i\}$. For binary polar signals, s_i has the possible values $-k$ and k, and for quaternary polar signals, s_i has the possible values $-3k$, $-k$, k and $3k$. In each case the $\{s_i\}$ are statistically independent and equally likely to have any of the possible values.

The relationships between the $\{q_i\}$ and the $\{s_i\}$, for the different partial-response channels, are given in Table 15.13. The output signal from the coder in Figure 15.10 is sampled at the time instants $\{iT\}$, for all values of the integer i, to give the sequence of impulses $\{q_i\delta(t - iT)\}$

fed to the baseband channel. Each of the different baseband channels is formed by the appropriate relationship between q_i and the $\{s_i\}$, which is generated in the coder. The impulse response of each channel is proportional to the corresponding $h(t)$ in Equation 14.42, 15.5, 15.14, 15.21 or 15.27, and in every case other than Equation 14.42 it is appropriately delayed relative to $h(t)$.

It can be shown that the average transmitted energy per signal-element is $\overline{q_i^2}$ (the mean-square value of q_i) so that the average transmitted energy per bit is $\overline{q_i^2}$ for binary signals and $\frac{1}{2}\overline{q_i^2}$ for quaternary signals. The transmitted signals are, of course, binary or quaternary, depending upon whether s_i has two or four possible values, regardless of the number of possible values of q_i. The $\{q_i\}$ are *correlated* and are *not* equally likely to have their different possible values. However, the $\{s_i\}$ are uncorrelated and have zero mean, so that $\overline{s_i s_l}$ (the mean value of $s_i s_l$) is zero whenever $i \neq l$. Thus it can be seen from Table 15.13 that in the case of a channel giving a cosine or sine signal-spectrum

$$\overline{q_i^2} = \overline{(s_i \pm s_{i-l})^2} = \overline{s_i^2 + s_{i-l}^2} = 2\overline{s_i^2} \tag{15.50}$$

where $l = 1$ or 2, and in the case of a channel giving a cosine^2 or sine^2 signal-spectrum,

$$\overline{q_i^2} = \overline{(\pm s_i \pm 2s_{i-l} \pm s_{i-2l})^2} = \overline{s_i^2 + 4s_{i-l}^2 + s_{i-2l}^2} = 6\overline{s_i^2} \tag{15.51}$$

where again $l = 1$ or 2. Furthermore, $\overline{s_i^2} = k^2$ for a binary polar signal and $\overline{s_i^2} = 5k^2$ for a quaternary polar signal. The values of the average transmitted energy per bit, for the different channels and for both binary and quaternary signals, can now readily be evaluated and are given in Table 15.14. The table shows also the possible values of q_i.

Since the sampled impulse-response of the transmitter filter, transmission path and receiver filter, in cascade, is $1\ 0\ 0\ 0\ \ldots$ with no delay in transmission, it follows that the sample value of the received waveform $r(t)$ at the time instant $t = iT$ is

$$r_i = q_i + v_i \tag{15.52}$$

where q_i is as given in Table 15.13 and v_i is a Gaussian random variable with zero mean and variance $\frac{1}{2}N_0$, as before.

In order to detect s_i from r_i it is necessary first to eliminate from q_i all components other than s_i. Following the correct detection of s_{i-1}, s_{i-2}, etc., the detector knows these terms, and with a knowledge of the relationship between q_i and the $\{s_i\}$, set by the coder at the transmitter, the detector now knows all components of q_i other than

Table 15.14   VALUES OF E_b FOR BINARY AND QUATERNARY SIGNALS OVER THE DIFFERENT CHANNELS

Signal spectrum at output of baseband channel	Possible values of q_i		Average transmitted energy per bit, E_b	
	Binary polar signal	Quaternary polar signal	Binary polar signal	Quaternary polar signal
Rectangular	$\pm k$	$\pm k, \pm 3k$	k^2	$2.5k^2$
Cosine or sine	$0, \pm 2k$	$0, \pm 2k, \pm 4k, \pm 6k$	$2k^2$	$5k^2$
Cosine^2 or sine^2	$0, \pm 2k, \pm 4k$	$0, \pm 2k, \pm 4k, \pm 6k, \pm 8k, \pm 10k, \pm 12k$	$6k^2$	$15k^2$

s_i. Thus the detector uses an arrangement of decision-directed cancellation of intersymbol interference, as previously described, to remove the intersymbol interference from r_i and to give the signal

$$x_i = \pm s_i + v_i \tag{15.53}$$

The term $+s_i$ occurs in Equation 15.53 in every case other than that of the sine^2 signal-spectrum, when the term becomes $-s_i$.

Since, in every case, adjacent possible values of s_i differ by $2k$, the decision thresholds used for the detection of s_i from x_i, which are set half way between adjacent possible values of $\pm s_i$, are at a distance of k from the nearest value (or values) of $\pm s_i$. Thus, at high signal/noise ratios, the average probability of error in the detection of s_i from x_i can in every case be taken to be

$$P_e = Q\left\{\frac{k}{\sqrt{(\frac{1}{2}N_0)}}\right\} \tag{15.54}$$

As an alternative to the arrangement just described, the cancellation of intersymbol interference at the receiver can be replaced by the corresponding precoding at the transmitter, which would of course be additional to the correlative-level coding used to shape the channel response. The detection process at the receiver now involves the appropriate set of decision thresholds, and the average probability of error in the detection of s_i is again given approximately by Equation 15.54.

For either a cosine or sine signal-spectrum, the precoding and correlative-level coding may be combined very simply, as can be seen from the example in Figure 15.17. s_i is here a binary signal and the

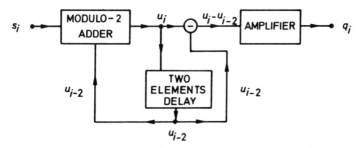

Fig. 15.17 Combination of precoding and correlative-level coding

Table 15.15 TRUTH TABLE FOR CODER IN FIGURE 15.17

s_i	u_{i-2}	u_i	$u_i - u_{i-2}$	q_i
0	0	0	0	0
0	1	1	0	0
1	0	1	1	$2k$
1	1	0	-1	$-2k$

resultant signal at the output of the baseband channel in Figure 15.10 has a sine spectrum, assuming as before that the transfer function of the transmitter and receiver filters in cascade satisfies Equation 14.40[442].

The signals s_i, u_i and u_{i-2} in Figure 15.17 have the possible values 0 and 1, so that $u_i - u_{i-2} = -1, 0$ or 1. The amplifier sets q_i to $-2k, 0$ or $2k$, depending upon whether $u_i - u_{i-2} = -1$, 0 or 1, respectively.

The truth table for the possible values of s_i, u_i, u_{i-2} and q_i is shown in Table 15.15. Clearly, q_i satisfies the condition for a sine signal-spectrum, given in Table 15.13, and s_i can be uniquely determined from q_i.

When s_i is a quaternary signal, a modulo-4 adder is used in place of the modulo-2 adder in Figure 15.17, and the signals s_i, u_i and u_{i-2} have the possible values 0, 1, 2 and 3. q_i is now a 7-level signal whose possible values are as given in Table 15.14.

In Figure 15.17, the modulo-2 adder and the two-elements delay circuit together form the *precoder*, and the subtractor and two-elements delay circuit together form the *correlative-level coder*. The latter, of course, acts as a filter that shapes the signal spectrum to its required form.

Consider now a more general arrangement of Figure 15.17, where the two-elements delay is replaced by an n-elements delay, where n is any positive integer. It may readily be shown that, with this coder, the

Table 15.16 RELATIVE TOLERANCES TO ADDITIVE WHITE GAUSSIAN NOISE AT A GIVEN AVERAGE TRANSMITTED SIGNAL ENERGY PER BIT

Signal spectrum	Probability of error		Relative tolerance to noise (dB)	
	Binary polar signal	Quaternary polar signal	Binary polar signal	Quaternary polar signal
Rectangular	$Q\left\{\sqrt{\left(\dfrac{2E_b}{N_0}\right)}\right\}$	$Q\left\{\sqrt{\left(\dfrac{4E_b}{5N_0}\right)}\right\}$	0	−4.0
Cosine or sine	$Q\left\{\sqrt{\left(\dfrac{E_b}{N_0}\right)}\right\}$	$Q\left\{\sqrt{\left(\dfrac{2E_b}{5N_0}\right)}\right\}$	−3.0	−7.0
Cosine^2 or sine^2	$Q\left\{\sqrt{\left(\dfrac{E_b}{3N_0}\right)}\right\}$	$Q\left\{\sqrt{\left(\dfrac{2E_b}{15N_0}\right)}\right\}$	−7.8	−11.8

spectrum of an individual signal-element, at both the input and the output of the baseband channel, has zeros at the frequencies $\{i/nT\}$ Hz, for *all* integers $\{i\}$ including zero, so that the resultant data signal has zero power-density at these frequencies[442]. It is, of course, the correlative-level coder that removes the frequencies $\{i/nT\}$ Hz.

The coder just described is a simple and effective means of shaping the transmitted-signal spectrum so as to avoid the transmission of particular frequencies. An application of this is considered in Section 11.7.

Using the relationships between E_b and k in Table 15.14, the error probability P_e in Equation 15.54 can be evaluated in terms of E_b and N_0, and hence the relative noise levels, for a given error probability and at a given average transmitted energy per bit, can be evaluated for binary and quaternary signals transmitted over the different channels. The results of this are shown in Table 15.16, where the tolerance to noise is measured in dB relative to that for a binary polar signal having a rectangular or raised-cosine spectrum. High signal/noise ratios are of course assumed here.

A comparison between Tables 15.12 and 15.16 shows that for cosine or sine signal-spectra, the partial-response channels, formed by correlative-level coding at the transmitter, give a tolerance to additive white Gaussian noise 0.9 dB below that for the alternative partial-response channels formed entirely by the transmitter and receiver filters, as for instance in Figure 14.6. In the case of cosine^2 or sine^2 signal spectra, the corresponding reduction in tolerance to noise is 1.8 dB. The reason for this is that, with correlative-level coding, the coder at the transmitter behaves as a linear filter that shapes the transmitted signal spectrum, in addition to the shaping of the signal spectrum performed by the transmitter filter itself. Thus the resultant or effective transmitter filter has a transfer function which is significantly different from that of the receiver filter. This means that neither of the Equations 14.34 and 14.21 are satisfied by the transmitter and receiver filters, so that the signal/noise power ratio at the output of the baseband channel no longer has its maximum value that is obtained in the alternative arrangement.

Since there is not a great reduction in tolerance to noise resulting from the use of correlative-level coding in place of the appropriate transmitter and receiver filters, there may sometimes be an advantage in the use of correlative-level coding to shape the signal spectrum. Where possible, however, the signal spectrum should normally be shaped entirely by the transmitter and receiver filters, which should satisfy Equation 14.21.

When binary signals are transmitted over the channel with a cosine^2 transfer function and correlative-level coding (but no precoding) at the transmitter, the received signal at time $t = (i + 1)T$ is

$$r_{i+1} = s_{i+1} + 2s_i + s_{i-1} + v_{i+1} \qquad (15.55)$$

as can be seen from Equation 15.52 and Table 15.13, where $s_i = \pm k$. Instead of using decision-directed cancellation of intersymbol interference to remove by subtraction $2s_i$ and s_{i-1} from r_{i+1} and hence to detect s_{i+1}, the detector now removes only s_{i-1} to form (with the correct detection of s_{i-1}) the signal

$$\begin{aligned} x_{i+1} &= r_{i+1} - s_{i-1} \\ &= s_{i+1} + 2s_i + v_{i+1} \end{aligned} \qquad (15.56)$$

s_i being then detected from the sign of x_{i+1}[509]. Practically all errors in the detection of s_i occur here when

$$s_{i+1} = -s_i \qquad (15.57)$$

which occurs with a probability of $\frac{1}{2}$, and under this condition

$$x_{i+1} = s_i + v_{i+1} \qquad (15.58)$$

Thus the probability of error in the detection of s_i, at high signal/noise ratios, can again be taken to be that given in Table 15.16. However, the error probability is in fact only about a quarter of that in the previous arrangement of decision-directed cancellation of intersymbol interference, and furthermore the detection process itself is somewhat simpler. Clearly, with binary signals, the detection process should be implemented as just described, rather than by the previous arrangement. A similar modification should be applied to the detection process in the case of the channel with a sine^2 transfer function, when binary signals are transmitted.

A very useful improvement in tolerance to noise can be achieved[508] by forming both x_{i+1} (Equation 15.56) and

$$x_i = r_i - 2s_{i-1} - s_{i-2}$$
$$= s_i + v_i \tag{15.59}$$

(assuming the correct detection of s_{i-1} and s_{i-2}) and detecting s_i from the sign of

$$x_{i+1} + x_i = s_{i+1} + 3s_i + v_{i+1} + v_i \tag{15.60}$$

Practically all errors in the detection of s_i from $x_{i+1} + x_i$ occur when $s_{i+1} = -s_i$ (as in Equation 15.57) and now

$$x_{i+1} + x_i = 2s_i + v_{i+1} + v_i \tag{15.61}$$

where again $s_i = \pm k$. Since Equation 14.60 holds under the conditions assumed here, the noise components v_{i+1} and v_i are statistically independent Gaussian random variables with zero mean and variance $\frac{1}{2}N_0$. Thus the resultant noise signal $v_{i+1} + v_i$ in Equation 15.61 is a Gaussian random variable with zero mean and variance N_0. The probability of error in the detection of s_i can now be taken to be

$$Q\left\{\frac{2k}{\sqrt{N_0}}\right\} = Q\left\{\sqrt{\left(\frac{4k^2}{N_0}\right)}\right\} = Q\left\{\sqrt{\left(\frac{2E_b}{3N_0}\right)}\right\} \tag{15.62}$$

from Equation 14.50 and Table 15.14. This means that, at high signal/noise ratios, the system gains an advantage of 3 dB, in tolerance to additive white Gaussian noise, over the previous arrangement, and so (from Table 15.16) loses only 4.8 dB in tolerance to noise relative to a system with a binary polar signal and a rectangular signal spectrum at the output of the baseband channel (Section 14.4). A similar modification with the same improvement in tolerance to noise can also be applied to the channel with a sine^2 transfer function.

A further improvement in tolerance to noise, over a channel with a cosine^2 or sine^2 transfer function, can be achieved by using in place of the arrangement just described a maximum-likelihood detector. This selects as the detected message the possible sequence of transmitted signal-element values for which there is the minimum mean-square difference between the corresponding received samples, for the given signal distortion but in the absence of noise, and the samples $\{r_i\}$ actually received. The detector can be implemented by means of the Viterbi algorithm[479] and, at high signal/noise ratios and a given average energy per transmitted signal-element, it loses only about 2 dB in tolerance to additive white Gaussian noise relative to a system with a binary polar signal and a rectangular signal spectrum at the output of the baseband channel (Section 14.4). In the corresponding arrangement, with a channel having a cosine or sine transfer function, the maximum likelihood detector loses only a fraction of 1 dB in tolerance to noise, the fraction reducing to zero as the signal/noise ratio increases. Thus, if a sophisticated detection process is used at the receiver, a partial response channel enables an excellent compromise to be achieved between the efficiency in the use of bandwidth and the tolerance to noise. The principles of maximum-likelihood detection are considered briefly in Chapter 6, further details on this and the Viterbi algorithm being given elsewhere[422,479,498]. The disadvantage of these techniques is that they involve considerable equipment complexity, whereas the arrangement given by Equations 15.59–15.62 can be implemented quite simply[508].

16

Modulated-carrier signals

16.1 Model of the data-transmission system

Practical data-transmission systems use transmission paths such as telephone circuits, HF radio links, satellite links, and so on. The majority of these not only use band-pass channels which are not well suited to the use of baseband signals, but they introduce frequency translation effects which prevent the use of baseband signals altogether. The frequency translation effects comprise shifts of one or two Hz in the whole of the signal spectrum. This prevents the correct detection of a baseband signal unless the frequency shift can be determined exactly at the receiver and suitably corrected for, which can be a difficult thing to do. A much simpler approach is to use the original baseband data signal to modulate a carrier, whose frequency is such that the spectrum of the modulated carrier signal lies within the pass-band of the transmission path. The modulated-carrier signal is transmitted, and suitably demodulated at the receiver to recover the baseband signal, which is then detected. The frequency translation effects are automatically corrected for in such a system. The data-transmission system is now as shown in Figure 16.1.

The data-transmission system is assumed to be a synchronous serial system with an element rate of $1/T$ elements per second, where T seconds is the duration of each signal element. The baseband data signal $s(t)$, used to modulate the carrier, is a rectangular waveform with transitions occurring at multiples of T seconds. A typical binary baseband signal $s(t)$ is as shown in Figure 13.1. The signal elements are assumed to be binary or quaternary, and may be polar or unipolar. As before, they are statistically independent and equally likely to have any of the possible binary or quaternary values.

There are three basic types of digital modulation employing the rectangular baseband waveform $s(t)$. These are amplitude-shift keying (ASK), phase-shift keying (PSK) and frequency-shift keying

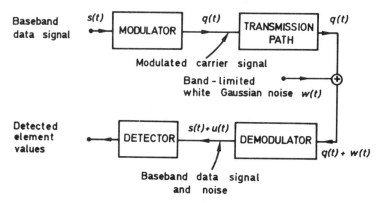

Fig. 16.1   Data transmission over a band-pass channel

(FSK). The modulated carrier signal $q(t)$, fed to the transmission path in Figure 16.1, is assumed to be an ASK signal.

The average transmitted element energy in $q(t)$ is assumed to be equal to that of the baseband signal $s(t)$, at the transmitter. Furthermore the signal carrier frequency in $q(t)$ is large compared with the signal element rate, so that there are many carrier cycles in each signal element of $q(t)$.

The transmission path is a band-pass channel of sufficient bandwidth not to introduce any significant distortion into the data signal, nor does it introduce any attenuation or delay. Thus the data signal at the output of the transmission path is the same as the data signal $q(t)$ at its input.

The additive white Gaussian noise, introduced over the transmission path, appears at its output as a Gaussian random process with a constant power spectral density of $\frac{1}{2}N_0$ over the frequency band (positive and negative frequencies) of the transmission path, the power density decaying to zero at frequencies away from the pass band of the transmission path. Thus the noise introduced by the transmission path can be considered to be the band-limited white Gaussian noise waveform $w(t)$, added to the data signal at the output of the transmission path and having a power density of $\frac{1}{2}N_0$ over the signal frequency band.

The signal at the input to the demodulator in Figure 16.1 is the waveform

$$r(t) = q(t) + w(t) \tag{16.1}$$

A high signal/noise ratio is assumed here.

The demodulator uses a process of linear coherent demodulation to convert the received ASK signal $q(t)$ into the corresponding baseband signal $s(t)$. At the same time it converts the received noise waveform $w(t)$ into the noise waveform $u(t)$ whose spectrum extends over the frequency band of the baseband data signal $s(t)$. Thus the signal at the output of the demodulator is the waveform

$$y(t) = s(t) + u(t) \tag{16.2}$$

The detector performs a process of matched-filter detection on each received baseband signal-element to give the detected element value. The demodulation and detection processes together give the best available tolerance to the Gaussian noise, under the assumed conditions.

The aim of this analysis is to compare the relative tolerances to additive white Gaussian noise of the different modulated carrier signals, assuming in each case the optimum detection process, regardless of whether or not this is feasible in practice. In this way the different modulated-carrier signals are compared on the basis of their relative tolerances to Gaussian noise, as determined by the signal waveforms themselves and not influenced by the particular detection processes most often used.

16.2 ASK signals

Consider an individual element of the baseband data signal $s(t)$, at the input to the modulator in the transmitter, where

$$s(t) = \begin{cases} s, & 0 < t < T \\ 0, & \text{elsewhere} \end{cases} \tag{16.3}$$

and s is equally likely to have any one of the m values $k_0 + 2lk$, for $l = 0, 1, \ldots, m - 1$. k has an appropriate positive value, and $k_0 = 0$ or $-(m-1)k$, depending upon whether the signal is unipolar or polar, respectively.

The modulator forms the product of the baseband waveform $s(t)$ and a sine-wave carrier $\sqrt{2} \cos 2\pi f_c t$, that has a constant instantaneous frequency f_c Hz and unit power level. The signal element at the modulator output, corresponding to $s(t)$ in Equation 16.3, is

$$q(t) = \begin{cases} \sqrt{2}\, s \cos 2\pi f_c t, & 0 < t < T \\ 0, & \text{elsewhere} \end{cases} \tag{16.4}$$

The carrier phase at time $t = 0$ is for convenience taken to be zero, since its value does not affect any of the important results derived here.

Clearly, when $s \neq 0$, a burst of carrier, of constant level and with

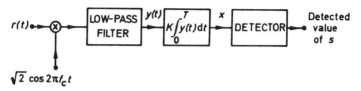

Fig. 16.2   Coherent detector for an ASK signal element

instantaneous frequency f_c Hz, is transmitted from 0 to T seconds. When $s(t)$ is a unipolar signal-element, $q(t)$ is an ASK signal-element. When $s(t)$ is a polar signal-element, $q(t)$ is a suppressed carrier ASK signal-element.

The energy of the transmitted signal-element given by $q(t)$ in Equation 16.4 is

$$\int_0^T q^2(t)\, dt = \int_0^T 2s^2 \cos^2 2\pi f_c t\, dt = s^2 \int_0^T (1 + \cos 4\pi f_c t)\, dt$$

$$= s^2 \left[t + \frac{\sin 4\pi f_c t}{4\pi f_c} \right]_0^T \simeq s^2 T \tag{16.5}$$

since it has been assumed that $f_c \gg 1/T$. Thus the average transmitted energy per element of the modulated-carrier signal $q(t)$ is approximately

$$E = \overline{s^2}\, T \tag{16.6}$$

which is the same as the average energy per element of the corresponding baseband signal $s(t)$. If f_c is any whole multiple of $1/2T$, Equation 16.5 holds exactly.

From Equation 16.4, the waveform at the input to the demodulator, during the time interval 0 to T, is

$$r(t) = \sqrt{2}\, s \cos 2\pi f_c t + w(t) \tag{16.7}$$

where $w(t)$ is a Gaussian random process with zero mean and a two-sided power spectral density of $\frac{1}{2}N_0$ over the signal frequency band.

The coherent detector for the received signal element is shown in Figure 16.2, where the multiplier and low-pass filter together correspond to the demodulator in Figure 16.1, and the integrator and detector together correspond to the detector in Figure 16.1

The signal at the input to the low-pass filter in Figure 16.2, over the time interval 0 to T seconds, is

$$r(t)\sqrt{2} \cos 2\pi f_c t = 2s \cos^2 2\pi f_c t + \sqrt{2}w(t) \cos 2\pi f_c t$$

$$= s + s \cos 4\pi f_c t + \sqrt{2}w(t) \cos 2\pi f_c t$$

$$= s(t) + s(t) \cos 4\pi f_c t + \sqrt{2}w(t) \cos 2\pi f_c t \qquad (16.8)$$

Since the bandwidth of $w(t)$ is assumed to be small compared with its centre frequency f_c, it may be shown that[428]

$$w(t) = w_c(t) \cos 2\pi f_c t - w_s(t) \sin 2\pi f_c t \qquad (16.9)$$

where $w(t)$, $w_c(t)$ and $w_s(t)$ are all Gaussian random processes, with zero mean and the *same* mean-square value or average power level. $w_c(t)$ and $w_s(t)$ each occupy the frequency band from zero frequency to $\frac{1}{2}B$ Hz, where B Hz is the bandwidth (over positive frequencies) of $w(t)$, so that $w(t)$ has *twice* the frequency band of either $w_c(t)$ or $w_s(t)$. Furthermore, both $w_c(t)$ and $w_s(t)$ have a constant power spectral density from zero frequency to nearly $\frac{1}{2}B$ Hz. Thus, from zero frequency to nearly $\pm\frac{1}{2}B$ Hz, the *two-sided* power spectral density of $w_c(t)$ and $w_s(t)$ is *twice* that of $w(t)$, over the frequency band of the data signal $q(t)$, and is therefore N_0. Clearly, the noise signal at the input to the low-pass filter is

$$\sqrt{2}w(t) \cos 2\pi f_c t = \sqrt{2}w_c(t) \cos^2 2\pi f_c t$$

$$- \sqrt{2}w_s(t) \cos 2\pi f_c t \cdot \sin 2\pi f_c t$$

$$= \frac{1}{\sqrt{2}} w_c(t) + \frac{1}{\sqrt{2}} w_c(t) \cos 4\pi f_c t$$

$$- \frac{1}{\sqrt{2}} w_s(t) \sin 4\pi f_c t \qquad (16.10)$$

Let

$$\frac{1}{\sqrt{2}} w_c(t) = u(t) \qquad (16.11)$$

Then $u(t)$ is a Gaussian random process with zero mean and a *two-sided* power spectral density of $\frac{1}{2}N_0$ over the frequency band of the baseband data signal $s(t)$ in Equation 16.3.

The low-pass filter in Figure 16.2 is assumed to have unit gain over its pass band and to pass without delay or distortion the baseband data signal $s(t)$ together with the noise signal $u(t)$. It removes the high-frequency components of the data and noise signals, in Equations 16.8 and 16.10, to give at its output the signal

$$y(t) = s(t) + u(t) \qquad (16.12)$$

Clearly $y(t)$ is a rectangular m-level baseband signal $s(t)$ in the presence of bandlimited additive white Gaussian noise. The optimum detection process for such a signal has been studied in some detail in Chapter 13 for the particular cases where $m = 2$ or 4. The process will now be summarised briefly.

The signal $y(t)$ is fed to the integrator (Figure 16.2) which integrates the signal over the time interval 0 to T seconds, to give the output signal

$$x = K \int_0^T y(t) \, dt = K \int_0^T \{s(t) + u(t)\} \, dt \qquad (16.13)$$

so that

$$x = KTs + v \qquad (16.14)$$

where

$$v = K \int_0^T u(t) \, dt \qquad (16.15)$$

From Equation 13.11, v is a Gaussian random variable with zero mean and variance

$$N = \tfrac{1}{2} N_0 K^2 T \qquad (16.16)$$

The fact that the noise waveform $u(t)$ is band-limited white noise and not true white noise, as assumed in Chapter 13, does not affect this conclusion, since it is assumed that the noise power spectral density has the value $\tfrac{1}{2} N_0$ over the signal frequency band, which implies that the noise power spectral density maintains the value $\tfrac{1}{2} N_0$ from zero frequency to a frequency very much greater than $1/T$ Hz. It can now be seen from Figure 13.2 and Equation 13.10 that the output noise component v from the integrator is essentially the same as that which would have been obtained if $u(t)$ had been true white noise, and no significant error results in Equation 16.16.

The detection process that minimizes the probability of error in the detection of s from x, selects the possible value of KTs closest to x. Thus the detector in Figure 16.2 compares x with $m - 1$ decision thresholds whose values are $[k_0 + (2l - 1)k]KT$, for $l = 1, 2, \ldots, m - 1$, and then selects as the detected value of s its possible value such that KTs lies between the same decision thresholds as x.

Since the distance from any possible value of KTs to the nearest decision threshold is KTk, it follows that at high signal/noise ratios the probability of error in the detection of s can be taken to be

$$P_e = Q\left(\frac{KTk}{\sqrt{N}}\right) \tag{16.17}$$

as in Chapter 13.

Not only is the expression for the error probability the same here as in Chapter 13, but the output noise power N from the integrator is the same function of the input noise power spectral density $\frac{1}{2}N_0$ in both cases. Furthermore, when the ASK signal $q(t)$ is formed by the product of the baseband signal $s(t)$ and the sine-wave carrier $\sqrt{2}\cos 2\pi f_c t$, as is assumed here, the average signal energy per bit, E_b, is the same for both $q(t)$ and $s(t)$, since each signal has an element energy of $s^2 T$. But each signal has, of course, also the same value of k. Clearly a given value of E_b for a baseband signal $s(t)$ and the corresponding ASK signal $q(t)$, implies the same value of k for both signals, and vice versa. Thus, at a given average transmitted signal energy per bit and a given error probability, the received noise power spectral density $\frac{1}{2}N_0$ in the case of an ASK signal is the same as that for the corresponding baseband signal, so that the two signals have the same tolerance to additive white Gaussian noise.

The error probabilities and tolerances to additive white Gaussian noise of various baseband signals and their corresponding ASK signals, are shown in Table 16.1. The tolerances to noise are expressed in dB relative to that of a binary polar signal and the corresponding binary suppressed carrier ASK signal. The quoted results are derived from Chapter 13 and assume high signal/noise ratios.

In the ideal coherent detection of an ASK signal-element (Section 6.5) the low-pass filter in Figure 16.2 is omitted. However, under the assumed conditions, where $f_c \gg 1/T$, the high-frequency components at the output of the multiplier are, for practical purposes, removed by the integrator, so that the presence or absence of the low-pass filter does not noticeably affect the performance of the detector. Figure 16.2 has been adopted to emphasize the difference between *demodulation*, that is, the extraction of the modulating (baseband) waveform from the modulated-carrier signal, and *detection*, which is essentially a decision process and involves the comparison of the filtered baseband signal with suitable decision thresholds.

Figures 16.1 and 16.2 also show how the ASK system can be modelled as the corresponding baseband system, because of the very close relationship between ASK and rectangular baseband signals. Thus the same tolerance to noise is obtained in the optimum detection of $s(t)$ from $y(t)$ (Equation 16.2) as in the optimum detection of $q(t)$ from $r(t)$ (Equation 16.1), there being a close equivalence between the waveforms in $y(t)$ and those in $r(t)$.

Assume, as before, that the signal elements are statistically

Table 16.1 RELATIVE TOLERANCES TO ADDITIVE WHITE GAUSSIAN NOISE AT A GIVEN
AVERAGE TRANSMITTED SIGNAL ENERGY PER BIT

Possible values of s	Baseband signal $s(t)$	Modulated carrier signal $q(t)$	Probability of error P_e	Relative tolerance to noise (dB)
$\pm k$	Binary polar	Binary suppressed carrier ASK	$Q\left\{\sqrt{\left(\dfrac{2E_b}{N_0}\right)}\right\}$	0
$0, 2k$	Binary unipolar	Binary ASK	$Q\left\{\sqrt{\left(\dfrac{E_b}{N_0}\right)}\right\}$	-3
$\pm k, \pm 3k$	Quaternary polar	Quaternary suppressed carrier ASK	$Q\left\{\sqrt{\left(\dfrac{4E_b}{5N_0}\right)}\right\}$	-4
$0, 2k, 4k, 6k$	Quaternary unipolar	Quaternary ASK	$Q\left\{\sqrt{\left(\dfrac{2E_b}{7N_0}\right)}\right\}$	-8.5

independent and equally likely to have any of the possible element
values. Suppose also that the transmission path has a wide bandwidth
and introduces no signal distortion, regardless of the signal element
rate within the range considered. If now a quaternary polar baseband
signal is replaced by a 16-level polar baseband signal, or alternatively,
if a quaternary suppressed carrier ASK signal is replaced by a 16-level
suppressed carrier ASK signal, the 16-level signal carries 4 bits of
information per signal element, which is twice that carried by the
quaternary signal. At a given average transmitted power level and a
given *element* rate, each signal has the same average energy per
element. But, if the number of levels (possible element values) of a
signal is doubled, without changing the average element energy, this
approximately halves the difference between any adjacent pair of the
possible element values (possible values for s for the given average
element energy), thus reducing the tolerance to additive white
Gaussian noise at high signal/noise ratios by about 6 dB[320]. It
follows that, at high signal/noise ratios and at a given element-error
rate, the tolerance to additive white Gaussian noise of the 16-level
signal is approximately 12 dB below that of the quaternary signal.
The 16-level signal has twice the information rate of the quaternary
signal and both signals occupy the same bandwidth. At a given
average transmitted power level and a given *bit* rate, each signal has
the same average transmitted energy per bit, and the 16-level signal
has half the element rate of the quaternary signal. Thus the average

energy per signal element of the 16-level signal is twice that of the quaternary signal. At high signal/noise ratios and at a given element-error rate, the tolerance to additive white Gaussian noise of the 16-level signal is now approximately 9 dB below that of the quaternary signal, and the 16-level signal occupies half the bandwidth of the other signal.

Suppose next that the 16-level signal is replaced by the corresponding 256-level signal which carries 8 bits of information per signal element. At a given average transmitted power level and a given *element* rate, the 256-level signal has twice the information rate of the 16-level signal. At high signal/noise ratios and at a given element-error rate, the tolerance to additive white Gaussian noise of the 256-level signal is approximately 24 dB below that of the 16-level signal. Both signals occupy the same bandwidth. At a given average transmitted power level and at a given *bit* rate, the 256-level signal has half the element rate of the 16-level signal, and the average energy per signal element of the 256-level signal is twice that of the 16-level signal. At high signal/noise ratios and at a given element-error rate, the tolerance to additive white Gaussian noise of the 256-level signal is now approximately 21 dB below that of the 16-level signal, and the 256-level signal occupies half the bandwidth of the other signal.

A transmitted m-level signal is normally generated at the transmitter from a binary signal that carries the information to be transmitted. This binary signal is fed to the transmitter from the associated equipment. Normally, $m = 2^n$ so that each transmitted m-level signal element carries n bits of information and corresponds to n elements of the original binary signal. The receiver, after detecting a received m-level signal element, recodes this into the corresponding n binary elements, for form the output binary signal which is fed to the associated equipment. When an error occurs in the detection of a received m-level signal element, at high signal/noise ratios, the wrongly detected element value (which is one of the m possible values of s) is normally *adjacent* to the correct element value. Thus if the m-level signal is related to the binary signal by the Gray code, an error in a detected element value of the m-level signal normally gives an error in only *one* element of the corresponding binary signal, which has of course n times as many elements as the m-level signal. Thus the element error rate in the binary signal, at high signal/noise ratios, is approximately $1/n$ times that in the m-level signal, when expressed as the average probability of error in a detected element value. This means that at a given element-error rate in the binary signal, the tolerance to additive white Gaussian noise is in fact a little better than that for the same element-error rate in the m-level signal. However, at high signal/noise ratios, the improvement is less than 1 dB even in the case of the 256-level signal and does not therefore significantly affect the relative performances of the different systems as just evaluated.

If the transmission (information) rate of any given signal is doubled by doubling the signal-element rate, at a given average transmitted power level and with the given number of signal levels, the average transmitted energy per signal element is halved, thus reducing the tolerance of the signal to additive white Gaussian noise by 3 dB. The bandwidth occupied by the signal is doubled. Clearly, where it is required to increase the transmission rate over any given channel, this is best achieved by increasing the signal-element rate rather than the number of levels (and hence the information content per signal element), just so long as the necessary bandwidth is available. A multi-level signal should not therefore be used where the required transmission rate can be achieved satisfactorily with a binary signal[422].

16.3 PSK signals

An individual transmitted element of a binary PSK signal is ideally

$$q(t) = \begin{cases} \sqrt{2k} \cos(2\pi f_c t + \phi), & 0 < t < T \\ 0, & \text{elsewhere} \end{cases} \tag{16.18}$$

where $\phi = 0°$ or $180°$, and $f_c \gg 1/T$. Thus

$$q(t) = \begin{cases} \sqrt{2s} \cos 2\pi f_c t, & 0 < t < T \\ 0, & \text{elsewhere} \end{cases} \tag{16.19}$$

where $s = \pm k$.

From Equation 16.4, the binary PSK signal is clearly a binary suppressed carrier ASK signal. The optimum detection process and properties of the binary PSK signal are therefore as described for the binary suppressed carrier ASK signal in Section 16.2.

An individual transmitted element of a quaternary PSK signal is ideally

$$q(t) = \begin{cases} 2k \cos(2\pi f_c t + \phi), & 0 < t < T \\ 0, & \text{elsewhere,} \end{cases} \tag{16.20}$$

where $\phi = \pm 45°$ or $\pm 135°$. Thus

$$q(t) = \begin{cases} \sqrt{2s_1} \cos 2\pi f_c t + \sqrt{2s_2} \sin 2\pi f_c t, & 0 < t < T \\ 0, & \text{elsewhere} \end{cases}$$

$$\tag{16.21}$$

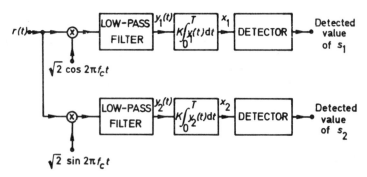

Fig. 16.3   Coherent detector for a quaternary PSK signal element

where $s_1 = \pm k$ and $s_2 = \pm k$. If ϕ is equally likely to have any of its four possible values in Equation 16.20, s_1 and s_2 are statistically independent and equally likely to have either binary value. The quaternary PSK signal is clearly the sum of two binary suppressed carrier ASK signals, whose carriers have the same frequency and are at an angle of $90°$, that is in phase quadrature. The corresponding baseband signal (that is the modulating waveform) for each of these binary signals is of course a binary polar signal.

The energy of the quaternary signal element is $2k^2T$, and the energy of each of the constituent binary elements in Equation 16.21 is k^2T, bearing in mind that $f_c \gg 1/T$.

The resultant waveform at the input to the coherent detector, during the time interval $0 < t < T$, is

$$r(t) = q(t) + w(t)$$
$$= \sqrt{2}s_1 \cos 2\pi f_c t + \sqrt{2}s_2 \sin 2\pi f_c t + w(t) \qquad (16.22)$$

and the coherent detector is as shown in Figure 16.3. It can be seen that the detector contains two separate coherent detectors, one for the signal $\sqrt{2}s_1 \cos 2\pi f_c t$ and the other for the signal $\sqrt{2}s_2 \sin 2\pi f_c t$.

Consider the response of the detector for the signal $\sqrt{2}s_1 \cos 2\pi f_c t$ to the signal-element $\sqrt{2}s_2 \sin 2\pi f_c t$. The signal at the output of the corresponding multiplier is

$$\sqrt{2}s_2 \sin 2\pi f_c t \cdot \sqrt{2} \cos 2\pi f_c t = 2s_2 \sin 2\pi f_c t \cdot \cos 2\pi f_c t$$
$$= s_2 \sin 4\pi f_c t \qquad (16.23)$$

This is a high-frequency signal which is blocked by the following low-pass filter to give no signal at the filter output and hence no signal at the output of the integrator. It may similarly be shown that the coherent detector for the signal $\sqrt{2}s_2 \sin 2\pi f_c t$ gives no output in response to the signal $\sqrt{2}s_1 \cos 2\pi f_c t$ at its input. Thus neither signal element gives any response from the optimum detector for the other element, and the two signal-elements are said to be *orthogonal*. This may be shown directly from the fact that the cross-correlation coefficient of the two signal elements is equal to zero. The cross-correlation coefficient is the integral of the product of the two signal waveforms $\sqrt{2}s_1 \cos 2\pi f_c t$ and $\sqrt{2}s_2 \sin 2\pi f_c t$, over the element duration from 0 to T seconds, divided by the element energy $k^2 T$ of each signal. It has the value

$$\frac{1}{k^2 T} \int_0^T 2s_1 s_2 \cos 2\pi f_c t \cdot \sin 2\pi f_c t \, dt = \frac{s_1 s_2}{k^2 T} \int_0^T \sin 4\pi f_c t \, dt$$

$$= \frac{s_1 s_2}{k^2 T} \left[-\frac{\cos 4\pi f_c t}{4\pi f_c} \right]_0^T \simeq 0 \quad (16.24)$$

since $s_1 s_2 = \pm k^2$ and $f_c \gg 1/T$.

It follows from the preceding discussion that the detection of each signal element by the corresponding coherent detector is unaffected by the presence or absence of the other element. Thus the tolerance of each signal to additive white Gaussian noise can be determined by considering the detection of that element in the absence of the other.

Each constituent binary element of the quaternary PSK signal is clearly a binary PSK signal element, and the average transmitted signal energy per bit for the quaternary PSK signal is

$$E_b = k^2 T \quad (16.25)$$

It may readily be shown that the performance of a coherent detector is unaffected by the phase of the signal carrier f_c Hz, so long as the phase of the reference carrier in the detector is the same as that of the received signal carrier. Thus the performance of the detector for the element $\sqrt{2}s_1 \cos 2\pi f_c t$ is the same as that of the detector for the element $\sqrt{2}s_2 \sin 2\pi f_c t$. It follows that the probability of error in the detection of each of the two binary signal elements is the same as that for the corresponding binary suppressed carrier ASK signal-element. Clearly, at high signal/noise ratios, the probability of error in the detection of a quaternary PSK signal element is approximately twice that in the detection of either of the constituent binary PSK elements, but no significant discrepancy is involved in taking it as being the same as for the binary elements.

Thus, from Equations 16.17, 16.16 and 16.25, the probability of error in the detection of a quaternary PSK signal-element can be taken to be

$$P_e = Q\left(\frac{KTk}{\sqrt{N}}\right) = Q\left\{\sqrt{\left(\frac{2E_b}{N_0}\right)}\right\} \tag{16.26}$$

It can be seen that at a given average transmitted signal energy per bit, that is, at a given information rate and at a given average signal power level at the input to the transmission path, both binary and quaternary PSK signals have the same tolerance to additive white Gaussian noise as a binary suppressed carrier ASK signal. However, at a given information rate, the quaternary PSK signal occupies half the bandwidth of the binary PSK or suppressed carrier ASK signal.

At a given element rate and a given error probability, the quaternary PSK signal has twice the power level of the corresponding binary PSK signal. Also, at a given element rate and at a given power level, for both quaternary and binary signals, the constituent binary elements of the quaternary PSK signal each have half the energy of the elements in the binary PSK signal. Hence, for the same error probability, the noise power spectral density at the input to the coherent detector for the quaternary PSK signal must be half that for the binary PSK signal. This means that, at a given element rate and at a given power level, the tolerance of the quaternary PSK signal to additive white Gaussian noise is 3 dB below that of the binary PSK signal, but its information rate is of course twice that of the binary signal. Both signals here occupy the same bandwidth.

If now a quaternary PSK signal is replaced by an 8-level PSK signal, at the same transmitted energy per element, the tolerance to additive white Gaussian noise is reduced by about 5 dB, the reduction being about 6 dB for each subsequent doubling of the number of levels (possible element-values). Thus, if an 8-level PSK signal is replaced by a 16-, 32-, 64-, 128- or 256-level PSK signal, at the same transmitted energy either per element or per bit, the reduction in tolerance to noise is similar to that in the case of a suppressed carrier ASK signal. It follows that an m-level PSK signal gains an advantage of about 5 dB in tolerance to additive white Gaussian noise over the corresponding m-level suppressed carrier ASK signal, for $m = 8$, $16, 32, \ldots$, and an advantage of 4 dB for $m = 4$. Again, when the transmission (information) rate of a PSK signal is doubled by doubling the element rate, at a given transmitted power level and assuming no signal distortion in transmission, there is a reduction of only 3 dB in tolerance to additive white Gaussian noise and the bandwidth of the transmitted signal is doubled. Thus, both ASK and PSK signals should be used with the smallest number of levels (possible element values) that is consistent with the required transmission rate and the available frequency band. Where possible, binary signals should be used.

16.4 FSK signals

An individual transmitted element of a binary FSK signal is ideally

$$q(t) = \begin{cases} \sqrt{2}k \cos 2\pi f_i t, & 0 < t < T \\ 0, & \text{elsewhere} \end{cases} \tag{16.27}$$

where $i = 0$ or 1, and i is the binary value of the FSK signal element.

$$f_0 = \frac{\frac{1}{2}l}{T} \quad \text{and} \quad f_1 = \frac{\frac{1}{2}l + 1}{T} \tag{16.28}$$

where l is a large positive integer. Clearly

$$f_1 - f_0 = \frac{1}{T} \tag{16.29}$$

so that an element with a carrier frequency f_1 has exactly one more cycle of the carrier than a signal element with a carrier frequency f_0. It follows that the FSK signal contains no phase discontinuities at the element boundaries and furthermore the carrier phase at the start of any signal element is independent of the binary values of the preceding elements. From Equation 16.27,

$$q(t) = \begin{cases} \sqrt{2}s \cos 2\pi f_1 t + \sqrt{2(k-s)} \cos 2\pi f_0 t, & 0 < t < T \\ 0, & \text{elsewhere} \end{cases}$$
$$\tag{16.30}$$

where $s = 0$ or k, depending upon whether $i = 0$ or 1, respectively, in Equation 16.27.

The binary FSK signal is clearly the sum of two complementary ASK signals each having half the peak amplitude of the binary ASK signal previously considered, and the energy of a signal element is $k^2 T$ for either value of s.

The coherent detector for the binary FSK signal is shown in Figure 16.4. It can be seen that the detector comprises two individual coherent detectors, each tuned to the signal element having the corresponding carrier frequency, the output signals x_0 and x_1 from the two integrators now being fed to a comparator.

The input waveform to the coherent detector, during the time interval 0 to T, is

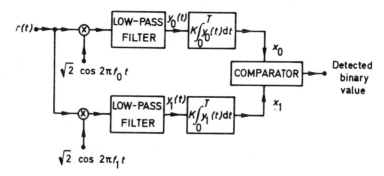

Fig. 16.4   *Coherent detector for a binary FSK signal element*

$$r(t) = q(t) + w(t) = \sqrt{2}s \cos 2\pi f_1 t + \sqrt{2}(k - s) \cos 2\pi f_0 t + w(t)$$

$$(16.31)$$

Thus, when $0 < t < T$, the signal at the output of the multiplier fed by $\sqrt{2} \cos 2\pi f_0 t$ is

$$2s \cos 2\pi f_1 t \cos 2\pi f_0 t + 2(k - s) \cos^2 2\pi f_0 t + \sqrt{2}w(t) \cos 2\pi f_0 t$$

$$= s \cos 2\pi(f_1 - f_0)t + s \cos 2\pi(f_1 + f_0)t + (k - s)$$

$$\quad + (k - s) \cos 4\pi f_0 t + \sqrt{2}w(t) \cos 2\pi f_0 t$$

$$= s \cos 2\pi \frac{t}{T} + s \cos 2\pi(l + 1) \frac{t}{T} + (k - s) + (k - s) \cos 2\pi l \frac{t}{T}$$

$$\quad + \sqrt{2}w(t) \cos \pi l \frac{t}{T} \tag{16.32}$$

The signal s here is strictly speaking the rectangular signal waveform $s(t)$, having the value s over the time interval 0 to T and the value zero elsewhere.

The low-pass filter passes the baseband signals $s \cos 2\pi(t/T)$ and $k - s$ with no attenuation, delay or distortion and blocks the high-frequency signals $s \cos 2\pi(l + 1)(t/T)$ and $(k - s) \cos 2\pi l(t/T)$. The noise signal at the output of the multiplier contains a low-frequency (baseband) component $u_0(t)$ together with a high-frequency component. The low-pass filter passes $u_0(t)$ without attenuation, delay or distortion, and blocks the high-frequency noise component. Thus the signal at the output of the low-pass filter is

$$y_0(t) = s \cos 2\pi \frac{t}{T} + (k - s) + u_0(t) \tag{16.33}$$

The signal at the output of the integrator, at time $t = T$, is

$$x_0 = K \int_0^T y_0(t)\, dt$$

$$= K \int_0^T \left[s \cos 2\pi \frac{t}{T} + (k - s) + u_0(t) \right] dt$$

$$= K \left[\frac{-s \sin 2\pi \frac{t}{T}}{2\pi \frac{1}{T}} + (k - s)t \right]_0^T + K \int_0^T u_0(t)\, dt$$

$$= KT(k - s) + v_0 \tag{16.34}$$

where

$$v_0 = K \int_0^T u_0(t)\, dt \tag{16.35}$$

Again, when $0 < t < T$, the signal at the output of the multiplier fed by $\sqrt{2} \cos 2\pi f_1 t$ is

$$2s \cos^2 2\pi f_1 t + 2(k - s) \cos 2\pi f_0 t \cos 2\pi f_1 t + \sqrt{2} w(t) \cos 2\pi f_1 t$$

$$= s + s \cos 4\pi f_1 t + (k - s) \cos 2\pi(f_1 - f_0)t$$

$$+ (k - s) \cos 2\pi(f_1 + f_0)t + \sqrt{2} w(t) \cos 2\pi f_1 t$$

$$= s + s \cos 2\pi(l + 2) \frac{t}{T} + (k - s) \cos 2\pi \frac{t}{T}$$

$$+ (k - s) \cos 2\pi(l + 1) \frac{t}{T} + \sqrt{2} w(t) \cos \pi(l + 2) \frac{t}{T} \tag{16.36}$$

and the signal at the output of the low-pass filter is

$$y_1(t) = s + (k - s) \cos 2\pi \frac{t}{T} + u_1(t) \tag{16.37}$$

where $u_1(t)$ is the low-frequency (baseband) component of $\sqrt{2} w(t) \cos \pi(l + 2)(t/T)$. As before, the signal s is, strictly speaking, the rectangular waveform $s(t)$.

The signal at the output of the integrator, at time $t = T$, is

$$x_1 = K \int_0^T y_1(t) \, dt$$

$$= K \int_0^T \left[s + (k - s) \cos 2\pi \frac{t}{T} + u_1(t) \right] dt$$

$$= K \left[st + (k - s) \frac{\sin 2\pi \dfrac{t}{T}}{2\pi \dfrac{1}{T}} \right]_0^T + K \int_0^T u_1(t) \, dt$$

$$= KTs + v_1 \tag{16.38}$$

where

$$v_1 = K \int_0^T u_1(t) \, dt \tag{16.39}$$

It can be seen from Equations 16.34 and 16.38 that x_0 contains no component in response to a received signal-element with a carrier frequency f_1 Hz, and x_1 contains no component in response to a received signal-element with a carrier frequency f_0 Hz. Thus x_0 and x_1 are the output signals in response to the corresponding complementary ASK signals, regardless of the presence or absence in each case of the other ASK signal.

The noise waveform $w(t)$ at the input to the coherent detector is additive white Gaussian noise which has been band-limited by the transmission path to the signal frequency band. $w(t)$ has zero mean and a two-sided power spectral density of $\frac{1}{2}N_0$ over the signal frequency band, the same as for the ASK and PSK signals. It is assumed here that the FSK signal is a double-sideband signal that suffers no significant distortion in transmission, as for the ASK and PSK signals. This implies that the Gaussian noise at the input to the coherent detector has a two-sided power spectral density of $\frac{1}{2}N_0$ extending over a bandwidth much greater than $1/T$ Hz, above and below each of the carrier frequencies f_0 and f_1 Hz. Since each of the two coherent detectors for the two complementary ASK signals that make up the FSK signal is the same as the coherent detector described for the ASK signals (apart from the comparator at the output and the frequency of the sine wave fed to the multiplier), and since each coherent detector is tuned to a frequency close to the centre of the bandwidth of $w(t)$, this bandwidth being small compared with f_0 and f_1, it is evident that $u_0(t)$ and $u_1(t)$ are Gaussian random processes with zero mean and a two-sided power spectral density of $\frac{1}{2}N_0$ over the frequency band of the baseband data signals in $y_0(t)$ and $y_1(t)$, for the reasons described in Section 16.2. Thus v_0 and v_1 are Gaussian random variables with zero mean and variance

$$N = \tfrac{1}{2}N_0 K^2 T \tag{16.40}$$

just as in the case of the noise component v for the ASK signal. Furthermore,

$$\int_0^T \sqrt{2} \cos 2\pi f_0 t \sqrt{2} \cos 2\pi f_1 t \, dt$$

$$= \int_0^T 2 \cos \pi l \frac{t}{T} \cos \pi (l + 2) \frac{t}{T} \, dt$$

$$= \int_0^T \left[\cos 2\pi \frac{t}{T} + \cos 2\pi (l + 1) \frac{t}{T} \right] dt$$

$$= \left[\frac{\sin 2\pi \dfrac{t}{T}}{2\pi \dfrac{1}{T}} + \frac{\sin 2\pi (l + 1) \dfrac{t}{T}}{2\pi (l + 1) \dfrac{1}{T}} \right]_0^T$$

$$= 0 \tag{16.41}$$

which means that the functions $\sqrt{2} \cos 2\pi f_0 t$ and $\sqrt{2} \cos 2\pi f_1 t$ are orthogonal over the time interval 0 to T. It may therefore be shown that v_0 and v_1 are *statistically independent* Gaussian random variables[426]. It also follows, of course, that the two binary elements of the FSK signal have a cross-correlation coefficient of zero, since Equation 16.41 shows that the two signal-elements are orthogonal.

From Equations 16.34 and 16.38,

$$\left. \begin{array}{l} x_0 = KT(k - s) + v_0 \\ x_1 = KTs + v_1 \end{array} \right\} \tag{16.42}$$

When the signal element has the binary value 0, $s = 0$, and when the element has the binary value 1, $s = k$. The relationship between the element binary value and the signals x_0 and x_1 is therefore as shown in Table 16.2.

Table 16.2 RELATIONSHIP BETWEEN THE ELE-
MENT BINARY VALUE AND THE SIGNALS x_0 AND x_1

Element binary value	0	1
x_0	$KTk + v_0$	v_0
x_1	v_1	$KTk + v_1$

The comparator in Figure 16.4 detects the binary value of the signal element as 0 when $x_0 > x_1$, and as 1 when $x_1 > x_0$. When the signal element is equally likely to have either binary value, this arrangement minimizes the probability of error in the detection of the binary value.

It is clear from the symmetry in Table 16.2 that the probability of error is the same whether the signal element has the binary value 0 or 1. Assume therefore that a binary value 0 is transmitted. Thus

$$x_0 = KTk + v_0 \quad \text{and} \quad x_1 = v_1$$

and an error results when $x_1 > x_0$.

The probability of an error is clearly

$$P_e = P(v_1 > KTk + v_0) = P(v_1 - v_0 > KTk)$$
$$= P(v_1 + v_0 > KTk) \tag{16.43}$$

where $P(v_1 > KTk + v_0)$ is the probability that v_1 exceeds $KTk + v_0$, and so on. The last step in Equation 16.43 follows from the fact that the probability density function of v_0 and v_1 is symmetric about zero, which implies that the probability density of $-v_0$ is the same as that of v_0.

The random variable formed by the sum of two statistically independent Gaussian random variables is also a Gaussian random variable, whose mean is the sum of the means of the two constituent random variables and whose variance is the sum of their variances. Let

$$v = v_0 + v_1 \tag{16.44}$$

so that v is a Gaussian random variable with zero mean and variance $2N$, where N is given by Equation 16.40. Thus the probability of an error is

$$P_e = P(v > KTk) \tag{16.45}$$

where v has the probability density function

$$p(v) = \frac{1}{\sqrt{(4\pi N)}} \exp\left(-\frac{v^2}{4N}\right) \qquad (16.46)$$

Thus

$$P_e = \int_{KTk}^{\infty} \frac{1}{\sqrt{(4\pi N)}} \exp\left(-\frac{v^2}{4N}\right) dv$$

$$= \int_{KTk/\sqrt{(2N)}}^{\infty} \frac{1}{\sqrt{(2\pi)}} \exp\left(-\tfrac{1}{2}v^2\right) dv = Q\left\{\frac{KTk}{\sqrt{(2N)}}\right\} \qquad (16.47)$$

The average transmitted energy per bit of the binary FSK signal is

$$E_b = k^2 T \qquad (16.48)$$

Thus, from Equations 16.47 and 16.40, the probability of error in the detection of the binary element value is

$$P_e = Q\left\{\sqrt{\left(\frac{k^2 T}{N_0}\right)}\right\} = Q\left\{\sqrt{\left(\frac{E_b}{N_0}\right)}\right\} \qquad (16.49)$$

For a given value of E_b this is the same as the probability of error in the detection of a binary ASK signal.

At a given average signal energy per bit, the tolerance to additive white Gaussian noise of the binary FSK signal is clearly 3 dB below that of a binary PSK signal and the same as that of a binary ASK signal.

An individual transmitted element of a quaternary FSK signal is ideally

$$q(t) = \begin{cases} \sqrt{2}k \cos 2\pi f_i t, & 0 < t < T \\ 0, & \text{elsewhere} \end{cases} \qquad (16.50)$$

where $i = 0, 1, 2,$ or 3, and i is the quaternary value of the FSK signal element. Also

$$f_i = \frac{\tfrac{1}{2}l + i}{T} \qquad (16.51)$$

where l is a large positive integer.

As before, there are no phase discontinuities at the element boundaries, and the carrier phase at the start of any signal element is independent of the quaternary values of the preceding elements. Again, the energy of a signal element is $k^2 T$ for each element value.

The coherent detector for the quaternary FSK signal is shown in Figure 16.5. Each of the four individual coherent detectors that make

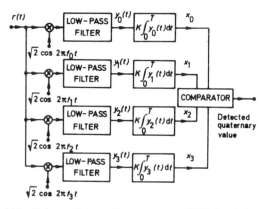

Fig. 16.5   Coherent detector for a quaternary FSK signal element

up the complete detector is itself a coherent detector tuned to the signal element having the corresponding carrier frequency. It also has the same basic properties as each of the two individual coherent detectors in Figure 16.4.

The four quaternary elements of the FSK signal are orthogonal, any two having a cross-correlation coefficient of zero, so that the individual coherent detector tuned to any one of the four elements gives no output signal from the integrator at time $t = T$, in response to any of the other three elements.

It follows from the analysis of the coherent detection of the binary FSK signal that at time $t = T$ the signals at the outputs of the four integrators in Figure 16.5 are as shown in Table 16.3. The noise components v_0, v_1, v_2 and v_3 are statistically independent Gaussian random variables with zero mean and variance N, given by Equation 16.40.

The comparator in Figure 16.5 determines which x_i has the largest (most positive) value and takes the corresponding value of i as the detected element value. This minimizes the probability of error in the detection of the quaternary value, when the received signal element is equally likely to have any of the four possible values, as is assumed here.

It is clear from the symmetry in Table 16.3 that the probability of error is the same, whatever the element value. Assume therefore that a quaternary value 0 is transmitted. Thus

$$x_0 = KTk + v_0$$

$$x_1 = v_1$$

Table 16.3 RELATIONSHIP BETWEEN THE ELEMENT QUATERNARY VALUE AND THE SIGNALS x_0, x_1, x_2 AND x_3

Element quaternary value	0	1	2	3
x_0	$KTk + v_0$	v_0	v_0	v_0
x_1	v_1	$KTk + v_1$	v_1	v_1
x_2	v_2	v_2	$KTk + v_2$	v_2
x_3	v_3	v_3	v_3	$KTk + v_3$

$$x_2 = v_2$$

$$x_3 = v_3$$

An error results when one or more of the following events occur

$$x_1 > x_0, \quad x_2 > x_0, \quad x_3 > x_0$$

The probability that one or more of these events occur is the probability of the *union* of the three events[425], which is

$$
\begin{aligned}
P[&(x_1 > x_0) \cup (x_2 > x_0) \cup (x_3 > x_0)] \\
&= P(x_1 > x_0) + P(x_2 > x_0) + P(x_3 > x_0) \\
&\quad - P[(x_1 > x_0) \cap (x_2 > x_0)] \\
&\quad - P[(x_1 > x_0) \cap (x_3 > x_0)] \\
&\quad - P[(x_2 > x_0) \cap (x_3 > x_0)] \\
&\quad + P[(x_1 > x_0) \cap (x_2 > x_0) \cap (x_3 > x_0)] \\
&< P(x_1 > x_0) + P(x_2 > x_0) + P(x_3 > x_0) \qquad (16.52)
\end{aligned}
$$

where $\cup$ signifies 'union' and $\cap$ signifies 'intersection'. $P(x_i > x_0)$ is of course the probability that x_i exceeds x_0. Thus the probability of an error is less than the sum of the individual probabilities of the three events

$$x_1 > x_0, \quad x_2 > x_0, \quad x_3 > x_0$$

From Table 16.3 and Equation 16.43, it can be seen that

$$
\begin{aligned}
P(x_1 > x_0) &= P(x_2 > x_0) = P(x_3 > x_0) \\
&= P(v_1 + v_0 > KTk) \qquad (16.53)
\end{aligned}
$$

so that, from Equation 16.47,

$$P(x_1 > x_0) = P(x_2 > x_0) = P(x_3 > x_0)$$

$$= Q\left\{\frac{KTk}{\sqrt{(2N)}}\right\} \tag{16.54}$$

Thus from Equation 16.52, the probability of an error in the detection of the quaternary FSK signal-element is less than $3Q\{KTk/\sqrt{(2N)}\}$ and greater than $Q\{KTk/\sqrt{(2N)}\}$, and at high signal/noise ratios the error probability can be taken to be

$$P_e = Q\left\{\frac{KTk}{\sqrt{(2N)}}\right\} \tag{16.55}$$

this being the same value as that given by Equation 16.47.

At a given transmitted signal power level and a given element rate, that is, at a given transmitted energy per signal element, k and T have the same values in Equation 16.55 as they have in Equation 16.47. Thus, at a given transmitted energy per signal element, the probability of error in the detection of a received signal element is, for practical purposes, the same whether it is a binary or quaternary FSK signal.

The average transmitted energy per bit of the quaternary FSK signal is

$$E_b = \tfrac{1}{2}k^2 T \tag{16.56}$$

since each element carries two bits of information. Thus, from Equations 16.55 and 16.40, the probability of error in the detection of a quaternary FSK signal-element can be taken to be

$$P_e = Q\left\{\sqrt{\left(\frac{k^2 T}{N_0}\right)}\right\} = Q\left\{\sqrt{\left(\frac{2E_b}{N_0}\right)}\right\} \tag{16.57}$$

For a given value of E_b this is the same as the probability of error in the detection of a binary PSK or suppressed-carrier ASK signal.

Clearly, at a given average transmitted signal energy per bit, a quaternary FSK signal has the same tolerance to additive white Gaussian noise as a binary PSK or suppressed carrier ASK signal, and it has an advantage of 3 dB over a binary FSK signal. At a given information rate, the binary and quaternary FSK signals occupy approximately the same bandwidth, which is a little wider than that occupied by the corresponding binary ASK and PSK signals. Furthermore, the quaternary FSK signal now has the same tolerance to additive white Gaussian noise as the corresponding quaternary PSK signal, but it occupies a little more than twice the bandwidth.

Suppose next that the quaternary FSK signal is replaced by a 16-level FSK signal, whose possible values of the instantaneous carrier frequency are spaced at regular intervals of $1/T$ Hz, where T seconds is the element duration. With statistically independent signal elements and equally likely element values, the 16-level FSK signal carries 4 bits of information per signal element, which is twice that carried by the quaternary signal. At a given transmitted power level and a given *element* rate, there is only a *small* reduction in tolerance to additive white Gaussian noise when the 16-level FSK signal replaces the quaternary signal, but the information rate is doubled and the bandwidth is increased by a factor of about four times. As the signal/noise ratio approaches infinity, so the reduction in tolerance to noise approaches 0 dB. At a given transmitted power level and a given *information* rate, the 16-level FSK signal has half the element rate of the quaternary signal, so that it has twice the energy per signal element. Clearly, as the signal/noise ratio approaches infinity, the 16-level FSK signal gains an advantage approaching 3 dB, in tolerance to additive white Gaussian noise, over the quaternary FSK signal, but its bandwidth is now approximately twice that of the latter signal.

Suppose next that the 16-level FSK signal is replaced by the corresponding 256-level FSK signal which carries 8 bits of information per signal element. At a given transmitted power level and a given *element* rate, at high signal/noise ratios, there is only a small reduction in tolerance to additive white Gaussian noise when the 256-level FSK signal replaces the 16-level signal, but the information rate is doubled and the bandwidth is increased by a factor of about 16 times. As the signal/noise ratio approaches infinity, so the reduction in tolerance to noise approaches 0 dB, as before. At a given transmitted power level and a given *information* rate, the 256-level FSK signal has half the element rate of the 16-level signal, so that it has twice the energy per signal element. Thus, as the signal/noise ratio approaches infinity, the 256-level FSK signal gains an advantage approaching 3 dB in tolerance to additive white Gaussian noise over the 16-level FSK signal, but its bandwidth is about eight times that of the latter signal.

If the transmission (information) rate of an FSK signal is doubled by doubling the signal element rate, at a given transmitted power level and with the given number of signal levels, the tolerance of the signal to additive white Gaussian noise is reduced by 3 dB and the bandwidth occupied by the signal is doubled.

Clearly, the tolerance to additive white Gaussian noise of an FSK signal can be significantly increased by increasing the number of signal levels, but only at the expense of a considerable increase in the use of bandwidth and an enormous increase in equipment complexity. In practice, the coherent detector would now be replaced by the corresponding *incoherent* detector. Each combination of a multiplier, low-pass filter and integrator (Figure 16.5) is here replaced by the corresponding 'quenched resonator'. This is an infinite-Q turned circuit, whose resonant frequency is equal to the appropriate signal carrier frequency, the tuned circuit being momentarily short circuited at the start of every element period to reduce its output signal to zero. At the end of an element period, the magnitude (envelope) of the output signal from each tuned circuit is measured and fed to the comparator (Figure 16.5) as the corresponding signal x_i. A tuned circuit gives no output signal at the end of an element period, in response to any of the possible carrier frequencies other than its resonant frequency, regardless of the phases of these signal carriers. As the signal/noise ratio increases, so the tolerance of this detector to additive white Gaussian noise approaches that of the corresponding coherent detector. Further details on the incoherent detector are given in Section 6.8 and Figures 6.4–6.6.

With *coherent* detection, the frequency shift between adjacent possible carrier frequencies can be reduced from $1/T$ to $1/2T$ Hz while still maintaining orthogonality between the different possible waveforms of a received signal-element (Equation 16.41), and so introducing no intersymbol interference at the output of any integrator in the detector (x_i in Figure 16.5)[320]. This approximately halves the bandwidth of the FSK signal. Unfortunately, coherent detection is too complex to be used here in practice, and with *incoherent* detection the different possible signal-element waveforms now introduce intersymbol interference in the detector, in the sense that a quenched resonator tuned to one possible frequency of the FSK signal no longer gives zero output in response to each of the other possible carrier frequencies. Thus, in practice, a frequency shift of $1/T$ Hz is normally used for a multi-level FSK signal.

Although of no practical value, the combination of a multi-level FSK signal having a large number of levels and the ideal coherent detection process of is great theoretical interest because it demonstrates both the structure of a 'wide-deviation' digital FSK signal and the mechanism whereby this signal achieves a high tolerance to additive white Gaussian noise. The mechanism essentially depends on the fact that, at a *given element rate*, a considerable increase in the number of levels of the FSK signal results in only a *small* reduction in tolerance to noise, at high signal/noise ratios, the reduction becoming negligible as the signal/noise ratio approaches infinity[320]. This means, of course, that the *information rate* of the FSK signal can be increased by the appropriate increase in the number of levels and the corresponding increase in bandwidth, without, however, noticeably reducing the tolerance to noise. This property is not shared by either ASK or PSK signals.

Table 16.4 RELATIVE TOLERANCES OF DIFFERENT SIGNALS TO ADDITIVE WHITE GAUSSIAN NOISE (EXPRESSED IN dB)

Binary polar baseband	0
Binary unipolar baseband	− 3
Quaternary polar baseband	− 4
Quaternary unipolar baseband	− 8.5
Binary suppressed carrier ASK	0
Binary ASK	− 3
Quaternary suppressed carrier ASK	− 4
Quaternary ASK	− 8.5
Binary PSK	0
Quaternary PSK	0
Binary FSK	− 3
Quaternary FSK	0

16.5 Comparison of signals

The relative tolerances to additive white Gaussian noise, of the different modulated carrier signals and the corresponding rectangular baseband signals, are shown in Table 16.4. In each case, the noise level, expressed in dB relative to that in the case of a binary polar baseband signal, is quoted for a given error probability and a given average transmitted signal energy per bit. High signal/noise ratios are assumed.

Some of the figures quoted in Table 16.4 are approximate, but the approximation becomes better the higher the signal/noise ratio, and at error rates around 1 in 10^5 the inaccuracy due to the approximation should in no case exceed $\frac{1}{2}$ dB.

The ASK, PSK and FSK signals are here assumed to be narrowband signals with ideal and undistorted waveforms. This has been done to demonstrate, with the minimum of mathematical complexity, the essential operations involved in the optimum detection processes for such signals, and hence to bring out the fundamental relationships that exist between the signals. However, the relative tolerances to additive white Gaussian noise of the different modulated-carrier signals usually apply also in the important case where the transmission path is a voice-frequency channel and the conditions are less ideal. The carrier frequencies are now only a little higher than the highest modulating frequencies, and the transmitted signals are bandlimited to make a more efficient use of bandwidth, with the result that they are no longer true ASK, PSK and FSK signals. The more general application of the results given in Table 16.4, for the modulated-carrier signals, can be seen from the References 297–351. These also show that, at high signal/noise ratios, the reduction in tolerance to additive white Gaussian noise, when *coherent* detection is replaced by *incoherent* detection, is around 1 dB for ASK, FSK and binary PSK signals, 2.3 dB for quaternary PSK signals and 3 dB for higher-level PSK signals. The frequency shift between adjacent possible values of the instantaneous carrier frequency of the FSK signal is here assumed to be $1/T$ Hz.

References

TELEPHONE CIRCUITS

1. Fuchs, G., 'Reflections in coaxial cables due to impedance irregularities', *Proc. IEE*, **99**, 121–136 (1952)
2. Fowler, A. D. and Gibby, R. A., 'Assessment of effects of delay distortion in data systems', *AIEE Trans. Commun. Electron.*, **77**, 918–923 (1959)
3. Alexander, A. A., Gryb, R. M. and Nast, D. W., 'Capabilities of the telephone network for data transmission', *Bell Syst. Tech. J.*, **39**, 431–476 (1960)
4. Mertz, P., 'The effect of delay distortion on data transmission', *AIEE Trans. Commun. Electron.*, **79**, 228–232 (1960)
5. Mertz, P., 'Model of error burst structure in data transmission', *Proc. Nat. Electron. Conf.*, **16**, 232 (1960)
6. Yudkin, H. L., 'Some results in the measurement of impulse noise on several telephone circuits', *Proc. Nat. Electron. Conf.*, **16**, 222–231 (1960)
7. Chittenden, P. A., 'Notes on the transmission of data at 750 bauds over practical circuits', *IRE Trans. Commun. Syst.*, **CS-9**, 7–12 (1961)
8. Wright, E. P. G., 'Error rates and error distributions on data transmitted over switched telephone connections', *IRE Trans. Commun. Syst.*, **CS-9**, 12–15 (1961)
9. Enticknap, R. G., 'Errors in data transmission systems', *IRE Trans. Commun. Syst.*, **CS-9**, 15–20 (1961)
10. Mertz, P., 'Model of impulsive noise for data transmission', *IRE Trans. Commun. Syst.*, **CS-9**, 130–137 (1961)
11. Williams, M. B., 'Present and future facilities for data transmission', *Computer J.*, **4**, 88–95 (1961)
12. Wildhagen, G. A., 'Some results of data transmission tests over leased telephone circuits', *IRE Trans. Commun. Syst.*, **CS-9**, 271–275 (1961)
13. Stoffels, R. E., 'Data transmission through Strowger automatic offices', *Automatic Electric Tech. J.*, **7**, No. 8, 301–305 (1961)
14. Gatfield, A. G., 'Delay distortion in telephone lines', *IRE Int. Conv. Rec.*, **9**, Pt. 8, 109–118 (1961)
15. Morris, R., 'Further analysis of errors reported in "Capabilities of the telephone network for data transmission"', *Bell Syst. Tech. J.*, **41**, 1399–1414 (1962)
16. Wegner, J. 'Data transmission tests on the telephone network of the Federal German Post Office', *Nachrichtentech Z.*, **15**, 629–634 (1962)
17. Minami, T., 'Circuit interruption and the effects of interruption on the quality of data transmission', *Japan Telecommun. Rev.*, **4**, No. 1, 34–38 (1962)
18. Sussman, S. M., 'Analysis of the Pareto model for error statistics on telephone circuits', *IEEE Trans. Commun. Syst.*, **CS-11**, 213–221 (1963)
19. Berger, J. M. and Mandelbrot, B., 'A new model for error clustering in telephone circuits', *IBM J. Res. Develop.*, **7**, 224–236 (1963)
20. Fennick, J. H., 'A report on some characteristics of impulse noise in telephone communication', *IEEE Trans. Commun. Electron.*, **83**, 700–705 (1964)
21. Elliott, E. O., 'A model of the switched telephone network for data communications', *Bell Syst. Tech. J.*, **44**, 89–109 (1965)
22. Williams, M. B., 'The characteristics of telephone circuits in relation to data transmission', *Post Office Elec. Eng. J.*, **59**, 151–162 (1966)
23. Buchner, M. M., 'Some experimental results on impulse noise classification', *IEEE Trans. Commun. Technol.*, **COM-17**, 659–663 (1969)
24. Fennick, J. H., 'Amplitude distributions of telephone channel noise and a model for impulse noise', *Bell Syst. Tech. J.*, **48**, 3243–3263 (1969)

25. Ridout, P. N. and Rolfe, P., 'Transmission measurements of connexions in the switched telephone network', *Post Office Elec. Eng. J.*, **63**, 97–104 (1970–71)
26. Duffy, E. P. and Thatcher, T. W., 'Analog transmission performance on the switched telecommunications network', *Bell Syst. Tech. J.*, **50**, 1311–1347 (1971)
27. Balkovic, M. D., Klancer, H. W., Klare, S. W. and McGruther, W. G., 'High-speed voiceband data transmission performance on the switched telecommunications network', *Bell Syst. Tech. J.*, **50**, 1349–1384 (1971)
28. Fleming, H. C. and Hutchinson, R. M., 'Low-speed data transmission performance on the switched telecommunications network', *Bell Syst. Tech. J.*, **50**, 1385–1405 (1971)
29. Hills, M. T. and Evans, B. G., *Transmission Systems*, Allen and Unwin, London (1973)
30. Karbowiak, A. E., 'Investigation of signal distortion in cables caused by imperfections in cable manufacture', *Proc. IEE*, **121**, 419–431 (1974)
31. Halliwell, B. J. (Ed.), *Advanced Communication Systems*, Newnes-Butterworths, London (1974)

HF RADIO LINKS

32. Rice, S. O., 'Distribution of the duration of fades in radio transmission', *Bell Syst. Tech. J.*, **37**, 581–635 (1958)
33. Bailey, D. K., 'The effect of multipath distortion on the choice of operating frequencies for high-frequency communication circuits', *IRE Trans. Antennas Propagat.*, **AP-7**, 397–404 (1959)
34. Goldberg, B., 'HF radio data transmission,' *IRE Trans. Commun. Syst.*, **CS-9**, 21–28 (1961)
35. Salaman, R. K., 'A new ionospheric multipath reduction factor (MRF)', *IRE Trans. Commun. Syst.*, **CS-10**, 220–222 (1962)
36. Polyzou, J., 'Data transmission for military communication; parameters and capabilities', *IEEE Trans. Commun. Syst.*, **CS-11**, 454–464 (1963)
37. Goldberg, B., '300 kHz–30 MHz MF/HF', *IEEE Trans. Commun. Technol.*, **COM-14**, 767–784 (1966)
38. Schwartz, M., Bennett, W. R. and Stein, S., *Communication Systems and Techniques*, Chapter 9, McGraw-Hill, New York (1966)
39. Shepherd, R. A. and Lomax, J. B., 'Frequency spread in ionospheric radio propagation', *IEEE Trans. Commun. Technol.*, **COM-15**, 268–275 (1967)
40. Brayer, K., 'Error patterns measured on transequatorial HF communication links', *IEEE Trans. Commun. Technol.*, **COM-16**, 215–221 (1968)
41. Bello, P. A., 'A troposcatter channel model', *IEEE Trans. Commun. Technol.*, **COM-17**, 130–137 (1969)
42. Watterson, C. C., Juroshek, J. R. and Bensema, W. D., 'Experimental confirmation of an HF channel model', *IEEE Trans. Commun. Technol.*, **COM-18**, 792–803 (1970)
43. Sastry, A. R. K., 'Estimation of bit error rates for narrow-band digital communication in the presence of atmospheric radio noise bursts', *IEEE Trans. Commun. Technol.*, **COM-19**, 733–735 (1971)
44. Lin, S. H., 'Statistical behaviour of a fading signal', *Bell Syst. Tech. J.*, **50**, 3211–3270 (1971)
45. Pickering, L. W., 'The calculation of ionospheric Doppler spread on HF communication channels', *IEEE Trans. Commun.*, **COM-23**, 526–537 (1975)

ELEMENT SYNCHRONIZATION AT THE RECEIVER

46. Sunde, E. D., 'Self timing regenerative repeaters', *Bell Syst. Tech. J.*, **36**, 891–937 (1957)
47. Bennett, W. R., 'Statistics of regenerative digital transmission', *Bell Syst. Tech. J.*, **37**, 1501–1542 (1958)

48. Edson, J. O., Flavin, M. A. and Perry, A. D., 'Synchronized clocks for data transmission', *AIEE Trans. Commun. Electron.*, No. 40, 832–836 (1959)
49. Aaron, M. R. and Gray, J. R., 'Probability distributions for the phase jitter in self-timed reconstructive repeaters for PCM', *Bell Syst. Tech. J.*, **41**, 503–558 (1962)
50. Gumacos, C., 'Analysis of an optimum sync search procedure', *IEEE Trans. Commun. Syst.*, **CS-11**, 89–99 (1963)
51. Selin, L. and Tuteur, F., 'Synchronization of coherent detectors', *IEEE Trans. Commun. Syst.*, **CS-11**, 100–109 (1963)
52. Anello, A. J., Ruocchio, A. C. and Van Gieson, W. D., 'A new digital method of bit synchronization derived from an analog theory', *IBM J. Res. Develop.*, **8**, 318–328 (1964)
53. Van Horn, J. A., 'A theoretical synchronization system for use with noisy digital signals', *IEEE Trans. Commun. Technol.*, **COM-12**, 82–90 (1964)
54. Wintz, P. A., 'A strategy for obtaining explicit estimates of signal delay', *IEEE Trans. Space Electron. Telem.*, **SET-11**, 23–28 (1965)
55. Wintz, P. A. and Hancock, J. C., 'An adaptive receiver approach to the time synchronization problem', *IEEE Trans. Commun. Technol.*, **COM-13**, 90–96 (1965)
56. Gardner, F. M., *Phaselock Techniques*, 117–119, Wiley, New York (1966)
57. Saltzberg, B. R., 'Timing recovery for synchronous binary data transmission', *Bell Syst. Tech. J.*, **46**, 593–622 (1967)
58. Mallory, P., 'A maximum likelihood bit synchronizer', *Proc. Int. Telemetry Conf.*, 1–16 (1968)
59. Lindsey, W. C. and Anderson, T. O. 'Digital transition tracking loops', *Proc. Int. Telemetry Conf.*, 259–271 (1968)
60. McBride, A. L. and Sage, A. P., 'Optimum estimation of bit synchronization', *IEEE Trans. Aerospace Electron. Syst.*, **AES-5**, 525–536 (1969)
61. Wintz, P. A. and Luecke, E. J., 'Performance of optimum and suboptimum synchronizers', *IEEE Trans. Commun. Technol.*, **COM-17**, 380–389 (1969)
62. McBride, A. L. and Sage, A. P., 'On discrete sequential estimation of bit synchronization', *IEEE Trans. Commun. Technol.*, **COM-18**, 48–58 (1970)
63. Lee, G. M. and Komo, J. J., 'PCM bit synchronization and detection by nonlinear filter theory', *IEEE Trans. Commun. Technol.*, **COM-18**, 757–771 (1970)
64. Hurd, W. J. and Andersen, T. O., 'Digital transition tracking symbol synchronizer for low SNR coded systems', *IEEE Trans. Commun. Technol.*, **COM-18**, 141–147 (1970)
65. Simon, M. K., 'Nonlinear analysis of an absolute type of an early-late-gate bit synchronizer', *IEEE Trans. Commun. Technol.*, **COM-18**, 589–596 (1970)
66. Simon, M. K., 'Optimization of the performance of a digital-data-transition tracking loop', *IEEE Trans. Commun. Technol.*, **COM-18**, 686–689 (1970)
67. Lee, G. M. and Komo, J. J., 'PCM bit synchronization and detection by nonlinear filter theory', *IEEE Trans. Commun. Technol.*, **COM-18**, 757–762 (1970)
68. Gitlin, R. D. and Salz, J. 'Timing recovery in PAM systems', *Bell Syst. Tech. J.*, **50**, 1645–1669 (1971)
69. Farrell, J. L. and Murtha, J. C., 'Statistical bit synchronization in digital communications', *IEEE Trans. Commun. Technol.*, **COM-19**, 487–491 (1971)
70. Takasaki, Y., 'Systematic jitter due to imperfect equalization', *IEEE Trans. Commun. Technol.*, **COM-19**, 1275–1276 (1971)
71. Stiffler, J. J., *Theory of Synchronous Communications*, Prentice-Hall, Englewood Cliffs, N.J. (1971)
72. Takasaki, Y., 'Timing extraction in baseband pulse transmission', *IEEE Trans. Commun.*, **COM-20**, 877–884 (1972)

73. Chang, R. W., 'Analysis of a dual mode digital synchronization system employing digital rate-locked loops', *Bell Syst. Tech. J.*, **51**, 1881–1911 (1972)

74. Takasaki, Y., 'Analysis of nonlinear timing extraction in pulse transmission', *Electron. Commun. Japan*, **55-A**, No. 12, 1–9 (1972)

75. Lindsey, W. C., *Synchronization Systems in Communication and Control*, Prentice-Hall, Englewood Cliffs, N.J. (1972)

76. Chow, L. R., Wang, P. P. and Owen, H. A., 'A linear bit synchronizer with learning', *IEEE Trans. Commun.*, **COM-21**, 226–230 (1973)

77. Singh, H. and Tjhung, T. T., 'FSK bit synchronization by combined AM', *IEEE Trans. Commun.*, **COM-21**, 1034–1037 (1973)

78. Huzii, A. and Kondo, S., 'On the timing information disappearance of digital transmission systems', *IEEE Trans. Commun.*, **COM-21**, 1072–1074 (1973)

79. Cessna, J. R. and Levy, D. M., 'Phase noise and transient times for a binary quantized digital phase-locked loop in white Gaussian noise', *IEEE Trans. Commun. Technol.*, **COM-20**, 94–104 (1974)

80. Chakrabarti, N. B. and Gangopadhyay, R., 'Performance of a differential coincidence-type self bit synchroniser at low s.n.r.', *Electronics Letters*, **10**, 190–191 (1974)

81. Garodnick, J., Greco, J. and Schilling, D. L. 'Response of an all digital phase-locked loop', *IEEE Trans. Commun.*, **COM-22**, 751–764 (1974)

82. Rich, M. A., 'Designing phase-locked oscillators for synchronization', *IEEE Trans. Commun.*, **COM-22**, 890–896 (1974)

83. Franks, L. E. and Bubrouski, J. P., 'Statistical properties of timing jitter in a PAM timing recovery scheme', *IEEE Trans. Commun.*, **COM-22**, 913–920 (1974)

84. Hagiwara, S., Hinoshita, S. and Kawashima, M., 'PCM-FDM: System capability and performance improvement on waveform equalization and synchronization), *IEEE Trans. Commun.*, **COM-22**, 1149–1154 (1974)

85. Roza, E., 'Analysis of phase-locked timing extraction circuits for pulse code transmission', *IEEE Trans. Commun.*, **COM-22**, 1236–1249 (1974)

86. Lyon, D. L., 'Timing recovery in synchronous equalized data communication', *IEEE Trans. Commun.*, **COM-23**, 269–274 (1975)

CHARACTER OR FRAME SYNCHRONIZATION AT THE RECEIVER

87. Barker, R. H., 'Group synchronization of binary digital systems', *Communication Theory*, 273–287, Ed. W. Jackson, Butterworth, London (1953)

88. Sekimoto, T. and Kaneko, H., 'Group synchronization for digital transmission systems', *IRE Trans. Commun. Syst.*, **CS-10**, 381–390 (1962)

89. Massey, J. L., 'Optimum frame synchronization', *IEEE Trans. Commun.*, **COM-20**, 115–119 (1972)

90. Nielsen, P. T., 'Some optimum and suboptimum frame synchronizers for binary data in Gaussian noise', *IEEE Trans. Commun.*, **COM-21**, 770–772 (1973)

91. Levitt, B. K., 'Optimum frame synchronization for biorthogonally coded data', *IEEE Trans. Commun.*, **COM-22**, 1130–1133 (1974)

START-STOP SYSTEMS

92. Oberman, R. M. M., 'Start-stop data transmission without the stop element', *IRE Trans. Commun. Syst.*, **CS-9**, 252–258 (1961)

93. Ransom, J. J. and Gupta, S. C., 'A discrete receiver structure for bit detection without synchronization for signals corrupted by additive and multiplicative noise', *IEEE Trans. Commun.*, **COM-22**, 1702–1705 (1974)

AM SYSTEMS

94. Sunde, E. D., 'Theoretical fundamentals of pulse transmission—1', *Bell. Syst. Tech. J.*, **33**, 721–788 (1954)

95. Horton, A. W. and Vaughan, H. E., 'Transmission of digital information over telephone circuits', *Bell Syst. Tech. J.*, **34**, 511–528 (1955)
96. Doty, C. R. and Tate, L. A., 'A data transmission machine', *AIEE Trans. Commun. Electron.*, No. 27, 600–603 (1956)
97. Clark, A. P., 'A high speed signalling system for use over telephone circuits', *ATE J.*, **15**, 157–172 (1959)
98. Clark, A. P., 'A high speed data transmission system for use over telephone circuits', *AGARDograph*, **43**, 111–139 (1959)
99. Gibby, R. A., 'An evaluation of AM data system performance by computer simulation', *Bell Syst. Tech. J.*, **39**, 675–704 (1960)
100. Girinsky, A. and Roussel, P., 'High speed transmission of numerical data over telephone channels', *Elec. Commun.*, **36**, 248–262 (1960)
101. Minami, T., Sanagawa, H. and Hamao, S., 'Binary data transmission on private telephone line', *Rev. Elec. Commun. Lab.*, **9**, 437–473 (1961)
102. Smith, J. G., 'On the feasibility of efficient multi-amplitude communication', *Nat. Telecommun. Conf. Rec.*, 20E.1–20E.5 (1972)

FM SYSTEMS

103. Cohn, J., 'A new approach to the analysis of FM threshold extension', *Proc. Nat. Electron. Conf.*, **12**, 221–236 (1956)
104. Gryb, R. M., '"Recorded carrier" system for high speed data transmission', *Bell Lab. Rec.*, **35**, 321–325 (1957)
105. Malthaner, W. A., 'Experimental data transmission system', *IRE Wescon Conv. Rec.*, Pt. 8, 56–63 (1957)
106. Price, R. and Green, P. E., 'A communication technique for multipath channels', *Proc. IRE*, **46**, 555–570 (1958)
107. Pierce, J. N., 'Theoretical diversity improvement in frequency shift keying', *Proc. IRE*, **46**, 903–910 (1958)
108. Weber, L. A., 'A frequency modulation digital subset for data transmission over telephone lines', *AIEE Trans. Commun. Electron.*, No. 40, 867–872 (1959)
109. Hollis, J. L., 'An experimental equipment to reduce teleprinter errors in the presence of multipath', *IRE Trans. Commun. Syst.*, **CS-7**, 185–188 (1959)
110. Boggs, A. and Boughtwood, J. E., 'Application of telegraph techniques in data transmission', *AIEE Trans. Commun. Electron.*, No. 44, 336–340 (1959)
111. Schmidt, A. R., 'A frequency stepping scheme for overcoming the disastrous effects of multipath distortion on high frequency FSK communication circuits', *IRE Trans. Commun. Syst.*, **CS-8**, 44–47 (1960)
112. Scheer, G. A., 'New system defeats multipath effect', *Electronic Industries*, **19**, 150–156 (1960)
113. Maniere, M. and Benoit-Gonin, R., 'Telegraph distortion on high-speed frequency shift data transmission systems', *IRE Trans. Commun. Syst.*, **CS-9**, 259–270 (1961)
114. Hinkfuss, I. C., 'A 1200 baud digital data transmission system', *Proc. IRE (Australia)*, **22**, 636–641 (1961)
115. Meyerhoff, A. A. and Mazer, W. M., 'Optimum binary FM reception using discriminator detection and IF shaping', *RCA Rev.*, **22**, 698–728 (1961)
116. Lowe, R. L., 'A frequency-shift data set for voice coordinated asynchronous transmission up to 1200 bauds', *Western Union Tech. Rev.*, **16**, No. 3, 112–120 (1962)
117. Bowyer, L. R. and Highleyman, W. H., 'An analysis of inherent distortion in asynchronous frequency-shift modulators', *Bell Syst. Tech. J.*, **41**, 1695–1736 (1962)
118. Smith, E. F., 'Attainable error probabilities in demodulation of binary PCM/FM waveforms', *IEEE Trans. Space Electron. Telem.*, **SET-8**, 290–297 (1962)

119. Meyers, S. T., 'An FM data set for voiceband data transmission', *Bell Lab. Rec.*, **41**, 2–7 (1963)

120. Shaft, P. D., 'Distortion of multitone FM signals due to phase nonlinearity', *IEEE Trans. Space Electron. Telem.*, **SET-9**, 25–35 (1963)

121. von Baeyer, H. J., 'Band limitation and error rate in digital UHF–FM transmission', *IEEE Trans. Commun. Syst.*, **CS-11**, 110–117 (1963)

122. Robin, H. K., Bayley, D., Murray, T. L. and Ralphs, J. D., 'Multitone signalling system employing quenched resonators for use on noisy radio teleprinter circuits', *Proc. IEE*, **110**, 1554–1568 (1963)

123. Bennett, W. R. and Salz, J., 'Binary data transmission by FM over a real channel', *Bell Syst. Tech. J.*, **42**, 2387–2426 (1963)

124. Splitt, F. G., 'Combined frequency- and time-shift keyed transmission systems', *IEEE Trans. Commun. Syst.*, **CS-11**, 414–421 (1963)

125. Head, N. E., 'A high speed data transmission system', *GEC J.*, **30**, 129–135 (1963)

126. Kennedy, R. D. and Lebow, I. L., 'Signal design for dispersive channels', *IEEE Spectrum*, **1**, 231–237 (1964)

127. Anderson, R. R., Bennett, W. R., Davey, J. R. and Salz, J., 'Differential detection of binary FM', *Bell Syst. Tech. J.*, **44**, 111–159 (1965)

128. Lender, A., 'A synchronous signal with dual properties for digital communication', *IEEE Trans. Commun. Technol.*, **COM-13**, 202–208 (1965)

129. Mazo, J. E. and Salz, J., 'Probability of error for quadratic detectors', *Bell Syst. Tech. J.*, **44**, 2165–2186 (1965)

130. Lender, A., 'Binary orthogonal FM technique with multiple properties', *IEEE Trans. Commun. Technol.*, **COM-13**, 499–503 (1965)

131. Klapper, J., 'Demodulator threshold performance and error rates in angle-modulated digital signals', *RCA Rev.*, **27**, 226–244 (1966)

132. Glenn, A. B., 'Analysis of noncoherent FSK systems with large ratios of frequency uncertainties to information rates', *RCA Rev.*, **27**, 272–314 (1966)

133. Roberts, L. W. and Smith, N. G., 'A modem for the Datel 600 service—Datel modem No. 1A', *Post Office Elec. Eng. J.*, **59**, 108–116 (1966)

134. Mazo, J. E. and Salz, J., 'Theory of error rates for digital FM', *Bell Syst. Tech. J.*, **45**, 1511–1535 (1966)

135. Groves, K. and Ridout, P. N., 'Effect of multipath propagation on performance of narrowband frequency modulation radiotelegraph systems', *Proc. IEE*, **113**, 1934–1942 (1966)

136. Hopner, E., Calfee, R. W. and West, L. P., 'A vestigial-sideband FM modem', *Proc. Nat. Electron. Conf.*, **22**, 375–377 (1966)

137. Smith, N. G. and Tridgell, R. H., 'Performance of the Datel modem No. 1A', *Post Office Elec. Eng. J.*, **59**, 250–254 (1967)

138. Schilling, D. L., Hoffman, E. and Nelson, E. A., 'Error rates for digital signals demodulated by an FM discriminator', *IEEE Trans. Commun. Technol.*, **COM-15**, 507–517 (1967)

139. Cook, F. W. and Lakhani, A. H., '200 baud data transmission systems', *Systems Technol.*, No. 3, 31–37 (1967)

140. McRae, D. D., 'Error rates in wideband FSK with discrimination demodulation', *Proc. Int. Telemetering Conf.*, 48–77 (1967)

141. Todd, J. K., 'Modems for data transmission', *Point-to-Point Telecommun.*, **12**, 15–23 (1968)

142. Schneider, H. L., 'Click comparison of digital and matched filter receivers', *Bell Syst. Tech. J.*, **47**, 301–313 (1968)

143. Montaguti, G., 'Marconidata modems for 1200 baud operation', *Point-to-Point Telecommun.*, **12**, 97–108 (1968)

144. Nelson, E. A. and Schilling, D. L., 'Response of an FM discriminator to a digital

FM signal in randomly fading channels', *IEEE Trans. Commun. Technol.*, **COM-16**, 551–560 (1968)

145. Kwan, R. K., and McGee, W. F., 'Digital computer simulation of a frequency-shift keying system', *IEEE Trans. Commun. Technol.*, **COM-16**, 683–690 (1968)

146. Hess, D. T., 'Equivalence of FM threshold extension receivers', *IEEE Trans. Commun. Technol.*, **COM-16**, 746–748 (1968)

147. Pasternack, G. and Whalin, R. L., 'Analysis and synthesis of a digital phase locked loop for FM demodulation', *Bell Syst. Tech. J.*, **47**, 2207–2237 (1968)

148. Mazo, J. E., Rowe, H. E. and Salz, J., 'Rate optimization for digital frequency modulation', *Bell Syst. Tech. J.*, **48**, 3021–3030 (1969)

149. Sakrison, D. J., McAulay, R. J., Tyree, V. C. and Yuen, J. H., 'An adaptive receiver implementation for the Gaussian scatter channel', *IEEE Trans. Commun. Technol.*, **COM-17**, 640–648 (1969)

150. Yavuz, D. and Hess, D. T., 'FM noise and clicks', *IEEE Trans. Commun. Technol.*, **COM-17**, 648–653 (1969)

151. Bayley, D. and Ralphs, J. D., 'The Piccolo 32-tone telegraph system', *Point-to-Point Telecommun.*, **13**, 78–90 (1969)

152. Spanton, J. C. and Connellen, P. L., 'Modems for the Datel 200 service—Datel modems No. 2A and 2B', *Post Office Elec. Eng. J.*, **62**, 1–9 (1969–1970)

153. Smith, B. M., 'Error behaviour of linearly distorted binary FM signals', *A.T.R.*, **4**, 36–42 (1970)

154. Yavuz, D. and Hess, D. T., 'False clicks in FM detection', *IEEE Trans. Commun. Technol.*, **COM-18**, 751–756 (1970)

155. Osborne, P. W. and Schilling, D. L., 'Threshold analysis of phase-locked-loop demodulators using most likely noise', *IEEE Trans. Commun. Technol.*, **COM-19**, 31–41 (1971)

156. Bobilin, R. T. and Lindenlaub, J. C., 'Distortion analysis of binary FSK', *IEEE Trans. Commun. Technol.*, **COM-19**, 478–486 (1971)

157. Glazer, A., 'Distribution of click amplitudes', *IEEE Trans. Commun. Technol.*, **COM-19**, 539–543 (1971)

158. Chadwick, H. D., 'The error probability of a wide-band FSK receiver in the presence of multipath fading', *IEEE Trans. Commun. Technol.*, **COM-19**, 699–707 (1971)

159. Davis, B. R., 'FM noise with fading channels and diversity', *IEEE Trans. Commun. Technol.*, **COM-19**, 1189–1200 (1971)

160. Bacher, W., 'Modems for serial transmission of data over telephone circuits', *Siemens Rev.*, **38**, Special Issue 'Remote data processing', 67–73 (1971)

161. van den Elzen, H. C. and van der Wurf, P., 'A simple method of calculating the characteristics of FSK signals with modulation index 0.5', *IEEE Trans. Commun.*, **COM-20**, 139–147 (1972)

162. Murarka, N. P., 'Detection of FSK signals using linear FM dispersion method', *Proc. IEEE*, **60**, 469–471 (1972)

163. Kelly, C. N. and Gupta, S. C., 'The digital phase-locked loop as a near optimum FM demodulator', *IEEE Trans. Commun.*, **COM-20**, 406–411 (1972)

164. de Buda, R., 'Coherent demodulation on frequency-shift keying with low deviation ratio', *IEEE Trans. Commun.*, **COM-20**, 429–435 (1972)

165. Gill, G. S. and Gupta, S. C., 'First order discrete phase locked loop with applications to demodulation of angle modulated carrier', *IEEE Trans. Commun.*, **COM-20**, 454–462 (1972)

166. Bayley, D. and Ralphs, J. D., 'Piccolo 32-tone telegraph system in diplomatic communication', *Proc. IEE*, **119**, 1229–1236 (1972)

167. Simon, M. K. and Springett, J. C., 'The performance of a noncoherent FSK receiver preceded by a bandpass limiter', *IEEE Trans. Commun.*, **COM-20**, 1128–1136 (1972)

168. Garodnick, J., Greco, J. and Schilling, D. L., 'Theory of operation and design of an all-digital FM discriminator', *IEEE Trans. Commun.*, **COM-20**, 1159–1165 (1972)

169. Tou, F. and Simpson, R. S., 'Optimum deviation ratio and observation interval for continuous-phase binary frequency-shift keying', *IEEE Trans. Commun.*, **COM-21**, 1067–1069 (1973)

170. Tomlinson, M. and Methiwalla, A. E., 'Good performance i.f. and pre-modulation filters for simple f.s.k. system', *Electronics Letters*, **9**, 620–621 (1973)

171. Sass, E. J. and Hannum, J. R., 'Minimum-shift-keying modem for digitized-voice communications', *RCA Eng.*, **19**, No. 4, 80–85 (1973–1974)

172. Kwan, R. K., 'Intersymbol interference in an FM–DCPSK System', *IEEE Trans. Commun.*, **COM-22**, 660–670 (1974)

173. Hurst, G. T. and Gupta, S. C., 'On the performance of digital phase locked loops in the threshold region', *IEEE Trans. Commun.*, **COM-22**, 724–726 (1974)

174. Pugh, A. R., 'The latest modem for the Datel 600 service—Datel modem No. 1F', *Post Office Elec. Eng. J.*, **67**, 95–101 (1974)

175. Cattermole, K. W., 'Digital transmission by frequency shift keying with zero intersymbol interference', *Electronics Letters*, **10**, 349–350 (1974)

176. Osborne, W. P. and Luntz, M. B., 'Coherent and noncoherent detection of CPSFK', *IEEE Trans. Commun.*, **COM-22**, 1023–1036 (1974)

177. Tomlinson, M. and Methiwalla, A. E., 'Improvements in coherent FSK performance', *Electronics Letters*, **10**, 393–394 (1974)

178. Tomlinson, M., 'Realizable filters which give zero intersymbol interference in an FSK system', *Int. J. Circuit Theory Appl.*, **2**, 291–297 (1974)

179. Prapinmongkolkarn, P., Morinaga, N. and Namekawa, T., 'Performance of digital FM systems in a fading environment', *IEEE Trans. Aerospace Electron. Syst.*, **AES-10**, 698–709 (1974)

180. de Buda, R., 'About optimal properties of fast frequency shift keying', *IEEE Trans. Commun.*, **COM-22**, 1726–1727 (1974)

181. Austin, M. C., 'Wide-band frequency-shift keyed receiver performance in the presence of intersymbol interference', *IEEE Trans. Commun.*, **COM-23**, 453–458 (1975)

182. Waylan, C. J., 'Detection of fast, noncoherent, frequency-hopped FSK', *IEEE Trans. Commun.*, **COM-23**, 543–546 (1975)

PM SYSTEMS

183. Costas, J. P., 'Phase-shift radio teletype', *Proc. IRE*, **45**, 16–20 (1957)

184. Hopner, E., 'An experimental modulation-demodulation scheme for high-speed data transmission', *IBM J. Res. Develop.*, **3**, 74–84 (1959)

185. Lawton, J. G., 'Theoretical error rates of differentially-coherent binary and kineplex data transmission systems', *Proc. IRE*, **47**, 333–334 (1959)

186. Cahn, C. R., 'Performance of digital phase-modulation communication systems', *IRE Trans. Commun. Syst.*, **CS-7**, 3–6 (1959)

187. Cahn, C. R., 'Comparison of coherent and phase-comparison detection of a four-phase digital signal', *Proc. IRE*, **47**, 1662 (1959)

188. Voelcker, H. B., 'Phase shift keying in fading channels', *Proc. IEE*, **107**, 31–38 (1960)

189. Tucker, D. G., 'Synchronous demodulation of phase-reversing binary signals, and the effect of limiting action', *IRE Trans. Commun. Syst.*, **CS-9**, 77–82 (1961)

190. Hopner, E., 'Phase reversal data transmission system for switched and private telephone line applications', *IBM J. Res. Develop.*, **5**, 93–105 (1961)

191. Masek, J. R., 'Carrier phase reversal transmits digital data over telephone lines', *Electronics*, **34**, 56–58 (1961)

192. Baker, P., 'Phase modulation data sets for serial transmission at 2,000 and 2,400 bits per second', *AIEE Trans. Commun. Electron.*, No. 61, 166–171 (1962)

193. Buterbaugh, J. N. and Toffler, J. E., 'HC-270 four phase data modem', *IRE Trans. Commun. Syst.*, **CS-10**, 464–466 (1962)

194. Widl, W., 'An experimental data transmission system', *Ericsson Rev.*, **39**, No. 3, 62–71 (1962)

195. Bussgang, J. J. and Leiter, M., 'Error rate approximations for differential phase shift keying', *IEEE Trans. Commun. Syst.*, **CS-12**, 18–27 (1964)

196. Proakis, J. G., Drouilhet, P. R. and Price, R., 'Performance of coherent detection systems using decision directed channel measurements', *IEEE Trans. Commun. Syst.*, **CS-12**, 54–63 (1964)

197. Clark, A. P., 'A phase modulation data transmission system for use over the telephone network', *Radio Electron. Eng.*, **27**, 181–195 (1964)

198. Rappaport, M. A., 'Digital computer simulation for a four-phase data transmission system', *Bell Syst. Tech. J.*, **43**, 927–964 (1964)

199. Hubbard, W. M., 'The effect of a finite width threshold on binary differentially coherent PSK systems', *Bell Syst. Tech. J.*, **45**, 307–319 (1966)

200. Lindsey, W. C., 'Phase-shift-keyed signal detection with noisy reference signals', *IEEE Trans. Aerospace Electron. Syst.*, **AES-2**, 393–401 (1966)

201. Halton, J. H. and Spaulding, A., 'Error rates in differentially coherent phase systems in non-Gaussian noise', *IEEE Trans. Commun. Technol.*, **COM-14**, 594–601 (1966)

202. Hubbard, W. M., 'The effect of noise correlation on binary differentially coherent PSK communication systems', *Bell Syst. Tech. J.*, **46**, 277–280 (1967)

203. Hubbard, W. M., 'The effect of intersymbol interference on error rate in binary differentially-coherent phase-shift-keyed systems', *Bell Syst. Tech. J.*, **46**, 1149–1172 (1967)

204. Hubbard, W. M. and Mandeville, G. D., 'Experimental verification of the error rate performance of two types of regenerative repeaters for differentially coherent phase-shift-keyed signals', *Bell Syst. Tech. J.*, **46**, 1173–1202 (1967)

205. Proakis, J. G., 'Probabilities of error for adaptive reception of M-phase signals', *IEEE Trans. Commun. Technol.*, **COM-16**, 71–81 (1968)

206. Bussgang, J. J. and Leiter, M., 'Error performance of differential phase-shift transmission over a telephone line', *IEEE Trans. Commun. Technol.*, **COM-16**, 411–419 (1968)

207. Bussgang, J. J. and Leiter, M., 'Error performance of quadrature pilot tone phase-shift keying', *IEEE Trans. Commun. Technol.*, **COM-16**, 526–529 (1968)

208. Bailey, C. C. and Lindenlaub, J. C., 'Further results concerning the effect of frequency selective fading on differentially coherent matched filter receivers', *IEEE Trans. Commun. Technol.*, **COM-16**, 749–751 (1968)

209. Einarsson, G., 'Polyphase coding for a Gaussian channel', *Ericsson Technics*, **24**, No. 2, 75–130 (1968)

210. Prabhu, V. K., 'Error rate considerations for digital phase-modulation systems', *IEEE Trans. Commun. Technol.*, **COM-17**, 33–42 (1969)

211. Calandrino, L., Crippa, G. and Immovilli, G., 'Intersymbol interference in binary and quaternary PSK and d.c. PSK systems', *Alta Freq.*, **33**, 337–344 (1969)

212. Kwan, R. K., 'The effects of filtering and limiting a double-binary PSK signal', *IEEE Trans. Aerospace Electron. Syst.*, **AES-5**, 589–594 (1969)

213. Jones, B. J. and Teacher, V., 'Modem at 2400 bits per second for data transmission over telephone lines', *Elec. Commun.*, **44**, 66–71 (1969)

214. Sherman, R. J., 'Quadri-phase shift keyed signals detection with noisy reference signals', *EASCON '69 Conv. Rec.*, 46–52 (1969)

215. Bello, P. A. and Esposito, R., 'Error probabilities due to impulsive noise in linear

and hard limited DPSK systems', *IEEE Trans. Commun. Technol.*, **COM-19**, 14–20 (1971)

216. Jones, J. J., 'Filter distortion and intersymbol interference effects on PSK signals', *IEEE Trans. Commun. Technol.*, **COM-19**, 120–132 (1971)

217. Prabhu, V. K., 'Performance of coherent phase-shift-keyed systems with intersymbol interference', *IEEE Trans. Inform. Theory*, **IT-17**, 418–431 (1971)

218. Davies, M. C., 'The effect of bandwidth on the performance of a phase-modulated digital channel', *Proc. IEEE*, **59**, 1622–1623 (1971)

219. Shimbo, O., Celebiler, M. I., and Fang, R., 'Performance analysis of DPSK systems in both thermal noise and intersymbol interference', *IEEE Trans. Commun. Technol.*, **COM-19**, 1179–1188 (1971)

220. Cacciamani, E. R. and Wolejsza, C. J., 'Phase ambiguity resolution in a four-phase PSK communication system', *IEEE Trans. Commun. Technol.*, **COM-19**, 1200–1210 (1971)

221. Claire, E. J., Couch, L. W. and Kalyanaraman, S., 'Properties of a class of signalling waveforms for digital phase modulation', *IEEE Trans. Commun. Technol.*, **COM-19**, 1252–1259 (1971)

222. Morgan, D. R., 'Error rate of phase-shift keying in the presence of discrete multipath interference', *IEEE Trans. Inform. Theory*, **IT-18**, 525–528 (1972)

223. Lindsey, W. C. and Simon, M. K., 'On the detection of differentially encoded polyphase signals', *IEEE Trans. Commun.*, **COM-20**, 1121–1128 (1972)

224. Tannhauser, A., 'High speed data transmission with differential phase modulation in telephone networks', *Nachrichtentech Z.*, **25**, 330–333 (1972)

225. Shimbo, O., Fang, R. J. and Celebiler, M. I., 'Performance of M-ary PSK systems in Gaussian noise and intersymbol interference', *IEEE Trans. Inform. Theory*, **IT-19**, 44–58 (1973)

226. Prabhu, V. K., 'Error probability performance of M-ary CPSK systems with intersymbol interference', *IEEE Trans. Commun.*, **COM-21**, 97–101 (1973)

227. Yanagidaira, H., Shintani, S. and Kawai, K., 'Modified 8-phase modulation system and its application to 4800-b/s data-transmission modem', *Electron. Commun. Japan*, **56-A**, No. 3, 1–9 (1973)

228. Allen, R. W. and Batson, B. H., 'A variable-data-rate, multimode quadriphase modem', *Conf. Rec. IEEE Int. Conf. Communications*, **2**, 37.18–37.25 (1973)

229. Koubanitsas, T. S. and Turner, L. F., 'A simple bound to the error probability in coherent multi-phase phase-shift-keyed systems with intersymbol interference and Gaussian noise', *Proc. IEE*, **120**, 725–732 (1973)

230. Chiu, H. C. and Simpson, R. S., 'Effect of quadrature and demodulation phase errors in a quadrature PSK system', *IEEE Trans. Commun.*, **COM-21**, 945–948 (1973)

231. Siglow, J. and Valenta, H., 'Data communication equipment Modem 4800 for leased telephone circuits', *Siemens Rev.*, **40**, 514–519 (1973)

232. Rhodes, S. A., 'Performance of offset-QPSK communications with partially-coherent detection', *Nat. Telecommun. Conf. Rec.*, **2**, 32A.1–32A.6 (1973)

233. Hentissen, V. O., Laiko, P. P. and Sarkilahti, R. M., 'A digital demodulator for PSK signals', *IEEE Trans. Commun.*, **COM-21**, 1352–1360 (1973)

234. Koubanitsas, T. S., 'Performance of multiphase coherent phase-shift-keyed systems with intersymbol interference and Gaussian noise', *Proc. IEE*, **120**, 1485–1488 (1973)

235. Zakharov, Y. K. and Sokolov, V. P., 'Analysis of detection of phase-modulated signals in the presence of noise', *Radio Eng. Electron. Phys.*, **17**, 2107–2110 (1973)

236. Mattsson, O., 'Modem ZAT2400 for data transmission', *Ericsson Rev.*, **50**, No. 3, 101–107 (1973)

237. Ruthroff, C. L. and Bodtmann, W. F., 'Adaptive coding for coherent detection of digital phase modulation', *Bell Syst. Tech. J.*, **53**, 449–466 (1974)

238. Ehlinger, J. C. and Wolf, W. J., 'Design and performance evaluation of eight phase data sets for use on telephone channels', *Conf. Rec. IEEE Int. Conf. Communications*, 9E.1–9E.6 (1974)

239. Rhodes, S. A. 'Effect of noisy phase reference on coherent detection of offset-QPSK signals', *IEEE Trans. Commun.*, **COM-22**, 1046–1055 (1974)

240. Koubanitsas, T. S., 'Performance of multiphase CPSK systems with intersymbol interference', *IEEE Trans. Commun.*, **COM-22**, 1722–1726 (1974)

241. Lee, J. S. and Miller, L. E., 'On the binary DPSK communication systems in correlated Gaussian noise', *IEEE Trans. Commun.*, **COM-23**, 255–259 (1975)

242. Salwen, H., 'Differential phase-shift keying performance under time-selective multipath fading', *IEEE Trans. Commun.*, **COM-23**, 383–385 (1975)

243. Wood, R., 'Performance of a multilevel d.c.p.s.k. system in the presence of interference and Gaussian noise', *Electronics Letters*, **11**, 152–153 (1975)

DETERMINATION AND INFLUENCE OF THE PHASE OF
THE REFERENCE CARRIER IN A COHERENT DETECTOR

244. Lindsey, W. C. and Didday, R. L., 'Subcarrier tracking methods and communication system design', *IEEE Trans. Commun. Technol.*, **COM-16**, 541–550 (1968)

245. Natali, F. D. and Walbesser, W. J., 'Phase locked loop detection of binary PSK signals utilizing decision feedback', *IEEE Trans. Aerospace Electron. Syst.*, **AES-5**, 83–90 (1969)

246. Oberst, J. P. and Schilling, D. L., 'Performance of self-synchronized phase-shift keyed systems', *IEEE Trans. Commun. Technol.*, **COM-17**, 664–669 (1969)

247. Nozaka, K., Muratani, T., Ogi, M. and Shoji, T., 'Carrier synchronization techniques of PSK modem for TDMA systems', *Conf. Rec. INTELSAT/IEE Int. Conf. Satellite Communication*, London, 154–165 (1969)

248. Mazo, J. E. and Salz, J., 'Carrier acquisition for coherent demodulation of pulse-amplitude modulation', *IEEE Trans. Commun. Technol.*, **COM-18**, 353–360 (1970)

249. Lindsey, W. C. and Simon, M. K., 'The performance of suppressed carrier tracking loops in the presence of frequency detuning', *Proc. IEEE*, **58**, 1315–1321 (1970)

250. Feistel, C. H. and Gregg, W. D., 'Performance characteristics of adaptive/self synchronizing PSK receivers under common power and bandwidth conditions', *IEEE Trans. Commun. Technol.*, **COM-18**, 527–536 (1970)

251. Lindsey, W. C. and Simon, M. K., 'Data aided carrier tracking loops', *IEEE Trans. Commun. Technol.*, **COM-19**, 157–168 (1971)

252. Kobayashi, H., 'Simultaneous adaptive estimation and decision algorithm for carrier modulated data transmission systems', *IEEE Trans. Commun. Technol.*, **COM-19**, 268–280 (1971)

253. Badessa, R. S., 'A communications detector with a signal-synthesized reference', *IEEE Trans. Commun. Technol.*, **COM-19**, 643–648 (1971)

254. Cahn, C. R., 'Comparison of phase tracking schemes for PSK', *Proc. Int. Telecommun. Conf.*, Washington, D.C., 172–180 (1971)

255. Lindsey, W. C. and Simon, M. K., 'Carrier synchronization and detection of polyphase signals', *IEEE Trans. Commun.*, **COM-20**, 441–454 (1972)

256. Yamamoto, H., Hirade, K. and Watanabe, Y., 'Carrier synchronizer for coherent detection of high-speed four-phase-shift-keyed signals', *IEEE Trans. Commun.*, **COM-20**, 803–808 (1972)

257. Ho, E. Y. and Spaulding, D. A., 'Data transmission performance in the presence of carrier phase jitter and Gaussian noise', *Bell Syst. Tech. J.*, **51**, 1927–1931 (1972)

258. Fang, Y., 'Carrier phase-jitter extraction method for VSB and SSB data transmission systems', *IEEE Trans. Commun.*, **COM-20**, 1169–1175 (1972)

259. Schollmeier, G., 'The effect of carrier phase and timing on a single sideband data signal', *IEEE Trans. Commun.*, **COM-21**, 262–264 (1973)

260. Matyas, R. and McLane, P. J., 'Data-aided tracking loops for channels with phase jitter and intersymbol interference', *Conf. Rec. IEEE Int. Conf. Communications*, 3.3–3.13 (1973)

261. Cahn, C. R., 'Phase tracking and demodulation with delay', *IEEE Trans. Inform. Theory*, **IT-20**, 50–58 (1974)

262. Simon, M. K. and Smith, J. G., 'Carrier synchronization and detection of QASK signal sets', *IEEE Trans. Commun.*, **COM-22**, 98–106 (1974)

263. Even, R. K. and Voulgaris, N. C., 'Carrier phase recovery scheme for a low-frequency vestigial sideband video transmission system., *IEEE Trans. Commun.*, **COM-22**, 897–903 (1974)

264. Matyas, R. and McLane, P. J., 'Decision-aided tracking loops for channels with phase jitter and intersymbol interference', *IEEE Trans. Commun.*, **COM-22**, 1014–1023 (1974)

265. Arnstein, D. S., 'Reliability bounds for coherent communications with maximum likelihood phase estimation', *IEEE Trans. Commun.*, **COM-22**, 1859–1862 (1974)

266. Ho, E. Y., 'A new carrier recovery technique for vestigial sideband (VSB) data systems', *IEEE Trans. Commun.*, **COM-22**, 1866–1870 (1974)

RELATIVE TRANSMISSION RATES OF DIFFERENT SYSTEMS

267. Nyquist, H., 'Certain factors affecting telegraph speed', *Bell Syst. Tech. J.*, **3**, 324–346 (1924)

268. Nyquist, H., 'Certain topics in telegraph transmission theory', *AIEE Trans.*, **47**, 617–644 (1928)

269. Hartley, R. V. L., 'Transmission of information', *Bell Syst. Tech. J.*, **7**, 535–563 (1928)

270. Gabor, D., 'Theory of communication', *IEE J.*, **93**, Pt. 3, 429–457 (1946)

271. Pushman, H. J., 'Spectral density distributions of signals for binary data transmission', *Radio Electron. Eng.*, **25**, 155–165 (1963)

272. Bennett, W. R. and Rice, S. O., 'Spectral density and autocorrelation functions associated with binary frequency-shift keying', *Bell Syst. Tech. J.*, **42**, 2355–2385 (1963)

273. Tjhung, T. T., 'Band occupancy of digital FM signals', *IEEE Trans. Commun. Syst.*, **COM-12**, 211–216 (1964)

274. Anderson, R. R. and Salz, J., 'Spectra of digital FM', *Bell Syst. Tech. J.*, **44**, 1165–1189 (1965)

275. Gibby, R. A. and Smith, J. W., 'Some extensions of Nyquist's telegraph transmission theory', *Bell Syst. Tech. J.*, **44**, 1487–1510 (1965)

276. Shimbo, O., 'General formula for power spectra of digital FM signals', *Proc. IEE*, **113**, 1783–1789 (1966)

277. von Baeyer, H. J. and Tjhung, T. T., 'Effects of pulse shaping on digital FM spectra', *Proc. Nat. Electron. Conf.*, **22**, 363–368 (1966)

278. Franks, L. E., 'Further results on Nyquist's problem in pulse transmission', *IEEE Trans. Commun. Technol.*, **COM-16**, 337–340 (1968)

279. Lundquist, L., 'Digital PM spectra by transform techniques', *Bell Syst. Tech. J.*, **48**, 397–411 (1969)

280. van den Elzen, H. C., 'Calculating power spectral densities for data signals', *Proc. IEEE*, **58**, 942–943 (1970)

281. Boykin, J. R., 'Spectrum economy for filtered and limited FSK signals', *IEEE Trans. Commun. Technol.*, **COM-19**, 92–96 (1971)

282. Glance, B., 'Power spectra of multilevel digital phase-modulated signals', *Bell Syst. Tech. J.*, **50**, 2857–2878 (1971)

283. Prabhu, V. K. and Rowe, H. E., 'Spectra of digital phase modulation by matrix methods', *Bell Syst. Tech. J.*, **53**, 899–935 (1974)

284. Baker, T. J., 'Asymptotic behaviour of digital FM spectra', *IEEE Trans. Commun.*, **COM-22**, 1585–1594 (1974)

VESTIGIAL-SIDEBAND SYSTEMS

285. Sunde, E. D., 'Theoretical fundamentals of pulse transmission—2', *Bell Syst. Tech. J.*, **33**, 987–1010 (1954)

286. Holland, G. and Myrick, J. C., 'A 2500 baud time-sequential transmission system for voice frequency wire line transmission', *IRE Nat. Conv. Rec.*, Pt. 8, 187–190 (1959)

287. Hollis, J. L. 'Measured performance of the Sebit-25 data system over wire line facilities at 2500 bits per second', *IRE Trans. Commun. Syst.*, **CS-8**, 134–137 (1960)

288. Hollis, J. L., 'Digital data fundamentals and the two level vestigial sideband system for voice bandwidth circuits', *IRE Wescon Conv. Rec.*, Pt. 5, 132–145 (1960)

289. Brand, S. and Carter, C. W., 'A 1650 bit-per-second data system for use over the switched telephone network', *AIEE Trans. Commun. Electron.*, **80**, 652–669 (1962)

290. Becker, F. K., Davey, J. R. and Saltzberg, B. R., 'An AM vestigial sideband data transmission set using synchronous detection for serial transmission up to 3000 bits per second', *AIEE Trans. Commun. Electron.*, **81**, 97–101 (1962)

291. Critchlow, D. L., Dennard, R. H. and Hopner, E., 'A vestigial-sideband, phase reversal data transmission system', *IBM J. Res. Develop.*, **8**, 33–42 (1964)

292. Farrow, C. W. and Holzman, L. N., 'Nationwide field trial performance of a multilevel vestigial-sideband data terminal for switched network voice channels', *Conf. Rec. IEEE Int. Conf. Communications*, 782–787 (1968)

293. Croisier, A. and Pierret, J. M. D., 'The digital echo modulation', *IEEE Trans. Commun. Technol.*, **COM-18**, 367–376 (1970)

294. Fang, Y., 'New methods to generate vestigial-sideband signal for data transmission', *IEEE Trans. Commun.*, **COM-20**, 147–157 (1972)

295. Hill, F. S., 'On time domain representations for vestigial sideband signals', *Proc. IEEE*, **62**, 1032–1033 (1974)

296. Hill, F. S., 'Optimum pulse shapes for pulse amplitude modulation data transmission using vestigial sideband modulation', *IEEE Trans. Commun.*, **COM-23**, 352–361 (1975)

COMPARISON OF DIFFERENT SYSTEMS

297. Blachman, N. M., 'A comparison of the information capacities of amplitude and phase modulation communication systems', *Proc. IRE*, **41**, 748–759 (1953)

298. Reiger, S., 'Error probabilities in binary data transmission systems in the presence of random noise', *IRE Nat. Conv. Rec.*, Pt. 8, 72–79 (1953)

299. Montgomery, G. F., 'A comparison of amplitude and angle modulation for narrow-band communication of binary coded messages in fluctuation noise', *Proc. IRE*, **42**, 447–454 (1954)

300. Mertz, P. and Mitchell, D., 'Transmission aspects of data transmission service using private line voice telephone channels', *Bell Syst. Tech. J.*, **36**, 1451–1486 (1957)

301. Masonson, M., 'Binary transmissions through noise and fading', *IRE Nat. Conv. Rec.*, Pt. 2, 69–82 (1957)

302. Reiger, S., 'Error rates in data transmission', *Proc. IRE*, **46**, 919–920 (1958)

303. Turin, G. L., 'Error probabilities for binary symmetric ideal reception through nonselective slow fading and noise', *Proc. IRE*, **46**, 1603–1619 (1958)

304. Sunde, E. D., 'Ideal binary pulse transmission by AM and FM', *Bell Syst. Tech. J.*, **38**, 1357–1426 (1959)

305. Beard, J. V. and Wheeldon, A. J., 'A comparison between alternative HF telegraph systems', *Point-to-Point Telecommun.*, **4**, 20–48 (1960)

306. Glenn, A. B., 'Comparison of PSK vs FSK and PSK–AM vs FSK–AM binary coded transmission systems', *IRE Trans. Commun. Syst.*, **CS-8**, 87–100 (1960)

307. Helstrom, C. W., 'The comparison of digital communication systems', *IRE Trans. Commun. Syst.*, **CS-8**, 141–150 (1960)

308. Wier, J. M., 'Digital data communication techniques', *Proc. IRE*, **49**, 196–209 (1961)

309. Sunde, E. D., 'Pulse transmission by AM, FM and PM in the presence of phase distortion', *Bell Syst. Tech. J.*, **40**, 353–422 (1961)

310. Zabronsky, H., 'Statistical properties of M-ary frequency-shift-keyed and phase-shift-keyed modulated carriers', *RCA Rev.*, **22**, 431–460 (1961)

311. Bodonyi, A. B., 'Effects of impulse noise on digital data transmission', *IRE Trans. Commun. Syst.*, **CS-9**, 355–361 (1961)

312. Lerner, R. M., 'Modulation and signal selection for digital data systems', *AIEE Trans. Commun. Electron.*, **80**, 661–669 (1962)

313. Weaver, C. S., 'A comparison of several types of modulation', *IRE Trans. Commun. Syst.*, **CS-10**, 96–101 (1962)

314. Clark, A. P., 'Considerations in the choice of the optimum data-transmission systems for use over telephone circuits', *J. Brit. IRE*, **23**, 331–355 (1962)

315. Bello, P. A. and Nelin, B. D., 'The influence of fading spectrum on the binary error probabilities of incoherent and differentially coherent matched filter receivers', *IRE Trans. Commun. Syst.*, **CS-10**, 160–168 (1962)

316. Splitt, F. G., 'Comparative performance of digital data transmission systems in the presence of CW interference', *IRE Trans. Commun. Syst.*, **CS-10**, 169–177 (1962)

317. Wolf, J. K., 'On comparing N-ary systems', *IRE Trans. Commun. Syst.*, **CS-10**, 216–217 (1962)

318. Jenks, F. G. and Hannon, D. C., 'A comparison of the merits of phase and frequency modulation for medium speed serial binary digital data transmission over telephone lines', *J. Brit. IRE*, **24**, 21–36 (1962)

319. Smith, K. L., 'Some recent developments in data transmission', *J. Brit. IRE*, **24**, 405–414 (1962)

320. Arthurs, E. and Dym, H., 'On the optimum detection of digital signals in the presence of white Gaussian noise—a geometric interpretation and a study of three basic data transmission systems', *IEEE Trans. Commun. Syst.*, **CS-10**, 336–372 (1962)

321. Rowlands, R. O., 'The relative efficiencies of various binary detection systems', *IRE Int. Conv. Rec.*, **10**, Pt. 4, 185–189 (1962)

322. Besslich, P., 'Error probabilities of binary transmission systems due to noise and fading', *Archiv Elekt. Ubertragung*, **17**, 185–197 (1963)

323. Bello, P. A. and Nelin, B. D., 'The effect of frequency selective fading on the binary error probabilities of incoherent and differentially-coherent matched filter receivers', *IEEE Trans. Commun. Syst.*, **CS-11**, 170–186 (1963)

324. Halstead, L. R., 'On binary data transmission error rates due to combinations of Gaussian and impulsive noise', *IEEE Trans. Commun. Syst.*, **CS-11**, 428–435 (1963)

325. Stein, S., 'Unified analysis of certain coherent and noncoherent binary communication systems', *IEEE Trans. Inform. Theory*, **IT-10**, 43–51 (1964)

326. Bello, P. A., 'Error probabilities due to atmospheric noise and flat fading in HF

ionospheric communication systems', *IEEE Trans. Commun. Technol.*, **COM-13**, 266–279 (1965)

327. Engel, J. S., 'Digital transmission in the presence of impulsive noise', *Bell Syst. Tech. J.*, **44**, 1699–1743 (1965)

328. Bennett, W. R. and Davey, J. R., *Data Transmission*, McGraw-Hill, New York (1965)

329. Bello, P. A., 'Bounds on the error probability of FSK and PSK receivers due to non-Gaussian noise in fading channels', *IEEE Trans. Inform. Theory*, **IT-12**, 315–326 (1966)

330. Bello, P. A., 'Binary error probabilities over selectively fading channels containing specular components', *IEEE Trans. Commun. Technol.*, **COM-14**, 400–406 (1966)

331. Zeimer, R. E., 'Character error probabilities for M-ary signalling in impulsive noise environments', *IEEE Trans. Commun. Technol.*, **COM-15**, 32–44 (1967)

332. Jacobs, I., 'Comparison of M-ary modulation systems', *Bell Syst. Tech. J.*, **46**, 843–864 (1967)

333. Cook, F. W., 'Medium speed digital data transmission', *Systems Technol.*, No. 1, 43–47 (1967)

334. Jones, J. J., 'Multichannel FSK and DPSK reception with three-component multipath', *IEEE Trans. Commun. Technol.*, **COM-16**, 808–821 (1968)

335. Salz, J., 'Communications efficiency of certain digital modulation systems', *IEEE Trans. Commun. Technol.*, **COM-18**, 97–102 (1970)

336. Prabhu, V. K., 'On the performance of digital modulation systems that expand bandwidth', *Bell Syst. Tech. J.*, **49**, 1033–1057 (1970)

337. Tjhung, T. T. and Wittke, P. H., 'Carrier transmission of binary data in a restricted band', *IEEE Trans. Commun. Technol.*, **COM-18**, 295–304 (1970)

338. Sharpe, J. T. L., 'Techniques for high-speed data transmission over voice channels', *Elec. Commun.*, **46**, 24–31 (1971)

339. Davey, J. R., 'Modems', *Proc. IEEE*, **60**, 1284–1292 (1972)

340. Bodharamik, A., Moore, J. B. and Newcomb, R. W., 'Optimum detection and signal design for channels with non- but near-Gaussian additive noise', *IEEE Trans. Commun.*, **COM-20**, 1087–1096 (1972)

341. Walker, A. and Rearwin, R., 'Digital modulation techniques', *Conf. Rec. IEEE Int. Conf. Communications*, **2**, 28.20–28.24 (1973)

342. Lyon, D. L. and Holsinger, J. L., 'Unified analysis of synchronous digital modulation schemes', *Conf. Rec. IEEE Int. Conf. Communications*, **2**, 43.24–43.30 (1973)

343. Edwards, J. R., 'A comparison of modulation schemes for binary data transmission', *Radio Electron. Eng.*, **43**, 562–568 (1973)

344. Fang, R. and Shimbo, O., 'Unified analysis of a class of digital systems in additive noise and interference', *IEEE Trans. Commun.*, **COM-21**, 1075–1091 (1973)

345. Edvardsson, K. and Nyman, H., 'Modems for data transmission on voice grade lines', *Elec. Commun.*, **48**, 110–120 (1973)

346. Jain, P. C., 'Error probabilities in binary angle modulation', *IEEE Trans. Inform. Theory*, **IT-20**, 36–42 (1974)

347. Pumpe, G., 'Modems and accessories for data transmission over telephone networks', *Siemens Rev.*, **41**, 104–109 (1974)

348. Benedetto, S., Biglieri, E. and Castellani, V., 'Intersymbol interference sensitivity of some multilevel digital transmission schemes', *Alta Freq.*, **43**, 377–389 (1974)

349. Thompson, R. and Clouting, D. R., 'Digital angle modulation for data transmission', *Systems Technol.*, No. 19, 14–18 (1974)

350. Massaro, M. J., 'The distribution of error probability for Rayleigh fading and Gaussian noise', *IEEE Trans. Commun.*, **COM-22**, 1856–1858 (1974)

351. Thompson, R. and Clouting, D. R., 'Digital angle modulation for data transmission', *Systems Technol.*, No. 20, 33–37 (1975)

DESIGN AND PERFORMANCE OF SYSTEMS OPERATING IN NON-GAUSSIAN NOISE

352. Wainwright, R. A., 'On the potential advantage of a smearing and desmearing filter technique in overcoming impulse-noise problems in data systems', *IRE Trans. Commun. Syst.*, **CS-9**, 362–366 (1961)

353. Shepelavey, B., 'Non-Gaussian atmospheric noise in binary-data, phase-coherent communication systems', *IEEE Trans. Commun. Syst.*, **CS-11**, 280–284 (1963)

354. Rappaport, S. S. and Lurz, L., 'Optimal decision thresholds for digital signalling in non-Gaussian noise', *IEEE Int. Conv. Rec.*, **13**, Pt. 2, 198–212 (1965)

355. Rappaport, S. S. and Kurz, L., 'An optimal nonlinear detector for digital data transmission through non-Gaussian channels', *IEEE Trans. Commun. Technol.*, **COM-14**, 266–274 (1966)

356. Millard, J. B. and Kurz, L., 'Adaptive threshold detection of M-ary signals in statistically undefined noise', *IEEE Trans. Commun. Technol.*, **COM-14**, 601–610 (1966)

357. Simon, M. K. and Kurz, L., 'Optimal processing and design of digital signals perturbed by Gaussian and non-Gaussian noise', *IEEE Int. Conv. Rec.*, **14**, Pt. 7, 72–84 (1966)

358. Ziemer, R. E., 'Error probabilities due to additive combinations of Gaussian and impulsive noise', *IEEE Trans. Commun. Technol.*, **COM-15**, 471–474 (1967)

359. Klose, D. R. and Kurz, L., 'A new representation theory and detection procedures for a class of non-Gaussian channels', *IEEE Trans. Commun. Technol.*, **COM-17**, 225–234 (1969)

360. Bello, P. A. and Esposito, R., 'A new method of calculating probabilities of errors due to impulsive noise', *IEEE Trans. Commun. Technol.*, **COM-17**, 368–379 (1969)

361. Silver, H. I. and Kurz, L., 'A class of continuous signal-design problems in burst noise', *IEEE Trans. Inform. Theory*, **IT-16**, 570–581 (1970)

362. Richter, W. J. and Smits, T. I., 'Signal design and error rate of an impulse noise channel', *IEEE Trans. Commun. Technol.*, **COM-19**, 446–458 (1971)

363. Omura, J. K. and Shaft, P. D., 'Modem performance in VLF atmospheric noise', *IEEE Trans. Commun. Technol.*, **COM-19**, 659–668 (1971)

364. Sastry, A. R. K., 'Estimation of bit error rates for narrow-band digital communication in the presence of atmospheric radio noise bursts', *IEEE Trans. Commun. Technol.*, **COM-19**, 733–735 (1971)

365. Miller, J. H. and Thomas, J. B., 'Detectors for discrete-time signals in non-Gaussian noise', *IEEE Trans. Inform. Theory*, **IT-18**, 241–250 (1972)

366. Silver, H. I. and Kurz, L., 'A class of discrete signal-design problems in burst noise', *IEEE Trans. Inform. Theory*, **IT-18**, 258–262 (1972)

367. Nirenberg, L. D., 'Low SNR digital communication over certain additive non-Gaussian channels', *IEEE Trans. Commun.*, **COM-23**, 332–341 (1975)

QUADRATURE AM AND COMBINED AM AND PM SYSTEMS

368. Cahn, C. R., 'Combined digital phase and amplitude modulation communication systems', *IRE Trans. Commun. Syst.*, **CS-8**, 150–155 (1960)

369. Hancock, J. C. and Lucky, R. W., 'Performance of combined amplitude and phase modulated communication systems', *IRE Trans. Commun. Syst.*, **CS-8**, 232–237 (1960)

370. Campopiano, C. N. and Glazer, B. G., 'A coherent digital amplitude and phase modulation scheme', *IRE Trans. Commun. Syst.*, **CS-10**, 90–95 (1962)

371. Lucky, R. W. and Hancock, J. C., 'On the optimum performance of N-ary systems having two degrees of freedom', *IRE Trans. Commun. Syst.*, **CS-10**, 185–192 (1962)

372. Lindsey, W. C., 'Error probabilities for Rician fading multichannel reception of binary and N-ary signals', *IEEE Trans. Inform. Theory*, **IT-10**, 339–350 (1964)

373. Lindsey, W. C., 'Error probabilities for coherent receivers in specular and random channels', *IEEE Trans. Inform. Theory*, **IT-11**, 147–150 (1965)

374. Weber, C. L., 'On optimal signal selection for M-ary alphabets with two degrees of freedom', *IEEE Trans. Inform. Theory*, **IT-11**, 299–300 (1965)

375. Weber, C. L., 'New solutions to the signal design problem for coherent channels', *IEEE Trans. Inform. Theory*, **IT-12**, 161–167 (1966)

376. Reed, I. S. and Scholtz, R. A., 'N-orthogonal phase-modulated codes', *IEEE Trans. Inform. Theory*, **IT-12**, 388–395 (1966)

377. Scholtz, R. A. and Weber, C. L., 'Signal design for phase-incoherent communications', *IEEE Trans. Inform. Theory*, **IT-12**, 456–463 (1966)

378. Dunbridge, B., 'A symmetric signal design for the coherent Gaussian channel', *IEEE Trans. Inform. Theory*, **IT-13**, 422–431 (1967)

379. Weber, C. L., 'A contribution to the signal design problem for incoherent phase communication systems', *IEEE Trans. Inform. Theory*, **IT-14**, 306–311 (1968)

380. Stone, M. S. and Weber, C. L., 'On the globally optimum M-ary noncoherent digital communication systems', *Proc. IEEE*, **57**, 1203–1204 (1969)

381. Ottoson, R., 'Performance of phase and amplitude modulated signals on a Gaussian channel', *Ericsson Technics*, **25**, No. 3, 153–198 (1969)

382. Salz, J., Sheehan, J. R. and Paris, D. J., 'Data transmission by combined AM and PM', *Bell Syst. Tech. J.*, **50**, 2399–2419 (1971)

383. Kawai, K., Shintani, S. and Yanagidaira, H., 'Optimum combination of amplitude and phase modulation scheme and its application to data transmission modem', *Conf. Rec. IEEE Int. Conf. Communications*, 29.6–29.11 (1972)

384. Lindsey, W. C. and Simon, M. K., 'L-orthogonal signal transmission and detection', *IEEE Trans. Commun.*, **COM-20**, 953–960 (1972)

385. Thomas, C. M., 'Amplitude-phase-keying with M-ary alphabets: A technique for bandwidth reduction', *Proc. Int. Telemetering Conf.*, **8**, 289–300 (1972)

386. Benedetto, S. and Biglieri, E., 'A comparison of digital PM–AM transmission systems over telephone lines', *Conf. Rec. IEEE Int. Conf. Communications*, **1**, 7.7–7.13 (1973)

387. Foschini, J. G., Gitlin, R. D. and Weinstein, S. B., 'On the selection of a two-dimensional signal constellation in the presence of jitter and Gaussian noise', *Bell Syst. Tech. J.*, **52**, 927–965 (1973)

388. Kernighan, B. W. and Lin, S., 'Heuristic solution of a signal design optimization problem', *Bell Syst. Tech. J.*, **52**, 1145–1159 (1973)

389. Simon, M. K. and Smith, J. G., 'Hexagonal multiple-phase-and-amplitude shift keyed signal sets', *IEEE Trans. Commun.*, **COM-21**, 1108–1115 (1973)

390. Foschini, J. G., Gitlin, R. D. and Weinstein, S. B., 'Optimization of two-dimensional signal constellations in the presence of Gaussian noise', *IEEE Trans. Commun.*, **COM-22**, 28–38 (1974)

391. Smith, J. G., 'A review of multiple amplitude-phase digital signals', *IFT J.*, **1**, 6–14 (1974)

392. Thomas, C. M., Weidner, M. Y. and Durrani, S. H., 'Digital amplitude-phase keying with M-ary alphabets', *IEEE Trans. Commun.*, **COM-22**, 168–180 (1974)

393. Harper, R. C., 'Adaptive phase and amplitude modulation on a frequency dispersive fading channel', *IEEE Trans. Commun.*, **COM-22**, 764–776 (1974)

394. Simon, M. K. and Smith, J. G., 'Offset quadrature communication with decision feedback carrier synchronization', *IEEE Trans. Commun.*, **COM-22**, 1576–1584 (1974)

395. Gitlin, R. D. and Ho, E. Y., 'The performance of staggered quadrature amplitude modulation in the presence of phase jitter', *IEEE Trans. Commun.*, **COM-23**, 348–352 (1975)

396. Smith, J. G., 'Odd-bit quadrature amplitude-shift keying', *IEEE Trans. Commun.*, **COM-23**, 385–390 (1975)

PARALLEL SYSTEMS USING SEPARATE FREQUENCY BANDS
FOR THE DIFFERENT CHANNELS

397. Jones, W. B., 'A comparison of frequency-shift anti-multipath signalling techniques for digital communication systems', *IRE Trans. Commun. Syst.*, **CS-9**, 83–87 (1961)

398. Johansen, D. E., 'Binary error rates in fading FDM–FM communications', *IRE Trans. Commun. Syst.*, **CS-9**, 206–214 (1961)

399. Saltzberg, B. R. and Sokoler, R., 'A multifrequency data set for parallel transmission up to 20 characters per second', *AIEE Trans. Commun. Electron.*, **81**, 101–105 (1962)

400. Pearce, J. A., 'Data collection systems, their application and design', *J. Brit. IRE*, **24**, 489–496 (1962)

401. Bello, P. A. and Nelin, B. D., 'Optimization of subchannel data rate in FDM–SSB transmission over selectively fading media', *IEEE Trans. Commun. Syst.*, **CS-12**, 46–53 (1964)

402. Brookner, E., 'The design of parallel-FSK systems for use in multipath channels', *Proc. IEEE*, **53**, 1162–1163 (1965)

403. Brookner, E., 'Nonorthogonal coding', *IEEE Trans. Commun. Technol.*, **COM-13**, 550–552 (1965)

404. Fischer, G. and Grunow, D., 'Modems for parallel transmission of data within automatic telephone networks', *Siemens Rev.*, **38**, Special Issue on 'Remote data processing', 73–80 (1971)

PARALLEL SYSTEMS USING OVERLAPPING FREQUENCY
BANDS FOR THE DIFFERENT CHANNELS

405. Doelz, M. L., Heald, E. T. and Martin, D. L., 'Binary data transmission techniques for linear systems', *Proc. IRE*, **45**, 656–661 (1957)

406. Mosier, R. R. and Clabaugh, R. G., 'Kineplex, a bandwidth efficient binary data transmission system', *AIEE Trans. Commun. Electron.*, No. 76, 723–728 (1958)

407. Bello, P. A., 'Selective fading limitations of the Kathryn modem and some system design considerations', *IEEE Trans. Commun. Technol.*, **COM-13**, 320–333 (1965)

408. Chang, R. W., 'Synthesis of band-limited orthogonal signals for multichannel data transmission', *Bell Syst. Tech. J.*, **45**, 1775–1796 (1966)

409. Zimmerman, M. S. and Kirsh, A. L., 'The AN/GSC-10 (KATHRYN) variable data rate modem for HF radio', *IEEE Trans. Commun. Technol.*, **COM-15**, 197–204 (1967)

410. Porter, G. C., Gray, M. B. and Perkett, C. E., 'Data at twice the speed eases h.f. traffic jam', *Electronics*, **40**, No. 20, 115–120 (1967)

411. Saltzberg, B. R., 'Performance of an efficient parallel data transmission system', *IEEE Trans. Commun. Technol.*, **COM-15**, 805–811 (1967)

412. Chang, R. W. and Gibby, R. A., 'A theoretical study of performance of an orthogonal multiplexing data transmission scheme', *IEEE Trans. Commun. Technol.*, **COM-16**, 529–540 (1968)

413. Schmid, P. E., Dudley, H. S. and Skinner, S. E., 'Frequency-domain partial-response signals for parallel data transmission', *IEEE Trans. Commun. Technol.*, **COM-17**, 536–544 (1969)

SERIAL SYSTEMS WITH A TRANSMITTED AMPLITUDE AND PHASE REFERENCE

414. Bello, P. A. and Nelin, B. D., 'Predetection diversity combining with selectively fading channels', *IRE Trans. Commun. Syst.*, **CS-10**, 32–42 (1962)

415. Rushforth, C. K., 'Transmitted reference techniques for random or unknown channels', *IEEE Trans. Inform. Theory*, **IT-10**, 39–42 (1964)

416. Walker, W. F., 'The error performance of a class of binary communication systems in fading and noise', *IEEE Trans. Commun. Syst.*, **CS-12**, 28–46 (1964)

417. Gagliardi, R. M., 'A geometric study of transmitted reference communication systems', *IEEE Trans. Commun. Technol.*, **COM-12**, 118–123 (1964)

418. Hingorani, G. D. and Hancock, J. C., 'A transmitted reference system for communication in random and unknown channels', *IEEE Trans. Commun. Technol.*, **COM-13**, 293–301 (1965)

419. Spilker, J. J., 'Some effects of a random channel on transmitted reference signals', *IEEE Trans. Commun. Technol.*, **COM-13**, 377–380 (1965)

420. Bussgang, J. J. and Leiter, M., 'Phase shift keying with a transmitted reference', *IEEE Trans. Commun. Technol.*, **COM-14**, 14–22 (1966)

421. Bershad, N. J., 'Optimum binary FSK for transmitted reference systems over Rayleigh fading channels', *IEEE Trans. Commun. Technol.*, **COM-14**, 784–790 (1966)

PRINCIPLES AND TECHNIQUES OF COMMUNICATION

422. Clark, A. P., *Advanced Data-Transmission Systems*, Pentech Press, London (1977)

423. Lathi, B. P., *Random Signals and Communication Theory*, Intertext Books, London (1968)

424. Schwartz, M., *Information Transmission, Modulation, and Noise*, 2nd Ed., McGraw-Hill Kogakusha, Tokyo (1970)

425. Davenport, W. B., *Probability and Random Processes*, McGraw-Hill, New York (1970)

426. Thomas, J. B., *An Introduction to Statistical Communication Theory*, pp. 614–620, Wiley, New York (1969)

427. Panter, P. F., *Modulation, Noise and Spectral Analysis*, pp. 131–161, McGraw-Hill, New York (1965)

428. Taub, H. and Schilling, D. L., *Principles of Communication Systems*, pp. 235–281, McGraw-Hill Kogakusha, Tokyo (1971)

PARTIAL-RESPONSE CHANNELS AND CORRELATIVE-LEVEL CODING

429. Brogle, A. P., 'A new transmission method for pulse-code modulation communication systems', *IRE Trans. Commun. Syst.*, **CS-8**, 155–160 (1960)

430. Aaron, M. R., 'PCM transmission in the exchange plant', *Bell Syst. Tech. J.*, **41**, 99–141 (1962)

431. Lender, A., 'Faster digital communications with duobinary techniques', *Electronics*, **36**, 61–65 (1963)

432. Lender, A., 'The duobinary technique for high speed data transmission', *IEEE Trans. Commun. Electron.*, **82**, 214–218 (1963)

433. Wolf, J. K., 'On the application of some digital sequences to communication', *IEEE Trans. Commun. Syst.*, **CS-11**, 422–427 (1963)

434. Lender, A., 'Correlative digital communication techniques', *IEEE Trans. Commun. Technol.*, **COM-12**, 128–135 (1964)

435. van Gerwen, P. J., 'On the generation and application of pseudo-ternary codes in pulse transmission', *Philips Res. Rep.*, **20**, 469–484 (1965)

436. Howson, R. D., 'An analysis of the capabilities of polybinary data transmission', *IEEE Trans. Commun. Technol.*, **COM-13**, 312–319 (1965)

437. Sipress, J. M., 'A new class of selected ternary pulse transmission plans for digital transmission lines', *IEEE Trans. Commun. Technol.*, **COM-13**, 366–372 (1965)

438. Kretzmer, E. R., 'Generalization of a technique for binary data communication', *IEEE Trans. Commun. Technol.*, **COM-14**, 67–68 (1966)

439. Lender, A., 'Correlative level coding for binary-data transmission', *IEEE Spectrum*, **3**, 104–115 (1966)

440. Sekey, A., 'An analysis of the duobinary technique', *IEEE Trans. Commun. Technol.*, **COM-14**, 126–130 (1966)

441. Becker, F. K., Kretzmer, E. R. and Sheehan, J. R., 'A new signal format for efficient data transmission', *Bell Syst. Tech. J.*, **45**, 755–758 (1966)

442. van Gerwen, P. J., 'Efficient use of pseudo-ternary codes for data transmission', *IEEE Trans. Commun. Technol.*, **COM-15**, 658–660 (1967)

443. Amoroso, E., 'On the efficient use of voice-channel bandwidth in data transmission', *IEEE Trans. Commun. Technol.*, **COM-15**, 669–679 (1967)

444. Nakagome, Y., Amano, K. and Ota, C., 'A multilevel code having limited digital sum', *Trans. IECE Japan*, **51-A**, 31–37 (1968)

445. Franaszek, P. A., 'Sequence-state coding for digital transmission', *Bell Syst. Tech. J.*, **47**, 143–157 (1968)

446. Lender, A., 'Correlative data transmission with coherent recovery using absolute reference', *IEEE Trans. Commun. Technol.*, **COM-16**, 108–115 (1968)

447. Gorog, E., 'Redundant alphabets with desirable frequency spectrum properties', *IBM J. Res. Develop.*, **12**, 234–241 (1968)

448. Smith, J. W., 'Error control in duobinary data systems by means of null zone detection', *IEEE Trans. Commun. Technol.*, **COM-16**, 825–830 (1968)

449. Pierce, J. R., 'Some practical aspects of digital transmission', *IEEE Spectrum*, **5**, 63–70 (1968)

450. Kaneko, H. and Sawai, A., 'Feedback balanced code for multilevel PCM transmission', *Trans. IECE Japan*, **52-A**, 24–31 (1969)

451. Danilov, B. S., 'Binary shift registers for generating a given signal spectrum in data transmission equipment', *Telecommunications*, **23**, 26–31 (1969)

452. Stevens, A. D., 'Data transmission on digital link sections', *Point-to-Point Telecommun.*, **13**, 91–101 (1969)

453. Johannes, V. I., Kaim, A. G. and Walzman, T., 'Bipolar pulse transmission with zero extraction', *IEEE Trans. Commun. Technol.*, **COM-17**, 303–310 (1969)

454. Gunn, J. F. and Lombardi, J. A., 'Error detection for partial response systems', *IEEE Trans. Commun. Technol.*, **COM-17**, 734–737 (1969)

455. Danilov, B. S., 'Binary shift registers for generating a given signal spectrum in data transmission equipment', *Telecommunications*, **23**, 26–31 (1969)

456. Kobayashi, H., 'Coding schemes for reduction of intersymbol interference in data transmission systems', *IBM J. Res. Develop.*, **14**, 343–353 (1970)

457. Croisier, A., 'Introduction to pseudo-ternary transmission codes', *IBM J. Res. Develop.*, **14**, 354–367 (1970)

458. Miyakawa, H. and Harashima, H., 'Channel coding for digital transmission', *J. Inst. Electron. Commun. Eng. Japan*, **53**, 1494–1497 (1970)

459. Chien, T. M., 'Upper bound on the efficiency of d.c. constrained codes', *Bell Syst. Tech. J.*, **49**, 2267–2287 (1970)

460. Kobayashi, H. and Tang, D. T., 'On decoding of correlative level coding systems with ambiguity zone detection', *IEEE Trans. Commun. Technol.*, **COM-19**, 467–477 (1971)

461. Kobayashi, H., 'Correlative level coding and maximum likelihood decoding', *IEEE Trans. Inform. Theory*, **IT-17**, 586–594 (1971)

462. Kobayashi, H., 'A survey of coding schemes for transmission or recording of data', *IEEE Trans. Commun. Technol.*, **COM-19**, 1087–1100 (1971)

463. Ferguson, M. J., 'Optimal reception for binary partial response channels', *Bell Syst. Tech. J.*, **51**, 493–505 (1972)
464. Franklin, J. N. and Pierce, J. R., 'Spectra and efficiency of binary codes without DC', *IEEE Trans. Commun.*, **COM-20**, 1182–1184 (1972)
465. Leuthold, P. E., 'A new concept for the realisation of data modems with integrated digital filters and modulators', *Philips Res. Rep.*, **27**, 223–243 (1972)
466. Preparata, F. P., 'Error detection and synchronization with pseudo-ternary codes for data transmission', *Alta Freq.*, **42**, 280–285 (1973)
467. Houts, R. C. and Green, T. A., 'Comparing bandwidth requirements for binary baseband signals', *IEEE Trans. Commun.*, **COM-21**, 776–781 (1973)
468. Kalet, I. and Weinstein, S. B., 'In-band generation of synchronous linear data signals', *IEEE Trans. Commun.*, **COM-21**, 1116–1122 (1973)
469. Lyon, R. F., 'Two-level block encoding for digital transmission', *IEEE Trans. Commun.*, **COM-21**, 1438–1441 (1973)
470. Schmidt, K. H., 'Data transmission using controlled intersymbol interference', *Electrical Communication*, **48**, 121–133 (1973)
471. Greenstein, L. J., 'Spectrum of a binary signal block coded for DC suppression', *Bell Syst. Tech. J.*, **53**, 1103–1126 (1974)
472. Asabe, T., 'Multilevel balanced code with redundant digits', *IEEE Trans. Commun.*, **COM-22**, 1136–1140 (1974)
473. Cohen, P., Adoul, J. P. and Goulet R., 'Optimum bandwidth compression for a class of correlative multilevel coding', *IEEE Trans. Commun.*, **COM-22**, 1140–1145 (1974)
474. Hill, F. S. and Lee, W. U., 'Binary transversal filters for PAM pulse generation with correlative coding', *IEEE Trans. Commun.*, **COM-23**, 483–486 (1975)

RECENT SYSTEMS

475. Wozencraft, J. M. and Jacobs, I. M., *Principles of Communication Engineering*, Wiley, New York (1965)
476. Lucky, R. W., Salz, J. and Weldon, E. J., *Principles of Data Communication*, McGraw-Hill, New York (1968)
477. Carlson, A. B., *Communication Systems*, McGraw-Hill, New York (1968)
478. Root, W. L., 'An introduction to the theory of the detection of signals in noise', *Proc. IEEE*, **58**, 610–623 (1970)
479. Forney, G. D., 'Maximum likelihood sequence estimation of digital sequences in the presence of intersymbol interference', *IEEE Trans. Inform. Theory*, **IT-18**, 363–378 (1972)
480. Terman, F. E., *Radio Engineering*, McGraw-Hill, London, pp. 609–661 (1951)
481. Maslin, N. M., 'High data rate transmissions over h.f. links', *Radio Electron. Eng.*, **52**, 75–87 (1982)
482. Gronemeyer, S. A. and McBride, A. L., 'MSK and offset QPSK modulation', *IEEE Trans. Commun.*, **COM-24**, 809–820 (1976)
483. Amoroso, F. and Kivett, J. A., 'Simplified MSK signaling technique', *IEEE Trans. Commun.*, **COM-25**, 433–441 (1977)
484. de Jager, F. and Dekker, C. B., 'Tamed frequency modulation, a novel method to achieve spectrum economy in digital transmission', *IEEE Trans. Commun.*, **COM-26**, 534–542 (1978)
485. Rydbeck, N. and Sundberg, C. E., 'Recent results on spectrally efficient constant envelope digital modulation methods', ICC79 Int. Conf. on Communications, Part 3, Boston, Mass., U.S.A., 42.1/1–6 (1979)
486. Oetting, J. D., 'A comparison of modulation techniques for digital radio', *IEEE Trans. Commun.*, **COM-27**, 1752–1762 (1979)

487. Muilwijk, D., 'Correlative phase-shift keying—A class of constant envelope modulation techniques', *IEEE Trans. Commun.*, **COM-29**, 226–236 (1981)

488. Fang, R. J. F., 'Quaternary transmission over satellite channels with cascaded nonlinear elements and adjacent channel interference', *IEEE Trans. Commun.*, **COM-29**, 567–581 (1981)

489. Murota, K. and Hirade, K., 'GMSK modulation for digital mobile radio telephony', *IEEE Trans. Commun.*, **COM-29**, 1044–1050 (1981)

490. Le-Ngoc, T., Feher, K. and Van, H. P., 'New modulation techniques for low-cost power and bandwidth efficient satellite earth stations', *IEEE Trans. Commun.*, **COM-30**, 275–283 (1982)

491. Batson, B. H., Seyl, J. W. and Smith, B. G., 'Experimental results for FSK data transmission systems using discriminator detection', Nat. Telecommunications Conf., Dallas, U.S.A. (1976)

492. Park, J. H., 'On binary DPSK detection', *IEEE Trans. Commun.*, **COM-26**, 484–486 (1978)

493. Stein, P. J. and Gibson, R. W., 'A 1200 b/s single chip microcomputer data modem', *IERE Conference Proceedings*, No. 49, 181–188 (1981)

494. Petrovic, R., 'On the performance of binary coded signals', *IEEE Trans. Commun.*, **COM-29**, 1403–1405 (1981)

495. Pawula, R. F., 'On the theory of error rates for narrow-band digital FM', *IEEE Trans. Commun.*, **COM-29**, 1634–1643 (1981)

496. Falconer, D. D., 'Application of passband decision feedback equalization in two-dimensional data communication systems', *IEEE Trans. Commun.*, **COM-24**, 1159–1166 (1976)

497. Akashi, F., Tatsui, N., Sato, Y., Koike, S. and Marumo, Y., 'A high performance digital QAM 9600 bit/s modem', *NEC Res. & Develop.*, **45**, 38–48 (1977)

498. Clark, A. P., Harvey, J. D. and Driscoll, J. P., 'Near-maximum-likelihood detection processes for distorted digital signals', *Radio Electron. Eng.*, **48**, 301–309 (1978)

499. Maejima, H. and Doi, T., 'Modem for 9600 bit/s data transmission', *Japan Telecomm. Rev.*, **21**, 118–121 (1979)

500. Muramo, K., Mochida, Y., Amano, F. and Kinoshita, T., 'Multiprocessor architecture for voiceband data processing (application to 9600 bps modem)', ICC79 Int. Conf. on Communications, Part 3, Boston, Mass., 37.3/1–5 (1979)

501. McLaughton, L. and Fagan, A. D., 'The time-domain simulation of high-speed data-transmission systems over the British P.S.T.N.', Int. Conf. on Computer Aided Design and Manufacture of Electronic Components, Circuits and Systems, Brighton, England, 223–226 (1979)

502. Gitlin, R. D. and Weinstein, S. B., 'Modulation and demodulation techniques for voicegrade data transmission', 1980 Int. Conf. on Communications, Part 1, Seattle, U.S.A., 8.2/1–5 (1980)

503. Adams, P. F., 'Speech-band data modems', *Electronics and Power*, **26**, 733–736 (1980)

504. Westall, F. A., 'Efficient digital signal processing realizations for PSK modem receivers', *IERE Conference Proceedings*, No. 49, 143–152 (1981)

505. Koya, M., Ishizuka, K. and Maeda, N., 'High-speed data modem using digital signal processor', Int. Conf. on Communications, Denver, U.S.A., 14.7/1–5 (1981)

506. Clark, A. P. and Fairfield, M. J., 'Detection processes for a 9600 bit/s modem', *Radio Electron. Eng.*, **51**, 455–465 (1981)

507. Godard, D. N., 'A 9600 bit/s modem for multipoint communication systems', IEEE 1981 Nat. Telecommun. Conf., New Orleans, U.S.A., B3.3/1–5 (1981)

508. Clark, A. P. and Hussein, B. A., 'Non-linear equalizers having an improved tolerance to noise', *Radio Electron. Eng.*, **52**, 145–153 (1982)

509. Clark, A. P., Lee, L. H. and Marshall, R. S., 'Developments of the conventional nonlinear equalizer', *IEE Proc.*, Pt. F, **129**, 85–94 (1982)

510. Clark, A. P., Ip, S. F. A. and Soon, C. W., 'Pseudobinary detection processes for a 9600 bit/s modem', *IEE Proc.*, Pt. F, **129**, 305–314 (1982)

511. Sondhi, M. M. and Berkley, D. A., 'Silencing echoes on the telephone network', *Proc. IEEE*, **68**, 948–963 (1980)

512. Powers, E. N. and Zinnerman, M. S., 'TADIM—a digital implementation of a multichannel data modem', IEEE Int. Conf. on Communications, Philadelphia, U.S.A., 706–711 (1968)

513. Salz, J. and Weinstein, S. B., 'Fourier transform communication system', Ass. Comput. Machinery Conf. on Computers and Communications, Pine Mountain, U.S.A. (1969)

514. Weinstein, S. B. and Ebert, P. M., 'Data transmission by frequency division multiplexing using the discrete Fourier transform', *IEEE Trans. Commun. Technol.*, **COM-19**, 628–634 (1971)

515. Clark, A. P., Kwong, C. P. and Harvey, J. D., 'Detection processes for severely distorted digital signals', *Electronic Circuits and Systems*, **3**, 27–37 (1979)

516. Clark, A. P. and McVerry, F., 'Performance of 2400 bit/s serial and parallel modems over an HF channel simulator', *IERE Conference Proceedings*, No. 49, 167–179 (1981)

517. Clark, A. P. and McVerry, F., 'Channel estimation for an HF radio link', *IEE Proc.*, Pt. F, **128**, 33–42 (1981)

518. Clark, A. P. and Asghar, S. M., 'Detection of digital signals transmitted over a known time-varying channel', *IEE Proc.*, Pt. F, **128**, 167–174 (1981)

519. Kabal, P. and Pasaputhy, S., 'Partial-response signaling', *IEEE Trans. Commun.*, **COM-23**, 921–934 (1975)

INDEX

Absolute value, 61, 68, 223
Adaptive detection process, 133–7, 150–3
Adaptive equalizer, 133–7, 153
Adaptive system, 133–7, 150–3
Additive noise, 25–31, 112, 115, 154, 183, 247
Alphabet, 8–10
Amplifier limiter, 79, 88, 92, 113, 122, 123, 127
Amplitude, 3, 25–31, 39
Amplitude modulation (AM), 6–7, 39–43, 223, 248–55
Amplitude modulation effects, 25–31, 113–5
AM-PM signal, 130–2
AM receiver, 60–2, 67–9, 84–5, 248–52
AM signals, 6–7, 39–44, 60–2, 67–9, 93–9, 103–5, 115, 237, 248–55, 271–2
AM system, 76–85, 93–9, 112–5
AM transmitter, 246–7
Antipodal signal, 4, 39, 43, 48, 141, 167
APR systems, 150–2
ASK signals, 39–44, 60–2, 67–9, 93–9, 103–5, 248–55, 271–2
Asynchronous systems, 36, 119–20, 125–8
Attenuation distortion, 11–20, 22–4, 135, 138, 140, 142
Attenuation-frequency characteristic, 17–20
Audio link, 12–15
Autocorrelation function, 206
Automatic gain controlled (AGC) amplifier, 79, 84–5, 112
Average energy per bit, 174–5, 178–9, 181, 194, 240
Average energy per signal element, 166, 174–5, 178–9, 181, 186, 188, 193–4

Band limited Gaussian noise, 49, 51, 155, 247–51, 262–3
Band limiting, 38, 80, 83–4, 154, 182
Band-pass channel, 246–8
Band-pass filter, 83–91, 109, 123, 127
Bandwidth, 3, 11, 100–11, 129, 132, 140, 181, 207, 235, 253
Baseband channel, 185, 192–4, 207, 221
Baseband signals, 4–5, 38, 100–3, 168–245, 253–5

Bauds, 4, 9, 20, 100–3
Binary signals, 4–6, 39–48, 76–128, 163–76, 222–7, 230–45, 259–65
Binary value, 170, 175, 259, 264
Bit of information, 8–9
Bits per second, 8–10

Cancellation of intersymbol interference, 209–21, 227, 233–4, 239–40
Carrier link, 12–20, 26–7
Channel, 1–2, 9, 13, 138–42
Channel transfer function, 195, 201–2, 208, 212, 214, 217
Character, 37
Carrier phase synchronization, 76, 78
Code converter, 121–2
Coder, 221–33, 238–42
Coding rule, 223, 231, 238
Coherent detection, 55–62, 76–83, 93–9, 104–6, 108, 129–37, 246–70
Coherent detector, 55–62, 77, 249, 256, 260, 266
Collins Kineplex system, 147–9, 152
Coloured Gaussian noise, 53, 160
Common-impedance coupling, 26
Comparator, 123–4, 127–8, 260, 264, 266
Complementary AM signals, 43–4, 56
Complementary ASK signals, 259
Complex conjugate, 158, 190–2
Complex number plane, 71, 190
Conditional probability density, 164
Correlated signals, 239
Correlative-level coding, 237–45
Cosine spectrum, 208–11, 222–8, 234–42, 245
Cosine^2 spectrum, 214–6, 230–45
Cross-correlation coefficient, 95, 257, 263, 266
Crosstalk, 25–6

Data channels, 9, 138–49
Data-collection system, 9
Data signal, 4–5
Data-transmission system, 112–53, 182–5, 192–5, 246–8
D.C. component, 168–9, 236–7
Decision-feedback equalizer, 135, 218–21

Decision threshold, 163–7, 171–9, 198, 209, 215, 218, 223–6, 230, 232, 251
Delay circuit, 92, 122
Delay distortion, 11–20, 22–4, 98, 113–5, 138–42
Demodulated waveform, 81–5, 123–4, 127, 247, 252
Demodulation, 7–8, 13, 21, 80–93, 122–4, 126–8, 247–8, 252
Detected data signal, 81, 84–5, 123, 125
Detection process, 49–99, 122–5, 126–8, 154–67, 170–80, 218–20, 243–5, 246–68
Differential coding, 5–6, 60, 69, 78, 121–2
Differentially coherent detection, 69–75, 92, 98–9, 105–6, 117, 122–5, 129, 147–8
Digits, 8–9
Discriminator, 84–90, 126–8
Distortion, 11–24, 98, 100, 109–11, 113–5
Doppler shift, 23, 30
Double-sideband signals, 6–7, 39–48, 103–9, 129–32, 135–53, 246–72
Duobinary system, 223

Echoes, 15–20
Element rate, 100–11, 178, 181–2, 207, 236, 253–5, 258, 268–70
Element synchronism, 9, 141
Element timing waveform, 32–7, 81–5, 116, 119, 123–4
Element value, 4–5, 8
Energy-density spectrum, 100–1
Energy spectral-density, 186–7
Energy of signal element, 186–7, 249, 259
Envelope detector, 64–6, 69, 73–5
Equalizer, 133–7, 218–21, 243–4
Equipment complexity, 9–10, 37, 57, 63, 79, 82–3, 109, 114–9, 128, 136, 139, 153
Error bursts, 210, 213, 215, 218, 220–1, 234, 243
Error-extension effect, 210, 213, 215, 218, 220–1, 234, 243
Error in signal estimate, 162
Error probability, 94–7, 163–7, 172–81, 198–9, 220, 234–5, 242, 244, 253, 258, 265, 268
Estimate of signal, 161–3
Exclusive-OR gate, 92, 123–4, 224

Expected noise power, 157, 159, 162, 173, 188
Expected value, 156, 162
Eye pattern, 204

Fading rate, 24, 30
FDM systems, 138–52
Flat fading, 28–31, 148
FM discriminator, 84–91
FM receiver, 54–7, 63–7, 84–91, 126–8, 259–68
FM signals, 39–50, 55–7, 63–7, 80, 86, 90–1, 93–9, 107–111, 115, 125–6, 129, 259–72
FM system, 84–91, 109–15, 119–20, 125–9
FM transmitter, 118–9, 125–6
Fourier transform, 3, 156, 160, 186–7, 190, 194–5
Frequency divider, 78
Frequency-division multiplexing (FDM), 13, 21, 137–52
Frequency modulation (FM), 39–50, 107–9, 125–6, 129, 259, 265
Frequency modulation effects, 13, 21, 25–31, 38, 62, 113–4, 140, 246
Frequency offset, 13, 21, 25–31, 38, 98, 140, 246
Frequency selective fading, 22–4, 148–9, 152–3
Frequency shift, 86, 90, 95–8, 107–9
Frequency spread, 30, 148–9, 152–3
Frequency translation effects, 13, 25–31, 38, 246
FSK signals, 39–50, 55–7, 63–7, 80, 93–9, 107–9, 125–6, 259–72
Full-wave rectifier, 78, 84–5, 126–7

Gaussian noise, 27–8, 30, 49, 51, 53, 94–8, 112–5, 154–5, 160, 167, 247, 250–1
Gaussian random process, 94–7, 155, 162, 173, 188, 193–4, 249–51, 262–3
Gaussian random variable, 161–5, 173, 177–8, 194, 198–9, 251, 263–5
Gray code, 180, 254
Group-delay characteristic, 11–20

HF radio links, 1, 9, 12, 14, 20–4, 27–31, 138–53
Hybrid transformer, 14–15

Impulsive noise, 25–8
Incoherent detection, 62–75, 83–99, 104–6, 115, 121–8, 147–9, 270–2
Incoherent matched filter, 64–7, 68–9, 73–5
Infinite-Q tuned circuit, 64–7, 73–5
Information, 5, 8–9
Information rate, 9, 100–1, 114–5, 149, 168, 178, 253–5, 258, 268–9
Instantaneous frequency, 39, 55, 80, 85, 88, 259
Instantaneous signal power, 155–9, 190
Integrator, 55, 58, 61, 64, 67, 69, 77, 82, 93, 172, 177, 249, 256, 260, 266
Interchannel interference, 28, 142–52
Intermodulation effects, 26
Intersymbol interference, 15–6, 19–20, 142–6, 167, 207–8
Inverter, 224, 227
Ionized layer, 21–2
Ionosphere, 21–4, 29–31

Jitter, 25, 27, 34, 80, 98

Lightning discharges, 28
Linear coding, 237–45
Linear demodulation, 7–8, 13, 21, 76–82, 246–52
Linear equalizer, 133–5
Linear estimation, 161–3, 172
Linear filter, 80–2, 154–67, 171, 186–218, 250–2
Linear modulation, 6–7, 13, 20, 38–42, 129–33, 141, 147, 150, 248–9
Linear operation, 161–3, 172
Listener echo, 15
Loaded audio link, 12–9
Local exchange, 14
Loop delay, 15
Lower sideband, 7
Low-pass filter, 80–2, 85, 88–9, 92–3, 118, 123, 127, 249–50, 256, 260, 266

Magneto-ionic splitting, 29
Matched filter, 154–62, 170–2, 190–2, 251
Matched-filter detection, 154–67, 170–80, 246–68
Maximum-likelihood detection process, 49, 244–5
Maximum signal/noise ratio, 155–9, 186–92

Maximum transmission rate, 113–5, 128
Mean-square error, 162
Mean-square value, 162, 186
Microphonic effects, 26
Microwave links, 12–4
Minimum error probability, 49–62, 93–9, 163–7
Mismatch, 14–20
m-level signal, 8–10, 50–72, 129–37, 150, 176–81, 186, 192, 248, 253–8, 265–72
Modem, 1, 112–37, 246–8
Modified duobinary system, 223
Modulated-carrier signals, 6–7, 38–48, 93–111, 129–53, 246–72
Modulating waveform, 39–41, 80–2, 93, 114–8, 121–2, 125–6, 130–2, 248, 255–6, 259, 265
Modulation, 6–7, 38–48, 116–8, 121–2, 125–6, 129–37, 246–8, 255–6, 265
Modulation methods, 38–48, 103–53, 246–72
Modulation noise, 26
Modulo-2 adder, 224–5, 231–2, 241
Modulo-4 adder, 227–9, 241
Modulus, 61, 68, 190, 223
MSK signal, 45–7
Multilevel signals, 8–10, 50–72, 129–37, 150, 176–81, 186, 192–248, 253–8, 265–72
Multipath propagation, 15–20, 22–4, 143–6
Multiplicative noise, 25–31

Narrow-band filter, 34–5, 76–8, 98
Narrow-band Gaussian noise, 250, 262–3
Narrow-band signals, 138–53, 246–70
Near-maximum-likelihood detector, 136
Noise, 2, 11, 25–31, 51, 53, 112, 154, 183, 247
Noise power, 156–9, 162, 173, 188, 193, 251
Noise power spectral density, 51, 53, 155, 157, 160, 173, 183, 188, 247, 250
Noise variance, 162–3, 173, 193, 251, 263
Noise-whitening filter, 53, 160
Noncoherent detection, 83–91
Nonlinear distortion, 20
Nonlinear equalizer, 135, 218–21

Nonlinear operation, 172
Non-physical system, 160, 196
Nyquist rate, 100
Nyquist's vestigial-symmetry theorem, 200–1

Offset QPSK signal, 46–7
Optimum detection process, 49–62, 154–67, 244–70
Orthogonal signals, 60–1, 75, 142, 257, 263

Parallel systems, 9, 34, 83, 93, 138–53, 169
Parseval's theorem, 157
Partial-response channels, 207–45
Peripheral equipment, 120
Phase angle, 190
Phase distortion, 190
Phase jitter, 25, 27
Phase-locked-loop FM discriminator, 89–90
Phase-locked oscillator, 34, 76, 78, 89, 124, 151
Phase modulation (PM), 38–48, 57, 80, 116–8, 121–2, 129–32, 135–6, 141, 147, 255
Phase quadrature, 45–7, 130, 141, 147, 150, 256
Physically realisable filter, 159, 196–7
Pilot carrier, 106, 133, 150–2
PM signals, 39–48, 57–60, 69–75, 80, 93–9, 105–6, 109–10, 114–9, 121–2, 129–32, 135–6, 147, 255–8, 271–2
PM receiver, 57–60, 69–75, 92–3, 122–5, 255–8
PM system, 78–84, 92–9, 109–25, 129–32, 135–6, 147–9
PM transmitter, 116–22
Polar signal, 168–74, 176–9, 183, 186, 193–4, 199, 248
Power density spectrum, 3–7, 103, 107, 111, 139, 141, 169
Power spectral density, 51, 53, 155, 157, 160, 173, 183, 188, 247, 250
Precoding, 221–33, 240–1
Prior knowledge, 51, 76, 83, 161–2, 167, 170, 174
Private line, 15–20, 38
Probability density function, 163–5, 173, 264–5
Pseudo-ternary system, 224

PSK signals, 39–48, 57–60, 69–75, 80, 93–9, 105–6, 114–9, 121–2, 255–8, 271–2

QAM signal, 130–2, 136–7, 150–2
Q function, 94, 165
QPSK signal, 255
Quadrature component, 104, 105–6
Quaternary signals, 10, 129–32, 176–81, 194, 199, 227–30, 235, 240–2, 253, 255–8, 265–8, 271–2
Quaternary value, 176, 179
Quenched resonator, 64–9, 73–5, 269–70

Raised-cosine spectrum, 201–6, 234–5
Random variable, 163
Rayleigh fading, 23, 29, 153
Receiver filter, 83–91, 109, 123, 127, 154–62, 170–2, 182–94
Rectangular baseband signal, 4–6, 101–3, 168–81, 246–55
Rectangular modulating waveform, 39–48, 55, 57, 60, 80, 93, 103–9, 116–8, 121, 126, 140–52, 246–72
Rectangular spectrum, 195–200, 234–5, 238, 240, 242
Reference carrier, 56, 59, 62, 76–80, 98, 106, 133, 150–2, 249, 256, 260, 266
Reflections, 16–20, 29
Repeaters, 14–5
Ripple in frequency characteristic, 16–7, 19, 23
Rounded baseband signal, 5–6, 80–2, 84–5, 101–3, 118, 182–245
Rounded modulating waveform, 41, 80–2, 84–5, 105, 109, 118, 271–2

Sample value of random variable, 163
Sample value of signal, 194, 197, 205, 207, 209, 212, 215, 218, 222, 225, 230, 231, 239
Sampler, 193
Sampling instant, 160, 171, 193, 197, 205, 209, 212, 215, 218, 222, 225, 230, 231, 239
Satellite links, 12–4
Schwarz inequality, 157, 189
Serial systems, 9, 38–99, 112–37, 152–3, 168–272
Sequence of impulses, 184–5, 193, 222
Sideband, 6–7, 103–6

Signal alphabet, 8–9
Signal carrier, 6, 39, 42, 44–6
Signal distortion, 11–24
Signal element, 3, 8
Signal energy, 4, 51, 53, 61, 155–6, 158, 166, 174–5, 178–9, 181, 186–94, 234–5, 239–40, 249, 252–3
Signal level, 18, 25, 30
Signal/noise ratio, 95, 153, 155–9, 188, 190, 192
Signal power, 4, 48, 51, 155–6, 159, 174–5, 178–9, 181, 186–90, 234–5, 252–5, 258, 268–9
Signal spectrum, 194–5
Signal value, 5, 6, 81
Sine spectrum, 211–3, 222–30, 233–242, 245
Sine^2 spectrum, 216–8, 230–45
Single-sideband signal, 7, 13, 20, 103–4, 237
Sinusoidal roll-off, 200–1
Sky wave, 20–4, 29–30
Spectrum, 3–4, 101–8, 111, 139, 141, 169, 186, 194–5
Start-stop systems, 35–7
Statistically independent noise samples, 62, 206, 263, 266
Sudden level changes, 25–6, 114–5
Sudden phase changes, 25–7, 40, 80, 98, 114–5, 120
Suppressed carrier AM signal, 39–42, 68, 78, 80, 103–5, 116–122, 130–7, 141–52, 248–58, 271–2
Suppressed carrier ASK signal, 39–42, 68, 103–5, 116–8, 141–52, 248–58, 271–2
Switched inverter, 73
Switched line, 15–20
Synchronizing signal, 37
Synchronization, 32–7, 56, 60, 62, 76, 78, 150–2
Synchronously multiplexed signals, 9, 140–52
Synchronous systems, 32–7

Telegraph distortion, 205
Telephone circuits, 1, 11–20, 25–7
Ternary signal, 224

Threshold level, 81, 163, 167, 172, 174–5, 177, 179
Time correlation, 53–5, 161–2
Time delay, 11
Time dispersion, 15–24, 143
Time guard band, 145–6
Time modulation effects, 30
Timing information, 32–7
Timing waveform, 35, 84–5, 123–4, 128, 200–5, 236–7
Tolerance to distortion, 20, 24, 37, 98, 104, 109–11, 113–5, 128–53
Tolerance to noise, 41–8, 74–5, 85–91, 94–8, 108–15, 149, 181, 199, 234–5, 242, 253–5, 258, 268–9
Transient interruptions, 25–6, 113
Transmission bridge, 16
Transmission path, 11–31, 182–3, 246–7
Transmission rate, 8–10, 100–11, 113–5, 128–137, 149, 253–5, 258, 268–9
Transmitter filter, 121–2, 125–6, 183–94, 237–8, 242–3
Transparent system, 33
Truth table, 225, 228–9, 232–3, 241
Two-dimensional signal, 130–2

Unbiased estimate, 162
Uncorrelated noise samples, 206, 263, 266
Union bound, 267–8
Union of events, 267
Unipolar signal, 168–70, 174–6, 179–81, 183, 187, 193–4, 199, 248
Upper sideband, 7

Vector, 190
Vestigial sideband signal, 103–6, 132–3
Voice-frequency channel, 1–2, 11
Voltage-controlled oscillator, 89–90, 125–6

Waveform, 5
Wide-deviation FSK signal, 268–70
Wiener–Kinchine theorem, 206
White Gaussian noise, 27–8, 30, 49, 51, 53, 94–8, 112–5, 154–5, 166–7, 183, 247
White noise, 25–6